BEYOND

the

GOLDEN DOOR

William O'Dwyer

edited by

Paul O'Dwyer

St. John's University   Jamaica, New York

© 1986 Paul O'Dwyer
All rights reserved
Published by St. John's University, Jamaica, New York
Manufactured in the United States of America
Library of Congress Catalog Card Number 86-62415
ISBN 0-87075-575-7

Library of Congress Cataloging-in-Publication Data

O'Dwyer, William, 1890–1964.
   Beyond the golden door.

   Bibliography: p.
   Includes index.
   1. O'Dwyer, William, 1890–1964. 2. Mayors--
New York (N.Y.)--Biography. 3. Irish Americans--
New York (N.Y.)--Biography. 4. New York (N.Y.)--
Politics and government--1898–1951. I. O'Dwyer,
Paul, 1907-   . II. Title.
F128.5.O28   1987   974.7'104'0924   86-62415
ISBN 0-87075-575-7

This Book is Dedicated

to

Patrick O'Dwyer of County Cork
Schoolmaster

and

Bridget McNicholas O'Dwyer of County Mayo
Schoolmistress

Who Guided Their Brood Through Childhood

and

Bade Them Reach a Different Plateau.

THE NEW COLOSSUS

Not like the brazen giant of Greek fame,
With conquering limbs astride from land to land;
Here at our sea-washed, sunset gates shall stand
A mighty woman with a torch, whose flame
Is the imprisoned lightning, and her name
Mother of Exiles. From her beacon-hand
Glows world-wide welcome; her mild eyes command
The air-bridged harbor that twin cities frame.
"Keep, Ancient lands, your storied pomp!" cries she
With silent lips. "Give me your tired, your poor,
Your huddled masses yearning to breathe free,
The wretched refuse of your teeming shore.
Send these, the homeless, tempest-tossed to me.
I lift my lamp beside the golden door!"

Emma Lazarus

TABLE OF CONTENTS

PREFACE

I made many efforts to get my brother to tell his story, particularly during the last decade of his life. He was a great storyteller and frequently his friends and his family, after being regaled with reminiscences, would urge him to have his stories taped. Bill's out-of-hand rejection of these urgings gives some insight into his character. I broached the subject seriously with him shortly after he resigned as Ambassador to Mexico. He was far from being an orderly person and I knew the idea of buckling down to writing an autobiography would be, to say the least, most distasteful. Outside of the time he spent in the Army or with the War Refugee Board he had always had an ample staff, and it would have been quite simple for him to direct any of them to make notes and to record the unusual and historic experiences in his life. It had never occurred to him to do it or if it had, he dismissed the thought from his mind.

In 1949 Gene Fowler wrote *Beau James*. It was a biography of Jimmy Walker. Fowler approached Bill that same year with an offer to do the same. Fowler was one of many writers who had made similar proposals. All offers including Fowler's were declined. Bill was Mayor during the last year of Jimmy Walker's life. Before his election, Bill had visited Walker in his apartment near Gracie Mansion, the Mayor's official residence. He became fond of Walker and felt Fowler's presentation was somewhat shallow. It is more than likely that *Beau James* was, at least partially, responsible for his reticence.

I knew that my persistence was often annoying, but I also felt that in the comparatively relaxed atmosphere of Mexico he might be induced to give himself over to the task. The time-consuming schedule of public office was now behind him and he was in a position to devote a part of each day to compiling the material he would need. Mexico City had another advantage. It was then a place of refuge for many talented writers whom he knew and who would be eager to help.

He had a way of discouraging my efforts. "Books," he would philosophize, "are a very special part of civilized existence. They have added immeasurably to human development, have increased man's store of knowledge, have provided a warehouse for historical experiences. They have provided enjoyment for all those who were privileged to read them in the earlier days. It is presumptuous for people to write books which they hope will take their place on library shelves alongside the classics that have withstood the test of time. My experiences were interesting enough, but they would for the most part do no better than to duplicate the many accounts of happenings which have already found their way into bound volumes." And that would, for the moment, bring an end to my exhortation.

I did not give up. I thought that if I made arrangements to have some skilled writer whom he liked and admired approach him on the subject, I might get a different response. I knew someone whom I felt sure would have a fair chance of success. His name was Joseph Freeman. He had been close to Oscar Bernstien (my law partner), his wife and Bill. Freeman's wife, Charmene Von Veigand, was also well known to us. Freeman and many others engaged in creative writing had come on hard times; they had gone down before the avalanche of abuse that was directly attributable to the neurotics then in charge of the legislative and administrative branches of our government. At my urging Joe Freeman set forth to visit Bill in Mexico. I paid his way. I heard from Mexico from time to time. I received no letter, but associates at our law office there explained that the Ambassador and Mr. Freeman were out of the city. I felt that was a good omen and I had visions of a volume as big as *Never Call Retreat*, the last book any publisher had accepted from this known Marxist. Joe Freeman returned without a note. He and Bill had traveled through Mexico from the Mayan country to the stronghold of the Yaquis. Seemingly, they enjoyed every minute of it, and Joe was more than ever enthralled with his Irish host in the province of the Aztecs. However, he felt it would have been impossible for him to write impartially on the man with whom he had spent the most interesting six months of his life. I had placed great store on that arrangement and the disappointment was debilitating.

Oscar Bernstien and I had opened an office in Mexico. One day when I was in the office there, I accidentally came across a letter written on the stationery of Columbia University by Louis Starr, who headed Columbia's oral history department. "Did you see this letter from Louis Starr?" I asked. "Yes, I saw it. Somebody wants an interview," he said. He discouraged interviews with reporters he did not know. He was not even familiar with Louis Starr's great efforts to perpetuate historical information by having the experience of prominent men and women taped and later transcribed. I explained the virtues of the Starr program and how successful it had been and urged him to cooperate with it. "All right," he said, "tell Louis Starr I will see Mr. Kelly." Soon after,

John Kelly, New York policeman, Rhodes scholar and now professor at the University of Delaware, began a series of taped interviews. Since then, permission has been given to at least a hundred researchers to review these tapes at Columbia.

In New York, I was approached by Carlton Cole, a literary agent, who said that several publishers were dying to get Bill's biography. This proved to be the exaggeration of the century. However, meetings with publishers ensued and deals were made but no book resulted from Carlton's efforts.

While I was engaged in the campaign to have my brother commit to writing an account of his eventful life, I had never for a moment given thought to writing about my own life. If I had entertained any such idea, my experience with publishers should have been enough to dissuade me. Then Linda Fisher broached the subject to me.

I had known Linda since 1967. She was issuing press releases in the Albany branch of the peace movement when I became aware of her special talents. In the 1968 Democratic Party primary, I was the peace candidate for U.S. Senator for New York on the ticket headed by Senator Eugene McCarthy. I. Philip Sipser, my campaign manager, assigned Linda to act as my press secretary while I traveled the 400-mile campaign trail in upstate New York. She was at the Commodore Hotel in New York on primary night when Gene McCarthy and I were swept to victory. She was also there to arrange my appearance, battered and forlorn, as we conceded defeat in the November election. We kept in touch from that time on and nothing daunted, she kept on issuing press releases for me as if we had won. She goaded me into considering an autobiography in about the same way I had prodded my brother 15 years earlier. Finally she arranged for me to have lunch with the publisher. Soon an advance was in place and I began the task of writing *Counsel for the Defense* with the assistance of my secretary, Virginia Polihrom.

I made the mistake of not getting an agent who would run interference between my publisher and me. To make matters worse the publisher assigned a young woman straight out of school to do some editing on the finished product. Her penciled notes to me in the margins of the manuscript indicated that she quarrelled with what she described as quaint expressions which revealed my early education and environment. This neophyte could not have been aware that she had struck a sensitive nerve, nor was I aware of how much of the emigrant was still intact after having lived the active life of a New Yorker for half a century. Reading the announcement that my publisher had become part of a conglomerate only added to my discontent.

My experience with publishers, as a lawyer representing clients against publishers, as Bill's representative and as an author, made it clear that if I wanted to get Bill's book published, I would have to travel some other road. I knew I could not accept the rules which would require me to crowd 50 interesting and exciting years into 300 pages.

As a brand new member of the Authors Guild I received their literature and read their articles avidly. The Guild presented some very interesting alternatives to distressed writers.

Encouraged by a feeling of liberation and with time to spare when I left City Hall in 1977, I turned to the task of gathering together the chapters of my brother's story which I found among his papers. It turned out that my prodding had not been in vain; the material he had put together covered most of the major events and people of his life. The story had been written at different times, mostly in Mexico. Jill Levine, who had been my executive secretary in City Hall, and I put the parts in chronological order, but I found some gaps in the story.

There was very little about the historic background of his people which would, at least in part, account for his attitudes towards life, his personality or his ambition. Where I felt it was necessary to present such information, I did so. The information about Ireland during the last century was derived from well-known and acknowledged historians, such as S.J. Lyons of Trinity College, Dublin, but much of it came from my own personal experiences.

My knowledge of the history of native Americans, blacks and religious minorities in this country derived initially from contacts with members of these groups. My curiosity was piqued by these encounters and I read extensively finding that several of the myths that Americans hold dear are distortions and that prejudice and injustice have been the lot of many in this land of the free.

My brother's description of the circumstances surrounding President Roosevelt's establishment of the War Refugee Board was less than complete. As a member of the American League for a Free Palestine in the mid-1940's, I was aware of activities of Jewish-American associations which would complement what he had written. Histories of the Holocaust provided additional information on the people and events of the period.

Furthermore, in his account of his stewardship as Mayor of New York, he made no mention of the newspaper editorials written about the most important happenings. They had been gathered together in preparation for his appearance before the Kefauver committee. I have added some of them to his descriptions of the solutions to the problems he faced as Mayor.

I had been his defender when he was under attack by the Kefauver committee. I had dealt personally with Senator Kefauver and Rudolph Halley, the committee's chairman and counsel, while Bill was in Mexico.

The information I had adds new dimensions to their actions.

When the manuscript was completed, I sent to Sloane, Bill's former wife, that portion of it in which she figured, for review or comment. It came back with corrections, but she also added her evaluation of what she had read. "So far this is reasonably factual and almost incredibly dull." It was a stinging criticism, but it came as no great shock. Further on she expressed her utter exasperation: "This certainly contains none of the charm, humor or anything else I remember about Bill O'Dwyer. I suppose it is all right for the record." Sloane had always been a straightforward person. Her deep affection for Bill did not end at their separation nor even with his death. It was never more manifest than in her reaction to his and my account of his life.

After reading the manuscript again, I concluded that the written pages may not satisfy one such as Sloane, but they do contain a basic source of material more reliable than would be found in sensational news headlines, the tapes of nightly newscasters or the columns of journalists hard-pressed to write something entertaining each day.

The finished book is neither a biography nor an autobiography, but rather a combination of the two. I knew it did not fit into any recognizable slot as publishers see these things, but the Guild advised it did not have to be that way. I had no doubt that the story of my brother's life would be enlightening and above all else a significant part of the history of New York.

I was convinced that the book could best be appreciated by an institution of learning—a university—and what better one than the university that gave me an opportunity to become educated in the law. When I applied for admission to St. John's Law School at 19 years of age, I had been in this country a little over a year. In 1985 I found St. John's University as imaginative as it had been in 1925 when it created a law school to tend the needs of Irish, Italian and Jewish immigrants who were hungry for the opportunity to learn. St. John's agreed to let me present my brother's story in its somewhat unconventional form. I had found a publisher that was interested in the history of New York and felt the book worthy of an institution devoted to higher education, as renowned for learning as it was for basketball.

Paul O'Dwyer
1986

PROLOGUE

*PO'D**

The romantic and oft-repeated story of William O'Dwyer's rise to fortune as well as fame was somewhat of a distortion. Since he did not seek wealth, he did not fit into Horatio Alger's mold and many people, mayor-watchers and others, found it difficult to understand him when he was in a serious mood. For instance, his was a rather violent reaction to the story, written as he was about to leave his post as Ambassador to Mexico by a careful and respected reporter, to the effect that as he was going to live in Mexico he was about to surrender his American citizenship. Bill enjoyed the friendship of the domestic and foreign press in Mexico and none of them could understand why his anger was almost uncontrollable. He called the press to meet him. The gathering was inaccurately described as a press conference. Bill became insulting and most abusive to the author of the story who was present in the room. Indeed, members of the press, who were present to witness what appeared to them to be strange behavior, knew a number of Americans who became Mexican citizens to avoid criminal and civil liability should they, while retaining American citizenship, fail to pay American taxes. Some newsmen with whom I spoke felt that after a long and creditable career in public service the abuse heaped upon Bill by a Senate subcommittee and a host of prosecutors might have provided a justifiable reason for taking out citizenship in a country that had extended the hand of friendship to him when he stood abused back home.

I never heard him give voice to patriotic claptrap and only this chance incident brought to the surface the difference in commitment between him and those who, for tax avoidance or otherwise, had surrendered what to Bill O'Dwyer was his most valuable asset and a status that was little less than sacred. Had the subject matter been some other bit of annoyance, I would have felt that Bill should have been cautious

---

*Most of the material in this book was written by my brother. However, I have added several chapters or portions of chapters. My contributions are indicated by the abbreviation PO'D. In the few instances where material by both of us in included in the same chapter, the part written by Bill is indicated by WO'D.

not to arouse the media to further antagonism. His outburst was out of character for him. Seldom, if ever, had he been guilty of bad manners. But here I found no quarrel with his reaction.

I remembered the day I swore away any allegiance I was reputed to have to George V whom they said was King of Great Britain and Ireland. There was no point in telling the judge I didn't have any such allegiance. Anyway, having removed that stigma, I, for the first time, acquired a country that I could honor and be proud of and complain about and argue with, with all the affection and emotion and bias of a father, a mother, a sister, a brother, a wife, a son, a daughter. I knew that repudiating that relationship would be the act of an ingrate. I was in total sympathy with my brother.

The difference between him and his fellow citizens who felt his reaction was unexplainable had to be related to the environment whence he came. To be understood it had to be viewed against the new freedoms which American citizenship had bestowed upon him and his newly acquired status as a child of and partner in the American Revolution. He was a history buff and we frequently had discussed the revolution. We were aware of the history of the colonies, of the religious intolerance and the discrimination against the men and women of no property and the oppression by the ruling class among the colonists which cried out for revolt. But Bill O'Dwyer's roots were not in New Amsterdam or in New England or Virginia. The conditions which helped to mold him were 3,000 miles away and his escape into freedom's world was not a distant experience.

So back to Ireland for some of the answers and for the rest—to the history of the city and state to which he came. The story about Bill O'Dwyer which most people liked to hear and to repeat dealt with the penniless immigrant coming to New York in 1911 and climbing to great heights in this friendly atmosphere. It was clear proof that in this country one could rise from the most humble circumstances to the most honored and important place in the land, and it established a rare generosity on the part of our nation. It was a romantic tale, but there was a flaw in it. It ignored the fact that the opportunities guaranteed by the Bill of Rights had been denied to New York's earliest inhabitants. It failed to explain why those great advantages available even to the European immigrant could not apply to a man of the caliber of Percy Sutton[1] whose career paralleled Bill O'Dwyer's in very many respects.

William O'Dwyer was the product of at least a century of hardship imposed on his people by alien greed and brutality. The same greed and the same brutality had been visited upon the black slaves and the native Americans. The place whence he came is still plagued by the same greed and the same brutality and the place he came to is still in the throes of wrestling with rank discrimination even while the Bill of Rights, like a voice from the honored past, tells the nation to deal decently with its minorities.

Oft I had heard it said and repeated that it took Tom Paine's *Common Sense* to give the patriots and soldiers an understanding of why there should be a revolution. While British tyranny was annoying, the tyranny of the colonists against each other was a much greater reason to strike for a new freedom. Nobody was saying it that way, however. It was easier to blame it all on Great Britain whose record made her suspect. Pointing the accusing finger at several generations of colonists who continued to institutionalize bigotry and intolerance was less acceptable.

When the story is told it brings new luster to the founders of the republic and those who established our basic principles. Hopefully, the lamp at the golden door will light the space inside it. It is to be hoped this effort will demonstrate the distance we have come and as the light from the lamp shines on the dark corners that need cleansing, it will bid us to be worthy of those who established the principles which have made us, with all our faults the only country to be able, through the constitutional process, to challenge the right even of our President to continue in office. If, notwithstanding those great accomplishments, the story may not fully reveal the warmth or the wit or the charm or the humor of Bill O'Dwyer, and if I have difficulty in shaping it that way, it is for want of skill rather than fact. I do hope, however, that the reader will understand the immigrant's deep feeling for a country that has brought itself out of the abyss of ignorance of its early settlers in colonial days, and through the inspiration of thinking and principled revolutionary leaders created a framework of liberty and bid all of us in the continuing revolutionary process to fill in the squares.

1. Sutton came to New York from San Antonio, Texas, was employed as a subway worker while he pursued an education in the law, served as a paratrooper in the U.S. Army in World War II while the Army was still segregated and suffered indescribable indignities as he travelled through the States in full uniform. When he gained admission to the bar, he was elected to the State Legislature from a black district. Following a distinguished career as Borough President of Manhattan, where he was recognized as an expert in city government, he sought the position of Mayor for which he was eminently qualified. Every reasonable observer knew he failed to get the votes in white districts because he was black. That election took place in 1977, a quarter of a century after William O'Dwyer, with a very similar background, was swept into office. It was obvious the City, as one Democratic leader expressed it, "was not ready for a black Mayor."

CHAPTER 1

THE FAMINE AND THE O'DWYERS OF TULLYLEASE

PO'D

The Famine of 1847-1850 had devastated the land. Half of its nine million population had melted away. Some died by the roadside. Most of those who starved got a Christian burial of sorts. Some never made it back to mother earth, their carcasses consumed by carnivorous animals. About two million made it somehow to the emigrant ship. Many of those died on board and were fed to the sharks. Others died of malnutrition and disease soon after landing. At Grosse Ile, Quebec, eight thousand of them died and were buried in a common grave. The fittest or the luckiest made it to Boston, New York, Philadelphia, Montreal and Quebec to start all over again. Some were recruited for the coal fields where they again suffered from the pangs of hunger. Hundreds of them died from black lung disease. Others died more violently deep in the bowels of the earth with no safety law to protect them and defenseless against the greed of the mine boss.

The Great Hunger brought mixed reaction from London. The *Times* gloated. "Soon," their editorial read, "there will be fewer Irishmen on the Banks of the Shannon than there are Red Indians in Manhattan." The British Parliament debated and debated on what measures the government should take. The House of Commons felt that to hand out relief to the suffering or to ration existing supplies would prove to be unfair to the merchant class who lived by the law of supply and demand. And so Ireland's food supply continued to flow to England. In each of the years in which death relentlessly reaped its human harvest, more than enough agricultural products to feed Ireland's population were shipped out of the country. As Thomas Gallagher points out in *Paddy's Lament*:

> The almost immediate starvation and distress that followed the
> failure of the potato crop in 1846 could have happened only in

1

Ireland, a country forced by its union with Britain to depend for its subsistence on this single crop. For although three-quarters of Ireland's cultivable land was in "corn"—a general term that included such grains as wheat, oats, and barley—almost all of it was shipped to England. The cattle and sheep grazed in Ireland, and the pigs fed, were likewise not eaten in Ireland but sent to Britain for consumption by either the British people or those maintaining her colonies.

To make matters worse, in the stricken areas merchants raised the prices and gouged the last few possessions from the victims while they were yet alive. The gombeenmen (usurers), most of them Irish Catholic, accumulated new and sizeable fortunes.

A number of compassionate men and women in England took issue with their government's attitude. They created a charitable trust to aid the starving. They called on the Queen, then a young woman, to take the lead, recognizing that a sizable donation from Her Majesty would spell success for the project. Victoria contributed £5.

The nation which had survived so many attacks now lay prone. Nature has its own way of drawing the blind on the individual tragedy, but the *shanachie* (storyteller), whose art made him the keeper of the people's experiences, wove these events into history, which was repeated by word-of-mouth in each affected locality and to each succeeding generation. It was about a century later that Liam O'Flaherty and Cecil Woodham Smith put the pieces together in two books—O'Flaherty's *Famine* and Woodham Smith's *The Great Hunger*—which became best sellers in both Ireland and America.

It was while these events were taking place that my grandfather, John O'Dwyer, of Tullylease in the county of Cork, took a wife. In those days marriages were generally arranged between the parents, and most frequently the matchmaker was the broker. On rare occasions the young got together on their own. That union was known as a love match. John and Catherine's was a love match. It had to be. She was Catherine Norcott and she came of Planter[1] stock. Her marriage to a despised papist was a shock to her family and her conversion to Catholicism ended her connection with her kinfolk. For John, marriage to one of a hated class, even a converted one, did not bring any cheers from his side of the marriage. But the hostile attitude of their environments obviously did not diminish their affection for one another. They had nine

---

1. Much of the lands of Ireland had been confiscated and given to English nobility who cleared the natives off their holdings and "planted" English or Scottish settlers on their places.

Patrick and Bridget O'Dwyer with children. The original picture with eight children was taken in Bohola in 1918; Bill and Jim were inserted later. Top (left to right): Bill, Tom, Frank, Jack and Jim. Middle: Linda, May, Kathleen and Josie. Bottom: Patrick, Paul and Bridget.

3

children. My father, Patrick, was born seven years after the worst period of the famine.

John and Catherine were in trade. They opened a small shop in Tullylease where they sold a variety of foodstuffs and enjoyed the privilege, from a government license, to sell whiskey and stout seven days a week. The legend over the door read, "John O'Dwyer—Tea, Wine and Spirit Merchant."

The opportunities were few in Tullylease. Patrick's options were limited to the teaching profession, migrating or joining the British Army in any one of five regiments, bearing names like the Connaught Rangers or the Munster Fusaliers (many of whose members had taken the Queen's shilling from the recruiting sergeant on a fair day and had gained fame and death). By 1887 the population of the village had been reduced to a few hundred people.

But Tullylease had seen better days. In the seventh century it was an important seat of learning. The name in Gaelic was Tullach Leis which means the hill of huts. Students came from far distant places and lived in huts on the side of the hill while they studied under St. Berihert. That was 1200 years before Patrick O'Dwyer was born, but the history and legend were an integral part of Tullylease. During his boyhood years, the 18th of February was celebrated as the saint's day. People came there to visit the ruins of the old church the saint had built. The story goes that St. Berihert came as a missionary to the North Cork area which was still a Druid stronghold and succeeded in converting the people to Christianity.

The church and the cell of St. Berihert are now gone and the replacement built in the 12th century is in ruins, but the holy well remains. Ireland has its full complement of holy wells. Most of them are associated with a saint or a learned monk. But on February 18th the people still come to Tullylease to drink from the well of St. Berihert, and some of the pilgrims come in the hope of being cured of some malady. Stories of past miracles are part of the local storytellers' repertoire.

It may be that the reputation of Tullylease as an ancient center of learning affected Patrick's decision, and it may be that the other alternatives were uninviting. In any event, he set out for Drumcondra College in Dublin on the first step of a journey which was to ultimately take him away from the Province of Munster and to the Western Province of Connaught.

4

CHAPTER 2

PATRICK O'DWYER AND
THE MURDER MACHINE

PO'D

Deplorable is the only appropriate description that could be reasonably applied to the Irish educational system until the end of the 19th century. It was then that Trinity College, the "bastion of Protestant ascendancy," opened the doors ever so little to Catholics and Dissenters.

Patrick O'Dwyer was in his 20's in 1883 when St. Patrick's College in Drumcondra, Dublin, opened *its* doors. The avowed purpose of the school was to bring professionalism into the primary educational system, which had staggered along illegally through the centuries. In practice the new schools were part of a larger plan to remove the Gaelic culture from Ireland.

The "hedge" schoolteacher, who had served to keep education alive for several centuries, imparted the rudiments of education to the children of the poor. While the Penal Laws were being enforced during the last decade of the 17th century and the first half of the 18th century, a lookout was posted on a nearby hill to warn the teacher of the approach of the redcoats. There was a £5 bounty on the teacher's head. The teacher lived on whatever the tenant farmer could afford to pay. Frequently in poor areas like Mayo, he or she survived on such food items as the local farmer supplied when no hard cash was available. The hedge school had seen its greatest day while the Penal Laws were being enforced, but in the absence of any other system available to the Catholic peasant, it continued to serve the people far into the 19th century.

The passage of the Catholic Emancipation Act in 1829 did not signal the immediate restoration of rights to the Irish Catholic population, and education became high on their list of demands. When eventually a system was put in place, the conditions attached to it made the school an instrumentality of Anglicizing the youth of Ireland.

An accommodation between the Catholic Church and the Empire

5

was established, which proved to be most helpful in controlling the natives and was successful in discouraging any general uprising for more than half a century. Where the British had failed through the use of oppression, brutality and violence, the new educational system proved to be a great success. Concession was granted the local church to dominate the system, in return for which the Celtic culture was well-nigh obliterated.

Two years after the passage of the Catholic Emancipation Act, Parliament gave £30,000 to the Lord Lieutenant of Ireland "to assist with the education of the people." Up to that time, all grants for education were allocated to such groups as the Dublin Society for Promoting English Protestant Schools in Ireland. The money was used to proselytize as well as educate.[1] In the same year the Board of Commissioners of National Education was created. It immediately ran into trouble and was thrown off balance by the fears of the Anglican, the Catholic and the Presbyterian churches. The religious institutions made it impossible for the children of Ireland to receive an education beside the children of another denomination. Finally, the Catholic schools came under the direct management of the parish priests.

The establishment of the Board of Commissioners of National Education had at first given hope that henceforth education would be available to Catholics and Dissenters as well as Protestants. But it took 52 years to open the doors of Drumcondra, the only teacher–training school for men, and of Our Lady of Mercy for women. Knowledge of the Gaelic language, still the spoken language in substantial areas of the country and the only avenue to an ancient culture, was not a requirement for entrance to either establishment, nor was knowledge of Irish history. If Irish classes were formed, they had to be after school hours. Even as late as 1900 there was nothing in the curriculum to differentiate the Irish school from the English school catering to children of similar ages. Any reference to the free spirit was prohibited. Indeed, poetry like "Breathes there a man" and "Freedom shrieked as Kosciosko fell" was banished from Irish national schools. Earlier, Archbishop Whately, one of the commissioners, expressed, "The aim of the commission is to make every pupil a happy English child." "Irish history was virtually ignored and Irish poetry might never have existed," concludes Trinity historian, F.S.L. Lyons. Padraig Pearse,[2] the schoolmaster at St. Endas, described the Commission of National Education as the "murder machine." "It is," he wrote, "because the English educational system in Ireland has

---

1. The Christian Brothers of Ireland, a teaching order, was formed to counteract the effects of the proselytizing which was then rampant, but only a small number of Irish children were fortunate enough to gain entrance to their schools.
2. Leader of the 1916 Rebellion who was captured and executed in that year.

deliberately eliminated the national factor that it has so terrifically succeeded. For it has succeeded in making slaves of us and it has succeeded
so well we no longer realize we are slaves . . . It remains the crowning
achievement of the . . . systems that they have wrought such a change
in this people that once loved freedom so passionately."

In 1888 when Patrick completed his teacher-training course, Drumcondra teachers were much in demand. The salary was fixed and small,
but the graduate could pick and choose the place in which he wanted
to settle. Several positions were available. The one he chose was in a
place called Bohola in County Mayo.

CHAPTER 3

IRISH DREAMS

For each age is a dream that is dying,
Or one that is coming to birth.
                    Arthur O'Shaughnessy

PO'D

LAND REFORM

Bohola was not even a dot on the map, but inquiry revealed its location to be in County Mayo. Mayo, the poorest county of the 32, had been the scene of the beginning of organizing activity against the absentee landlords who extracted unconscionable rents from the poorest tenants. A few miles away, Michael Davitt, the socialist revolutionary and organizer of the Land League, was born. During his college days in Dublin, Patrick O'Dwyer had come to know and admire Davitt, as well as William O'Brien, a fellow Corkman and Davitt's alter ego, and these years had a great effect on my father's politics.

It was understandable that Patrick O'Dwyer would be a staunch supporter and admirer of both leaders. Both men were the products of a period of great unrest. In infancy, Davitt and his parents had been evicted from their small farm in Straide in the county of Mayo. Straide was the next parish to Bohola. At the age of 11 he lost an arm in an accident in a factory in England where he was employed. Later while serving seven years for sedition in an English jail, he perfected his writing skills and because of his special knowledge of Jewish persecutions, the *New York Tribune* sent him on an assignment to Russia. His stories on the Russian pogroms, which were raging at the time, brought him to the notice of American journalists and politicians.

O'Brien was a brilliant writer, newspaper editor and pamphleteer. He was the strong, quiet radical voice at every conference of Irish political leaders of the time. This new theory of government called socialism was, curiously enough, then espoused by the more affluent and the intellectuals. O'Brien's chief interest was in the plight of the small farmers of Ireland. Since Mayo had become the early proving ground of the land reform movement, it was natural that Mayo was to see more and more of O'Brien. He and Sophie, his wife, moved their home to Westport in West Mayo, some 30 miles away from Straide and Bohola. From then until his death, the O'Briens were in the forefront of every humanitarian and nationalist movement and were the instigators of many of them.[1]

Michael Davitt also took up the cause of the Irish tenant farmer. An incident occurred on April 20, 1879, which was to bring many of the pieces together. A parish priest named Canon Burke, who doubled as a landlord in Irishtown, County Mayo, was about to evict a tenant farmer for inability to pay the unconscionable rent the good priest demanded. Davitt rallied the tenants of Mayo, thousands of whom surrounded the priest's house and the little farmhouse where the eviction was to take place. The priest surrendered to the intimidation.

The news of the success of the effort spread quickly. A week later, the Land League was formed. It became the most effective and formidable organization of its time and made Davitt a leader to be feared and respected. A principal objective of Davitt and the Land League was land reform. In less than two years, the House of Commons responded to the tenants' demands with the passage of the Land Act of 1881. The agitation continued and the law was amended and improved several times over succeeding years. For the first time, the Irish tenant farmer had won the "three F's": fixity of tenure, fair rent, and the right of free sale. The success of the Land League was all the more remarkable since the bishops of Ireland had joined the Tory Party of Great Britain in roundly condemning the Land League as the instrumentality of the devil.

1. Sophie O'Brien's background was no less interesting than her husband's. They met for the first time in Paris, the gathering place of world reformers and revolutionaries. O'Brien had been jailed in England in 1891. A journalist from Paris named Rafalovich interviewed him in his jail cell. Rafalovich was a Jewish refugee from a Latvian pogrom. Later, when O'Brien visited Paris, he called on Rafalovich and met the journalist's daughter, Sophie. They married and returned to Ireland. In Westport, Sophie used the considerable fortune she had inherited to finance the newspaper and pamphlets which her husband published. Finally, in the 1930's all her money was spent. Her husband had died. She returned to France only to be caught up in the house-to-house Nazi search for Jews. Only her identification, as Sophie O'Brien, saved this now elderly lady. With friends, she escaped to a small town on the Garonne River at the foothills of the Pyrenees. I visited her there in 1947.

HOME RULE

The success of this land reform movement gave new impetus to the rather modest demand for Home Rule for Ireland. During a visit to America, Davitt met with John Devoy and the other Fenian leaders to convince them to throw their weight and support to Charles Stewart Parnell, an Anglo-Irish Protestant member of Parliament who had welded his fellow Irish members of Parliament into a strong unified force known as the Irish Parliamentary Party.

Davitt's plan included joining the revolutionary forces and the parliamentary or constitutional forces together with the Land League. The purpose was to create a voting block in the House of Commons to support Gladstone's Liberal Party, in return for the enactment of Home Rule. In fact, Davitt had little enthusiasm for either the Home Rule movement or the Irish Parliamentary Party, but nevertheless he joined Parnell as the most likely leader to bring about much-needed national unity.

The demands of the Irish Parliamentary Party were mild in comparison to the movements of earlier periods. About 80 years earlier, Theobald Wolfe Tone, waving the separatist banner of the United Irishmen, had led his people, Protestant and Catholic, in open rebellion against the Crown. A few years later, Robert Emmett, son of an Anglican merchant, had followed the same path. Nor did the Irish Parliamentary Party have the intellectual credibility of the Young Ireland movement headed by a revolutionary group which came into existence soon after the Famine. The Young Irelanders broke with Daniel O'Connell, the pacifist, and like the United Irishmen, demanded that the ties to England be completely severed.[2]

The radicalism of the Fenian movement, which got its start in the United States just before the Civil War and which was committed to physical force as the only means of driving the British out of Ireland, came into open rebellion in 1867 and was crushed. Its methods found no favor with the Irish Parliamentary Party. The "stepping stone theory" was the vehicle by which they believed Ireland would attain its ultimate destiny. They were committed to attaining liberty through "constitutional means." They believed that a sort of dominion form of government would pass the British House of Commons with the help of Gladstone

2. In the repudiation of O'Connell, the man responsible for the passage of the Catholic Emancipation Act, the highly educated Young Irelanders lamented the necessity for their actions. "After careful deliberation it was determined to indicate our dissent from the course O'Connell had taken, as clearly as would be generous in the face of a triumphant enemy, and towards a chief whom that enemy aimed to humiliate. For the rest we could wait for the future. The future belongs to the young and self-reliant, and the policy of the country could not long be directed by a man who had passed his grand climacteric."

and the Liberals.

William Ewart Gladstone had become a sort of folk hero in Ireland.[3] During the years Patrick O'Dwyer was pursuing his studies in Dublin, the Liberal Party of Great Britain was under Gladstone's leadership. He had shown a sympathetic understanding of at least part of the Irish problem when in 1869 he brought an end to the hateful law which had required Irish Catholics to pay "tithes" for upkeep of the Anglican Church in Ireland.

In this context, Davitt and the Irish Parliamentary Party then brought the issue of Home Rule into the forefront, including a new movement to repeal the Act of Union, which had been passed in Dublin by "treachery and fraud" in 1800 and which removed the Irish law-making body to the British House of Commons. "Home Rule" was a far cry from the separatist republican doctrine of the preceding century, but even that rather mild measure needed the strong and credible leadership of Parnell.

Only Davitt, a man of many parts, a strange combination of idealist and political pragmatist, could accept Parnell as one who could be developed to unite and lead the Irish Parliamentary Party and the Irish people. There was little in Parnell's background which would fit him for the role that Davitt had created for him.

On his father's side, Parnell's family dated back a century when the ancestor came from England to buy land in Limerick and other areas of Ireland. His maternal grandfather, Charles Stewart, served in the American armed forces in the war against Great Britain in 1812. The Parnells had become Irish landlords to Irish peasant tenants, and while they had not been condemned for the imposition of rack-rents, they were still part of the hated Protestant ascendancy.

Parnell received his education in England and had not in his early years participated in any nationalist movement. Sometime after 1870 he decided that life as a country squire in Limerick was boring and that he ought to enter the political arena. In 1872 he stood for Parliament in Dublin and was defeated. In 1875 he was a candidate for Tipperary and lost. He had not yet convinced either the Catholics or the Fenians that he was a genuine nationalist.

In the same year Parnell again put himself forward as a candidate for Parliament. This comparative stranger to the scene had learned much from his two defeats. In his previous attempts to gain public office he had the blessing of a friendly priest. It hadn't helped. Then in 1875 a

3. I well remember a row of mugs with the Prime Minister's picture emblazoned on them as they looked out to us from the kitchen "dresser," 25 years after he had retired from office. This place of honor conveyed the impression that he was a good Englishman and no *Sashanach* (Gaelic for Saxon, a term of derision). The mugs remained until the Rebellion of 1916, after which they were no longer on display.

vacancy occurred in Meath, and Parnell became a candidate. This time, under the wise counsel of Davitt, he sought out the Bishop. Immediately following the meeting with His Lordship, he addressed a large gathering on April 12th in Navan. All the priests of the diocese were there to listen. Parnell described his platform. After a few references to land reform and home rule, he got to the point. He believed, he said, "in denominational education under the proper control of the clergy." Loud cheers came from the assembled Catholic clergy. This act of faith of the heretic was duly reported to His Lordship the Bishop, and on election day Parnell reaped the rewards that flowed from listening to his mentor.

Parnell took his seat in Parliament, became a dynamic and committed leader and held his party together for the next 15 years. In 1881 the Crown had him jailed. Confinement in Kilmainham Jail[4] cemented his hold on the people of Ireland. It established his sincerity and proved he was ready to follow in the Irish tradition. Having passed the test, his religion, once a drawback, now became a distinct asset.

While Parnell guided the destinies of the Irish Parliamentary Party, Gladstone was the acknowledged leader of the Liberal Party, and during six of those years he was Britain's Prime Minister. With a united Irish Party and a friendly Gladstone, the prospects for the enactment of Home Rule for Ireland were never brighter. Never since the year of the Catholic Emancipation Act had the people's hopes been higher. If they could have crowned Parnell king of Ireland, they would gladly have done it.

The Fenian influence waned. "Home Rule for Ireland without pistol or gun," the slogan of the constitutionalists, drowned out the cry of the last of the Fenian brotherhood. Their warning that England would leave Ireland only when blasted out, became less and less audible as Parnell's prestige increased.

Then the bubble burst. In 1889 Captain W.H. O'Shea, previously a member of Parliament, had sued his wife Katherine (Kitty) for divorce and named Charles Stewart Parnell as the co-respondent. Gladstone seized on the occasion to scuttle the Home Rule bill. He had an obligation to the dissenters (Protestants not in the established church), he said, who would take a dim view of his dealing with a leader who figured in a public scandal.[5] The Irish bishops followed meekly on Gladstone's

---

4. Kilmainham was one of the jails to which the Crown sent Irish political prisoners.
5. While the British, some Irish politicians and the clerical leaders of all faiths expressed shock at the love affair of Parnell and Kitty O'Shea, their righteousness seemed to have been selective. During the same period Edward VII, then the Prince of Wales, married and the father of a family, was openly maintaining Lilly Langtry as his mistress. There were clumsy efforts to hide the sordid relationship including an arranged public meeting between Edward's wife and Mrs. Langtry and the assignment of Mrs. Langtry to Edward's nephew, Louis, by whom she had a child. They also included a monthly payoff to Mrs. Langtry's husband to keep him silent.

heels. They denounced Parnell. His colleagues, including Davitt and O'Brien, advised him to resign until the divorce was over and he could marry his love. An ambitious young leader, Tim Healy, sought Parnell's mantle. In the election which followed, in a biting attack, Healy proclaimed that the great nationalist leader who had led the fight for Home Rule was more interested in: "Eight hours work and eight hours play and eight hours sleep with Kitty O'Shea."

In 1890 Home Rule, "the dream that was dying," developed a terminal illness in the London divorce court. It showed occasional flashes of life, as Parnell courageously faced the electorate in meetings throughout the country, but the division within the party was evident in every street corner and meeting place. Its death rattle could be heard at the end of the historic election rally at Sligo.

Parnell had nominated a nondescript candidate to carry his banner in the Sligo constituency that included two dioceses in Mayo. In a widely publicized appearance he spoke in favor of his candidate. But he was really speaking for himself, in what proved to be his last hurrah.

The Irish Parliamentary Party was now hopelessly divided, Parnell's continuance as its leader being the sole issue. The Irish hierarchy, as might be expected, followed the lead of Archbishop Croke, who warned that to support Parnell at election time would be to give "public scandal" to one who "committed a serious offense" and who had "not repented." His constituency encompassed the Diocese of Achonry, which included Bohola. The priests in Achonry, in a display of independence unheard of in other areas, revolted against the Bishop's decision. They had come from Fenian stock and openly supported Parnell. The bishops of two Mayo dioceses retreated to a neutral position. Parnell's candidate carried the day in Mayo, but lost the seat when the voters in Sligo town came out strongly in support of the Church. It was truly the end of an era.

As soon as Kitty was free, she married Parnell. Their happiness was shortlived. In 1891, he died a broken man. The contemporary Irish historian, A.M. Sullivan, wrote of his passing:

> Parnell, the high-souled patriot, the farseeing statesman, the fearless unflinching champion of Erin's rights who had struggled and battled and led the people within sight of the promised land of freedom—Parnell was no more.

His death occurred at Brighton, England on October 6, 1891. The long funeral cortege that escorted his remains to Glasnevin Cemetery[6] attested to the universal grief of the people of Ireland for the loss of Ireland's greatest son.

6. A Dublin cemetery where many Irish Revolutionaries are buried.

13

By 1891 the Fenian guns were silent, with no plans to take them from their place of hiding. What was left of the Young Ireland Movement was scattered. For the next two decades Ireland was to produce no armed rebellion.

That year, a few rhymes of a young and yet unknown poet, W.B. Yeats, reflected the people's despair:

> Seek then no learning from the starry men
> Who follow with the optic glass
> The whirling ways of stars that pass-
> Seek then for this is also sooth
> No word of theirs—the cold star-bane
> Has cloven and rent their heads in twain,
> And dead is all their human truth.

FREEDOM

A woman who was to play an important role in both the political and cultural aspects of the next dream was present at the Sligo meeting that had brought thousands to the town to hear Parnell. Constance Gore Booth, young daughter of a well-known Anglo-Irish landlord, rode her horse sidesaddle from her elegant estate 10 miles away into Sligo town. She had little interest in the issues of the campaign. She and her sister, Eva, went there to be seen and admired and out of curiosity to see this one-time popular hero who had risked his career for the love of Kitty O'Shea.

The Gore Booths were by far the best of their class. Indeed, the well-preserved legend around their mansion in Lisadell proclaims their concern for their tenants, whom they fed during the Great Hunger. Yet, they were of the aristocracy and accepted its generous privileges. On St. Patrick's Day, four years before Parnell's appearance in Sligo, Constance and her sister, having arrived at the age where young women of their station should be afforded the privilege of meeting Victoria Regina, Defender of the Faith, Queen of Great Britain and Ireland and Empress of India, were presented at court in England.

Now, at the Sligo meeting, a "dream that was coming to birth" was conceived. Parnell had been in the forefront of the fight for tenants' rights. He addressed the issue that day in a bitter attack on the system which had sustained the Gore Booths in luxury through the centuries. Eva was unaffected by it, but it seems to have been the turning point in the life of Constance Gore Booth. Soon after, she began to examine her relationship with her surroundings and with those whose misery had kept the "ascendancy" in its position of pomp and power.

During the next five years, Constance became embroiled in cultural interests and in the Feminist movement. In her first public act of faith, she organized the Sligo Woman Suffragists. It was by no means the extent of her interests. She agitated in her own home for her emancipation and finally gained permission to go to Paris to study art. There she married Polish Count Casimir Markievicz, and they returned to live in Ireland.

By the time a new birth of freedom came kicking and squalling from the quiet of the Irish womb, the Countess had become an avid follower of socialist labor leader James Connolly and was herself a leader in the Irish Citizen Army. In 1915, a year of preparation for the Rebellion, she exhorted the women of Dublin, "Leave your jewels in the bank and buy a revolver. Don't trust to your feminine charm . . . but go your own way depending for safety on your own truths and your own common sense . . ." and "We have got to get rid of the last vestige of the harem before woman is a free body as our dream of the future would have her."

It was clear she was a half a century ahead of her time, but even inside the revolution she demanded her own personal liberty and got it.

On Easter Monday, 1916, the Rebellion broke out. Countess Markievicz took her place as second in command of the Citizen Army division at the College of Surgeons at Stephen's Green. Her regiment, if one could call it such, consisted of 103 men and 15 women. After a week of fighting she and her contingent were directed by their commanders to surrender. She kissed her Luger pistol as she turned it over to her captors. Her subsequent sentence of death was commuted to life imprisonment, and she was transported to a British prison as a dangerous convict. Of her time in prison she said, "It's only a mean spirit that grudges paying the price."

The British committed the colossal blunder of executing the leaders of the Rebellion. The utter arrogance turned Ireland into an armed camp. Their second mistake was to release the other prisoners after one year in jail. Countess Markievicz returned to Ireland to carry on the fight that for her did not end until her death in her 60th year. In the intervening period she represented her people in the Irish Parliament from its establishment in 1919.

CHAPTER 4

THE McNICHOLASES OF BOHOLA

PO'D

Bohola is located 150 miles west of Dublin, and it is but a short distance from there to the western sea. From there the Druids said you could, betimes, see Tir Na-Nóg, the land of the ever-young, where good Irish men and women went after life in Erin was ended. Notwithstanding 15 centuries of one kind or other of Christianity, there was much of Druid belief left under the cloak of the new religion.

On the 21st day of June our nearest neighbor would build a fire in front of the house and say the rosary as she walked around it. It was St. John's Day. The fire was burning in his honor. She knew nothing about St. John and less about the ritual she performed. Before the coming of Patrick, in the fifth century, the people worshipped that way too. The movement around the fire was an act of worship to Bael Chinna, the God of Fire. Seemingly, Patrick and his missioners engaged in some compromises. They avoided head-on collisions. It might be too much to ask the people of Ireland to abandon their tribute altogether. The wise proselytizers continued the custom but prevailed on the converts to change the date from May 1st to June 21st, which coincided with the Feast of St. John.

Bohola was our parish. Besides the Catholic church, the home of the parish priest and the curate, it boasted of three pubs and a post office. Included in the parish were 23 villages or townlands, with a total population of 2,580, according to the 1911 census. Lismirrane, the village in which I was born, was two miles from Bohola "center." Its 17 houses were scattered over 300 acres, and when my mother was growing up, all 17 answered to the same name as hers, McNicholas.[1] The nearest

1. They were descendants of Jordan de Exeter, who had come to Ireland as Norman conquerors under King Henry II in 1171. The Normans in time became Irish, throwing in their lot with the people against England, and almost all their descendants became as impoverished as the rest. The land around Bohola was owned by the Knox Gore family, aristocrats who followed the English manners, dress, customs and religion. The village of Lismirrane, however, was owned by the Moores, who lived in Moore Hall, 30 miles south, and who did little to commend themselves to the oppressed tenants.

railroad station was in a neighboring town, and it took six and one-half hours by train to travel the 150 miles to Dublin.

The people around us were poor and frugal. They were small farmers who worked hard on the land, and for several months of the year they worked on farms in England and Scotland. "Spalpeen" was the name given to these migratory farm laborers, and the title was mostly used in derision.

The farmers preferred to have sons, who could fend for themselves, rather than daughters, for whom they would have to provide a dowry. The matchmaker had to know how much the dowry or "fortune" was and, on the basis of the amount, he could choose a suitable man. And the size of the dowry determined the amount of land which the prospective husband brought to the marriage. One son was usually selected to inherit the homestead. The old people invariably held on to the land for as long as they could, making marriage for the man at a young age unlikely. He almost invariably married a woman many years his junior who usually survived him by many years, thus creating a matriarchal society which, with few exceptions, made for a more than unusually unpleasant relationship between mother-in-law and daughter-in-law.

However, just as John O'Dwyer and Catherine Norcott's marriage was a love match, and not "arranged" according to custom, so was the marriage between my other grandparents of Bohola.

My grandfather, called Pat–"Peggy"[2] McNicholas to distinguish him from three other Pat McNicholases in the same townland, was the owner of 20 acres of good land. But he was not content with being a farmer. He also operated a shop where he sold salt, sugar, oatmeal, Indian meal, flour and American bacon. He bought his merchandise in Ballina, 15 miles away, and he used a team of mules to cart it home.

On his return journey, he usually stopped at a local inn to rest the mules and refresh himself. It was on such a day he met Penelope Caffrey, the niece of the owner of the establishment. She caught his eye, and the trips to Ballina became more frequent.

Penelope had a good education, was fond of music and was a hard worker. She was never favored with a marriage proposal for the reason that she had no dowry. Pat-Peggy was against the dowry system, calling it barbarous, revolting and disgusting, and Penelope's lack of a dowry therefore proved to be somewhat of an advantage. They were married in 1857.

Penelope attended to her husband's shop in Lismirrane but did not work on the farm or feed the livestock. Although she had no money,

2. Peggy was Pat's mother's name, and her children were referred to as if "Peggy" was their surname.

17

she was a cultured young woman who had many of the social graces. She was an accomplished musician and often played the harmonium when her day's work was done.

She bore many children. Bridget McNicholas, my mother, was the eighth of their nine children. She was one of three sisters. Ann was redhaired, Mary was flaxen-haired, and Bridget's *cool* was dark as night and went down to her waist.

During the time my mother was growing up, it was regarded as decidedly lower class to speak in the Gaelic tongue, and in response to the Anglicizing process, at 21 years of age she was unable to converse in the native language of both her father and mother. Her formal education was limited. She had been the smartest girl in the class, and that qualified her as a teacher because the parish priest said so. Whatever her qualifications in the beginning, the improvement was constant, and she could intelligently converse with my father when he first came to Bohola from a far-off place.

When Pat O'Dwyer arrived, she was already an assistant schoolteacher in the new school with the slated roof. The old one with a thatched roof had recently been burned down. The day's activities in the classroom did not exclude social contact or exchange of views between the new master and his assistant teacher. A courtship followed which was a matter of speculation to some, a matter of great interest to others and a matter of concern to those closer in kinship. Finally, Patrick and Bridget decided to tell her parents.

For Pat-Peggy it was a welcome proposal, more welcome than the usual feeling of satisfaction of a father whose daughter is about to marry an eligible man of promise, if not property. Before Patrick, there had been no suitors at her father's door. The prospective ones knew that Pat-Peggy McNicholas would part with no money to marry off his daughters. But Patrick O'Dwyer from Cork and college-trained in Dublin was also opposed to the dowry system. And so, in 1889 Bridget McNicholas and Patrick O'Dwyer were married.

CHAPTER 5

PAT O'DWYER OF BOHOLA

PO'D

The school to which Pat O'Dwyer was assigned to teach had recently been given a new slated roof. The teacher preceding him was a native Irish petty landlord, like Canon Burke of Irishtown. Even before the Land League agitation, some English landlords sold out parts of their holdings. Some enterprising natives, seeing a golden opportunity to acquire landlord status, bought tenanted lands in smaller quantities. The new owners were as avaricious or more so than their greedy predecessors. One of these squireens doubled as the teacher in the school to which Patrick O'Dwyer was later to come. The people burned down the school. The landlord teacher had the good judgment to sell out and depart the scene in the dead of night. It was into this restless atmosphere that Patrick O'Dwyer came.

He had travelled by train to Tuam in the adjoining county, some 40 miles away, and made the rest of the way into Mayo by stagecoach. For reasons that were not clear, the same people who burned the school gave the Corkman notice he was not welcome. He was, however, seasoned to meet hostility. His parents before him had overcome local resentment, but this surly opposition to one assigned to teach their own children was most difficult for him to understand. The new teacher had much knowledge to impart, but he also had much to learn about his new environment. The Gaelic culture had long ago been replaced in Cork by a semi-Anglicized version, and while both areas shared the resentment against the Crown, the conditions and environment in his new place of abode made him a stranger in their midst.

In North Cork, the land was rich. In Mayo, people tilled the pieces of earth between the rocks. Indeed, the place where the school was located was known as *Baile na Carraig*, the rocky townland. If he wanted to live here he would have to learn the names of the fields in Irish. He would need to respond to *"Bol o dia an an obair"* (God bless the work) or to know enough to take his turn at the churn as he entered a cabin.

It was said that if the visitor failed to observe this custom, the churned milk would produce no butter. Neither should he take a live coal from the fire to the outside field to light his pipe while the churning was in progress, lest the butter disappear. He would need to know at what location ghosts appeared as he travelled the boreens late at night. He would have to know that if the ghosts so confused him that he could not find his way in the darkness, wearing his coat inside out would bring an end to his confusion. And he would need to know as the older people spoke to each other in the Gaelic tongue, they were not doing so to exclude him from the conversation, but only because Gaelic, the language of their childhood, came more easily to them. While they discouraged the use of Irish among the younger ones as harmful to their future, they still cherished the old ways.

His discretion also would be needed as he discovered that it was in the bog field near the school that poteen (illegal grain whiskey) was distilled, and that he would have to take his place with the *mehil* (group of neighbors who gathered to bring in the crop for the widow). Nor could he drive a beggar or a tinker or a tramp from the door without responding to his outstretched hands—whether the giver had little or much and whether the suppliant was deserving were not matters of consequence. He would have to learn not to inquire into the identity of the poachers who, on a cold wintry night, gaffed salmon in the Gweestian and stole it from the London man who owned the fish in that river.

It took some time for Patrick O'Dwyer to learn the local customs and way of life so different from his native Cork. Gradually, he learned to bid goodbye to the spalpeens. They set out on foot to Kilfree 30 miles away, where they took the train to the East Coast and across the Irish Sea to work for an English farmer. And he learned to welcome them back, thin and wiry, in time to put in the crops on their small acreage and to sire another child.

Things were made easier for him when it became known that he had known and admired Michael Davitt and William O'Brien. His skill as a land surveyor, his familiarity with the world of commerce, and his ability to draw a marriage agreement brought him still more respect. And when he married Pat-Peggy's daughter, the hostility vanished altogether, and he was fully accepted as one of their own.

WO'D

Father John, the parish priest to whom my father reported, installed him as head teacher in a three-teacher school accommodating a hundred pupils. Patrick O'Dwyer was the only one who had received Drumcondra training, the other two having been selected by Father John because of their self-acquired erudition. His predecessor had infuriated the parents of the school district, and they looked with suspicion on the stranger who had come from Cork to take his place.

There was one lone Protestant in the parish. He became a Catholic at the time of his marriage and bravely maintained limited, but stubborn, independence from that time on by appearing for mass on Christmas and Easter only. Nevertheless, he was universally liked, and his dereliction was never mentioned. It was said there was a nest of Free Masons in Ballina, 15 miles away, where the children of the planters held their large holdings of land without challenge. The Free Masons, it was said, were in league with the devil and went through all kinds of frightening rituals at their meetings.

In 1888 most of the people in Bohola were still bilingual but confined their use of the Gaelic to swearing at the farm animals or at one another. To make the transition from Gaelic to English, the government agents took a leaf from St. Patrick's book. They maintained the colorful greetings, but in English, with the passage of time, "God bless the work" was the way the passerby spoke to the man at the plow. The changeover brought words into the prayers which lost their Gaelic flavor. People did not fully understand the "Hail" in Hail Mary. Did it have something to do with hailstones? Before second mass on Sunday, it was easy again when Pat Ryan recited the rosary in Irish. "*Se dho Bheata A Wurra*," he would start, and that made more sense than Hail. It was the simple greeting in common use. "May you live, Mary," it said, in an atmosphere where life had more than normal uncertainties.

My father not only was hired by Father John,[1] as schoolmaster at the "Soggarth's" will. Even though the teacher was paid his small salary by the British government, it was the parish priest who had the unbridled right to hire and fire according to his fancy.

Father John cared little for the eight teachers who taught in the four schools in our parish. He harbored a burning hatred for the Irish National Teachers Organization, and my father was one of its secret organizers. Growing up in this atmosphere, I hated Father John.

In my father's case, it was generally believed that when a nephew of Father John became qualified as a teacher, Dad would be out of a job and the nephew installed. I found myself at the age of eight praying behind the hayrick with my brother Jim that the priest's kinsman would fail his tests. We must have prayed to the wrong saint, or the neophyte

1. Father John O'Grady was a relentless tyrant, a sworn enemy of the Land League, the Fenians and all those opposed to the Crown. During the Reformation, Elizabethan and Cromwellian atrocities, and while the Penal Laws against Catholics and Dissenters were being enforced, the clergy took a leadership role in opposing England. But by the time Patrick O'Dwyer reached maturity, all that was past history. By special arrangement between church bodies and the Crown, the parson or parish priest throughout Ireland became the school manager and the teacher's boss.

teacher must have prayed to one with a closer relationship with the Deity. However, the Irish National Teachers Organization was in its creative period and won its bout with the government, and the priests. The change in status guaranteed my father his tenure. That may have been the way our saint worked it.

Nevertheless, with the passage of time the relationship fostered no Christian spirit in either the parish priest or in my father. And with each surrender to the priest-manager's acts of tyranny, the resentment increasingly developed into downright hatred. The relationship disturbed my mother, whose respect for the clergy had but one exception. Both of my parents allowed themselves a limited sense of spiritual rebellion, privately drawing comfort in the faith which placed limitations on infallibility, allowing it to the Pope, but denying it to Father John. My parents were sure that the pastor's hunger for money was not fully part of Christ's teaching and, while they were warned not to judge, they didn't see how Father John, even though he be anointed, would really make it to heaven on judgment day.

CHAPTER 6

PAT-PEGGY AND THE FENIANS

Pat O'Dwyer's aggressive politics, which followed in the Fenian tradition and came out of his life experiences, was the one thing about his son-in-law that Pat-Peggy McNicholas didn't like. Pat-Peggy's sentiments against the Fenians went back a long way and had partly to do with his oldest brother, Seamus.

In the early 1860's, Seamus had been on his way to England to work for a farmer near Ripon. He broke his journey in Dublin at the boarding house of a Mayo family named Gibbons, who had set up in business to accommodate the spalpeens from Mayo on their journey across. On his way to the North Wall he stopped to hear the recruiting officer. He had heard them before at the fair of Swinford, urging the young lads to take the Queen's shilling.[1] This recruiter was different. He spoke with a Yankee accent. He said there was trouble in the States. The pay was good and the cause was right. The army he was recruiting was in favor of keeping the States together and was against slavery.

Seamus wasn't quite sure what a slave was, but he heard that in the Penal Days Irish men and women were "transported" as slaves to the islands near America. Seamus wasn't a slave, but he figured he wasn't far from it when he worked in England, with the long hours, poor fare and the hayloft which was his bed at night. The final argument won him over: England was on the side of the slavers. Weighed against what he knew was ahead of him in England, he did not take long to make up his mind. Before the sun went down, he was a soldier in Uncle Sam's Army.

During the war his letters home were few. After the news came that the American war was over, Seamus wrote a letter to Peggy telling her he was all right. It was true, he said, that the American war was over, but the Irish war was beginning. He said he had joined the Fenians in

1. The recruiting officer gave the new recruit to the British Army a shilling as soon as he signed up.

Cincinnati and signed up to fight with General John O'Neill. They were going to strike another blow for Ireland and were marching on Canada.

Pat-Peggy in the meantime, had become settled in on the land and was Peggy's sole support. He had married Penelope and was raising a family. He wrote back to Seamus that news of his relationship with the Fenians was not to his liking. He said he thought very little of the Fenian movement, and besides it would be more fitting for Seamus to work hard and make out in his new country. In Ireland, he said, there was a rumor that every man who fought for Uncle Sam got 40 acres of land and a mule. (Pat-Peggy was considered well-off with 20 acres.) Seamus apparently resented the advice, for he was not heard from again directly. In 1866, when the news came that General O'Neill was defeated, Pat-Peggy and the family became worried about him. Some years after, a neighbor who lived in America told them that Seamus had become a contractor and built a big bridge at Parkersburg, West Virginia.

Pat-Peggy's opposition to the Fenians was not confined to letters to his brother. The local leaders wanted him to join. He refused and the more popular the Fenians became in and around County Mayo, the less popular he became. His prestige as a hardworking and industrious farmer made his opposition to the Fenian movement all the more irritating to its local leadership.

Among his neighbors were Harry Walsh and his aggressive wife, Catherine, who felt that talking ill of the Fenians was a blow at Ireland. The leadership met to deal with the situation. They considered the use of threats against Pat-Peggy to force him into membership. One morning he found a dagger stuck in his cabin door with a warning note on it. Late that afternoon Catherine and Harry Walsh were driving the mule and cart past his house on the way to the bog. Pat-Peggy took the note and the blade and threw it into the cart. "Catherine," he said, "you may need that yet to defend yourself against the ruffians you cherish."

At the next meeting of the Fenian Brotherhood, they voted to take revenge against Pat-Peggy as a lesson to others. They concluded that the news that his house was burned to the ground would travel far and quickly. They arranged for three men from a parish of Kilkelly, 10 miles away, to do the job. Catherine and Harry heard of the decision. "You fools," she said, "you just voted to burn my house. The day after Pat-Peggy's house is destroyed," she said, "he will burn mine in broad daylight."

The bitter rivalry continued until long past the Fenian Rising in 1867 and up to the day Harry took sick and died, leaving Catherine a widow with 10 children and one on the way. "The first man to my door," she told her listener 25 years later, "was Pat-Peggy." The ranks closed, and that ended the Fenian feud in Lismirrane.

CHAPTER 7

THE MASTER'S SON

PO'D

"Before you marry, prepare a house wherein to tarry," was an oft-repeated admonition to young people in Ireland with nuptials on their minds. The failure of the young schoolmaster and his schoolmistress to heed that warning gave rise to much speculation in the village. It heightened the curiosity of those who looked on a love match with much suspicion. In a "love match" situation, contrasted to the customary arranged marriage, the participants were on their own, the courtship was extended, and, unlike many other countries, there was no duenna-chaperone along to make the lovers keep their distance. Invariably, there was plenty of speculation regarding such a union. The O'Dwyer-McNicholas decision received its full share of comment.

"Let ye be counting," said the old village virago. The advice was not needed. As the months rolled by and the unborn began to develop and kick against a slender figure, the whispers became almost audible. But the count of nine came and went. Friends gave a sigh of relief and the relatives with their own misgivings had more than one reason to celebrate. The disastrous consequence of the "woman's folly" or the unbridled lust of man need not be faced.[1]

After Patrick and Bridget were married, Pat-Peggy and Penelope put them up for a year in their home. During this time the young couple built a thatched cottage on four acres of land they had acquired[2] and awaited the birth of their first child.

There were a few preparations for the event, that summer of 1890.

1. In the Penal Days when there was a price on the head of teacher and priest, candidates for the priesthood had to be smuggled to Europe for clerical training. There they became infected by Jansenism, which bore down heavily and branded forever those found to have engaged in sex without wedlock. The people accepted the new teaching but seemed to have forgotten about redemption.
2. The acreage now accommodates the O'Dwyer Chesire Home for the physically handicapped and has become the center of attraction for the surrounding parishes.

Pat-Peggy knew that Molly, the McNicholas' Conemara horse, would soon be needed for a special and important journey. About the middle of June the animal's right rear shoe became loose. Pat-Peggy was concerned, lest she be disabled when she would be most needed. He took her in from "the long green field" (as road grazing was referred to), mounted her, bareback, and drove her slowly over the river to his cousin, Martin Billy, the blacksmith.

On the way to the shop the shoe clattered. As they crossed the river Pat-Peggy feared he might lose it in the water, but it was still on when they arrived at the forge. Martin Billy picked up the hind foot, stretched it out to almost its full length, talked quietly and reassuringly to the animal while he hammered in some nails. "That will do till harvest," he said. Upon her return home, Molly was no longer released in the road for pasture but housed in the stable adjoining the house.

When Penelope returned from mass on St. Peter-Paul Day, the side car was not backed into its accustomed place in the cart house. Pat-Peggy's sons, Willie and James, moved it to a convenient place and left it in front of the door with its shafts resting on the pavement. The side car was an odd-looking vehicle. Its design was peculiar to Ireland. This one was built by Stanton, the carpenter. Two thin, wooden shafts reinforced with iron plates, were set wide enough apart to fit against each side of the one horse which pulled it along. The side car could accommodate two or three passengers on either side. They sat on a narrow seat with their feet resting on a board. A couple of feet nearer the ground the wheels moved directly under them. There was no railing in front of the passengers to halt a quick descent to mother earth, should the horse take off or the side car hit a deep rut in the road. Sometimes, to accommodate six passengers, the driver sat on top facing the same direction as the horse.

A little past midnight on July 7, 1890, Penelope shook her husband. "Wake up, Pat," she said. "It's time to go." The kerosene lamp by the kitchen fire had been lit and the household was wide awake. Bridget O'Dwyer was sitting on a chair in the kitchen looking anxious and frightened. She was about to go through an experience for which she was psychologically ill-prepared. She was, of course, aware of the fact that her time had come, but she knew little more.

Except for some polite and guarded conversation with Penelope, she had little or no knowledge of the true nature of what was taking place within her. The occasional shooting pain made her wince, but she suppressed an outcry. Her young husband was hovering nearby, looking sheepish and guilty. Bridget's brothers, James and Willie, had already harnessed Molly. Pat-Peggy lifted the shafts chest high and James backed the horse in between the shafts. "Be careful on the bog road," Penelope

26

warned. "It'll be good to have Brigeen here, but I don't expect she will be needed till after sun up." "No telling," Pat-Peggy responded, as he touched the whip to Molly's back.

There was not likely to be traffic on the road, and dawn came early in July. Yet, Pat-Peggy put candles in the lamps on the left and right sides of the vehicle. That was the law, and he was a sober and law-abiding man. He drove down the bog road through the darkness. There was little light from the candles. It was essentially up to Molly to avoid the holes in the road and take her charge safely through the narrow strip seven feet above the deep bog on either side. Pat-Peggy relied on her. She was a full-bred Conemara, small, steady and intelligent, with steel-grey coat, long black mane and tail. Out they came safely onto the Swinford road and over the stone bridge which spanned the Gweestan at Ballymiles and further on over the stone arch which spanned the Trimogue. The curlew and the lapwing screeched their protest after being disturbed, and the *minawn earach* uttered its stacatto cry from the darkness high above the road. The sound of the *minawn earach* was never completely identified with bird or other animal life. Its eerie sound was one of the unsolved mysteries, so the people in Bohola associated the sound with the world of ghosts, fairies and the "little people." The corncrake in the meadow gave signal to its young and mate, and its customary voice was stilled until the sound of the horse hoofs had established that there was a safe distance between them and the early morning traveller.

By the time Pat-Peggy reached his destination, the sun had come up over the Ox Mountains and was about to chase away the morning dew. The horse came to a halt at the small door of the mudwall-thatched cabin occupied by Brigeen na Broig, referred to frequently as An Beann (the woman). Seldom was she spoken about as the midwife, although that was her sole calling. No one was quite sure how Brigeen na Broig came by her name. Some theorized it was because she lost a shoe in her haste to get to her task. Anyway, "little Bridget of the one shoe" stuck, and people never referred to her by any other name.

The conversation between Pat-Peggy and Brigeen was in the Gaelic. Brigeen knew no English. "God save all here," said the visitor, as he rattled the wooden latch on the kitchen door. "Brigeen, I'm sorry to wake you so early." She lived alone and wasted no word in useless conversation. She pulled herself together. "I've been expecting you with months," she said good-naturedly. "You turn your head to too much slander," Pat-Peggy said reprovingly. "As God is my judge, Pat-Peggy," she said apologetically, "I didn't mean that." Sigmund Freud was around about that time, but they had not yet heard of him in Bohola.

There has never been any comparative study of the respective skills of the Irish country midwife and the modern accomplished obstetrician. Fortified as the new specialists are by the modern teachings and the most up-to-date methods, the odds are all on the side of today's sterile operating room, where hands cleansed of germs usher in new life. Yet, in our village there were no stillbirths. How much of that was due to the hard work country women endured during pregnancy and how much to the skill of the midwife is a matter of speculation. One thing was certain. In 1890 and for three decades thereafter, An Beann was greatly in demand in Bohola. She had no social standing and how she did what she did was not a subject for discussion.

The sex taboo was strong in Catholic Ireland and it included any reference to the wonders of reproduction. The special moment when new life came from the womb in all its beauty was to be shared only by the mother and Brigeen. Others may not have respected her, but she knew deep down in her heart that she was God's servant and was helping the Creator more than even the Bishop himself. She often thought it was not right for the people to tell little children that they were found under a head of cabbage, but she knew better than to say so.

Pat-Peggy returned with the midwife not a moment too soon. Bridget, now frightened out of her wits, screamed with the unbearable pain that would alternately ease off and begin again. Penelope and her daughters, Ann and Mary, had been trying to help. Now, Brigeen took over, directing them to leave the bedroom. She placed Bridget in position, gave barely-understood instructions, murmured half-sung assurances, and settled her strong arms about the now writhing and moaning Bridget. Her fingers worked slowly and gently to help the baby's head. With the utmost care and patience, Brigeen brought some measure of reassurance, as Bridget followed instructions and bent to her task. The darling dark head, the mark of the McNicholas clan, appeared, but that only seemed to be the occasion for even more violent pain than before. With more urging and with the skilled, firm and gentle hands, the small shoulders were eased out. With a half-sob and high-sigh, Bridget completed the birth. Brigeen tended to the umbilical cord, and the young woman leaned back in the bed, body warm and perspiring, her black eyes grateful and glowing.

Minutely, Brigeen examined the baby, each and every part. Once, with the Lavans' baby, she noticed that one of the little legs seemed smaller than the other. Brigeen knew that the baby would never follow the plow, nor hoe the corn, nor milk the cows, and she prayed he would be strong enough to be apprenticed to the cobbler and maybe open his own shoemaker's shop in Bohola or Swinford. She knew the custom of her people. They accepted a deformity as part of the Creator's plan. If a girl was not too badly deformed, it was arranged that she would learn to be a dressmaker, and one afflicted by deafness was likely to learn the tailor's trade, like "Dummy" Kilgallon who made all the suits for the people of Bohola.

To her observing eye, this baby was healthy in limb and body and would surely hold his own with the best. He was the schoolmaster's son and someday, with the help of his parents, he might be a priest.

The young father, unable to withstand the feeling that he had been responsible for such pain, had been walking in the road beside the house, alone. With the first outcry from the newborn, he returned to hear Brigeen. "It was not a difficult birth for the first one," the midwife was saying to Bridget. The young mother only half-understood the remark, still in a daze and too relieved that the dread of death from childbirth had passed to quarrel with her benefactor.

Brigeen wrapped the little one in a cloth and brought him to the anxious mother, who also examined the baby before she placed him to her breast to nestle, to feed, and to be nursed in body and soul. A great happiness came over the mother. The remnants of pain did not matter, and as Pat came to her side, she was proud. After a while, Penelope, Mary and Ann came and said a prayer of gratitude. Then Brigeen took the newborn to the crowd of relatives and neighbors which had gathered in the kitchen.

Almost immediately after Brigeen na Broig made her announcement, word went through the village on wings. The master's baby was born, and a boy at that. Males were desirable in Bohola. There was no need to provide a handsome dowry for the man child.

On the following Sunday after mass, the newborn was given his name in the ceremony in which the parish priest bid the devil leave the body. To ensure his total dismissal, holy water from the font was poured on William's head, while he, through his sponsors acting as his surrogate, renounced the devil "with all his works and pomps." William showed little enthusiasm for the total repudiation of the prince of darkness. He let out a most ungodly yell as the priest doused him with what seemed like a totally unnecessary amount of water, and the newborn seemed to move his head in rejection as the priest put his thumb to his lips and transmitted spittle to the small, delicate lips of the child. In an unnerving ritual to ensure that the devil would not return, the priest made the sign of the cross over the whole body. It was a sure defense. Beelzebub stops dead on his tracks when confronted with the cross of Christ.

Pat O'Dwyer stood with his in-laws outside the chapel gate as the parishioners came to offer congratulations. He wouldn't miss this part of it. It established his manhood. Now he did not need to worry that he would be like Pat Michel, who had no child to carry on his name, to help him in the springtime to plant the crops or haul the turf home with the donkey and cart or to break in a young horse or to go with him to England in "the back end" to reap and bind the oats and dig the potatoes for the rich farmer who hired him each year. He had a son who he hoped some day would represent the great traditions of his people. But when Pat Michel came to shake his hand, Pat was saddened and the pride left him.

Two weeks afterwards the young mother held back after mass until the parishioners had left the chapel. She and two other women waited by the alter rail to be churched.[3] Bridget McNicholas O'Dwyer was a well-educated person, but certain things she accepted without question. "Many things," the priest said, expressing the great wisdom that came with his sacred calling, "many things we know but cannot understand or explain. For instance, if you boil an egg, it gets hard and if you at the same time boil a potato it gets soft. We don't know why. That is the way with the mysteries and that is why we must have faith." She did not question why she had to be churched. It had something to do with a sinful condition she was in as a result of conceiving and bringing forth a baby, something private between her and the priest that one should go and be done with.

The 1890 conversion of Constance Gore Booth to Irish radicalism went without public notice. So also did the birth of a boy-child to Patrick and Bridget O'Dwyer in July of that year. He came to life in an atmosphere of confusion and utter despair, with no hope for Ireland but a continuation of tyranny, and in Mayo little to look forward to but the immigrant ship, the army or the clergy. In Ireland in 1890 it would be unthinkable that a Gore Booth, and a woman at that, would one day be in the company of a radical socialist, or be leading a company in armed rebellion against the Crown which her forebears for generations had faithfully served.

And it would have been just as presumptuous to suggest that the O'Dwyer first-born coming into life that year would one day become the Mayor of the world's largest city, a general in the Army of his adopted country, the confidante of two wartime Presidents of the most powerful nation in the world, an appointee as wartime minister to Italy, chairman of the Allied Economic Commission to save the children of Italy from starvation, head of the War Refugee Board, and United States Ambassador to the Republic of Mexico, the second most important post in the diplomatic service of the United States.

3. A church service for a woman after childbirth.

CHAPTER 8

"WHEN WAS I BORN?"

My date of birth was the 7th of July. On the records at Castlebar the date is entered as July 11. This was neither error nor did it have any effect on my "legitimacy." It was a deliberate entry made by my father and perpetrated on the 11th of August, 1890, a pleasant conspiracy to deprive the Crown of two shillings and sixpence, the regular fine for having been four days late in signing me in. At least that's one version. Another had to do with a hot discussion about Parnell.

It seems that the clerk in Castlebar, who was responsible for the registering of births, was an ardent Parnellite, and what began as a low-key discussion over his desk soon developed into an argument so heated that the registration was neglected in favor of a moveover to a nearby tavern. The clerk had the popular side and relished the expressions of approval from both sides of the bar. Parnell's staunch supporters could not agree with the new father that Parnell should have listened to Davitt and temporarily resigned party leadership until such time as he could marry Kitty. Pat O'Dwyer argued that Davitt was Parnell's mentor, if not his creator.

A debate on the role of the clergy in politics never failed to develop during any arguments about England's occupation, and with it a healthy anti-clericalism usually surfaced. This time, however, many laurels were thrown to the priests of Mayo for their bravery. The crowd around the principal debaters grew larger. Soon many others joined in the heated discussions which continued long past closing hours and on into the second day.[1] The young schoolmaster was at a distinct disadvantage. William O'Brien, his fellow Corkman, whom he had long admired, had split with Davitt and was advancing his defense of Parnell from Galway Jail.

1. The length of the debates may have accounted for the error in William O'Dwyer's recorded birth document. Those in charge of compiling vital statistics for his political campaign 50 years later and who wished to be deadly accurate, had trouble reconciling the dates in the county record and the baptismal certificate. (PO'D)

The next morning when Dad came home, he found Mother and "Willie" in good shape, but Mother was as mad as a wet hen. Dad's condition had suffered from the evening's revelry, and Mother threatened to give me away to the "tinkers" and call the whole thing off.

Mother could go up in the air and come down again with one motion. That is how I lost a great opportunity. Think of growing up with the Tinker McCawleys on a road that went nowhere and the same coming back, bartering with the neighbors, hunting for food, stealing chickens and ducks, watching cockfighting and dogfighting, and fishing along the riverbanks. At night in the tent by the roadside or on windy nights in Edward McDonald's sand pit, the pot boiling over a bright fire, supper and a tale or two until our eyes drooped and then a sound sleep until late the next day. No school to worry about, no money problems, no wars, no feeling of responsibility to anyone, eat when the hunger comes and drink the hard, cold water from the nearest spring. Instead of that I drew heartaches and headaches and felt the world on my shoulders until I was mentally and physically humpbacked, all because Mother cooled down too soon and did not give me away to the tinkers.

Soon after my birth, we moved into the new thatched cottage where the ten remaining O'Dwyer brothers and sisters were to be spawned.

CHAPTER 9

THE HOUSE THE GOBAWN BUILT

PO'D

The homes for large families such as Pat O'Dwyer's were small. It was the custom of the landlord, when he observed an additional cow barn, to raise the rent. So the people housed their milch cows in the end of the house. The custom lasted for seven years after William had left Ireland for the last time. Pat-Peggy's family had pioneered in building a special cowhouse, and when the O'Dwyers built their new house, there was little enough room for the large family they expected to have and none for domestic animals. Building the home for the master became a very special event.

It was in 1890 that the young O'Dwyers made the decision to build their nest. In Ireland for thousands of years the gobawn played a most important role in the lives of those able to afford his services. Whatever may have been the skill of the original "Gobawn Saoire", as time went on legend took over, and he became a mythical figure who was credited with designing and building lordly mansions in every part of Ireland, in places so far distant and in numbers so great that it seemed logical and very reasonable that he was possessed of special powers.

Many stories were circulated about his powers. The original gobawn could be compared in a way to our own Paul Bunyan or Johnny Appleseed, except that neither one of those gentlemen set up apprentices all over America, as the gobawn seems to have done in Ireland. Indeed, in 1890 there was one in Bohola with skills equal to the famed original and his given name was Tom Byrne. Pat O'Dwyer and his bride prevailed on Tom Byrne to give his talents, his time and his amazing skill to building them a home suitable for two schoolteachers. Since money was a scarce commodity, even the gobawn was compelled to operate within certain restrictions. Setting the foundation was no big problem. Since the frost line seldom went deeper than a few inches, and since the water table in Mayo was high for ten months of the year, there was no point to building a cellar.

Cow manure, with its binding qualities, and horsehair gathered locally was mixed with sand to make the mortar which the gobawn used. The mixture served to bind the stones he had selected for the building of a fine house. He knew what local wood to use which would not rot in the roof in that wet, wet climate and skillfully prepared the roof for the thatch of rye. The gobawn acquired helpers, two neighbors who could only be influenced to do this tedious job by a plentiful supply of Guinnesses or Murphy's porter, delivered to the job by two Clydesdale horses big enough it seemed to pull down the nearby steeple of Meelick. The helpers were not accustomed to having brew served on the job, and a sort of panic took over as they realized there would soon be an end to the task that had such delightful fringe benefits.

Finally, the job was finished. The new cottage was set on a slight slope, with its front looking north into the Ox Mountains and a smaller mountain to the south and west. It commanded a view of the Gweestan Valley for nine miles, and from one of the master's fields, the parish church steeple could be clearly seen on a sunny day. The Fairy Hill in Killaden, where the Gaelic poet Anthony Raftery was born, was only a mile away, and a half a mile from the house was the road to Swinford, over which the French and Irish armies, with General Humbert at the head, traveled, fresh from the victory at Castlebar and on their way to disaster at the Battle of Ballinamuck in 1798.

Pat planted gooseberry and currant bushes and apple trees all of which prospered and fruits of which would be later referred to by the priest as the occasion of sin. They were a temptation to steal, and that caused a commotion that came as surely as the season for ripe fruit came into our village.

The well that was to supply them with drinking and cooking water was located in the neighboring field owned by Jimmy Brennan, but that made no difference. By *brehon* law, by which Ireland was ruled up to the 17th century, each neighbor had access to the well no matter where it was. The rainwater, and there was lots of it, came off the roof and was channelled into a barrel. It was pure and soft without chemicals, was used for washing, and required little or no soap. Bridget did not use soap, only oatmeal, soft and cleansing, on her delicate skin, and she used the rainwater to wash her long jet-black hair.

The neighbors came to bid them welcome. There had not been a schoolteacher living in the village now since the hedge schoolmaster, who had his lean-to near the road a few hundred yards north of the schoolhouse. Mary Mack, the wife of Michael Durkan, had a special feeling for her cousin the bride. She got some special wool from a black sheep her cousin Tom Carrowmore had, and she carded the wool, spun it into yarn and knitted the black socks for the master and a "jersey" for his wife. The gift required a special, if hidden, performance. In order to card the wool, it was necessary to put some grease on it so that the hairs would roll out, and when the garment was finished, it remained greasy and the grease had to be removed. Acid was necessary to do the job, and where would one get it but urine? So in back of Michael Durkan's house was the barrel, and each day there was the contribution of both Michael and Mary, and without it the master would never have been able to wear his stockings nor his wife her jersey.

The crane over the open fire in the kitchen was the gift of Martin Billy, the blacksmith. He had taken it from the widow White's house, which had long been in ruins as a result of the landlord's battering ram.

There were two unoccupied rooms in the cottage. But not for long. Bridget O'Dwyer gave birth to her second child in 1891. It was a son, and they called him after Bridget's brother, James. They said that Patrick O'Dwyer preferred to think of him as being named after Seamus the Fenian, he who raised the American flag on Canadian soil. In two years, a girl, Kathleen (later known as Katty) was born (she was called after her grandmother, Catherine Norcott, who braved the displeasure of her family by marrying John O'Dwyer the papist), and then Jack (who was called after the man who risked being ostracized for marrying this dissenting Protestant). Mary Rose (May), Josephine and Frank each came a year or two apart.

After the birth of seven children, it became apparent there was a need for more room. So in 1899, two rooms were added, one on top of the other. It took the great skill of Tom Byrne and another gobawn, a man named McDermott, to connect the two parts of the house.

In order to get the full use of both rooms, the gobawn had to twist a wooden stairs until you could not describe its shape, but in any case it found its way into the upper room without losing any room upstairs, and if one had to twist like a reptile going up and coming down, well what harm? The people came in and wondered how the gobawn could have accomplished so great a feat and concluded that sure enough it took powers which no mere mortal could possibly have.

The second part of the house, that part which was two stories, was slated, and so it stood for two decades—a home half-thatched and half-slated. Into this renovated O'Dwyer residence were to be born the remaining O'Dwyer children: Thomas (Tommy), Linda and Paul. (The tenth child died in infancy.) The house the gobawn built was symbolic of its occupants. The first-built part was not unlike the home of every small farmer in the village, and the later, slated addition was more pretentious, symbolizing a family reaching for a higher plateau. The slate came all the way from a quarry in Tipperary, 150 miles away. The gobawn said it was the finest slate to be found outside of Belgium. He said he once heard from a Yank returning from America that there was better slate in a place called Vermont, but he had charged that up to Yankee boasting.

CHAPTER 10

CHILDHOOD IN BOHOLA

My contemporary, James Joyce, in 19th century Anglo-Irish Dublin, could learn about Gaelic myths, but we *lived* them. The Round Tower of Meelick was located a mile away and could easily be seen from our door. It had withstood at least 20 centuries of the Irish weather, and it was still sturdy and strong. Some said it was built in the time of Tuatha De Danaans, a race long gone, who had inhabited the island before the Milesians came. Others said it was built to house the holy vessels from the marauding Norsemen. But it stood out boldly. It was there long before the written word was used to record its message. It kept its secret and stands in mysterious grandeur.

There was little chance for us boys growing up in Bohola to get acquainted with Joyce's Jesuits. We did not know anything about them, and so we were not exposed to the theological controversy between them and the secular clergy who monopolized the teaching in the outlying areas. Nor were we made aware of the suspicion that existed concerning them and the determination of God's own church that they be barred from competing for the throne of Peter.

We did know all about Abraham and Isaac and Jacob, but that was long ago, and we were taught that their successors were bad people who had rejected Jesus Christ and then had him crucified. The account of what happened to them after that was spotty. Later on, Shakespeare made us acquainted with one who frequented the Italian stock exchange. His name was Shylock. He had a beautiful daughter named Jessica, who left her parent, and we approved. Joyce had not yet written about them, and even if he had done so earlier, the chances are that the news about his fantasy would not have been approved by Father John, or by my parents, for that matter.

The only thing about Dublin that crept into the life of Bohola was a class system, and in our own way, the O'Dwyers had sought to belong to what might be referred to as the middle class.

Raising so large a family left little time for diversion. As a child, my mother had been taught to play the concertina without the benefit of written music. After I was born, my impoverished parents bought a harmonium, which set us apart and brought a bit of culture into our home.

As the children grew, the girls were required to take lessons in playing the piano and singing. We frowned on the folk music all around us and, musically speaking, moved in the direction of such songs as "I Dreamt I Dwelled in Marble Halls" or "Juanita" or "How Can a Poor Gypsy Maiden Like Me Ever Hope the Proud Spouse of a Noble to Be?" The girls were also taught to sing "Soft o'er the Mountains" in parts.

The education my father had acquired gave him the right to be a schoolteacher, but it also provided him with the opportunity to spread his learning and extend his influence. He was a surveyor of sorts and owned his own "chain;" he kept the books for some local merchants; and he held adult education classes after hours in the school. (Many of the older neighbors were without schooling of any kind.)

He usually sent to town for the paper. He would read it by the light of a candle or a kerosene lamp, and then he would put the paper away and explain what he had read. The reading sessions did not find much favor with my mother, but they were popular, especially when my father would inject his humor into the occurrence he was describing. In 1897, Bob Fitzsimmons defeated Gentleman Jim Corbett and won the World's Heavyweight Boxing Championship. The people in Mayo felt badly, since Corbett's family came from Mayo and the people regarded Corbett as one of their very own. Many years earlier John McNicholas had left Ireland and had never written home or returned. Rumor had it that he had gone to America and had become a prizefighter. In reading the account of the fight, Dad substituted John McNicholas' name for Fitzsimmons' for the benefit of his audience. Soon the gleeful news was brought to old Tom McNicholas, John's father. Instead of being happy, the old man wept. "You ought to be happy, Tom," one of the neighbors said. "No," Tom countered in his broken English, "now someone will beat him and that will take all the good out of it."

Another occasion when my father became the center of influence had to do with a famous storm which battered our island in January of 1839. In our village, the neighbors referred to it as "the night of the Big Wind." Bad as that night was—for it did quite some damage—it might have been forgotten in Bohola if Dad had not revived the memory of it. The government had authorized a small pension for those who had reached three score and ten. One night, ten old men came in with their forms to be filled out, but none of them had ever been registered at birth. (Births were not registered until 1860.) Dad had a habit of looking over his pipe when he wanted fun. He asked the first man if he re-

38

membered the night of the Big Wind. The man said he remembered it very well indeed. It was the night of Uncle Johnny's wake and he was laid out in the "outshot" and the wind blew away the thatch. They had to remove the remains of Uncle Johnny up to the "room."[1] The other nine also said that they were at the wake. The following night twice as many men came with their forms and they, too, were all at Uncle Johnny's wake on the night of the Big Wind. The last one was Tom Owen, and Dad said, "Tom, this wake is getting too big. Didn't anyone at all besides Uncle Johnny die on that night?" And Tom, good-natured Tom, replied, "I wish, Master, I could help you out."

The scourge of our day was consumption, the name given to tuberculosis. When it struck, villagers sought to deny its existence, but it affected the lives of all of them in one way or another. Suspicion of it deprived the young girl of the opportunity to marry. There seemed to be no cure for it, but exposure to the cold was prescribed, and some places were reputed to be helpful to halt it. Switzerland and Denver, Colorado, were recommended. It penetrated my mother's family and accounted for the deaths of three of her eight sisters and brothers at an early age.[2] As a baby, I must have contracted it. I had never been aware of it until I entered the Army in 1942. A lung x-ray revealed scar tissue. I could not account for it. I must assume that I had contracted it during the first year of life, when I was housed in the home in which three aunts had recently been stricken by it. Consumption took a greater toll and was more feared than cancer, and heart ailments were unknown. The fever, when it struck, was deadliest of all, but it disappeared as suddenly as it struck. The unexplained phenomenon of long livers throughout it all could be found in almost every household. Pat-Peggy McNicholas was in good health until the day of his death at 92, and Penelope died in her 84th year.

We had little or no contact with the medical profession. Broken bones were set by the local "bone setter." Mr. O'Hora was a gifted man and his handiwork won widespread approval. As for other sicknesses, my grandmother, Penelope, was called in frequently. She had known about the uses of herbs. It is hard to say which had some legitimate healing qualities and which were based on pure superstition, but she and, later, my mother were sought after when sickness came. I remember mustard and linseed oil were in common use as cures. Other herbs

---

1. The "outshot" was a small extension protruding from the wall, sufficient to accommodate a bed close to the fire in the kitchen. The "room" was the bedroom in a small thatched cottage located in back of the fireplace. (PO'D)
2. One of her brothers, James, had a thriving tailor business in Swinford when he was stricken with it. He sold his possessions and went to Denver with his sister Anna, a vivacious red-haired young woman. He died shortly after their arrival, and she decided not to return to Ireland.

were used but which ones I cannot now say. Goose grease was preserved against the day someone was suffering from chest congestion.

And there were others in Bohola with some knowledge in the field of medicine. Upstream at the bridge was the forge of Tom Durkan. They used to say that Tom could shoe a horse or a mule in the dark, but this was by no means the total of the blacksmith's accomplishments. Men of his calling were expected to know much about horses and even the human frame.

One day, Martin McNulty, a cousin and classmate, came to school nursing a swollen jaw. The poor boy spent a miserable day with his toothache. That evening he told me he could stand it no longer, that he was going to have the tooth pulled out. "Who is going to do it?" I asked and he said, "Tom Durkan, the blacksmith." Tom tied a leather sling to the ailing tooth and the other end to the anvil. "Now," said he, "say five Our Fathers and five Hail Marys out loud." When Martin came to the middle of the three Our Fathers, the blacksmith poked a red-hot iron under his nose. By the time Martin recovered his balance, the tooth was swinging from the anvil.

Up the road in the middle of the bog was the shanty of the "three Devine persons"—Johnny and Tommy and Biddy. The Devines had a brew which had been a family secret for centuries, made out of herbs that grew on the bog. Anyone who thought they had skin cancer went there for a poultice, which removed the sore and left behind it a hole as big as a crater. Johnny and Tommy were the first to go, and then went Biddy with the secret, leaving behind only the ruins of the shanty.

There were pleasures of life to be experienced, too. I remember Christmastime celebrations, when what seemed like tons of currants and raisins were on display, and oranges from Spain to put in our stockings on Christmas Eve.

And I remember the two Clydesdale horses pulling a tank of paraffin oil all the way from Ballina to fill the barrel. Oil was then retailed by the pint to neighbors to give kitchen light for the long winter night. Darkness came late in the afternoon.

There was fun in lingering on the bridge over the Gweestan on my way home from school, watching the trout jump for flies or a wild duck train her small brood to swim under water and avoid the predators. There was hunting, not so much as a sport, but a means of providing food. There was little sportsmanship about the hunt, and there were no "in seasons" and "out seasons." The salmon in the streams were the property of an English family who never saw Ireland, and poaching salmon was not only for fun and food, it was also regarded as a patriotic duty.

Nearly every boy has his heroes. Mine was Martin J. Sheridan, also of Bohola, who became the champion discus star in three Olympiads for the United States and was still vigorous until his death in New York in 1918.

We had others in Bohola who would become celebrities. A boyhood friend was William Keary, who came to New York five years after me, went into the banking business, and served for several years as Al Smith's successor as president of the Empire State Building.

When it came to our connection with famous people, we were inclined to be boastful. Ellen Philbin, a neighbor, never let an occasion go by without making mention of her cousin, Mrs. MacDonald, "her that had the bishop."

A few miles from the schoolhouse was the birthplace of a scholar and blind poet. In my time little was known of him. It was long after, during a Gaelic revival, that his works were gathered by Douglas Hyde and set in print. The English visitor standing within a hundred feet of the place he had lived asked a neighbor where Raftery's home was. "There were no Raftery's here," the neighbor said. The poet's fame had traveled far but not near.

PO'D

It was the custom in Ireland to start the children on their way to education at the earliest possible age. It was expected that the children would be put to work as soon as they were able to help on the farm and it was prudent to have the children receive as much education as they could while they were yet not very productive.

At the age of three William was taken to the schoolhouse. He resisted the sudden change in his life and made his feelings known. The fact that his Da was at the other end of the schoolroom helped, but not much. Patrick O'Dwyer followed in the custom of Irish fathers. He suppressed any urge he may have had to publicly show affection for his son; anything approaching special attention would constitute favoritism and would hurt his standing with the other children. All of this brought no comfort to Willy. His mother was teaching in a school a mile away and his day in the classroom was a sad and bitter experience.

From May to October the children shed their shoes and went barefoot to school, a ritual to which they greatly looked forward. A stone bruise occasionally marred their joy for the moment, but it did not in any way dampen their enthusiasm as they ran through the fields or walked along the grassy patch on the roadside or let the soft bog ooze delightfully between their toes. What glass came into the parish was preserved, and broken glass posed no problem for Willy's bare feet on the way to school.

As to the children's clothing, there was little distinction between boys and girls until they reached the age of five or six. Both sexes wore dresses.

When childhood had ended and boyhood began, his mother constructed a suit of clothes for him. She had the benefit of a contraption known as the Singer sewing machine, which was the talk of the village. The seams of old clothes were broken down, the thread removed, and the separate pieces of cloth turned inside-out to make the cut-down suit. The end product lacked the skill of the tailor "Dummy," but it served its purpose adequately.

As far as his schooling was concerned, Willy and his classmates had narrowly prescribed subjects, and no discretion was given to the teacher to vary the curriculum. The rudiments of learning were imparted and, as far as it went, the education was equal to or better than its European contemporary. The books of Euclid and algebra and a study of English, which included Shakespeare, were part of the requirements in the mixed school (boys and girls), which took the scholars to their 13th year.

But there was no hint of the surging movement, centered in Dublin and led by such Anglo-Irish poets and writers as A.E. Russell, Lady Gregory, G.B. Shaw and William Butler Yeats, to unearth and revive the neglected and forgotten literary and cultural tradition of Ireland. Willy wasn't able to read Yeats' 1893 ode, "To Ireland in the Coming Times," that was really a declaration of faith:

> Know that I would accounted be
> True brother of a company
> That sang to sweeten Ireland's wrong,
> Ballad and story rann and song;
> Nor may I less be counted one
> With Davis, Mangan, Ferguson.

Measured in miles, Mayo was a long way from Dublin, and much farther if measured by the opportunity to study or be part of this great revival. No hint of the Dubliners' work found its way into the daily curriculum in Bohola.

And later on, when the seminary door was opened wide and bid Willy enter, there was even less chance in those surroundings to engage in a study of his birthright. Another quarter of a century was to pass before Willy, by accident, would become aware of the rich tradition these people had unearthed.

As for the rest of Willy's daily life in Bohola as a young boy growing into adolescence, it was much regulated. He was required to do all the chores that his contemporaries did. There was seed to be sown and a harvest to be reaped and fuel for the long cold winter nights to be gathered in and animals to be fed and sheltered. But the master's son would not have to leave school at 14 to follow his migratory laborer father at harvest time to "lift" oats for an English farmer in a field in England. Old Tom Byrne would tell Willy how lucky he was. Lifting oats was not a hard job but for the "thristles," as the Bohola people called the thistle. When young boys with soft hands began that work, the thistle thorns stuck into their unhardened flesh. Many a night, Tom Byrne said, he had cried in the hay loft where they were sleeping, and he had to smother his face deep in the hay so that the older men, including his father, would not hear him. Sometimes he would not sleep all night with his hands swollen and he in pain.

The Great Hunger required that protection against the potato blight be developed, and Willy, the oldest of a growing brood, had to take his turn with the spraying machine. The contraption was created specially to meet the needs of the Irish farmer. It was a small tank, carried on the back by shoulder straps, containing water mixed with copper sulphate to make a blue-colored spray. The nozzle was aimed at the potato stalks and the mixture spread on the leaves. A generous portion found its way onto the sprayer, and by the end of the day he was wet inside and out and sick from inhaling the poisonous mix. Whatever the inconvenience or difficulty, it had the effect of halting the progress of the dread disease which had destroyed the crops a half century before.

Next to the potato, turnips were the most common food and could, like potatoes, be preserved all winter long in outdoor pits shielded from the frost by straw and two feet of earth. Cabbage, the other staple, was planted individually in April by Willy and his father after school, and it continued to grow in the field until well into the new year. The outside young green leaves were boiled with bacon or ham.

Patrick O'Dwyer introduced onions, carrots and parsnips to the village, but farmers from the village did not feel they were worth the considerable trouble it took to produce them. There was not much variety in our diet, and tea and soda bread (sometimes with butter) was the closest thing to a dessert.

At the end of the village there was a grist mill. The water from the Gweestan was channelled down a runway for a quarter of a mile to turn the wheel that ground the oats, which provided the oatmeal breakfast for the village. The oats seed was sown by hand and reaped with a scythe. Willy, like the other children, was not required to sow, but lifted the oats immediately after they were cut and formed them into sheaves, later to be thrashed by hand with a flail and winnowed in a doorway to eliminate the chaff and dust. There was a period between the reaping and the thrashing during which the oat sheaves were put up in stacks and thatched with straw. Twisting the hay rope was a job for Willy, using a handmade twister of bent wire and two pieces of wood with holes to permit the bent wire to go through. Finally the rope of hay was made and placed on the thatch to keep it in place over the stormy winter. At first Willy was fascinated by the process, but after a while he became bored.

Occasional visitors to the village would bring Willy and his friends some hints of the outside world. One day a tinker came to Bohola to fix the kettle or saucepans or cans. The boys went to the roadside not so much to see him work, but to observe the stump of his left hand. He said he had just returned from the Boer War. He had signed up with the recruiting officer at the fair of Swinford, he said, and a Boer blew his hand away. Willy and the boys felt sorry for the tinker, but they were confused. The people of the village used to come into the master's kitchen to hear from the master's newspapers about how the Boers were fighting the British in South Africa, and the people were hoping the Boers would win.

Towhy, the dancing master, came to Bohola on his rounds. He was a tall, thin man in his late fifties and light on his feet. He would stay a month in the winter. He taught the youngsters how to dance the jig, the hornpipe and the reel, and to the older ones he taught all the movements of the Walls of Limerick and the Waves of Tory. He did not need to instruct them in the "set," as the quadrille was called. The people knew that and danced at a country home to the music of Martin na Carraig, the blind fiddler, and Austin Swift, the *piborach* (piper), who could play the Uileann pipes, which he was not required to inflate with his mouth and which suited dance music much better than the war pipes. The piper would sit near the open fire with the pipes on his knees, and he would work his elbows to make the air leave the bag, working his fingers deftly along the openings to create the sweetest music ever. The Uileann pipes filled the kitchens in the small country homes. The war pipes with their loud noise were more suitable to the hillside.

Willy was not permitted to attend Saturday night or Sunday night dances, even though youngsters of his age were given a chance to go there. His was to be a different upbringing, and his parents, particularly his mother, knew that in such a place, "He would learn more than his prayers." He could, however, join boys of his own age to fish the streams and to play handball against the gable of the schoolhouse on a Sunday afternoon.

Economic conditions, however, placed great limitations on Willy's sporting activities, and a football had to last a long time. When it became worn or the inner tube gave out, a pig's bladder became its substitute. All small farmers kept a special pig to be slaughtered each year. The screams of the animal about to be stuck with a knife between the two front feet could be heard a mile away. Strong men held the four feet firmly till the animal was lifeless. The shaving of the skin to remove the coarse hairs and the cutting and carving of the meat were shunned by Willy and his younger brothers, James, Jack, Frank and Tom. (Paul was not yet born by the time Willy left for Spain.) Their only interest was in the removal of the bladder, which would serve them when the shop-bought football gave out.

Through most of these growing-up years, Bridget found time to bear children and care for them *and* teach school a mile away from her home. Taking time off to bear children was acceptable to all but the parish priest, who saw in these lapses from the classroom an excuse to rid himself of the wife of one who had become a thorn in his side and to appoint a favorite in her place. After the birth of her seventh child, Bridget no longer had a job.

The result was near economic disaster. Sixty pounds a year was not much, but £40 for a schoolmistress added to it gave some hope. When that sum (small though it was) was withdrawn from the family budget, it was a blow. But Bridget had worked in her father's country store, where the measure of profit was small and the volume low. To meet the emergency, she turned half of one room into a shop. She stocked and sold Rickets Blue and strong-smelling bars of soap and Irish tobacco from County Meath, bonded and pressed together and cut and weighed and sold to the customer by the ounce. She also stocked flour in cotton sacks. The Pride of Erin was the brand, and the bags were white, and when their one use was over, they became the undergarments for the farmers' wives and daughters. They were indeed the pride of Erin, as the garments proclaimed. Nothing was wasted. The shop venture was not a howling success, however, and it didn't make up for the £40-a-year loss.

CHAPTER 11

RELIGION

PO'D

Before he acquired coordination, Willy was taught to "bless himself." His mother took his right hand (it seemed to be ineffective if the left hand was used) in hers and guided it first to his forehead, then to his lower chest, then to left shoulder and then to his right shoulder completing "the sign of the cross." As coordination came, he could do it by himself, and he was praised for his accomplishment. Then the time came for him to learn to pray to God.

In school for a half-hour every day at about the age of five he was taught the catechism (which had Maynooth approval and was the standard book used in all schools in Ireland under the control of the Catholic clergy). At seven, preparation for his first communion was commenced. A long period of instruction was required, and during the last three months Willy was, with all the other children, prepared to take his examination for this awesome and solemn event.

Three inspectors came to his school periodically to examine the pupils and check on the teacher's performance—giving special attention to the master. Two of these inspectors came from the Department of Education in Dublin. The master was never notified about their coming and Pat O'Dwyer feared them. When he had the feeling that the inspector was due or heard through the grapevine that he had been in a school nearby, he kept one eye always cocked on the road. He had an uninterrupted view of the road for a quarter of a mile. Not many strangers came down that road, and never was the master caught unawares.

The children, Willy among them, moved easily into the conspiracy to deprive the inspector of the element of surprise. They adopted an angelic attitude, which lasted all through the inspector's examination and until he was again out of sight. The inspector always stopped off to see the parish priest before visiting the schools. He got his evaluation of the teacher's performance from the man of God who held the teacher's destiny and life in his hand. The report was invariably biased and depended to a great extent on how much time and cooperation the teacher had given to the pastor on matters having little to do with the school or the pupils.

The third inspector was a priest known as the diocesan inspector, and his examination depended on the age of the child. The younger ones were confined to an inquiry as to "Who made you? Who made the world?" The older ones would be required to know much more. For example, Willy would have to know the design and dimensions of the Temple. The diocesan inspector conducted his examination in the school, frequently bypassed the local clergy, and reported his findings directly to the Lord Bishop himself. This was to remind the parish priest and the curate where the power lay, as if they needed any reminder. In the diocese of Achonry the bishop was Dr. Lister.

Religious instruction again received great attention and time when Willy and his companions became of age for confirmation. In the final stages of instructions all the children of the parish came to the church on weekday evenings where they were told that Dr. Lister himself would ask them about what they had been taught, and every one of them would have to know the answers before he or she would be confirmed into the Catholic faith.

Not everyone in Willy's class came up to Dr. Lister's standards. One of the Durkan lads was asked by Dr. Lister to name the Three Divine Persons. "Anthony, Biddy and Tommy," was the reply. The Bishop was astonished. The boys and girls on either side, about to become true soldiers of Christ, tittered. It was infectious and broke out into a laugh. The Lord Bishop was astounded and the curate was embarrassed and the parish priest was mortified. The schoolmaster somehow knew he would pay the price ultimately and took the initiative. "The boy is confused, Your Lordship," he ventured. "In this parish Biddy, Anthony and Tommy Devine are the best-known names in East Mayo. They have the cure for the cancer." The bishop wanted to get on with the job. He was not fully satisfied that the explanation was sufficient to wipe out the parish disgrace, but he was rushed for time. It seems he gave Martin Durkan, the miscreant, a harder blow to the cheek than was necessary to convince him of the solemnity of the occasion and to establish that he was henceforth required to defend his faith even at the sacrifice of his own young life. The blow to the cheek in the instance had an element of punishment to it, and well deserved too, for young Durkan had provoked levity while the Holy Sacrament of Confirmation, which only his lordship could administer, was taking place.

There were moments when it was obvious the great moral teachings about love of God and fellow man seemed not to have practical application. The religious instructions were often followed by clashes on the way home between boys from different schools within the parish. It seemed clear that the Sermon on the Mount had not been fully explained, or in any event its lesson was not sufficient to prevent the boys from the mountain from showing their prowess in the manly art of aggression to their fellow parishioners from the Gweestan Valley. Willy denied participation in these acts of "rowdyism," as his mother described them, and if his denial was less than truthful, he was shielded by the strong spirit of resentment against the informer, which infected the young, the old and the in between.

CHAPTER 12

FAIRIES & GHOSTS

PO'D

Belief in the existence of the kingdom of life other than earth, hell, heaven, purgatory and limbo (the state in which unbaptized children existed forever) was forbidden. But in Ireland that rule was ignored. Patrick and his missionaries were content to substitute heaven for Tir na Nog and did not challenge the people's belief in the fairies. It would, in the mind of the new aggressive, committed Christians, be the rock on which their mission might well perish. So, from the fourth to the twelfth century, in good times, which were few, and bad times, which were many, there was a peaceful coexistence. No one, least of all the hierarchy, said there was a conflict between belief in fairies and the story of Genesis, of Adam and Eve, the Angel Gabriel and Satan, the one God, the infallibility of the Pope and the one true Church, only members of which would ever see heaven.

The belief in the fairies was almost universal and a favorite topic of conversation during gatherings of the villagers late on a winter's night while visiting in a neighbor's house. Belief in ghosts was sometimes challenged. The incidents reported abounded and the circumstances were bizarre. But no one ever raised any questions about fairies. Not the ones referred to in the fairy tales, but the ones that were around McDonagh's Fort. Now, the people well knew that there were different kinds of fairies, that they lived their own lives, and that sometimes their activities clashed with the habits of humans.

Some, like the leprechaun, played tricks on humans. The leprechaun let it be known that if a human caught him and kept his eye fixed on the mite, the leprechaun would show the mortal where the pot of gold was hidden. But, as the Bard said, there was the rub. The wily article (who also spoke English if he had to) had perfected the art of "diverting" his captors' attention away from him, and that was the signal for his complete disappearance. Bridget O'Dwyer told Willy and her other children that such was the experience of her grandmother. She had gone

49

on a picnic to the Ox Mountains near Foxford. The party was drinking tea when the dwarf appeared. Bridget's grandmother knew what to do. She caught him and held him in the palm of her hand and spoke sharply to him in English, while he pretended not to understand. She then spoke in Irish and boldly demanded that he disclose to her where the gold was buried. He shouted in a shrill voice in Irish, "Look, look Foxford is on fire," and for the split second, she looked in the direction of the town. Needless to say the diminutive deceiver had his way. Foxford was not on fire and the leprechaun had disappeared from sight.

Bridget O'Dwyer was a wise, sophisticated and intelligent woman. It is hard to know whether she really believed the incident took place. Judging from the stories she related, the odds are that she believed it happened, and in any event her children were convinced that it was true. The presence of the fairies at specific locations in the parish was also universally accepted.

These were not stories told merely to please Bohola's children. The immortal tales of Hans Christian Andersen and James Stephens could be classified as fiction, but the true state of "The Kingdom" was oft revealed to the people who lived in Bohola, and the experiences of those to whom the fairies appeared were repeated as established truths.

Another story involved a presumed sacred playground for the fairies about a mile from our house. There was a hill above Peadar's house with an old fort at its very crest. In the center of the fort there was a cave that went so deep into the surrounding range of hills that no one ever came to the end of it. One day, as Willy and the boys were on the way home from school, they determined to explore the cave, and Peadar told them the story of what had happened to him. It seems that Peadar once took his mules and plow to the summit where he planned to turn over the sod in preparation for planting a crop. The mules were a fine pair of animals, sturdy and reliable, and far better for plowing than any team of horses in the village. They were bred from an Irish draft mare and one of the large donkeys which had been imported from Spain. Peadar had plowed his acres with them and harvested the land. He had broken them in gently, not like his neighbors who beat their animals into submission.

Oats and flax were hard on the land and Peadar needed to return several of his fields to pasture to restore the nutrients needed for hay. Despite the stories he had heard about the cave and its inhabitants, he determined to run the risk: he would plow the center of the fort. It was rich with cow manure, the accumulation of a thousand years—maybe more. He was not without some misgivings as he took hold of the plow's two handles. He looked around him but everything seemed normal. He held the reins on the handles of the plow and gave the command to the mules. The plow dug into the sod. The mules bent to their task. The earth was soft from the April rains and turned over easily, but after going a few paces, they stopped still. They seemed nervous and balky. Peadar thought they may have hit a beehive, but it was too early in the year for the bees to have enough life to sting the animals. Peadar spoke to the animals reassuringly and urged them forward in the language they had always obeyed. They would not budge. He cut an ash plant from a clump of bushes nearby and struck them on the rump. It was no use. They merely went sideways and tangled the traces around their feet. Peadar got them back in place after much persuasion. Now he tried leading them, but that did not work either.

Finally, a little man appeared in front of him, standing high on the ridge that surrounded the fort. "You're plowing up our race course," he said to Peadar, "and unless you make up your mind to leave, the four feet of your mules will be stuck to the ground forever." A great fear came over Peadar. He made up his mind to do as he was bid. He turned to leave the fort as quickly as he could, without mule or plow. He was only halfway down the hill when he heard a great noise behind him. The mules were coming after him at a gallop dragging the old plow behind them. They didn't halt till they reached the barn door. Peadar did not cry halt till he reached the comfort of his kitchen.

The following morning he went up to the adjoining hill where he could observe the old fort. The sod had been put back in place. He could not see anything unusual, but he heard the noisy laughter of the little people. He assumed they were enjoying the races.

Peadar did not want to spoil Willy and the boys' fun and waited until they had come out of the caves before he told them the story. The cave was really not a cave at all. It was a hand-built passage made of stone walls and big stone flags for a roof. A grown man could stand at its entrance, but in several yards it narrowed so a man would have to crawl through the hole. Inside were rooms where men could again stand upright. The boys mentioned to Peadar that they had neither seen any person nor heard any noise of any kind in the cave. Peadar said the fairies did not mind humans visiting provided that they did not disturb anything, and he said that the day he and the mules ran away he promised he would never again offend them. Since that time Peadar said they seemed to be in perfect agreement, and they played no more tricks on him or his mules.

There were other kinds of fairies like the Ban Shee (the woman fairy). She keens against the night wind in a bitter wail when one of the Milesian family dies. The Milesians were among the first of the races to come to the island thousands of years ago. The Ban Shee's cry is weird and lonesome and not like a human's or any wild animal's, but when the people hear it, they go to the house where a person is known to be dying so sure are they that the Ban Shee's cry is the signal of death. Once Tomas Oige walked four miles in the dead of night, after his wife heard the Ban Shee on the side of Carrowmore Hill, to be present when his uncle would breathe his last. (Tomas Oige was good at attending to such matters, and he would put the *mariv faisk* around the head to keep the jaws closed before rigor mortis would set in.) When he arrived, the old man's condition had changed for the better. He was sitting by the fire sucking his *dudgeen* (pipe). "What brings you here so early in the morning?" "I was going to the fair of Kiltimagh to buy a calf," Tomas explained. "I wanted to get there early before all the cattle jobbers bought up the best of the lot." "Tis a queer man you are, Tomas." the old man responded. "Going to buy a calf on Wednesday and that's the pig fair day. You'll have your journey for nothing. The cattle fair is tomorrow." Tomas was flustered. He was caught in a lie. "If someone in Lismirrane heard the Ban Shee," the old man added, "you had better look somewhere else. I feel in my bones I'm good for another ten years."

Tomas left delighted that his uncle was better, but with his faith in the Ban Shee a bit shaken. When he got home he heard the news a near neighbor had died suddenly.

It was hard to understand how the Ban Shee knew who in our village was descended from a Milesian family and who wasn't. In the 3,000 years since they came Erin had absorbed waves of Vikings, Spaniards, English, Normans and Parthalonians from Greece and made them her own.

Avasteen O'Maille must have had some Milesian blood in him because the Ban Shee cried long and loud down by the wooden bridge the night he died. He was not native to the village but came from over on the west of Mayo from the O'Maille country, and he claimed relationship to Queen Grace O'Maille, an amazon of a woman who sailed and managed pirate ships and got Elizabeth I really mad at her. Queen Grace was later called Granuaile, the name given to Ireland. Renowned and respected, she selected a leader of the O'Flahertys to father her children. Avasteen claimed relationship to her even though she reigned 300 years before he was born, and Willy heard the village people say that old Avasteen was related to Granuaile herself.

Avasteen was a *piborach* and he married a *piborach's* daughter. They both lived at the end of the bog. His family went away and his wife died leaving him alone and old. When he died, his neighbors came to bury him "decent." The older women came and washed the body and laid it overboard in the outshot, a projection which provided the family bed. A relative went to Michael Howley's to get the pipes and tobacco. They were new clay pipes, and as each visitor came he took a pipe and said, "The Lord have mercy on the dead." A few said it in Irish. Willy and Mike Durkan and three other boys took the pipes with tobacco in them. They got matches and went behind a sod fence to do what they saw their elders do. Each boy became deathly sick. They tried to hide their guilt, but their theft and disobedience called for the severe punishment that God had meted out to them. Their parents were satisfied that the Diety had taken over their job and done it well.

At the wake that night, because of the age of the deceased and the long vigil, games were played and there was no crying like when young Joe Lavin died. The games consisted of slapping the palm of the hand which was left open at the rump. The other players took turns at slapping it and then the slappers' turn came. It was a primitive show of strength. At young Joe Lavin's wake, the relatives came from afar. As each new one came, Willy noticed that the women came towards the coffin and cried aloud in a song praising the boy and quarrelling with his death. It usually ended with "Why did you die?"

Then there is the Shi Giodh or fairy wind. It sometimes whirls around in a circle, even on a day when there is not even a zephyr blowing. It carries dust and other objects with it and deposits them far away from the point of departure. The Shi Giodh must have migrated with the hordes that left Ireland for the Promised Land. John Steinbeck described the antics of the Shi Giodh, although he did not call it that, in his description, in *The Grapes of Wrath*, of the topsoil being carried away (the rape of the earth) in whirling circles (the anger of the wind fairy).

The Shi Giodh is also known to ride ahead of the storm, warning humans of its wrath as a gesture of friendship. Anyway, that's the way it worked when Big Wind blew across Ireland. The older ones referred to the night it happened as the *Iocha Na Giodha Mor* (the night of the Big Wind). It took place on the 6th of January, 1839. The Shi Giodh on that day was seen by the fisherman on the coast of Mayo and Galway warning them not to put out that night, even though up until then the night was calm and the water dark. It was a good thing they heeded her.

The storm was so strong that it killed 200 people. It ripped the stone flags off the roofs of the town of Swinford and crumbled the walls of some of the sturdiest buildings. In the parish of Meelick, only the Round Tower stood as it had for 2,000 years when the Tuatha de Danaans (or was it the Fir Bolgs?) built it. One of those ancient peoples constructed it, and it remains as a monument to their skill and even the Big Wind could not shake it. Willy could see the Round Tower from the door of the O'Dwyer cabin, and he heard all about the night of the Big Wind at his father's kitchen from the neighbors who were making application for the old age pension. It was that same year that Willy set off to Ballaghaderreen to become a priest.

CHAPTER 13

LEAVING HOME

Having grown up under the sharp eye of my mother, properly disciplined in one of her straitjackets, more than once I toyed with the idea of joining Tinker McCawley and his friends, whom she had once threatened to give me away to shortly after I was born.

I harbor a sullen recollection of a sally rod that rested on two nails over the fireplace. When Mother reached for the weapon, which she frequently did, I knew I was in for a hiding. By the time I was 13, Mother, satisfied that her "bronco" was well "busted," offered what was left of me, with pious pride, as "suitable timber for the holy calling."

That year, 1903, my skies began to show up cloudy. There was whispering between Mother and Dad, and Mother and Grandfather, even in my presence. For a while I felt hurt to be excluded from their confidences. After a little while it occurred to me that I, myself, was somehow involved. Had I been blessed with the gift of suspicion, I might have known that there was something in the wind not much to my liking, especially when I was taken to the local tailor, "Dummy" Kilgallon, for a new suit. At last, in August, I was approached on the subject, and my mother explained that they were determined to send me in October to St. Nathy's College, the diocesan high school in Ballaghaderreen, miles and miles away from Bohola. It was the only secondary school in the diocese and was under the patronage and direct control of the bishop, and it was to be hoped that under that atmosphere I would acquire a vocation for the priesthood.

My trunk was in the well of the side car, the horse and harness brightly polished, and Mother said, "Now, before you go, say good-bye to your Aunt Mary." I knew then what a vacuum was because I felt it in my stomach. A hopeless feeling it was, as I crossed the fields and stood at an old familiar corner on the hill just above Kattie Byrnes' and stopped to look around. It was a nice morning. The sun's rays reflected slantwise from the roof of the church two miles away. From where I stood I could see the river and the herons flying slowly upstream with their eyes on the water. Beyond the neighboring hill were the meadows by the river and the stone steps rising above the water leading to the well on the island near the little sandbank where the salmon spawned. "This evening," I reflected, "when the hungry trout are leaping for the flies, I will not be there." I passed the whin bushes where the hare's nest was and where fat, old Prince (almost my age) would follow her and she, playing with him, running and stopping and turning and then getting lost—Prince beside me with his tongue hanging out, his way of cooling off, without the strength to wag his stump of a tail, his eyes laughing and looking at me anxiously for a compliment: "Prince, you are stupid. You could not catch her in an empty sugar barrel!"

I could see Mickey Dillon climbing the hill from his house with a spade on his shoulder. Mickey the cranky one! The picture of Mickey standing in the race track at Swinford with a basket on his arm containing three oranges—the fruit woman gave it to him while she looked for change and she didn't come back, ever. When a neighbor, whom he hated, came by and asked him "how much" for the three oranges, that was too much. He put the oranges, he said, in his pocket. "And what did you do with the basket?" he was asked. Resuming his anger, with his chin whiskers shaking, "I kicked the bloody basket in the air."

And there was Nancy Fatch, always looking for wakes. She was the best "crier" in a thousand parishes. Once she joined some strangers leaving Swinford from the market because she heard them talk about a wake. The people over in the next parish were perplexed. They had never heard such crying, such abject grief. It was beautiful, Nancy swaying back and forth and reciting the great deeds of the deceased so loudly and so long, that a member of the family, taking pity on her for her sorrow, invited her up to the "room" where she was given a "half wan" of poteen so that she might be comforted. When Nancy got a chance she asked a woman seated beside her in Irish, "Who is the dead one?"

And there was Manie Owens coming up the road, no longer gay, but looking down at the toes of her shoes and shaking her head. Her old friend, Mary Gillen, no longer spoke well of Manie. After half a lifetime their friendship ended in a feud. Manie, on a winter's evening, looking into the fire, was always talking about Luke, her dead husband, and "how sick he was and him dying and how he opened his eyes for a minute and he said, 'Manie, I have just seen the Blessed Death who whispered to me that I was tired after my long journey and that I must come away with Him to take my rest.' " When Mary Gillen heard this she could not contain herself. Raising her left hand above her head, she commanded Himself to be her witness that in her life she never lied about the dead. "Manie and her inventions," she snorted. "Making things up out of her mind. Who was there but myself," she said, "while she was ranting and crying and making such noise as to almost waken the dead." "Who but myself," she said, "had the two pennies to put in his eyes and in my pocket was the *mariv faisk* (the death band) to pull up his poor jaw and close his mouth. Not a word did Luke say within my hearing." "Blessed Death," she added. For the moment the empty feeling within me had gone. There is so much in life that is new to the young, that the vacuum is only temporary. It came back, however, as I looked for the last time at my world.

And there was Michael Forkan, who was "beginning to age;" a few years ago he was "going on 90." There are troubles in living beyond your time and being alone. At 85 he married Ellen who "would never see 70 again." It turned out to be a good marriage. He got what he wanted, "someone to answer the rosary," and she expressed her joy in her own way: "Michael snoring by the fire is better than being alone."

Young and old must have companionship. That is how we are born, for a life without sharing is not living, it has no measurement by time, it is not a year, or a day, or an hour, or even a minute. It is an unconscious journey to the cemetery gate without any feeling, except perhaps the shock of the final release. "He has comprehended wisdom," writes Seneca, "who dies as free from care as he was born." Now that he was a companion, Michael Forkan was doing all right.

I went down the hill and crossed the stream and went up by Cormick's well, and sure enough there was Aunt Mary with her two empty buckets. All my life I had been in love with Aunt Mary. She had lived a hard life and had her share of early wrinkles to prove it. She had seen her brothers and sister die of consumption and her own little Sissy burning up with fever. Her children had gone away to foreign places. The going of the boys was natural to her, but saying good-bye to the little girls going off into the world, almost alone, was more than she could accept. With all her suffering she had the kindest eyes I have ever seen; the neighbors said that "with all her troubles, Aunt Mary was not one to envy or begrudge."

"Willy," she said, "that's a great suit. I suppose it was the 'Dummy' and he made it big, but you will grow into it in a year or two. Maybe the sleeves are a little short, but it is a fine suit." I said, "Aunt Mary, I came to say good-bye." She nodded, "I know. It's the only word that we have in our sad lives—good-bye to the living and good-bye to the dead." The tears in her eyes were for Sissy. "It is a fine thing your father and mother are doing for you," she added, "taking you out of the rain and the mud. There are many boys and girls who are on their way now. It's the hunger. For them it's good, but for us at home it's good-bye and the sadness and the longing that stays with us."

I don't remember leaving Aunt Mary, but I do recall by sundown the big gates were opened to St. Nathy's and I saw for the first time the old British soldier barracks that were used as a school. Jimmy, the porter, came out and took my trunk. He led me upstairs while Dad went inside to close out the business arrangement with college authorities.

It was an awkward good-bye of an Irish father who will admit of no sentimentality and a son with a longing for a word of kindness he will not get, and soon he was driving out of the big gates and I was by myself. Never before or since have I felt so alone.

CHAPTER 14

ST. NATHY'S & SALAMANCA

During one of her trips to the United States my sister May told reporters I was more mischievous than studious as a youngster. My secondary school record in St. Nathy's tends to justify her opinion. The students were divided between boarders and day boys. The boarders were divided between the sons of the wealthy and "the shabby genteel." Teachers I most remember were Father Joseph O'Gorman, Father Michael Kevin Connelly and Father Ambrose Blaine. I was never out of trouble with Father O'Gorman. I felt he had a disrespect for me from the way he curled his upper lip when he spoke to me. It seemed to me that he was kinder to the children of the rich. Father Blaine had fault to find with my essays. He noted once, in red pencil, "You are a red-hot Socialist." My father enjoyed this comment but mother viewed it with some alarm. No one was ever kinder to me or to anyone else than Father Ambrose Blaine. Father Connelly also appeared to like me.

In our class work in English we read the poets and such essayists as Addison, Steele and Lamb, along with a few short works of Macaulay. Macauley, a bigot, could never find comfort in the mind of an Irish boy. He wrote the history of the siege of Limerick, I remember. To a young mind living with pride in the unequal struggle of his people, Macaulay, with his fit of honeyed cadence, prostituted his talent before the heartless thrones that claimed him for a slave. His quill, however, was dulled by the mental power and the elegance and sense of justice of Edmund Burke. His essays did not obliterate the simple truth of Finley Peter Dunne contained in a single sentence: " 'Hennessy,' said Mr. Dooley, 'the British colonize in a silk hat and striped trousers with a Bible under the arm and the piece of lead pipe in the tail of the cut-away coat.' "

Some of the poetry we liked had to do with the feats of valor of Sarsfield and the Irish Brigade who escaped from Ireland to fight in the French Army. The poem that rang in my head 50 years later depicts the Irish Brigade on the night before the Battle of Fontenoy:

The mess tent was full and the glasses were set;
The gallant Count Thommond was President yet;
The veteran arose like an uplifted lance
Saying "Comrades, a health to the Monarch of France,"
God prosper Old Ireland, You'd think them afraid,
So pale grew the cheeks of the Irish Brigade.

I have never read the French account of the Battle of Fontenoy, but according to the version heard around Bohola, it was the Irish Brigade that came to the rescue and delivered a sound thrashing to the British.

The poems of Spenser found little favor with us. To this "sweet singer of pastoral joys and sylvan scenes" must go the credit for submitting a written recommendation to his Crown. The proposal would have the effect of exterminating the Irish. He had recently been granted a hugh area of confiscated land in Ireland. To ensure peaceful possession to him and his associates, his plan was to create a famine and pestilence so the people would consume each other. He may have been a great bard but it was a little difficult to separate the poem from the poet. Our literary inclinations were heavily influenced by our national outlook.

Father Connelly was generous to me with his books, for he knew I liked to read. From him I received the moderns—O. Henry, Bret Harte, Mark Twain, Swift, Sterne, and great tales of the plains, of the buffalo and the Indian. From them the thought was born that my destiny was in a new fabulous world. It called to me in a voice stronger than I had ever heard before. I believe that Father Connelly knew then that my life had to be free, and who could tell but that he, himself, shared my new-found longings?

There were tales among the boys of daring things that happened in other days. The one I liked best was of Willie Carty twirling his books over his head by the leather strap and hurling them into the Lung River in a dramatic good-bye to St. Nathy's. The next day he left for England.

Those were the days when the Irish people were struggling to find themselves in a self-sufficiency in realistic and artistic fulfillments. Stephens was dying and Joyce was struggling with his soul. Lady Gregory and Yeats were busy with the new theatre movement. Jack B. Yeats and A.E. were on the way in. Synge and George Birmingham were finding their places, and Patrick Henry Pearse was struggling with a higher education program in native Gaelic. A youngster named John McCormack in a school in Sligo was beginning to blossom as a tenor.

Father Connelly leaned towards Gaelic revival. Many a Sunday the students walked the five miles to Hyde Park to give him an opportunity to share his enthusiasm with Mr. Douglas Hyde, the great Protestant Gaelic scholar who found his inspiration in his visits to the United States.

Hyde founded the Gaelic League and was later President of Eire. Both men, well over six feet, chatted for a mile or two on the way home before parting.

St. Nathy's nestled under the brow of a black mountain. Somewhere behind the hill there was an isolated village called Dernacarta. The ladies of "D" were demure and handsome, but the men were rough in their liquor. When they came to town on the evening of a fair day, shutters went up in the stores and bars were closed.

A little railroad train made a round trip once a day to the junction of Kilfree to catch the main line from Sligo to Dublin. It was a ramshackle engine with a first-class carriage, a third-class carriage and the guard's van. Pat Snee, the engineer, smoked his pipe quietly while leaning over the little door of the engine room. When the train was ready to move, the guard waved a green flag and Pat, without turning, reached back and pulled a cord. After a few minutes the engine shook and groaned and that was the signal that the trip to Kilfree had begun.

It was an October day and the fog was thick when the word was passed to the students that at a certain hour they must be present at the station to bid farewell to the aging Bishop, Dr. Lister, who was going for the winter to the Canary Islands. The word was also passed around that Willie Carty had come back to the precious grandmother with whom he lived and who spoke nothing but Gaelic. Willie, it was said, was now a poet in Gaelic. There were so few around who knew Gaelic, Willie Carty had it easy. The point was, where was he? He was lost, he wasn't home, he had left for town and the big boys of the college were detailed to cover every pub in an effort to find him. At last he came, mud to his knees, with a tousled head of hair, looking like anything except a poet. We, the students, were lined up two by two in the station. Pat Snee was at his place at the trottle. The Bishop was sitting by the window in a first-class carriage and down at the end was the fife and drum band that came, of all places, from Dernacarta. Father Connelly and Douglas Hyde, with Willie between them, marched to the carriage window and greeted the Bishop. Then Carty took a paper from his coat pocket and read a Gaelic poem which the Bishop didn't understand. The guard waved his green flag, Snee pulled the rope and the engine began to move while the band played the only number they knew—"The Girl I Left Behind Me."

I had come to St. Nathy's with good training in mathematics, for Dad was a patient, helpful and insistent teacher who drilled me in seven books of Euclid. He also gave me a generous coverage in what was then called natural philosophy. This included such topics as gravity, inclined planes, falling bodies and water power. He also had taught me some trigonometry and arithmetic. During the next five years at St. Nathy's, the concentration was on Latin and Greek.

The school itself had at one time been a British barracks, and we sometimes felt the old atmosphere prevail about us. Then as now, student activities were greatly restricted. St. Nathy's did, however, provide us with an introduction to the classics, to Livy the historian, Horace the poet, and Caesar and his commentaries. In this isolated oasis of learning the doors were opened for us and we were invited to enter the great world of culture and knowledge.

Our introduction was casual but enough to whet our intellectual appetites. We, of course, took the word of Caesar that the battle with the Helvetii raged so furiously at one time that he in person was compelled to seize a sword from a soldier and join in the fray to turn the tide of battle. Much later we were to learn what his soldiers had to say about him and his didos, reported on what would be the counterpart of modern army latrine walls. I can't say I ever excelled in either Latin or Greek.

When I was 15 years old, Aunt Annie came from Chicago to visit us. She brought with her a leather-bound history of the United States and a bound volume of Longfellow's poem "Evangeline." Both made fascinating reading and turned my thoughts to America. All that summer the thought of going there haunted me. After the vacation came to an end, I begged Aunt Annie to ask Mother and Dad to allow me to go with her to Chicago instead of returning to St. Nathy's. Aunt Annie, delighted, moved quickly by first talking to Grandfather, who had great influence with Mother. One afternoon they both came up to our house to discuss my going back with her.

That afternoon, I think Mother was closer to the moon than any human being has been before or since. As the result of this explosion, poor Aunt Annie went back to Chicago with a clear understanding that if she ever came around again she would not be welcome. Strangely enough, Mother didn't cool off for a long time, and I went back to St. Nathy's with strict instructions not to communicate with Aunt Annie. For a while I was tempted to disobey and undoubtedly would have, except for the knowledge that she had learned her lesson and would not further interfere. Meanwhile, I settled down to the life of a student designated by wish, if not vocation, to a clerical life.

I struggled through the courses, and obtained grades which qualified me for acceptance to Maynooth, now a famous Irish seminary, or to Salamanca, the world-famous Spanish university. There are two reasons why I chose Salamanca in preference to Maynooth. The first was economic. Irish students at Salamanca were there under scholarship, whereas fees had to be paid at Maynooth. However impelling that reason was, I can't say it was the real one. While the question was under

61

discussion at home, I learned something about Salamanca from my friend and adviser, Father Connelly. It was one of the oldest universities in Europe (founded about 1230) and was first under the patronage of Alphonso IX, a well-educated monarch with great pride in this endowment. Years later St. Ferdinand of Castile reestablished it, and from that time on it became more and more renowned as a center of learning.

The Irish College at Salamanca was established in 1592, two years before Sir John Norris was to wreck his brilliant military career in North East Ireland. Seven years before then, in the same region, Elizabeth's favorite, the Earl of Essex, was to go down to defeat at the Pass of Plumes. In 11 years O'Neil was to suffer a crushing defeat at the battle of Kinsale. The Irish College, sometimes called the "Colegio de Nobles Irlandeses," was one of three European colleges established to supply priests to Ireland, the other two being in Louvain and Rome. Ireland had been torn apart by the religious wars that followed the rupture between Henry VIII and the Pope, and the priests were caught in the middle, becoming the greatest victims of the Reformation.

Columbus lectured at the University of Salamanca on his voyages of discovery, and a bust of Hernan Cortez was set among the famous students of the past in a plaza near the main building. Father Connelly had a great respect for Cortez as the man who brought the Catholic faith to Mexico. Even then, I viewed the story of Cortez with some mixed emotions.

In earlier days the Irish student was obliged to take three oaths. One of them required the student to commit himself to go to the Irish mission and devote his life there no matter what its hardships or dangers.

The university took pride in the fact that its courses in laws, lay and canonical, attracted students from all over Europe. The Copernican system was taught there long before it was accepted in other places. At the time the Irish College was established, the university had more than 8,000 students on its rolls, evidence of its standing and prestige everywhere. It was very heavily endowed, and its alumni could be found in any part of the known world.

By the time Father Connelly had finished telling me about Salamanca, whatever doubts I had about my vocation had disappeared. I'm sure he didn't mean to have it that way, but he was a hopeless romantic, and it came through in all his descriptions. I felt my calling was set in stone and concrete. I later found out the foundation was not quite so solid.

When I took leave of my parents, Mother was full of hope. She said it was the happiest day of her life and would be surpassed only when I returned to say my first Mass in St. Mary's Church in Bohola. Dad showed no such enthusiasm. He had taken me aside for about the nearest thing to a man-to-man talk that could be expected in those days. He asked me if this was my real wish. I told him it was. As I looked back at that later I realized he knew more of me than I did myself. His advice did not compare with that of Polonius to Laertes. It was much less complicated. It was simply to the effect that whatever path a man chose for himself, he should strive to excel at it. He himself had practiced that philosophy, although I am sure that if he had his life to live over he would have travelled farther. My brothers and sisters were bewildered. Jim, May, Katty and Josephine snickered at the idea of my becoming a priest. The younger ones, Frank, Jack, Tommy and Linda, were excited about the prospect. They thought of me as having been already ordained and giving them my blessing.

The night before I left, the neighbors had come to call. It was the custom of the country when a young son or daughter was to leave for far-off places to come to wish them luck and give them a shilling or two. The custom was born during the Famine. Those who couldn't make it to the ship gave what they could afford to those who were determined to make the try. When the neighbors had left, I had 30 shillings in my pocket. I knew they could ill-afford such generosity.

The train pulled into the station at Kiltimagh. My grandfather's side car, borrowed for the occasion, took me to the station. On the way, the horse, shying at something, broke part of the harness, and it took some time to bring the frightened animal under control. We were late for the train, but the whole town knew I was going, and Tom Wallace, the town porter, persuaded Owen Mack, the engineer, to wait. When 10 minutes had passed, the engineer must have concluded that my vocation had come a cropper. He had gone about 50 yards when a frantic stationmaster waved him to return. As I came into the station, the engine was puffing, panting and backing up. I left amid the cheers of neighbors and townspeople. It was my first railroad problem. I often wished the ones to come later were solved as easily. Obviously, it was not a "rapid transit system."

The journey to Spain was uneventful. Aboard the train were some spalpeens, in no mood to talk, several men from western areas speaking among themselves in Gaelic. I, too, was in no mood to talk or listen. I thought of the men who had gone before me and since I was in a clerical state of mind, my thoughts were preoccupied with St. Columb-Kill more than with the "Wild Geese."

St. Columb-Kill in the sixth century obtained a book to read which another had written. Columb-Kill copied it. Demand was made upon discovery and Columb refused to give up the copy. The case was taken before the King. The King made the first copyright decision: "To every cow her calf and to every book its copy." Columb-Kill mustered his followers to defend his right to the copy, and in the ensuing battle, a thousand persons were slain. Columb-Kill repented and imposed a punishment on himself. He would never again see Ireland. He would go into pagan country and convert one to the true faith for every one lost in that battle. He kept his pledge, returning from Iona only once to plead for the bards who had been outlawed. He came and went blindfolded.

But there were new and strange accents, and trains and boats and more trains, and in the new countries all thoughts of Columb-Kill and the bards and the tinkers and the landlords went out of my head and it seemed as though the past had never happened, and the new places seemed like fairyland.

All of a sudden I was in Salamanca. No one could go through the place without marveling at it. It was important in 220 B.C. when Hannibal captured it, and it remained under Rome until the coming of the Goths. Between the 8th and the 11th centuries it was under Arab rule. In 1811 the army of the Duc de Raguse was defeated south of Salamanca by an army under Wellington, and the city suffered severely. The sandstone buildings show signs of both Moorish and Roman architecture.

I was greeted at the university by Father Michael Doherty, rector of the Irish College, later Bishop of Zambo Anga in the Philippines. Two days later he introduced the new students to the great philosopher and thinker, Miguel Unamuno. Rector of the university, he was later exiled from Spain for his nonconformist ideas.

The Irish section of the university housed about 35 students. After formalities, we began classes, taught in Latin. I then realized why the emphasis was on the classical languages in St. Nathy's. The rules were strict, but no more so than at St. Nathy's, where we were permitted outside the grounds only on Sundays for a walk under supervision. However, university life of necessity—even in an ecclesiastical college—permits some exploration, and after a while there came a feeling that somehow childhood and boyhood had gone, and the age of manhood had arrived. Here one was not treated as a child anymore.

Dr. Doherty was helpful to each student who came under his care. The secure ones he left alone. Those who fell within the doubtful class bore close watching. He encouraged me a great deal, and for a while I got along well. I liked the university and its surroundings and I especially liked the feeling that I had passed the boyhood-student stage. But within the year the old feeling of discontent came over me, and I began to think more about America. I read everything I could find on the subject. Columbus and Cortez now were closer to me. I began to feel on occasion that the years in St. Nathy's were wasted. I would think of Laurence Sterne's comment on the "seven wasted years"—"the accusing spirit, which flew up to Heaven's chancery with the oath, blushed as he gave it in, and the recording angel as he wrote it down dropped a tear upon the word and blotted it out forever."

As time went on I thought more of Spain, dreamed more of overseas, and gave less attention to Ireland and the task before me. I found Spain saturated with romantic interest, although the tempo of life was slow. Spain seemed elegant, but old and fighting decay. The agrarian explosion of 25 years later was already in the making. The same grumbling against absentee landlords living high in European capitals on the profit of the sharecroppers at home paralleled in part the atmosphere in which I grew up in Ireland. In Ireland, however, the bomb had been touched off many years before and was rapidly bringing a solution. Spain was not yet ready to make the move.

There were the stories of Cortez. He had been a student at the university. One night, as he left his quarters to meet a young lady, he leaped from a window and broke his leg. According to the legend we heard at the university, he was expelled because of this escapade.

In my mind's eye I could see Cortez and his followers and hear the hoofbeats of their burros as they headed south to Cadiz. They were restless men of adventure in a hurry to pit their brains and energy against the storms of an unknown ocean. Answering a call from a world that was new and challenging, they knew what sacrifices had to be made. There were rivers and deep-cut gorges to cross. There were high mountains, with here and there a rugged pass that would have to be carved into a highway. But there was an excitement that would never be found in Spain.

I felt less sure of my calling with each passing month. If ever I had a vocation, this atmosphere was not the place to cultivate it. And yet the atmosphere did not have the same effect on my classmates. My inner struggle, as it became more pronounced, jelled into a lack of confidence in myself. There were times when I envied Willie Carty and wished I could take my books, climb the high bridge with its old Roman arch, and drop them one by one, watching their pages flutter like birds of prey into the river 500 feet below.

Father Doherty caught my mood. He would often take me aside, pointing out that for each student there were misgivings and a feeling of rebellion at the outset. Even St. Anthony, he said, had not been without his moments of doubt. These talks had a great effect on me. I thought of them often later when confronted with the problems of life, for they seemed to have a universal application. Their effect, however, was soon to wear off, and there I was, again, confused and groping.

Finally at the end of the second year I found he had left me alone longer than usual. He was leaving it up to me to decide.

When I told him of my decision, he nodded slowly. "Go," he said, "with our blessing. I think it is better this way. The laws of the Church are exacting and obedience to superiors is the most important. I may tell you now that Father Connelly predicted this would happen. You have his blessing also."

Now came the most unpleasant task of all—writing Mother. The letter came to Bohola with the disquieting news. I explained that I had come near the completion of my two years and was convinced I no longer had a vocation. The news was received with no little disappointment. The response from my mother suggested prayer for guidance. But if her first born's mind was made up, he should write Aunt Annie in Chicago. She would surely help. I mailed a letter to Aunt Annie. I felt a great weight had been lifted from my shoulders, as if shackles had been removed, leaving me free.

Annie was a worldly woman. She had accompanied her consumptive brother to Denver and stayed there long enough to bury him. She came back to Chicago and married a saloon-keeper who died leaving her with three small children and a saloon. She took her place behind the bar as its proprietor. She responded that she was sympathetic to the plight of her sister's boy and he would be greatly welcome in her home in Chicago. In any event, she would write to ask Tom Rouse to claim me when I arrived in New York. I sold my bicycle, and in no time I was in Cherbourg, where a ship was waiting to take me to America.

CHAPTER 15

NATIVE AMERICAN CONTRAST

PO'D

The 16th, 17th and 18th centuries had reaped havoc on the people of Ireland—or what was left of them—on their language, customs, culture, laws, art and, above all else, their self-esteem and dignity. The conquerors were truly masters, riding to the hounds over peasants' crops and treating them as waste beneath their feet. This was the legacy that Patrick and Bridget O'Dwyer grew up with.

In the Ireland of William's youth, the O'Dwyers, like their neighbors, kept their best side out. The best was none too good. Continuous waves of emigration had drained the youth out of the countryside and kept the people impoverished and discouraged. Some money came from America to pay the debts of the older people to the merchants and the gombeenmen who kept them alive, but at a very high cost. The Irish-elected representatives in London were content to beg for some sort of dominion arrangement. Malcontents had been driven to the badlands, the unproductive mountains or the bogs, or else found their way to America.

On the other side of the Atlantic in the place to which destiny was to carry William O'Dwyer, a devastating tragedy equal to the Irish experience had overtaken its native inhabitants over the course of the same three centuries.

In earlier times various European explorers, including Brendan the Navigator and Eric the Red, had dared the ocean, but it was the Columbus discovery that set the scene for every pirate, adventurer and privateer to cross the ocean bent on thievery or becoming rich entrepreneurs at the native population's expense.

At first these marauders stayed just long enough to rob and cheat the inhabitants and to carry off to Europe the products of their plunder. As time progressed, the merchant companies who had been granted rights over the hemisphere proceeded to populate the area and to involve the native population in all their wars. If the territory to which these

Europeans had come had a prior name, few took the trouble to find out what it was, and only a handful of historians felt any urge to give more than a short introductory reference to those who were about to be displaced by trickery and deception.

The Church of Rome, the largest of warring Christian sects, joined with the invading armies as they took over the southern and part of the northern portion of the discovered territory. The newcomers emanating from Spain and Portugal moved on the inhabitants with the sword, the sign of death and oppression, and beside it, the cross, the symbol of love. Fire and torture awaited those who resisted conversion. Many accepted death as the only alternative. One native about to die expressed the fear that if he did convert, he would meet only Christians in the next world. The newcomers' commitment to Christianity did not hinder them in any way from robbing the cultured natives of sacred vessels used in the practice of their religion. Gold became the object of all their murderous adventures.

Other factions came from England, Holland and France carrying their national rivalries with them, perpetuating their racial and religious hatreds. Rival factions, pursuing theories enunciated by Calvin, Knox, Wesley and a dozen others, each claimed for themselves a monopoly on eternal salvation. Their bitterness towards each other created an atmosphere of hate. Their common belief was in a vengeful, all-powerful Creator, who demanded that his creatures love and fear him under pain of burning through all eternity. It was truly a God created in their own image. Their intolerance made life together unbearable. The weaker were banished by the stronger, who brooked no opposition to their special religious dogma. They had long repudiated and done violence to the most noble concepts of the gentle founder who brought their beliefs into being.

The European intruders came to these shores waving written "authority" to occupy land they could not even vaguely describe. Starting with the early part of the 17th century, land grants were to appear, purporting to give to the monarch's favorites full and clear title to lands which were never theirs to give. These spurious documents presupposed that the lands conveyed were uninhabited, and the ritual of placing a flag on a wooden pole was somehow ordained by God as absolute proof of ownership.

Together or separately, the European plunderers brutalized many peaceful tribes, frequently provoking some of them to the oppressors' own level of savagery.[1] When the victims responded in kind, the Eu-

---

1. Even scalping, which was pointed out as clear evidence of depravity, was the invention of European exploiters.

ropeans wrote back home about how treacherous the "savages" were, how badly they responded to acts of kindness, how they had resisted conversion to the "true religion," and how the blessings of eternal salvation generously offered to them had been rejected. Among the "gifts" bestowed upon the natives by these Caucasian intruders were venereal diseases, alcohol addiction and smallpox.

In New Amsterdam the story was slightly different. The myth that on May 6, 1626, a shrewd German named Peter Minuit bought the island of Manhattan from its primitive owners for baubles worth $24 has been taught in every school and college. It is presented boastfully as proof of how shrewd the strangers were and how gullible the natives.

Given the period of time (less than a year) during which the West India Company settlers were around, it is doubtful that this legendary sale ever took place. There were very few Europeans who could communicate or speak the dialect of the native population, and it would have been difficult to explain the European concept of ownership to a people who had never known and undoubtedly would have resisted the idea of private ownership or the exploitation of land and environment.

The Hollanders were as aggressive as the settlers to the north or south with one significant difference—they did not share the same commitment to the religious life or the same intense religious hatred. New Netherland was created as a business venture, and with the exception of some French-speaking Huguenots, the settlers did not come here to escape persecution, but rather to engage in trade or farming.

When the first settlers' ships arrived, it was caution and wisdom which dictated to the captains of the *Nieu Neikelandt* in 1624 and *Orange Boom* in 1625 to land their families, cattle and farm implements first on Nut (now Governor's) Island and later to transfer them to Manhattan. It was apparent that those who inhabited the island and maintained it were surprised but not hostile at the intrusion of the strangers into their villages. Had they chosen to do so, they could easily have wiped out this small early contingent of invaders.

As for the presumed sale of Manhattan to Minuit, one must remember that to the Indians, reverence for the soil and the plant and animal life which grew and lived in it, from it and around it, was part of their very being. At that stage, they would no more have countenanced the allocation of exclusive use to anyone than they would have believed that the fish in the Hudson were the private domain of the intruders. The custom of giving gifts, however, was a deeply inbedded part of the life of the eastern Indian. They often engaged in the practice to the point of what whites would describe as pauperization. But it is most unlikely that they would have believed the *acceptance* of gifts from Minuit, if that ever happened, was any more than a gesture of friendship.

Furthermore, far from being an uninhabitable area, the site where the transaction was said to have occurred, at the tip of the island of Manhattan (now known as the Battery), was then and for a long time had been an important Indian settlement. Roadways from that village connected with other villages. The present lower Broadway had, for centuries before, been a well-travelled trail which went northward and later divided into two trails, one ending at the village called Sapohanikan (now Greenwich Village). The other branch went in a northeasterly direction over what is now Park Row. It passed a swamp, where the Beekman Hospital now sits, and continued alongside a fresh water pond, which for decades supplied New Amsterdam (thereafter New York) with drinking water. The pond long ago disappeared from sight. The filled-in ground, where once the Indian fished, is now Foley Square and Thomas Paine Park. The federal building and the state courts are on either side.

Abandoning a territory was not unknown among Indian tribes. It might happen for any number of reasons. Under such circumstances, another band moved into the area. It was then theirs to live in and enjoy for as long as they chose to occupy it.

This was the situation at the time of the supposed sale of Manhattan. Whatever the truth may have been about its particulars, the story does seem to have been the signal for various subsequent arrangements, which then became the excuse for a relentless war of extermination. And in any event, there was no suggestion that the Minuit claim was supported by any formal contract. In fact, the only evidence of the event seems to have been a notation in a ship's log. The entry lacked any description of the land alleged to have been conveyed.

The insistence on written documents came later. At first, the West India Company warned its representatives to deal fairly with the native population and to take no unfair advantage of them, but at least one of their early governors, Director-General Willem Kieft, was not listening. First, Kieft sought to impose a tax on the Indians, but none on the Europeans. And then, with little excuse, he made savage war on his Indian neighbors. In 1643, he was responsible for the massacre of the Weckquaesgeeks at Corlears Hook, beginning a sad history of annihilation and spurious land deals, which, to quote the language in one contract, required the Indians to "transport themselves to some other place."

Staten Island, occupied mainly by Hackensacks and Raritans, was sold three times. In the 1670 deed of sale, one finds among the "underwriters" several natives, including a baby boy and a baby girl. This sort of practice was typical. The purchasers were careless about title. Names appear on the so-called Indian deeds for property which was in the territory of other tribes. New owners were not very sure of their deeds. Confirmatory deeds were frequently drawn many years after the first transaction.

Whether the Indians knew the meaning of these treaties is not clear. What is not in doubt is the failure of the Europeans to live by their terms. Hundreds of treaties were signed and sworn to, and one with the Quakers was signed by William Penn in 1683 but not sworn to. Every treaty witnessed by God was broken. Only the Quakers honored their compact.

The first to come to what we now refer to as the Southern states carried with them the arrogance of the Established Church, the official religion of England. These strangers carried the disease of intolerance and were so severely infected by it that they sent Quakers to the gallows and Presbyterians, Lutherans, Anabaptists, Moravians and Huguenots scurrying for their lives.[2] They preached adherence and devotion to a gentle Christ who had pleaded for understanding for the most despised citizen. In the same breath they nurtured and fostered a system of human bondage. Their most revered leaders, without a word of condemnation from the ardent advocates of strict morality, engaged in the slave traffic with Moslem chiefs and amassed fortunes trading in human flesh.

The activities of the Europeans were not confined to trading with the shipowners whose vessels were specially equipped with chains to keep their cargo confined to the stinking holds during the long voyage from the African coast to the New World. Another equally profitable home trade developed which cast the white colonial Christian in the role of peddlers of the bodies of men, women and children in the land to which they had come seeking freedom. Native Americans were literally kidnapped in every colony, including New Amsterdam and New York, and a brisk slave trade went on within the colonies.[3]

Some of these native Americans were sent to Europe. Some of their women were especially selected for breeding. Young men who became apprenticed to business or trade were, at the end of their apprenticeships, committed to slavery, their employers becoming their masters.

The traffic in enslaved native Americans was not confined to the colonies. Dutch Governor Willem Kieft sent four native American slaves as a present to the British Governor of Bermuda. There they met African slaves and Pequods and Mohicans, who had been sold to the Bermuda

---

2. A century and a half later, new people, enlightened strangers, developed the First Amendment and put an end to these corruptions. But again there was an exception: it was not until the 1930's that freedom of religion was guaranteed to American Indians.
3. For the most part our histories of colonial times have omitted these episodes. The special exceptions are Almon Wheeler Lauber's *Indian Slavery in Colonial Times within the Present Limits of the United States* (Williamstown, Mass.: Corner House Publishers, 1913) and James E. Smith's *Slavery in Bermuda* (New York: Vantage Press, 1976).

71

colonists by New England traders. In Bermuda at that time there were many Irishmen who had been transported there by Cromwell. Seemingly, the Africans, the native Americans and the Irish met and discussed their experiences and their possible deliverance. They were all charged with conspiring to revolt against their masters, and with a plot to kill all the Englishmen and take over the island. The Irish and native Americans were all banished to a far corner of the island where ironically our military base is now located. The facial outlines of the local residents and their descendants are distinctly native American.

Bermuda was not the only place where Irish slaves have been recorded. Concurrent with the enslavement and extermination of native Americans, the Cromwellian campaign to bring about a final solution to the Irish question brought about an imbalance in the 600,000 souls that somehow had survived. By 1650, the women of Ireland greatly outnumbered the men. The commissioners whom the Lord Protector had left in Ireland to finish off his genocidal campaign realized that those they had condemned to "Hell or to Connaught" were worth more alive than in hell. A plan to deal with the surplus Irish women was put into effect. They were rounded up and "sold to merchants and transported to Virginia, New England, Jamaica or other countries." This profitable business was continued for several years.

A French Jesuit named Father Garganel, in charge of the society's missionary activities in Martinique, was made aware of a problem existing in a neighboring isle. After personal investigation, he wrote to the Jesuits in Limerick that the islands were "full of Irish," and that "every year shiploads of men, boys and girls were carried off by force for the purpose of the slave trade and conveyed by the British from Ireland." The slaves had pleaded with the Jesuit to get them a priest. The call was answered by a Limerick Jesuit named Father Hartegan, who spoke Irish, French and English. He assumed a French name and pretended to be a timber merchant. He succeeded in getting 150 Irish slaves from St. Kitts to Guadeloupe, leaving them there in the hands of the French to return to his mission. He was not heard of thereafter.

Some of the Irish slaves were said to have found their way to the mainland. Whatever Catholics there were in the colonies were not talking about it, and history does not record any separate account of them thereafter. Irish slaves were not mentioned in laws and other records documenting the plight of native American and black slaves.

The use of native American slaves was widespread and official New York was not far different in that respect from the rest of the colonies. In 1693 Indian and Negro slaves were used by the city in mending its fortifications. The New York newspapers periodically carried notices offering a reward for the return of "Indian slaves." A 1676 law excluded

Indians from being carters and they were prevented from the use of local inns for relaxation.[4] In 1702 by instruction from Queen Anne, a law was passed providing that baptizing "Indians" did not mean the end of their enslaved condition. The budget of the New York Colony was enhanced by the import tax on black and native American slaves moved from outside the colony of New York. In 1712 a law was enacted to prohibit free Indians from holding title to the land that was theirs in the first place. (A similar law was enacted in Ireland at the same time aimed at native Irish.) In 1715 New York passed a law making the children of Indian slaves, slaves for the rest of their lives.

In 1712 native Americans were charged with participating in a plot to destroy their white masters and take over the colony. It was discovered that Spanish Indians, who were charged with involvement in this plot, had been kidnapped in one of the Spanish colonies and served eight years as slaves in New York.

The Indians also played an integral part and became tragic victims in the white nations' New World conflicts. Just as Ireland became a battleground during the Reformation, the Counter Reformation and the Puritan Reformation, with disastrous consequences to the peasantry, so did the Indian country east of the Rocky Mountains become a battleground in the almost continuous war between the French and the English. New York was at its core.

The territory of the powerful Five Nations[5] bordered on both French and English territory, where the two countries battled over the fur trade. The vast territory around the Great Lakes was the principal battleground. There was no serious attempt by whites at that time to settle the area and farm it. The bitter experience from the slaughter of neighboring Indians by Governor Willem Kieft was not forgotten by the Five Nations, but the coming of Arent Van Curler (or Van Corlaer), a Dutch leader, made a most favorable impression on the Five Nations and softened their attitude to the Hollanders.

Years later, after the Dutch had surrendered to the English and New Amsterdam had become New York, Thomas Dongan, the colony's only Catholic governor, built on that foundation. The French had made a peace treaty with some enemies of the Five Nations, and in response, Dongan took the trouble to study the situation, thereby gaining the trust of the Five Nations tribes. It was to be feared that since Dongan was an Irish Catholic, whose lot was thrown in with the Duke of York, he would make peace with the Catholic French and so weaken the position of the

4. At the same time Darcy McGee, a native Irishman, was fined for pushing a peddler's cart within the Dublin Pale.
5. The Five Nations were the Mohawk, Oneida, Onondaga, Cayuga and Seneca tribes, and, after the 18th century, the Tuscarora.

Five Nations. But they found Dongan's attitude to be continuously hostile to the Canadians. At a later period, however, Dongan was ordered to make friends with the French Canadians. It was a crushing blow to the Five Nations, who regarded it as another betrayal.

The losses sustained by the Indians in these wars reduced their number, their strength and their influence. Even during the battles, in which they fought side by side with the English, their most persistent complaint was that the English made them pay an exorbitant price for the gun powder they were using in battle.

Things went from bad to worse when, in 1686, James II appointed Governor Edmund Andros to take charge of the New England colonies. Andros undid all the good work that Dongan had accomplished in New York.

Rumblings were heard along the Indian trails of the settlers' general discontent with their king back home. If the sachems of what was left of the Algonkians or the Five Nations were to draw comfort from such expressions, they were due for bitter disappointment. Finally, in July 1776 the Declaration of Independence listed grievances that could just as well have expressed the complaints of the native population's treatment at the hands of most of the European powers.

If the Indians drew comfort from the early paragraphs of that historic document, the clear and libelous description of their people as "merciless Indian Savages" must have dashed any hopes they may have had that they were to benefit from the declaration that it was "self-evident" that all men were created equal. It was clear that the new order held little in store for the native Indians, and the passage of time has proved that, for them, nothing has changed.

It should be added that since 1816 New York has enacted its own laws dealing with Indians within its borders, and has almost exclusive right to deal with the state's native American population. As a result, the remaining native population in the New York City area (now consisting of 300 Shenecocks) was driven eastward into a patch of land on the tip of Long Island, and all the Algonkians from the area have totally vanished.

As to the Five Nations, the few remaining Onondagas are ghettoized into a miserable patch of reservation near Syracuse, totally incapable of living according to their customs. They exist in shameful poverty, and even candidates for state and federal offices do not call to see them at election time. The Senecas in their reservation at Salamanca are not even allowed representation on the school board, which is hostile to their language, customs and culture, and rights guaranteed by law are frequently ignored by law enforcement officials. A reservation of the once-powerful Mohawks includes an island in the St. Lawrence River. When it became necessary to erect a bridge over the St. Lawrence, the reservation was chosen for the site, and the Mohawks were charged a toll to cross the structure, and a duty and excise charge was imposed on the groceries they brought to their families, across the structure which defaces their landscape. The fate of what is left of the Oneidas and the Tuscaroras can be described in similar terms.

Today, the total native American population in New York State does not exceed 50,000, and that of New York City, 15,000. In the entire country, the total native American population is less than a million with about 700,000 of these living on reservations.

CHAPTER 16

SLAVERY

PO'D

The first cargo of Negro slaves had come to New Amsterdam when it was new. They were bought by and then came under the care of the West India Company. At some time thereafter the shame of extending the institution into the colony of New Netherlands moved the company to adopt a policy which favored gradual manumission.

The West India Company officials made arrangements to have parcels of land along the Bowery and at Broadway, north and south of Prince Street, deeded to individual members of the town's black colony. A large number of slaves and freedmen built homes along these thoroughfares, planted crops on the land, and harvested the produce. Peter Stuyvesant, for all his reluctance to honor his employer's directions regarding freedom of worship, carried out this policy to the letter. He personally signed the conveyances. After the British takeover, Governor Nicolls and later Governor Loveland confirmed every one of their titles.

British, Portuguese and Dutch shipping interests were all gainfully engaged in ripping Africans away from their loved ones, committing them in chains in the stinking belly of a ship for delivery to the new land of despair. Upon their arrival here, males and females were sold singly or in pairs. It was expected that good, healthy ones would present the master with healthy babies who would soon prove to be valuable slaves. Some masters, however, preferred to buy a female who could not have children.

Fifty years after the Declaration of Independence annunciated the principle that all men are free and equal, New York, the most progressive state, was still engaged in a painfully slow process of ridding itself of this most disreputable of institutions. Eighty years before William O'Dwyer's arrival at Ellis Island, slavery was still legal in New York.

Notwithstanding the Holland merchants' activity in the slave trade, New Netherland's and New Amsterdam's attitude was less harsh towards blacks than that of the slaveholders of the rest of the hemisphere.[1] During the Dutch period, there was no fear of a slave uprising, nor was there an ever-present atmosphere of hostility and suspicion on the part of the white settlers. After the English gained control of the colony things began to change. The first clear evidence of maltreatment was the Negro and Indian slave insurrection of 1712.

New York City fully recognized slavery. Indeed, in 1709 the Common Council designated Markett House at the foot of Wall Street as the place for hiring "Negro and Indian slaves." The presence of the official hiring hall seemed to be the signal for the slaves, then about a third of the population, to join into a poorly planned and very desperate attempt to seek freedom. What took place was reported on June 23, 1712, by Governor Hunter to the Lords of Trade. "On April 7, 1712," he wrote, "there was a bloody conspiracy of some slaves to destroy as many of the inhabitants as they could to revenge themselves for some harsh usage from their masters." There was no further description of the "harsh usage." It was charged that between 23 and 33 slaves participating in the plot met at "the going down of the moon." In the attempted uprising, nine "Christians" were killed and four others wounded. About 70 Negroes and some Indians were rounded up by the militia, 27 brought to trial, and 21 executed. "Some were burnt, others hanged."[2] Six of the accused committed suicide.

The revolt occurred on April 7th, the trial and sentence in General Session Court took place on April 11th, and the executions were carried out between April 14th and 21st. Tom, the "Negro man slave of Nicholas Roosevelt," was singled out for special attention. He was sentenced to be "burned with a slow fire that he may continue in torment for eight or ten hours and continue burning in said fire until he be dead and consumed to ashes."

By December of that year, the legislature enacted a sheaf of laws dealing with "Negroes and other slaves" and specifically authorized the master or mistress to punish their slaves "not extending, however, to life or member." Typical of laws enacted that year by the legislature was one which provided that no freed slave, Indian or mulatto could own real property.

1. In the 17th century the public executioner in Europe was not considered a mean or particularly distasteful occupation, and it was classified more in the nature of a special skill. Pieter, a Negro, was appointed public executioner by the Dutch in New Amsterdam. In 1662 he demanded a raise.
2. Two of those executed were members of the church of Rev. John Shape, chaplain of the garrison. Reporting on the revolt to his superiors in London, Rev. Shape wrote that one of the two executed was later generally conceded to be innocent. Since there was no one close enough to the others of sufficient influence or standing, we can only speculate on the basis of similar hysterical reaction how many innocent ones were caught in the net.

The episode in 1712 was not the worst example of people in fear of a slave uprising. It seems the more the white population feared the Negro slave and black freed man, the more hysterical the political establishment became. As a consequence, unreasonable and brutish laws gave the masters the right to inflict sadistic punishment on their slaves. It was this state of mind that in 1741 was responsible for the hysteria and slaughter of innocent human beings.

It all started when a number of suspicious fires broke out in different parts of the town. The first consumed the Governor's home and other buildings within the fort[3]. The city fathers concluded that there was a plot by slaves to destroy the white population and to gain their freedom. Recorder Daniel Horsmanden took up the crusade, and rumor fed on rumor. The suspicion gained substance when a woman named Mary Burton gave evidence that a Negro named Ceasar had given to her and one Hughson, a tavern owner, the proceeds of a burglary committed in the home of a Mr. Hogg. She later extended her role to informing about a "plot," for which she was handsomely compensated by the Common Council. Her statements were the signal for mass arrests of slaves.

Confessions, obtained by bribery[4] or unusual brutality, were made public. They in turn gave credence to the stories, and so it went. Informers were the root source on which the populace relied to snuff out the lives of numerous slaves, a white family, and one white dissenting Christian, John Ury, who was branded as a papist priest. In a letter to Cadwallader Colden,[5] Recorder Horsmanden charged that Ury had created this "Catholic" plot. As part of the conspiracy, Ury was charged with having come into New York and "there celebrating Mass and granting Absolution."

At the time of the trials, there was a law in force for the trial of Negroes. However, the judges in these cases made special rules requiring the trials to be conducted "with great secrecy." There were no lawyers to stand by the side of the slaves or the "Papist priest," what lawyers there were in the colony having offered their services to the prosecution. Daniel Horsmanden became investigator, prosecutor and judge.

In contradistinction to the uprising of 1712, no slave committed suicide in 1741, but 18 were hanged, some put in chains, and 14 others burned at the stake. Hughson, Peggy Kerry, who was said to have been

3. The fort, at the Battery in lower Manhattan, had been first established by the Dutch and continued after the British takeover.
4. Proclamations were issued granting amnesty to those coming forward with information: £25 and freedom were offered to any slave, £45 to any Indian or freed Negro, and £100 to any white, who would supply the recorder with information about the plot. Soon the jail was packed.
5. Colden was one of the colony's most prominent and respected politicians.

a prostitute and in league with Hughson, and the doomed slaves went to their deaths displaying great dignity, all protesting their innocence.

By 1744, according to Horsmanden, "There had been some wanton wrongheaded persons amongst us, who took the liberty to arraign the justice of the proceedings," asserting that "there was no plot at all." The judge felt that such allegations required him to write a book on the subject. The book did not sell sufficient copies to pay the printer's costs. So ended the greatest disgrace in the history of the colony and a much greater reason for a revolution than a tax on tea.

The Declaration of Independence and the Constitution of the United States were instruments which gave hope to the oppressed people of the world. The colonies had produced a set of leaders who, remarkably, adopted views at variance with the mores of their society and laid the groundwork for the Revolution. The wisdom of Benjamin Franklin in bringing Tom Paine, a true revolutionary, to help in the tremendous task ahead is but one of the many examples of Franklin's genius. When *Common Sense* went into its many printings, there was added reason to believe that the Revolution was on solid ground and its objectives understood by the people of the colonies.

It is true that the flag displayed by the Sons of Liberty carried the inscription, "No Popery," in its folds, and that all through the War of Independence slavery remained a legal institution in all 13 states. Yet the Constitution had within its framework the capacity to make significant changes, and the full implementation of the objectives of the Declaration was clearly attainable. Additionally, freedom of religion was made possible not only by constitutional provision, but because Washington and Jefferson and other leaders openly acknowledged the contribution of Presbyterians, Catholics and Jews, among others, to the Revolution.

Slavery, however, was another matter, and black American slaves found it difficult to understand why they were excluded. Sometime between the Declaration in 1776 and the passage of the Bill of Rights, the Creator had turned his back on his black creatures, or at least so said those who framed the Bill of Rights. The ever-dissenting voices of Sam Adams and Tom Paine could not be heard above the howl, and their proposals to outlaw slavery were rejected. Others of the revolutionary figures who opposed slavery felt that pressing the issue would cause defections from the slaveholders of the Southern provinces, thereby jeopardizing the success of the revolt. The recognition that slavery was a blot on our national escutcheon had to wait for almost another century.

The continuation of slavery had a lot to do with their economic usefulness. However, with the passage of time, the Northern economy had no need for slaves, and those who railed against the system on moral grounds were beginning to enjoy a measure of success. The South, on the other hand, having from its very inception fostered a landed aristocracy with large plantations, found slaves essential to the maintenance of its special privileged existence. Finally, it took a bloody war to discontinue the practice of slavery. That war had its repercussions in the North, where the victim was made to suffer in the home territory of his supposed benefactors.

The memory of the Draft Riots of 1863 still hovers over our heads when we tend to put on airs of righteousness. Those riots claimed the lives of a thousand New Yorkers, among them black children made homeless for the second time as a hate-filled mob burned down their orphanage.

This most disgraceful occurrence was triggered by the passage of a law which permitted any draftee to buy his way out of military service for $300. The working class, impoverished and insecure, accepted the propaganda of many friends of the South in the Northern states. The agitators said that with emancipation, Negro freedmen would swarm into the Northern cities and take the jobs then held by white workers. New York Governor Horatio Seymour added his bit to the passion of that period when he declared the draft unconstitutional. Draft riots occurred in many parts of the country. Regretfully, New York was recorded as the leader.[6] To black America, the Emancipation Proclamation, issued on January 1, 1863, was not without its drawbacks.

When William O'Dwyer landed in New York, he was by no means universally accepted, but his position in New York society was far more secure than black citizens who had paid their taxes as free Americans for three generations. By the time he became Mayor in 1946, the black population had grown extensively throughout New York. Yet there was not even a token black in a leadership position in any of the New York City departments nor any recognition of their existence even in the lesser positions in city government. The lot of a black fireman or black policeman who might, through dogged persistence, have qualified for the jobs, found ostracism awaiting him at the back room of the stationhouse or in the firehouse bedroom. On the opening day of the baseball season, there was not a black face on the playing field at the Polo Grounds, Yankee Stadium or Ebbets Field, and Jackie Robinson, the next year, was the first player to break through the exclusion barrier.

Mayor O'Dwyer learned that the system of patronage within both

---

6. Irish workers, who made up the bulk of the New York working class, were all too well represented among the rioters. With their own history as the victims of exploitation and oppression going on in New York at that very same time, it is difficult to understand their outrageous behavior. The shame was not New York's alone.

the Democratic and Republican Parties had made it unlikely that any black would gain recognition. Blacks constituted a small part of the political machines, and no appointment trickled down to them. At the Mayor's suggestion, a black group in Harlem chose J. Raymond Jones as its spokesman, and William received his plan for appointment of blacks to positions of importance. Under that plan, the new appointments included commissioners, heads of departments and the first member of the Board of Higher Education; and additionally, Edward R. Dudley was appointed Ambassador to Liberia by President Truman on the Mayor's recommendation.

The days of Reconstruction had been a nightmare, and even the court of justice was, to the black population of America, just another symbol of oppression. Prejudice and ill-treatment continued unabated during World War II and regretfully did not end with the Army desegregation order of Harry Truman, nor even with the passage of the Civil Rights Act in 1963. In 1982 the black and Hispanic minority population of New York City was 50 percent of its total. Yet, there was not one minority elected representative in the city's governing body (the Board of Estimate), and even in the rather powerless City Council, the United States Courts found (that same year) that the district councilmanic lines were so gerrymandered as to rob these minorities of true representation in that body. Fifteen years after the United States Supreme Court held against segregation in the schools of America, President Reagan approved the decision by one member of his Cabinet to permit tax exemption to an institution of learning guilty of segregation. The more things changed, the more they remained the same.

CHAPTER 17

RELIGIOUS FREEDOM

PO'D

In New York during the last half of the 17th century, Catholics led an undercover existence. Despite the presence of a substantial Catholic population, no church was established, nor was any assembly permitted under pain of dire consequences. The differences between colonists with regard to religious beliefs did not prevent them from making common cause against both Catholics and slaves.

Catholics, under Calvert in Baltimore, had already lived to see the religious tolerance they had fought for literally obliterated. The Puritans, whom they had welcomed as refugees from the Established Church in Virginia, caused the enactment of laws against Catholics reminiscent of the Penal Laws in Ireland. Elsewhere, William Penn had made a noble effort to allow the Catholics who had flocked to Pennsylvania from Ireland to practice their religion. However, on his return to England the complaints from powerful sources were so extensive that he was forced to make an exception in the case of Catholic worship to his otherwise perfect record of tolerance.

Catholics were not the only ones to know loss of their religious freedom in New York. Earlier in the city's history, under the Dutch, New Amsterdam had been spared some of the excesses of intolerance, strife and hatreds, which marked the earlier days of the occupation of its northeastern neighbors. Its citizens, speaking 18 different languages, were altogether too preoccupied with settling in their new homes and with matters of commerce to become involved in warring religious factions. In contradistinction to the New Englanders, the Dutch were not so deeply committed to the religious life, nor were they subservient to the Dutch Reformed Church leadership.

However, Holland's great reputation for religious tolerance was undermined by some of the governors of the West India Company. Calvinist zealots who had been sent from Holland to establish the Dutch Reformed Church in Fort Orange (Albany) and New Amsterdam exerted a greater influence on the local officials. Director General Peter Stuyvesant was one who was particularly vulnerable to their pressures, and it led him into error.

A small group of Sephardic Jews looking for a safe haven in the New World had come to Manhattan in 1654. A group of Quakers fleeing from discrimination, hostility and persecution in New England sought refuge in Flushing, then under Dutch control. Lutheran residents, who felt they should be as free in New Netherland as they would have been in the Netherlands, sought permission to obtain a minister of their own persuasion. Stuyvesant took action to suppress the first two groups and ignored the Lutherans' petition.

There was no evidence that Stuyvesant was particularly religious, but he was a dictator in every fiber of his being, and all manner of dissidents annoyed him. The presence in the colony of those not adhering to the Dutch Reformed Church, he felt, was likely to be upsetting to the church's leaders and thereby be the cause of religious strife.

The Jewish community was shocked at what threatened to become a familiar pattern of anti-Jewish laws and regulations. They could not imagine this behavior being sanctioned in New Netherland since Jews had found safety in Amsterdam for over two centuries. A petition for redress was faithfully smuggled back to the Netherlands. The petition was brought to the attention of a Jewish merchant who had a heavy financial interest in the West India Company and was a member of the company board of directors. As might be expected, Stuyvesant's departure from the Dutch tradition brought a fast response. He was told to halt his discriminatory attitude. The instruction did not eliminate anti-Semitism entirely, but it helped ward off attacks and discrimination, and without it Jews would have encountered severe difficulties in New Netherland.

In Stuyvesant's eyes, the rules laid down by the company and the Stats General were to be applied to the Jewish residents, but not to any other sect, and especially not to Quakers. John Bowne, a Quaker resident of Flushing, came to Stuyvesant's attention when he gave his co-religionists the right to worship in his home. For that he was punished. Almost all the people of Flushing, those who were Quakers and those who were not, gathered together and petitioned Stuyvesant and the officials of Holland to abandon the persecution of Quakers. "The Flushing Remonstrance" became part of our history, as did the return instructions from Holland to Stuyvesant. The 1663 letter from the directors of the West India Company reads in part: "You may therefore shut your eyes, at least not force people's consciences, but allow everyone to have his own belief . . ."

Notwithstanding these early pronouncements, religious intolerance became more pronounced as the colony developed and the influence of the Netherlands diminished.

With the Treaty of Breda in 1667, New Amsterdam became New York. The city's undercover Catholics got a brief respite and a measure of hope with the appointment of Thomas Dongan as the province's only Catholic Governor. He was a member of a wealthy Catholic family from Limerick. Dongan's performance in New York was most constructive. In addition to creating close ties with the Five Nations, he was responsible for charters banning religious qualification for office and decrees that public worship by any sect would be henceforth permitted. Surprisingly, his otherwise exemplary records sustained him in spite of the feeling of antagonism towards Catholics.

His performance came to an abrupt end with the dethroning of James II in 1688. Upon leaving office, he took up residence in Long Island, but the government in New York was seized by Jacob Leisler, a rabid anti-Catholic, and Dongan had to flee for his life. When he got to England, he found that his ancestral home and lands had been confiscated. In 1691 the New York Assembly declared all Dongan's laws null and void and created new laws depriving Catholics of basic rights and declaring, "Nothing herein mentioned or contained shall extend to give liberty for any persons of the Romish religion to exercise their manner of worship contrary to the laws and statutes of their Majesty's Kingdom of England."

In 1697 even more severe anti-Catholic laws were enacted. One such proclaimed that a priest coming into the province after November 1700 "should be deemed an incendiary and disturber of the public peace and safety," and if captured, would be sentenced "to suffer perpetual imprisonment."

The 18th century started on a similar note. In 1701 the Assembly enacted a law prohibiting Papists "and Popish recusants from voting for any office whatsoever."[1]

Another significant event in the history of religious intolerance in New York City took place in 1707, when Rev. Gaulcherus du Bois, a Dutch Reformed minister, invited one Francis Makemie to halt his journey to Massachusetts long enough to preach in New York. Rev. Francis Makemie was an ordained Presbyterian minister from Ireland, who had come to Maryland at the invitation of a congregation that needed a spiritual leader. The announcement of Rev. Makemie's arrival in New York was brought to the attention of Lord Cornbury, the Governor, who promptly issued an edict forbidding Makemie from preaching. The

1. Even after Independence the New York Constitution contained a provision prohibiting a Catholic from holding office. This provision was not changed until 1806.

84

preacher, unwilling to get the church involved, arranged to have services in the home of a layman. At the same time that Makemie conducted his New York service, John Hampton, his assistant, preached in Newtown, Long Island. Four days later, Lord Cornbury had both Makemie and Hampton arrested and charged with having preached "their pernicious doctrine to the disturbance of the church by the law established and of the government of this Province." Both ministers served six weeks in jail awaiting trial since Makemie refused to promise not to preach were he released on bond. Hampton's case was dismissed, but Makemie stood trial, serving as his own counsel. Even though the jury was specially picked to do Lord Cornbury's bidding, Reverend Makemie was acquitted.[2]

As late as 1767, the New York Colony's Presbyterians requested that they be allowed to incorporate. They appealed to the King, who on the advice of the Lord's Committee of the Council for Plantation dismissed their request. It wasn't until the close of the Revolution that dissenting Protestants were permitted to meet, if not to incorporate.

With the Declaration of Independence and the spirit of defiance it fomented, the signs of relaxation took on new form. During the War of Independence, through seven long years ending with Evacuation Day in 1783, the writings of Paine, the logic of James Otis, and the forthright positions expressed by Sam Adams had now become familiar to the colonists. It was made abundantly clear to the majority, especially in the towns, that anything less than neutrality towards religion by the new government was not going to be acceptable.

Immediately after the war, Trinity Church in New York, a virile, independent, and influential religious institution, used its considerable wealth and prestige to help the various sects that had come together before the Revolution but did not have full sanction to engage in religious activities until freedom had been won. The church sold at a cheap price or simply gifted parcels of ground to many groups who wished to establish their own churches. Presbyterians, Catholics and Lutherans were given suitable sites on which to construct houses of worship. The Catholics erected their first church, St. Peter's, on Barclay Street. Since New York was the nation's capital, a Roman Catholic church was needed to accommodate the diplomatic corps arriving in New York from France and other Catholic countries. An appeal was made to France to supply a priest, and a Father Whelan, who was a chaplain in the French Navy, was assigned to St. Peter's.

But the war of exclusion was not over, and the battles against discrimination had yet to be fought out in many an arena. For one hundred

---

2. Lord Cornbury, nevertheless, required that the acquitted defendant pay the costs.

years after the surrender of the British at Yorktown, where so many Irish soldiers fought, the signs "Man wanted—no Irish need apply" were prominently displayed in New York store windows and at factory gates.

The Alien and Sedition Acts (1798), enacted while the populace was still chanting freedom songs, were the earliest national manifestation that there was a long fight ahead if our nation was to implement the inspiring language of the Bill of Rights. It was clear that, to begin with, the immigrant class would have to battle its way through ignorance and bigotry if its grandchildren were ever to enjoy their national inheritance.

Famous names in American history were participants in the election of 1807, in which the Irish population of New York was castigated, maligned and abused. The French also came in for a great measure of abuse, but the strongest language was reserved for the large influx of Irish emigrants that had so recently fled from Irish battlefields. The Federalist Party, which had sought to ride to power on anti-Irish slogans, was put to rout in New York, and during the days that followed, the Irish population engaged in post-election demonstrations. On the one side, carrying the banner of the Republican Party, were former Governor George Clinton and his nephew Mayor Dewitt Clinton, aided by Thomas Addis Emmett, a prominent Irish refugee. On the other side were leaders like former American Minister to Great Britain, Rufus King. The Federalist newspapers bitterly attacked the Republican Party for championing "the tribe fresh from the bogs of Ireland." In 1807 the Irish won the first skirmish. It was the first battle in a war that lasted a century.

The next significant migration from Ireland took place when New York entered into its canal-building adventures. Having completed the construction, many of the workers settled in the towns near its locks (and there, incidentally, created small outposts of the Democratic Republican Party). Their performance in the construction of these waterways was without equal and was responsible for the phenomenal growth of New York. It was difficult and dangerous work, devoid of any measure of protection for the workers or their loved ones. When they met with crippling accidents (as they frequently did), their dependents survived on the charity of friends or in the orphanage.

Each wave of Irish immigrants faced the most virulent hostility from the Anglo-American population. The worst came when the floodgates opened in 1847–1850, letting in over two million people. Their suffering in the home of the brave was a disgrace to the nation. Yet, with all the hardships, the voice of those who treasured the beginning of our tradition was heard above the mob, and it gave hope to the Irish in the middle of their misery that they would survive.

If on the day William O'Dwyer was born he had been an immigrant in New York, he would have encountered great difficulty getting any kind of employment. In the last half of the 19th century the media, by and large, showed clear hostility towards the Irish, with the cartoons of Thomas Nast in *Harper's Weekly* and *The New York Times* matching the equally vicious cartoons in London's *Punch*. Each depicted the Irish as primitive, with features not unlike an ape.[3] As the Irish increased in numbers here and gained political prominence, the cartoons changed from snide to near panic, frequently depicting Irish-Americans as a mob of aborigines led by some local political leader.[4]

The Irish War of Independence (1916–1923) ended in a divided country and a bloody civil war, and thousands left Ireland for New York in the 20's in utter disillusionment. By then, the war against the Irish was over in the United States. In the last part of the 19th and the early 20th century the stereotyped stage Irishman had been driven from the New York theatre. Thomas Nast was dead and gone. No longer did religious sects have to fight for the right to conduct their own schools, and the "No Irish Need Apply" signs had disappeared. And when Paul Blanchard, later La Guardia's Commissioner of Accounts, wrote books of dire warnings about "Catholic Power" and "Irish Power" in New York, nobody listened to his diatribe.

In other areas, bigotry was still alive. Alfred E. Smith was defeated when he carried the Democratic banner in the Presidential election in 1928, and in 1960 John F. Kennedy had to assure a large assembly of Protestant ministers in Texas that he was not a direct agent of the Pope. But the rank and file of Irish-Americans, now several generations of them, were free to work (except on the very highest level) and to educate their children in a Catholic or a public school as they saw fit.

It was a long struggle. By 1920, when William O'Dwyer began to study law at Fordham University, the Jewish and Irish populations were in charge of Democratic politics in New York. When he resigned from the Police Department to practice law, John F. Hylan was Mayor, and William was free to pursue a career on the bench, which would one day permit him the privilege of becoming a confidante of two Presidents of the United States.

Whatever may have been the case in other areas of the country, New York had eliminated its prejudice against the Irish. Nearly limitless

3. Cartoons in the British newspapers from 1965 to today follow the same theme—Irishmen with faces resembling the earliest humans to appear on earth.
4. In 1981 Nicholas Murphy of Rockland County, a suburb of New York, bought a share of stock in a greeting card company that had created several particularly offensive St. Patrick's Day cards. He waged war on the company through three succeeding annual stockholders meetings. Finally, the company decided to reverse its policy, and the caricatures were withdrawn from publication.

opportunities awaited those who passed through the golden door.[5] However, yesterday's travail has little to do with today's attitudes. So it was with Irish-Americans. Hardly had they gained the rights of equality with their WASP neighbors, when they joined the white majority in keeping the heel on the black minority, whose suffering was so much like their own. It has taken a new Irish-American generation and a sad and spectacular hunger strike to bring them to the realizations that the war was not really over and that there is so little difference between ghettos, whether they be in Birmingham or Belfast.

---

5. Yet, it should also be noted that 150 years after the Revolution the product of Irish high schools and colleges were not yet admitted into the board rooms of the New York banks or insurance companies, and at the Bicentennial in 1976, their number in the higher echelons of the large financial and industrial institutions was far from proportionate to their education, training and competence.

CHAPTER 18

ARRIVAL IN NEW YORK

On June 29, 1910, the S.S. *Philadelphia* steamed towards New York Harbor. It slowed down and its anchor was dropped. A Jacob's ladder was thrown over the side, the bottom of the ladder reaching to the water. A boat came alongside the ladder and a man climbed on board. Someone asked, "What's happening?" "It's the Sandy Hook pilot," he was told. "He must steer the ship from this point." Sure enough, the man went onto the bridge. Then a whistle blew. The boatman shouted some orders, and the anchor moved inch by inch out of the water up the side of the vessel to its resting place by the bow. I didn't know what a Sandy Hook pilot was, but one thing was clear. The captain was no longer the austere man he had been as we crossed the Atlantic. He was now standing to one side as the pilot guided the vessel into the Narrows which separates Brooklyn from Staten Island—two communities called after towns in Holland whence came the earliest European settlers.

The grounds sloping to the water on Staten Island's side were well kept and green. I had read about the American Revolution and tried to identify the scenes with the battles of that time and later. Coney Island was behind us and nearby there must be the place where General Howe landed his troops. Or was that Admiral Howe? On the right, that must be Governor's Island, with its round fortress built in 1809 to defend the city from attack by the British, and a companion fortress of similar design across the way by Battery Park. And up ahead, that must be the Brooklyn Bridge, still new and one of the world's wonders. No one could fail to recognize it, or the high buildings of Manhattan. Over there on the left must be New Jersey where Alexander Hamilton was killed by Aaron Burr in a duel.

I was only guessing about the landmarks. The ship had slowed down now and seemed to be moving cautiously up the mouth of the river. I turned to a deckhand who had come aboard at Sandy Hook. He was adjusting a cable. "Sir," said I, "where is Weehawken?" "It's right in front of you across the river," he answered. "Is that where Hamilton was killed in the duel?" "For Christ's sake," said the man. "You ask questions like a cop and you haven't even landed yet." "Excuse me, sir," I said, "I meant no harm." "Twenty-two," he said. Whereupon, I remarked. "I don't understand you, sir." "Skidoo," he said. I left him hurriedly because of his attitude. I didn't know then that "twenty-two skidoo" was current slang for "Get the hell out of here and let me work!"

The vessel moved past the Statue of Liberty. At Ellis Island, a stone's throw further on, its human cargo, "the wretched refuse," was herded into a room where some were claimed by friends or relatives. The rest were tagged and delivered to those who imported them. The ship then proceeded to a North River Pier where, with much more care, the rest of the cargo was unloaded.

Among the passengers debarking at Ellis Island was a "tempest-tossed" student, who had felt his vocation slip from under him in Salamanca. I took my place in line. I was spared the embarrassment, anxiety and fright of some of my fellow passengers when Tom Rouse, a distant cousin, claimed me. Tom had no special desire to rescue young emigrants, but he had long been in love with this migrant's aunt, Annie Pat-Peggy. The object of his affection had been married three times. Tom had pursued her without success on each occasion when she was eligible. True to her promise, as I knew she would be, she wrote from her home in Chicago announcing that her nephew was coming with no one to claim him. To make matters worse she said I was a "spoiled priest." Faithfully, her rejected lover stood in wait at Ellis Island for Mayo and Salamanca's gift to the land of hope. It was an awkward meeting. Outside of the lingering hope, there was nothing to bind this mature middle-aged man and the immigrant. Even the normal feeling of concern and support for the new arrival was missing.

This was not the classic case of the penniless stranger coming to seek a better world. Penniless I was, but I knew the classics and came ashore with knowledge of Latin and Greek and fluency in Spanish. This was hardly the stuff to move a saloonkeeper to lend assistance. A call from Chicago changed all that, and the student diverted from a godly calling was taken in tow by his disgruntled compatriot.

Things happened quickly and in an orderly manner. I was questioned and shown through a door. I had no baggage problem. I had no baggage. A ferry ride from Ellis Island to the Battery to a saloon under the Third Avenue "El" near the ferry house. Tom and I sat on high stools at the bar and had lunch. "You are now about to experience your first subway ride," Tom told me. We didn't talk in the subway and I didn't want to. It was all so new.

The long train slid into the station smooth as silk. Ever so many doors opened at the same time and thousands of people, it seemed to me, of all ages and types, came out to the platform, using a three-step rhythm as they went on their way. Thousands entered in three steps, the doors closed and the train moved on. Neither an engine nor an engineer was visible. The whole performance was like a ballet led by some supernatural baton.

No one seemed astonished at this wonderful arrangement. It was just taken for granted. Imagine the reaction to a thing like this in Bohola. Let us say that this train came down the hill from the school at midnight and stopped in front of Jimmy Brennan's turf shack, discharging and loading in a few seconds thousands of people and then slithering on down the bog road. Doors would be bolted in mad haste, into their beds they would jump with one movement, heads under the bedclothes, praying to some favorite saint for help and forgiveness. That is something I myself would not have wanted to see for all the money in the world. By the way, whatever happened to the quiet subway? The day came when this service would be noisier than thunder, and Michael Quill was not the only one contributing to the rumpus.

This was the fastest ride I had ever had up to that day. The subway came up into the air at 149th Street and Third Avenue, and we got off at the Prospect Avenue Station and walked a block to the corner of 161st Street to Tom Rouse's saloon. It was late afternoon and the hurdy-gurdies were playing, and the little girls were doing impromptu sidewalk dances with a grace I had never seen. There were telephones and taxicabs and Pabst signs across the street. There was coming and going and men shook hands and didn't say "God bless the work" or "How's your health," but "How's business?" That, too, was a strange greeting. This was the first notice I had of the depression of 1907. It was still here in 1910.

"There are several Irishmen who have been successful in the grocery business," said Tom Rouse. "I talked to a manager of one of them. If you mind your business and work hard, there is no reason why you should not succeed." It was the beginning of what proved to be a short career, but it was not to end my contact with Tom Rouse. I came to work for him later.

I had a furnished room in a boarding house in the South Bronx, and I had a job, thanks to Aunt Annie and Tom Rouse. New York was strange and big and speedy and a bit bewildering. "It will be all right," I assured myself. "Thank God. I am now at home."

CHAPTER 19

MAKING A LIVING

I had two jobs up to February 1911. Both paid me $9.00 a week. At first I was a delivery boy in one of James Butler's grocery stores at 143rd Street and Third Avenue. The hours were long and the pay was small, but then I was new and Tom Rouse predicted for me a nice future in the grocery business, and yet, from the beginning I began to learn that nothing in life is perfect. The job had two main drawbacks. Mr. Madden, the grocery clerk, had a twitch in his yellow mustache, and when he had nothing else to get angry about, he had me. In his temper he was always careful of his language to the customers, but when we were alone he dropped his restraint.

My second complaint was the condition of my push-cart. The wheels were loose, and on the cobblestones of Third Avenue the vehicle once in a while got out of control. On occasions of this kind I had something on my mind to say that was far from flattering about James Butler, but I did not have to say the word. Every time I pulled the rope of a dumb waiter, the housewife would say, "Stay there boy," and now and then after she had checked her purchases, she would say the word for me.

One day in September a big newspaper ad announced a sale of strictly fresh eggs in all the Butler stores at 25 cents a dozen. That morning there was quite a rush on eggs. I was on my knees packing Kirkman's soap on a bottom shelf, when a woman came in and got into an argument with Mr. Madden regarding the age of the eggs. She was very angry and said many harsh things in a loud voice about Mr. Butler and Mr. Madden too. But Mr. Madden stood his ground and didn't return the 25 cents, and she said, "Keep the quarter and keep the eggs too," and broke them on the counter. And to me the woman was right, they were not "strictly fresh."

I am afraid I had the bad taste to laugh, because Mr. Madden, in the presence of the woman, called me a name that no man likes to hear about himself. Mother would have been offended by it, too. If I had counted ten, as I was often advised I should in such cases, I might still be deeply concerned with the grocery business. It happened, however, that I did not count at all, not even the cakes of soap that I threw at Mr. Madden. I took off my apron, and the customer and myself walked out of Butler's forever. In September, I went to work for P.J. Heaney Company Building Materials at West Farms in the Bronx. Miss Schoultz, the bookkeeper, and myself did not get along well together. The relationship deteriorated in the following months to a point where one of us had to leave, and she, being the more important one, remained.

During my stay in Salamanca, Father Jordon and Father Blaine had paid us a visit on their way home to Ireland from Argentina. Having thus become interested in Argentina, I signed up on the S.S. *Dochra* as an ordinary seaman for $15.00 a month. We loaded coal at Norfolk, and after touching a few ports in Brazil, we dropped anchor in the harbor of Montevideo. As we sailed up the Río de la Plata for Ensenada, the coal was all in the bunkers, none on deck. After a week at Ensenada we moved to the new Pier No. 3 in front of the Paseo Colon in Buenos Aires.

I found Buenos Aires a lively, well-planned city of about a million and a half people. William Bulfin, the editor of the *Southern Cross*, whom I knew of, had died. The brilliant author of *Tales of the Pampas* had taken his children to Ireland to school and there died of pneumonia. Gerald Foley was the new editor. I went up the creaky wooden steps of 172 Chacabuco and he greeted me warmly. From Mr. Foley I learned a good deal of the history of the Irish in the Argentine from the days of Archdeacon Dillon. He had done a good deal of research on Thurmond O'Brien, who served during the revolution as the right arm of José de San Martín. In fact, when San Martín was a guest of Simón Bolívar in Lima after the final battle at Ayachucho, Bolívar presented San Martín with an umbrella once used by Pizzaro in parades. San Martín accepted and then begged leave to present it to Thurmond O'Brien, the greatest tactician in the Republic of Argentina, who was standing beside him. Bolívar, too, had as his personal aide one Colonel O'Leary born in Cork or Kerry, and his personal physician was a Dr. Daly from Dublin. Foley explained to me something in which I took great pride: the flagship of the Argentine Navy is called the *Almirante Brown*. The Admiral was born in Foxford, County Mayo, seven miles from Bohola. Foley had also done considerable research on the three O'Higgins, grandfather, son and grandson, from Chile, who originated in County Wicklow. He took a great delight in telling me the story of William R. Grace, who came from Ireland to work on Dr. Gallagher's farm, near Lima, Peru, and ended his career as Mayor of New York City.

On the way back to the U.S., the coal passer, a sly fellow, pretended to be sick and the boatswain, a lanky one from Newfoundland, assigned me to the engine room for the whole trip. In the tropics shoveling coal between decks is hot work. No one could find fault with the coal passer for getting out of this chore. There was some sort of a lesson in that too, and I was learning it. If you ever lend $10.00 to a boatswain, don't try to get it back until you land; if you do, you might end up a coal passer, barring, of course, that you are the captain of the ship.

We returned to Boston in May and a week later we were back in New York. When I came down the gangplank my mind was already made up that New York was what I wanted. I had seen enough already to show me that.

I had drawn some of my pay in Buenos Aires, so that when I left the ship in Brooklyn, I had only money enough to buy a suit of clothes, shirts and underwear, a pair of shoes, and enough to live on for about a week. I looked for a job on land in a few places, without any result. When my money ran out, I went back to the river boats and put my know-how to work, firing first the *Frank Jones* and after that the *Caaterskil*, from Christopher Street to a dock under the railroad bridge in Albany. They were night boats. There was no trouble in getting these jobs; the pay was $40.00 a month with meals, and the men were not steady. The majority worked for a day or two, drew what was coming to them, and went on a drunk.

There is no river that I have ever seen that compares in beauty with the Hudson River: the sheer cliffs on the New Jersey shore; Sleepy Hollow and thoughts of the fine tales of Washington Irving; Storm King Mountain and West Point; the grim prison at Ossining; the little camp at Red Hook where Bob Fitzsimmons trained for his fights; Hyde Park, then the home of a young politician named Franklin Delano Roosevelt and destined to become a shrine of indestructible memories; Kinder-hook, the birthplace of Martin Van Buren, the first President of the United States to be born in the United States; across the river, towns like Athens and Catskill; and in the early morning sunlight above the hills, the flashes from the dome of the State Capitol; and then Albany, New York, itself. When I saw it first, it was on the 4th day of July, 1911, three days before I became 21.

In the middle of July, I got deathly sick from drinking too much ice water in the fire room. My temporary co-workers pointed out to me that I was dehydrated, and, depending on their wisdom, I walked two blocks from the pier to Dolan's Saloon, where I drank my first glass of beer and ate a bowl full of small onions. I found out later that the "boys" would have advised the same medicine for a broken ankle. I had kept my promise to my mother not to drink intoxicating liquor of any kind until after my 21st birthday. As for obtaining any benefit in Dolan's, I should have promised her not to touch it until my 41st birthday. In the

94

end, I saw a doctor in New York who examined me carefully and said that my teeth were bad. Perhaps it was youth and natural resistance, but I began to feel better as I left the doctor's office, and the improvement was noted with every shovelful of coal that I threw into the firebox.

When October came, the river began to freeze, and the ride on the night boat became less romantic. Following a half-century-old custom, the boat was tied up, and then followed the business of looking for another job. I had helped the captain on one occasion when the boys found it comfortable to sleep under the table in Dolan's backroom and I was alone. I had managed on that occasion to clean my fires in the downstream current to Poughkeepsie, giving me enough steam to take her into New York against the incoming tide. "My boy," said Captain Clarke, "I am going to make a marine engineer out of you. I am going to spend the winter on the Chesapeake Bay and I'm taking you along." The thought flashed across my mind that opportunities are everywhere, even in a job like this. Had I at last found myself? Unfortunately, the next day in Hanover Square the captain dropped dead of heart failure, and that meant beginning all over again.

Next, I conducted a trolley car from Newark to Hackensack and sometimes to the river for about three weeks. I was sent to a factory with a special car; the workers coming home jammed the car full. I got all the fares I could, but a "spotter" in the car counted the heads. He said I was short ten fares and I was fired. I went looking for the "spotter" and found him, a little man well over 60 with big eyeglasses. I walked past him and went back to New York.

Within a few days, I met a distant relative of my mother, Tom Durkan from Chicago, the general superintendent of construction of a new building at 80 Maiden Lane. Soon I was a member of the Hodcarriers Union Local 3, and the edge of the triangular hod chaffed the skin of my shoulder as I climbed the ladder to where the bricklayer was waiting for his load. The local union I joined was Irish and was in competition with an Italian local. Both groups were pitted against each other and both were much exploited. The competition was fierce everywhere. I was fascinated by the men who walked surefootedly along the narrow steel beams many stories above the ground. "They are Mohawks," a compatriot informed me. "What's a Mohawk?" I asked. "A red Indian. He has no fear of heights." I was told they came down from Canada and swarmed about Dean Street in Brooklyn during the construction season and went back home to the reservation when deep winter brought building to a standstill in New York.

The pay was $19.25 a week, but with overtime it was more, and one week I earned over $33.00. While this work was not my life's ambition, I had found what Archimedes was looking for: "A place to stand on to move the world."

Saturday night and Sunday afternoons that summer were something to remember. The barber under the house where I lived knew his business. He gave me a hair trim, shave, shampoo and iodine treatment over a hot towel to get the plaster out of my pores. Then I donned a navy-blue suit, black shoes, white shirt and a gray tie, a new straw hat for 85 cents, and I was off to Healey's West 66th Street. At a corner table Dumphy the waiter, who owned two apartment houses, trained me in reading the menu and using the silver. The little oyster fork looked like a cunningly contrived hand tool. On the fourth Saturday night when business eased up, Dumphy said, "Now you can take care of yourself. You don't have to come back until you can afford it. The wines can wait for later. Don't you be a show-off ever. I can tell a show-off by the way he talks to the hat check girl or the cigarette girl or the waiter. Some of them could play the menu on the piano without having the taste to order nice. I make as much money as most of them by the end of the year. I have six at home, thank God, all doing well, even the two in school. I would not want any of them in the company of a show-off. I like nice people, rich or poor, who take one cocktail and order properly, a drink with the meal and up they get and go away. That kind always says thank you, waiter. That makes me feel good. When you have a steady job, get married to a nice girl and stay home with her and the friends. Places like this give a lad bad habits." "Thanks for everything, Ed," I said leaving. "God bless you, Bill," he said. That was the last time I saw Ed Dumphy. I felt I had been talking to a real man.

Sunday afternoon was Celtic Park out in Sunnyside, Queens: the 34th Street ferry, the trolley ride to the neighborhood, and a six-block walk to the park itself. It was owned and operated by the Irish American Athletic Club. There were bars, a dancing pavillion, a well-kept field and a grandstand. I saw Martin J. Sheridan, Pat McDonald, Matt McGrath, Johnny Joyce beat their own records there. I saw Abel Kiviat in the mile, and Melvin Shepard broke Lunghi's half-mile record there. The hurdle champions, Ralph Rose and Gordon Duke, were there. George Horine broke Mike Sweeney's 20-year record for the high jump there. A big league of the Irish Gaelic football teams played their series there every Sunday. At the end of the day it was home to bed and Monday morning.

One Sunday I met Andy Sheridan. The four brothers, Dick, Joe, Martin and Andy, were great and all-around athletes. Andy had hurt his knee, which threw him out of competition. He was the wine steward at the Ritz-Carlton, 46th and Madison. Within a month, I was working for him in the service bar. Dumphy was right; the wines came later. Now bins full of all kinds of imported wines became familiar with practice. Andy was studious, intelligent, conservative. The Sheridans were and still are the pride of Bohola. They were all popular, but Andy was my favorite. He became a lawyer with an expert knowledge of appellate work and was in this field, in every field he entered, a successful man. In a few months Andy and I were in the Vanderbilt, 34th and 4th Avenue, and after a year-and-a-half, we spent the summer in the old Grand Union in Saratoga.

It was in the Vanderbilt I met Kitty Lenihan, a telephone operator. She was an accomplished musician, especially at the piano. Whenever I could, I would sit and listen to her. Her timing, feeling and finger control could only come from one who loved music and the instrument. Her mother had a great sense of humor. She loved to tell of the evening when she and Mrs. Carey were coming home riding in a crowded horse-drawn trolley car. A man in overalls and along in years, with an unwashed face and a sad look and reeking of perfume, was standing in front of them holding on to the strap. The two women looked at one another, not knowing what to make of it and after a while began to giggle and then broke out in laughter. The man said, "Ladies, I know what you are thinking, but you are wrong. I work in a perfume factory."

From Saratoga, I worked for a short time for Tom Rouse, donning my white bartenders' apron after a short apprenticeship. I learned to conquer the urge to respond sharply to those who spoke disparagingly of Ireland, the Irish, and greenhorns. However, I was not warned sufficiently about who was to be granted and who denied the toilet privileges. The key was kept behind the bar, and I was the enforcement officer. The system was easy enough to control when one was not busy. But one warm night, when the show next door let out, the bar was crowded three deep with thirsty people. Beer had to be served promptly, change made with dispatch, and people made happy on their way home to their beds. Just then, there was a man asking for the key at the same moment that the entire orchestra from the theatre, all eleven of them, ordered milk punches. With some concern for the consequences of my refusing the first man's request, I gave the key and returned to making the punches. Suddenly, the wrath of Rouse descended on my head: the man I had given the key to was not a customer. I told Tom to what use he could put the key, and I paid the price for my vulgarity. I finished the routine of the evening, and at a suitable opportunity took off my apron and gave it to Tom.

A week later I was hired to work in the wine cellar from six in the morning to three in the afternoon, seven days a week, at the Hotel Plaza, 59th and Fifth Avenue. The hours were perfect for night school, which I was to attend for the next three years. I concentrated on my law school certificate, Spanish, English, civics and American history, and I took a course in shorthand and typewriting.

It was the history of New York which fascinated me. The river Hudson, I was told, got its name from an English sea captain who came across it by accident in 1609, and New York got its name from the Duke of York, who received it as a present from his brother, King Charles II. "Did the Duke actually come here to rule the province?" I inquired. "No," I was told. "All he gave was his name. He later became King James II." "I've come 3,500 miles," I mused, "to meet Seamus a Chacah once more." "What did you say?" the teacher asked. "Oh, nothing," I said. It would take too much effort to explain that James was despised by the Irish. Three centuries earlier James had run from the River Boyne to Dublin and got to the town to announce his defeat ahead of the rest of his army. "James of the fecal matter" is a literal Norman-English translation of "Seamus a Chacah."

During the succeeding three years in night school, nothing was taught of the native American Indians, some of whom I had observed putting the steel beams together on the land their people once owned. During American history class, we were taught that New York City dated back to 1664, when the British captured it. It was a bit of propaganda which those of Dutch extraction deeply resented, for they had set up shop here, I was later to discover, in 1625, the year in which their first colonist arrived from Holland.

I was also later to learn that the great river had a name long before Henry Hudson came across it by accident. New Amsterdam came to be the new Dutch name for the Manhates. Most historians of that time, before, and since, made little reference to the people who occupied this island and had held it as a sacred trust for more than 10,000 years.

The story of those who had come into the beautiful land from Europe, as it was told to the class, could not but leave the impression that somehow God had ordained that the strangers had entered another Promised Land, where some miserable Philistines lurked behind trees in defiance of the Creator's favoritism.

CHAPTER 20

POLICEMAN (1917-1924)

Nineteen seventeen was a momentous year for me. Within that year, I completed my credits, received my law school certificate,[1] got married to Kitty, and became a citizen of the United States. I took the New York Police Department examinations, and on July 17, 1917, I entered the school of recruits for two months of physical and academic training with a shield in my pocket—#6406.

A class of about 60 recruits met in the gymnasium at 240 Centre Street. There was a semi-military atmosphere about the room. We fell in according to height, two by two. Bill Whalen and Mike Richter were among the tallest, Bitanno Christiano and James J. O'Neil were somewhere in the center of the lineup, and John Gorman and myself were the shortest. We were at the end. We were told by a tall, blonde young Swede named Arthur Wallander what was expected of us, what clothes to buy, and where to get our uniforms and equipment. We were dismissed for the day to report the following morning.

That night I put my law school certificate away in a safe place. Police work was divided into three tours: day, evening and midnight. Until I could get an assignment of one straight tour, I could not use the certificate while a policeman.

The next day we swung into routine action, an hour of drilling and an hour of school work. The class consisted, for the most part, of studying the rules of the department and the city ordinances. We had two professors: one was Sergeant Con O'Leary and the other, Sergeant Billy File. After two months, four of us were assigned to 43rd Street and Fourth Avenue, Brooklyn—Cristiano, O'Neil, Whalen and myself. (It was a strange set of circumstances that years later would bring Gorman, Wallander, Richter, Whalen, O'Leary and myself together again.) Following instructions, we left the subway for the street at Fourth Avenue

---

1. Receipt of the law school certificate meant that Bill had completed the secondary school courses required for entrance into law school. (PO'D)

and 36th Street. Not one of the four had ever been in that part of Brooklyn before. A block away was the iron fence of Greenwood Cemetery. Three blocks in the other direction, down the hill, was New York Bay.

With our bright new uniforms, shining shields and unmarked nightsticks, we held a conference on the corner to settle a burning question. In what direction was the station house? The insignificant things that trouble a young policeman, such as worrying about a station house, when we were standing on one of the most historic spots of the Revolutionary War. Down on Atlantic Avenue at the Smith Street corner, George Washington stood watching the Marylanders come down the hill from Prospect Park to the old stone house on Fifth Avenue. He saw them make a stand and also saw them slaughtered. We did not know that morning that a few blocks away, buried under a junkyard, were the sacred bones of the men who died for freedom in that battle. Nor did we know that Terry McGovern did his daily run outside the cemetery wall when he trained for the fight with Peddler Palmer.

With the help of a bemused neighborhood bartender, we found our way to the station house, and reported to Captain James Brannan, a swell-headed little tyrant, who knew in his heart that where he rightly belonged was in the chair of the mayor of the city. But everyone else who knew him, knew in their hearts that he should never have been a police captain. He was a strict disciplinarian who never gave a policeman a break. My colleague-to-be, George Joyce, who knew him well, once remarked that if Brannan owned the lake in Prospect Park, he would not give a duck a swim. We were divided into squads, and each man fell into line as of noon that day.

The New York Police Department traditionally thinks of itself as the finest in the world and no man who wears the blue but thinks of himself as "one of the finest." In the decades that have elapsed since I first put on the shield, the New York Police Department organization has been radically transformed by startling technical developments and new trends in technique, methods and application of ideas, as well as by great social changes, and it is today truly an impressive and unique organization.

But in 1917 it was, like the rest of life around it, in what now seems the semi-handicraft stage. There were no radio or motor patrols, no multiplicity of devices to flash the signal of trouble, no mechanized action to follow. There were no ingenious checks, indexes and controls in routine such as we now have and no precise supervision.

Men on bicycles or on mounts still patrolled remote districts. There were sprawling, thinly-populated posts, in Brooklyn especially, where the cop was monarch of all he surveyed, and what he surveyed in my post were two farms, a cemetery, some squatters' shacks and the hopeful

Patrolman O'Dwyer on his beat in Brooklyn flanked by soldiers from the nearby Army post, 1917

beginnings of a real estate development.

I joined in time to see the old-type cop going out and the new-type coming in. I am very glad that I was in time to know the old-timer in the days when a college-bred man on post was undreamed of. The old-timer had a juicy character and colorful individuality that is absent now. Some sense of being autonomous bred a great variety of temperament in him. He was no intellectual giant. He passed his examination for the force on a minimum live-weight of 200 pounds in first-class working order and the equivalent of a grammar-school education. He was thereafter haunted by no more intellectual aspirations than were native to him, because promotion had not been by competitive civil service but by appointment. It was therefore far more important for him to know the district leader and the idiosyncrasies of the lieutenant than to know what was the hypotenuse of the triangle. He was prevailingly Irish, first or second generation, and looked upon those strangers of other nationalities who wandered into the department as merely signs of a decline in the age.

He came into the department very often direct from a job of driving horses—behind the plough, the forward end of a streetcar or a truck—and he had the authority and sense of how animals behave that was very useful in dealing with the human animal. He lived in fear of nothing but the book of rules and the plain-clothes sergeant, and the latter he feared more than the former.

One of the most colorful and experienced of the many old-timers I came to know was Matt Kinnaine, who stood six feet two in his stocking feet. He had the strength of a twenty-mule team in his right arm, but was never known to be brutal except to criminals like the "Kid Cheese" gang, who were on his post. As a matter of fact, Matt Kinnaine was a sweet, kindly man, but he hated Mayor Gaynor, who prohibited policemen from using their night sticks. One night a young couple on Kinnaine's post came home to find every indication of a burglary. Matt went up to the apartment and found the burglar under the bed. He pulled him out and hit him with the night stick to subdue him. Mayor Gaynor suspended Matt and fined him five days' pay.

One of the Kid Cheese gang once stomped his foot at Matt, calling him an Irish flatfoot, and then ran into a hallway. Matt's intuition told him to take out his tiny pocket billy. Experience had taught him that a long stick was useless in a fight in a narrow hallway. Fifteen minutes after Matt went into the hallway, out came eight hoodlums, all spread on the sidewalk with Matt looking on calmly waiting for the patrol wagon to take them in.

Big Nell Flaherty, the stepmother of prize fighter Terrible Terry Montgomery, was known to be rough in her liquor and to resist arrest with a dedication, and members of the law were more than once tossed out by her. In her younger days she was a handsome woman of almost six feet. In her neighborhood, she exercised an influence for good among the children and made more peace within the families than all the judges in Brooklyn.

One night Matt was directed to go down to 28th Street, where Nell was "cutting up." When he got there, she was sitting on the stoop in an ugly state of mind. Several policemen stood around, all somewhat tattered. Matt looked upon Nell with the sympathy of a man who knew that a great champion was on her way out. "Nell," said Matt, "ya're cutting up again." Nell said, "Nothing to it, Matt, just having a little fun." "Nell, sitting on that stoop won't do you no good. You ought to have a doctor." "Talk square, Matt," she replied. "You wanna take me in?" "No," said Matt, "I don't want to, but I think it's better for ye." "If you think it is Matt, let's go," and with that she and Matt walked into the station house.

Matt sent out for black coffee and a sandwich. Nell drank the coffee but didn't touch the sandwich. In the morning she went to the Magistrate's Court, where John McGuire was presiding. He once asked a defendant, "Do you want 30 days in this court or go to special sessions and get justice?" In Nell's case, the judge asked Matt, "What do you suggest?" "Your Honor," said Matt, "I think I should take her for an examination to Kings County Hospital." The doctor at the hospital asked for three days for observation. "Is it all right, Matt?" said Nell, and Matt said, "It's the best thing for you, Nell." They gave her some powerful purgatives, and on the second day she was dead in her bed. Her death preyed on Matt Kinnaine's mind until his dying day. He was bitten by a dog, given the wrong medicine and died.

On our first day in the station house each of us four newcomers was given "the book of rules." The book of rules had been bequeathed to the department a decade or more before my time by Commissioner Bingham. He had modeled it on the West Point manual, unfortunately with no sense that the material in hand might have some relationship to the given result.

The book of rules (which even after it was officially retitled the Police Manual still went by its familiar name) described every object and objective of a policeman's life on duty. It prescribed every article of his dress and bearing, it wound him up in a limitless web of observances and infractions, and it ordained for him endless zeal in the quest of knowledge leading to the solving of crimes.

Each succeeding commissioner, not to be outdone in this vision of perfection, added to it voluminously. Whenever a situation arose that no one knew how to handle, often susceptible to no known departmental procedure, a chapter was added, until it began to resemble the Talmud and its commentaries, in which one had to seek hair-splitting interpretations, leading into some pretty fancy dilemmas. Most men, having to choose between keeping their eye on the post or their nose in the book, solved it by learning it reasonably well, doing the best they could, and hoping for the best.

As for myself, I learned very early on that the book of rules didn't cover everything. On one of my first nights on the beat, I came upon a drunk, six feet tall, stretched across the sidewalk on First Avenue. What did the rules say? I was new to the uniform and innocent in police usage. It was 11:45 P.M., my relief was due in about 20 minutes. Call an ambulance? Call the wagon? Try to walk him in? Yes, that, but walking him was difficult. I gave him a heave, got him on my back, his feet dragging, and as I puffed under the load, I met "Father" Denny, my relief. "Good evening," he said, smiling blandly. "Wither bound?" "To the station house," I said. "Is the gentleman in custody?" he asked. "Protective custody," I said. "I felt he might come to some harm." "Young man," said Denny, "what I am looking at would make every policeman blush all the way back to the 'rattle watch! Tomorrow, the drunk won't thank you, the judge will mock you for not having brains, your Sunday will be ruined, and if you get a hernia, who will suffer and who will pay?" "But how about the book of rules?" I asked. "The book of rules to a lieutenant is a jumble of words, except when he is writing out a complaint. Then, and then only, does it become the word." "What do you suggest?" I asked. "Here is a vacant lot with many attractive heaps of clean dirt." I dropped my burden into place, at which the drunk said, "Where am I?" "You are now, sir," said Denny, "in the Waldorf-Astoria, and the maid has just dimmed the lights. In the morning ask for ice water and the bellboy will be happy to oblige." As we walked away, the drunk began to urinate. "You see what you missed," said Denny, "an uncomfortable design on the back of your uniform."

In my time, the old-timers found the book of rules bewildering and irritating but, conditions of supervision being slow and lumbering, not too oppressive. It was still the time when the old-type cop carried a quid of tobacco for consolation on a lonesome beat, when he could slip in on dead winter nights for a chat and a glass of something warming without the slightest idea that he was betraying his trust, or any chance of being betrayed by some strict constructionist.

I have said the he felt himself to be autonomous. He actually felt himself the monarch of his post. This bred in him faults as well as virtues. They were not all lovable old characters. There were men who were despots and tyrants, who were far too handy with the club. I have known men who would lurk in the shadow of a building, and seeing some amiably drunk Swede weaving his way down the street, would lie in wait to take a crack at him.

Take, for example, Jerry Sullivan. My post was on the waterfront, and the area became a sea of every racial stock, so that the man on post might expect trouble inside of every saloon door. On Third Avenue one day, in broad daylight, a large gentleman of Nordic extraction took into his muddled head to have a go with the cop on post. The attack was unexpected and the cop, Pat Murnane, found himself sitting on the sidewalk with his back to the wall and out for a count of a hundred. Jim Shortell came to his aid and ended up sitting beside Murnane. Next, Willie Tjarks answered the call. The neighborhood children had never seen anything like this before: three policemen in full uniform in broad daylight sitting beside one another on the sidewalk and the Nordic strutting around "for more worlds to conquer." Our station house had a chauffeur on the patrol wagon named Jerry Sullivan who welcomed any opportunity to swing his blackjack. Jerry pulled up to the scene, the Swede made for him, and Jerry whacked him with the jack and stepped back a pace to see his knees slowly wilt. Jerry put his arms around him as he was falling and threw him into the wagon. "When I hit them, they drop," said Jerry.

Then there was William Hurley, whose well-merited nickname was "Blackjack." Hurley had been a policeman for 30 years and he had studied "good English" for 25 cents a lesson when he first arrived from Ireland. No doubt he concentrated on big words. He never used a short one if a big word would do. He was a solemn man with no humor. When he became a policeman and had a legal right to carry a weapon, he used the stick at every opportunity.

He told, with his sense of glorious memory, of going upstairs in a house on Second Place to arrest on a warrant a man who had abandoned his wife. The man told him, "There is my wife. She does not want me locked up, and I came back to make this my home." "Sir," said Mr. Hurley, "it is duty, sir. I have a warrant which I must execute." The man said, "Mr. Hurley, please don't put the cuffs on me, I will come quietly." "That sir," said Mr. Hurley, "is a proper request." "When I got to the street," said Hurley, "he gave me the boot and threw me on a snow bank. I followed him on the run and lucky for me he turned into a blind alley, yes sir, a blind alley. I drew my jack, sir, and split his head open. I'll learn you, said I, to respect a policeman."

But I was acquainted with far more old-timers who knew their posts as no young cop knows his today. They knew every family and its problems, they shooed the young ones away from trouble, they soothed the old ones. They knew how to settle neighborhood squabbles so that they never came into court, they held juvenile courts on the curbstone, they held domestic relations court on the stairways, and if you had told them they were interpreting the book of rules too freely, they would have stared at you in simple wonder. Why in heaven's name be dragging everything into Magistrate's Court? This way it saved the people the shame of arrest and himself the trouble of going to court to make the charge—the people made up, the kids went straight, what was wrong with that?

Book of rules or no book of rules, the old-timers, who had been 20 and 30 years on the force when I first came in, remained unreconstructed to the end, disregarding theory for more or less quick-witted action. We young ones, who of course eventually became the old-timers, learned a lot from them both on post and in the station house.

There was a good deal more life in the station house, around the old round stove, than there was in later years. The old nine-squad system demanded that one night in three be spent on reserve there. That was a great time for exchange of gossip and of police lore.

And being a police officer, it always interested and amused me to see the way the precinct and the post put its stamp on a police officer. A "sparrow-cop" for instance is always unmistakable. Left alone in the park a good part of the time with the grass and the squirrels, he develops a contemplative manner. He need not be a nature lover to start with; sooner or later in sheer self-preservation, he learns the beauties of contemplation. A cop in a neighborhood where the children are a constant source of worry develops the manner of a severe schoolmaster. In traffic he develops a majestic irritability or calm. In well-to-do neighborhoods, where the complaints develop from the nerves of householders lacerated by small boys tearing up the shrubbery or unexplained noises in the garret or defects in the city housekeeping, the cop develops the soothing manner of a psychiatrist. In neighborhoods where great property interests are at stake, the cop develops a prowl and a menacing manner. On posts full of potential emergencies, like the Great White Way or Coney Island, the habitual bearing of the cop becomes a hawk-like alertness.

There was always a gulf between the Manhattan cop and one from any other borough. To the Manhattan cop we were all semi-rural characters. Later, the patronizing manner became somewhat softened, but it still existed, and it was always galling to us. Our consolation was the fact that we were nevertheless equals before the book of rules.

Most of the cops of my time, and certainly on the patrolman level, were honest men who worked long hours for low pay, plodding their unsophisticated way and doing their duty as they saw it.

There was a somewhat notorious system, however, that created what we called the "Murphy Lieutenant." A standard sum (it was, I believe, then set at $4,000) passed through the trustworthy channels of the district leader to the enigmatic Charley Murphy, who ruled over the Fourteenth Street clubhouse, and automatically released the spring for the merest rookie, so that he could take his ease as a lieutenant for the rest of his life. Every precinct had its tale of some rookie who had scarcely mastered the book of rules and who, following some legacy left to him or his wife, was mysteriously called to a lieutenancy.

For the average patrolman earning $1,000 a year, with a maximum of $1,200, $4,000 was a fairly unattainable sum. The low salary served, along with the stiffest competitive exams, to eliminate the majority. The rookie had a good big slice of his first year's pay lost to him at the start. When he had finished outfitting himself with the required two uniforms at $50 apiece (worth $20), obtainable by police regulations only from a certain firm that held the valuable concession for equally valuable consideration, two pairs of shoes at $10 a pair (no better than the $3 pair the rookie had always worn), the $10 club, the $20 gun, the rubber boots, the storm capes, and the odds and ends, all specified by regulations which forced him to buy at exorbitant prices, he was lucky if he could eat during the first year. Thereafter, there were replacements, and always a smart upkeep. Later the Patrolmen's Benevolent Association in its militant phase, attacked this problem and forced an honest commissariat to deal honestly with the cop.

A man could not hope to save much on $1000 to $1200 a year and, contrary to the general belief, the sources of graft were meager for the man on the beat. Unless he drew the royal flush of a post in one of the bright light areas or in some dim noisome quarter, he was generally perforce honest. The standard sources of graft were gambling and prostitution. The glaring revelations of the Lexow Report on vice certainly showed that the police force was corrupt at the head, but that the body of the police force was generally sound. Oh, yes, a cop on a beat might accept a drink slipped to him from a side door, he might wink at the flouting of the Raines Law (the liquor licensing law), but he might do this as much through fear or favor as in consideration of cash, and the most he might get out of it was a box of cigars or a present of a merchant's wares.

I did become aware of police corruption on other levels, however. At one time I was assigned to a large building where the workers were on strike. Once a day the pickets were taken into the station house on a charge of disorderly conduct. The detectives were constantly around them to the neglect of the felonies and misdemeanors that under the rules were their concern. I asked the older policeman I was assigned with why the detectives were doing that. "No doubt it is an arrangement between the captain of the precinct and the employers," he answered. "If you will notice, the captain goes up to see the employer and comes down and gives the word for the arrest." "But why should the police do that?" He answered simply, "Money."

When I had been a patrolman on post in the precinct for about a year and a half, I was taken off patrol duty and assigned to the Poplar Street station as chauffeur to Tom Murphy, the borough inspector. Motor supervision was not yet universal in the Police Department. It was at this time confined to inspectors and accomplished undreamed of results in developing more efficient control of the precincts. Driving the inspector around his tour over Brooklyn and Queens, and indeed through the five boroughs, was a wonderful opportunity for me to learn the city. I learned from this the physical character of the city, its length, breadth and density of population, the strata of life it enclosed and the peculiar characteristic of each locality.

In these tours I began to lose my provincial character as a waterfront patrolman. I began to glimpse the city as a whole in all its massive strength and power, the immense scope of its activity, the industry, commerce and trade that sustained it, its glittering highlights and its sombre depths. I learned to distinguish between one kind of slum and another. I learned where it took its pleasures and how. I learned the impact on it of its tides of immigration and the vast web of nationalities of which it was composed.

Still later in my career as a policeman, I spent several years as a plainclothesman, following the half-world of gamblers, racetrack touts, crapshooters, lottery-ticket vendors, policy-slip distributors, and a host of other merchants of illusion. Robbery and murder during that period were rampant. Household burglaries were the same. Men who had been taught to kill during the war flocked into New York from all over the country. There was a great deal of restlessness in the city because of these conditions.

The experience enriched me with a wonderful gallery of portraits of odd characters, and a knowledge of the foibles and fancies of the human animal that I would not have traded for anything. But the most invaluable possession of all given me was a realistic understanding that within the community that lives by explicit laws and observances, there exists another world that lives by an unwritten set of laws and observances, and to them those laws have the same binding force and furnish the same protection. It was the realization of this, not theoretically but practically understood, that was of the greatest possible value to me when I came to deal with the shadowy kingdom of organized crime. Using the same logic one did in the daylight world of the normal citizen, I had only to learn what constituted rational action in that kingdom to break into it.

The half-world of gambling in those days was not really part of the underworld of crime. The criminal tendency may have been there, but the fact remains that comparatively few of the gamblers and sharks whom I followed emerged later into big-time organized racketeering. A few bookmakers did go into bootlegging and rumrunning, the most notable example being Big Bill Dwyer, who turned from bookmaking to rumrunning, but the majority, perhaps lacking initiative, kept within their limits.

Racetrack betting was illegal, but to nail a charge there had to be someone to see the money change hands. Money did not change hands at the racetrack, but through runners and at the pools. I came to see that the whole business of making the big book and the little book, hedging and covering, was pretty much a business or a craft, not unlike the market or the curb, surrounded with a little more voodooism, but with something more tangible to put the money on, and in infinitely pleasanter surroundings. The great American public having declared itself piously on the wickedness of horse racing and betting, then proceeded to stream out in great numbers to enjoy it.

I can remember how it was in the old days when there was still racing at Brighton Beach. There were always two ways of going home. If you won, you came out grandly the front way, and, with the winnings to heighten your sense of the material world, looked grandly around for some party to join at one of the tony places, where there were celebrities and actresses and pretty women to be seen, or you came home in the steam train which cost a dollar. If you lost, you went out through the entrance leading on to the beach and from there made your way around to the trolleys.

The waterfront, which for a long time was my beat, was a rough place, but organized racketeering as we know it had not yet developed. There were a few gangs that carried through some organized crimes, but it was not racketeering; that developed with prohibition. The gangs operating around the waterfront in those days were only embryonic compared to the latter-day variety, though I saw some of those characters develop into the modern gangster. Their enterprises were violent but sporadic. There was the Kid Cheese gang, Matt Kinnaine's nemesis, which terrorized night watchmen and broke into warehouses and boxcars. And the Kilduffs, led by the Kilduff brothers, operating floating crap games and a variety of other wily enterprises, who had a hand in everything from petty larceny to piracy.

A few years later, prohibition transformed the sporadic gangsterism into organized racketeering, which operated with the precision of machine-driven big business, and also opened up a new source of big money—narcotics. The fields of operation overlapped. But the biggest source of racketeering wealth was not yet tapped—labor racketeering.

That came later. By that time, I was off the waterfront beat.

The Police Department was simply not prepared to cope with the enforcement of a law that was so thoroughly resented and so actively resisted by the public as was prohibition. Strange though it may seem, the law enforcement arm is really sensitive to public cooperation or resistance. With laxity in enforcement regarded as a finer, braver performance than severity, it was no wonder that some men saw no reason why they should not take advantage of their opportunities. And the opportunities were fantastic.

The bootleg dollar, compared to what was called the "woman's dollar," seemed "clean", coming as it did from people who looked and acted like businessmen rather than pimps and fences. Everyone knew its source was in respected big business. It was a safer dollar too. There might be rumblings, but there would be no public clamor. The hooch was murderous? Well, whose fault was that? There might be hijacking and piracy and rumrunning, but where were the Federal men? Taking their cut like everyone else. The moralists who saw the sinister possibilities for the future in this new code had to make their case on a very unpopular principle.

The map of graft suddenly shifted. It was no longer the bright light areas that yielded up the richest booty, but waterfront precincts which were former places of banishment, obscure highways, dismal little outposts where a man had been sent to die of loneliness.

Beginning early in my career as a policeman, I had developed other ambitions. In the summer of 1920, during the period I was assigned to Inspector Murphy, I confided in him that I wanted to become a lawyer. A kindly man, he shrugged his shoulders as much as to say, "How ridiculous!" However, he gave me permission to attend law school, and I entered Fordham that year.

About the time I began law school, we moved to 53rd Street and Third Avenue to the home of Minnie Kerschner and her aunt and her Uncle Karl. They lived on the ground floor, we lived on the second floor, and another family lived on the third.

Kitty was not in good health. She had never been too robust. After two operations and our move to Brooklyn, she was still not responding. She lost weight and was frequently in pain. She required constant treatment by her doctor, and she suffered occasionally from nerves. After a long period of time, it seemed to me that she wasn't getting any better.

May of 1920 also brought bad news from Ireland. My brother Tommy died at 18. He was tall, athletic and daring, and always claimed the privilege in our village of being the first to ride the horse that needed breaking. He was struck down by appendicitis and died six months later. Tommy was my father's favorite and his death was quite a blow. Father followed him the succeeding January. He died of pneumonia after a very brief illness.

Letters came to my brother Jim[2] and myself from my sisters May and Kathleen and my mother. The same parish priest, Father John, now an old man, still was in charge of the affairs of the parish. He ordered the school opened the day after my father's funeral. The neighbors regarded the order as a mark of disrespect and took things into their own hands. They kept their children from school and stood by the crossroads in turns, in case the word had not been heard. It was their way of writing a legend on the tombstone of the master who had labored among them for 40 years. Then they waited for Sunday's sermon for repercussions, but the old man ignored the incident and that was the end of it.

The letters showed considerable emotion. Mother was hurt, but forgiving. The other seven, Kathleen, Mary, Josephine, Linda, Paul, Frank and Jack, were angry and rebellious. However, the action of the neighbors took the sting out of the insult.

As for my law ambitions, I was making headway and continuing at Fordham until February of 1922, when my position with Inspector Murphy was abolished, and I was back again in uniform. The dean of Fordham Law School was the great Father Francis LeBuffe. I explained my troubles to him, and with great sympathy he looked at my record and said, "To whom shall I go, the police commissioner or the mayor? I don't know either one." I suggested the police commissioner, and a few days later he was seeing Commissioner Enright. That night he reported. "Like all great men, the commissioner was non-committal," but shortly after that interview I was assigned as clerk to Commissioner Daly and continued my studies at Fordham until my graduation in 1924.

My lot as a policeman had not been an unhappy one. It had afforded me a variety of views of human behavior, and of the motivations that move and frequently rouse people to do the things they do. I had been given the opportunity to understand the people and their problems. In the neighborhoods that I patrolled I felt that I knew almost everyone and could see the seeds of nervous discontent there. I also could see the need for a program of disease prevention, proper medical care, adequate recreation areas and proper housing, and when I finally left the Police Department, I knew that I was not leaving these problems, and my concerns about them, behind.

I also took away from those years hundreds of indelible memories of some great characters, perhaps none greater than a cop named "Dod-

2. Jim, my second oldest brother, came to America in 1912. (PO'D)

dle" MacManus. Doddle was a rare type of policeman. In our day, from the moment a man put on his uniform, his biggest dream was promotion. The price of promotion was constant study, which began at once with courses at Civil Service School, and rarely did anyone miss a class. Doddle MacManus was not a book student. He had no interest in promotion. His only ambition was to be a "holy terror." He cultivated no relationships in or out of the department, except those that helped him reach his goal.

In preparing his cases, difficult work did not bother him. He studied wiretapping, and on the coldest days you could see him disguised as a telelphone repairman at a box on the pole, waiting for or listening to conversations sometimes a mile or two away. He developed his own methods of getting over a backyard fence or wall. He was abrupt with lawyers who practiced in the criminal courts. No "fixer" would dare offer him a present. He was careless in the matter of dress, sometimes appearing in court unshaven and unkempt, almost belying the detective shield pinned to his lapel. When the Baums Law became effective and four-time losers drew a mandatory life sentence, Doddle went in search of third offenders with a change in heart. He found his share of them, obtained jobs for them, and kept his contacts with them in a "friendly way," and they in turn, in a spirit of appreciation, were expected to be "of use" to their "protector."

There were several cases in which these gentlemen took an active part. In one of them, Doddle sealed the safe of Harry McKane while he got legal authority to open it forcibly based on "information and belief." The information came from one of his "sources." As he walked away, it occurred to him that Harry, if given a chance, might heat the wax, remove the evidence, and seal it again. It was true there was a uniformed policeman stationed there, but Doddle did not consider that an adequate protection. He went back to Harry's place and called up a "protégé" named "Irish John"—one of his third offenders—and asked him to report at once with his tools. Irish John was a perfectionist in his line, which was cracking safes long before the use of explosives. He had the reputation of being the best "hammer and chisel man" in the world. In those days some men filed their finger tips to make them sensitive to the "click," but Irish John knew where to place the chisel on the lock, and with one blow only, the safe came open. He was so adept that the Safe and Lock Squad recognized his style. His perfection was his downfall. He had nowhere to go except into the arms of Doddle MacManus. When Harry saw Irish John show up with his hammer and chisel, he opened the safe himself.

One of Doddle's nemeses was "His Honor," the presiding judge in one of the criminal courts. Like Doddle, a "righteous" man, the judge detested criminals, browbeat both defendant and counsel for the defense and, with the jury as his audience, would act as both judge and prosecutor. He was a strong supporter of the Ten Commandments, and when it suited him he was not above adding one or two of his own. As might be expected, the judge looked upon Doddle as an upstart who had somehow invaded his territory, and no one who came before him drew the vitriol of his tongue as did Doddle. Doddle could not win a case before His Honor.

One night, after the judge's behavior had left Doddle a disheartened and disgusted man, he made his usual rounds of his "official family." One of them was a janitor, a tired old man whom Doddle had given up as a dead loss. This particular night, however, he informed Doddle, "Dere's a young dame in da tent' floor. She don't work and she makes up good. I tink she got two 'Johns.' " "Who are they?" asked Doddle. "I dunno, but one of 'em's a judge." Doddle pricked up his ears. From the description that followed, Doddle concluded it could only be His Honor.

A few nights later the janitor, on instructions, left the latch of the window leading to the fire escape open. Doddle saw His Honor go in through the main entrance. No need for hurrying now—a little time would not hurt. After an elevator ride to the roof and a leisurely descent on the fire escape, Doddle crawled through the window and stepped into the room—there was the girl and His Honor. There were a bottle of whiskey, water and ice, and two highballs on the table. His Honor was relaxing, but with his pants off. The personable female was trying them on! "Good Evening, Your Honor," said Doddle to the startled jurist. "Whiskey, is it, and women, is it, and you bleating about the return to the Ten Commandments! And I am McManus the unbelievable one, the disgrace to the Police Department, the liar! If I were to tell the world exactly what I am looking at they would not believe their ears."

His Honor became fidgety. MacManus said, "Take it easy, Judge. I am leaving now. Your business is yours, and mine is mine. I have no time for loose talk, but tomorrow I expect to be referred to as 'Mr. MacManus,' and I expect my cases before you to be adjourned to another part." His Honor agreed. The next day the courtroom was astonished to find His Honor so friendly to "Mr. MacManus," and his case was adjourned as agreed. That evening, Doddle went around to see the janitor to thank him for his "cooperation" and to slip him a fin. "How are things upstairs?" he asked. "Flat's empty," said the janitor. "Da broad blew."

CHAPTER 21

LAWYER (1925-1932)

I completed my law courses at Fordham University in 1924, the same year my youngest brother, Paul, was finishing his studies at St. Nathy's Secondary School back in County Mayo, from which I was graduated 17 years earlier. Even though I had received my B.L. degree and passed the bar examination, there were still critical decisions to be made. I was 34 years of age and had spent seven years in the Police Department. Even among my friends in the department, going to law school had seemed a bit ambitious. However, there was precedent for it. A man named Maurice Carmody had become a lawyer while in the department, and he had found it advantageous as he rounded out his years as captain and inspector.

But no one within the memory of headquarters had ever left the department, forfeiting its comparative security and relinquishing its pension, to venture into the practice of law. "What do you think?" I asked Jimmy, my brother. Back from the war, Jimmy had joined the Fire Department and was preparing for the lieutenant's examination. He was a believer in civil service as a career. "Bill," he said, "you were never cut out to be a cop. Your summons book is unused and what kind of a sergeant do you think you'll make?" Jim was the family conscience and the one to whom everybody went for advice. It was unlike him to suggest something as daring as venturing out into the new world of law.

I knew I had many obstacles to overcome. I was required to fill out one year of clerkship in a law office, and I sought out my friend Mike Delahanty, who had a most successful civil service school on 15th Street. "I can help you a bit," he said. "There is a promotion class in the Police Department about to begin, and you can teach criminal law and procedures." Another friend introduced me to a lawyer named Harry Houlihan. He was the attorney of record for some casualty insurance companies. "Clerks I don't need," he said. "I can get them for $5 a week, but an ex-cop as an investigator and court preparation man I could use. It will get you acquainted with court procedure at the same time. I can pay you $40 a week and whatever expenses you are required to pay out—dollar for dollar." Between the two jobs I knew I could stagger out the year while I was waiting to qualify for admission to the bar. For a year I carried on, half cop and half law clerk, with about enough salary to support a healthy appetite and a sickly wife.

The following April, Paul, the last of the O'Dwyer's, made it to New York. "He's awful small," Frank said, the evening we all met to bid him welcome at a family gathering at Mrs. Maguire's 103rd Street boarding-house, where Frank and Jack[1] still lived. "What do you think he weighs?" asked Jack. "He says he's nine stone," said Frank. Frank was the most recent arrival and understood Irish expressions. "How much is that in pounds?" asked Jim. We figured it out that a young immigrant weighing 125 pounds, almost 18 years of age, and 5 feet 5 inches presented us a family problem. "He'll grow," said Jim. "And we can get him a job which will let him. And in the meantime, Bill, you can take him with you on your rounds. It will get him used to the country." "You're not afraid what the exposure will do to him?" Jack the cynic chimed in. He was always uncomfortable about Jim's concern that our personal behavior should bring no blush to our family.

Three months afterward, I was admitted to practice law. To celebrate the event, Andy Sheridan proposed that a dinner in my honor be arranged by the Mayo Men's Patriotic and Benevolent Association which he promised would be worthy of the momentous occasion.

It was a night to be remembered—tuxedos for the men and evening gowns for the women, and Andy, who had served so long at the Vanderbilt, supervised the menu. More than a thousand friends and relatives gathered at the Hotel Commodore to mark the occasion, and to climax the evening I was presented with a set of law books. The dinner committee was hard-pressed for a toastmaster who would do justice to the event, and Sheridan would not be content with anybody but the most eloquent. Magistrate Leo Healy, before whom I was later to appear, had acted as toastmaster on several occasions where Andy had been, and his performance had measured up to the high standards to which Sheridan insisted. There was one drawback. I had heard of Judge Healy, but we had never met. As a matter of fact, the judge had never heard of me.

As it turned out, that seemed to be no hindrance to the good judge. In the old-time oratory so much admired by Andy and the Mayo men, he bent to his task. "On one snowy night in particular," he said, "I saw this handsome young officer standing under a street light, nightstick in

1. My brothers Frank and Jack had arrived in New York about five years earlier. (PO'D)

115

one hand, and a law book in the other. His ambition knew no bounds and like a kite he rose against the wind. He is beyond any peradventure of a doubt a worthy descendant of the doughty ancestor, that same General O'Dwyer, who so fearlessly charged up San Juan Hill beside Teddy Roosevelt with a few of the other more daring Rough Riders." My admiration for the judge was only exceeded by my curiosity. The following day I checked the records of Roosevelt's Rough Riders and found no one to fit either the name or the description.

I was full of hope but with no immediate prospects. "Are you a lawyer yet?" asked Detective Jim Powers. He was attached to the Butler Street police division, and we met on Court Street, Brooklyn. "Just got admitted last week and I'm still looking around," I said. "Have you ever met George Joyce, the alderman from Gowanus?" he asked. "Never heard of him," I said. In no time we were entering an office at 44 Court Street. The sign on the door said "Holmes and Bernstien, Lawyers," and over in a corner another name in smaller letters, "George Joyce." We talked awhile. "A typical Irish-American," I thought. "Knows nothing about his antecedents and cares less. But an affable product of Red Hook." In the large office were two other men. Frank Wing Holmes, tall, heavyset, a graduate of Hamilton College, began in Brooklyn as a school teacher, then took up law. His middle name came to him from a well-known upstate family. He was dignified and well mannered and seemingly tolerant. The other man, Oscar Bernstien, was small, with the brightest blue eyes I had ever seen in anyone. The humor in the conversation bounced from Bernstien, the product of Odessa, and Joyce, the storyteller from Brooklyn's Smoky Hollow.

"Oscar, I want you to meet an Irish cop—thinks he's a lawyer." "Don't they all," said Oscar, revealing the sharp rejoinder to which I was soon to be accustomed. A few days later, having passed muster with my new associates, the name Joyce on the entrance was rubbed off and was replaced by a new sign reading, "Joyce and O'Dwyer, Attorneys at Law," giving both of us the privileges of access to Oscar Bernstien, one of the brightest lawyers I ever knew. With business cards and stationery printed, we were to venture forth into the new world of business in Brooklyn in the late 20's.

Six months afterward, Joyce was appointed to the bench. While he never really left our lives, our meetings were rare. My time in the office brought me more and more in contact with Oscar Bernstien, and it continued after hours in his home on Madison Avenue. The experience with Oscar and his wife, Becky, opened up a new world for me and gave me self-confidence. A new and strange assortment of people frequented their home: artists, writers, and radical labor leaders, who somehow seemed as fascinated with me as I was with them. In time I came to enjoy this altogether different environment, and they seemed to wonder at the language and the expressions of an immigrant cop turned lawyer. Kitty's health was not improving and she did not altogether enjoy the conversation.

In the meantime, friends who did not list many professionals among their acquaintances made sure that I was invited to speak at or to install the officers of the local fraternal associations. At first I was shy and fearful of the task. I was much relieved when it was over. On the way home I usually remembered the smart things I could have said. But as time progressed, and I began to take stock of myself, I became aware of an improvement. Oscar Bernstien was not a public speaker, and, although he was born in Russia, his diction was perfect and his brief-writing ability was known and respected in every appellate court in the city. After he knew I did not resent it, he assumed the position of law teacher and a most severe critic of my public posture. And with Kitty as an additional listener and critic, before the end of the year I was beginning to find myself comfortable in the courtroom and at ease in addressing an audience. "You haven't mastered either," Oscar would say. "You've got a long way to go. And you've got a lazy streak." And then the blow would be softened. "You're Irish, so where's the O'Casey?" Sean O'Casey was Oscar's favorite modern playwright.

The next year, we opened an office across the street from the Magistrate's Court on Coney Island to catch the summer trade and those who got into trouble on the weekends. It was financially a success but professionally left a lot to be desired. I tried one case after another until they became routine. They paid the rent with money to spare, but the cases became a bore, and I knew that one day I would have to move on. However, one case was different from the rest.

William Alexander, a pilot flying a craft which resembled the first product of the Wright brothers, got lost in the fog at Coney Island and landed on the crowded beach killing two bathers. He was placed under arrest and charged with homicide. I was retained to defend him. "Would you do that for me in the air?" I asked. It was about the time Lindbergh made his historic flight and we were becoming air-minded. "I'll be glad to show you, if you're not too nervous to make the trip," he said. "On reflection," I said, "perhaps it would be a good way to demonstrate to the court that you were in a fix and did the best you could."

Leo Healy was the magistrate and a Mr. Eno was the prosecutor. Sam Bernstein was the court stenographer. They agreed to witness the demonstration from above New York. On my specific instructions Alexander shunned alcohol during lunch. Up over Manhattan we were wobbling with the up current. I had hoped to dramatically make my motion to dismiss as the plane hovered over Coney Island, but as we came over the Narrows, the plane fell twenty feet. I attempted to speak, but nothing intelligible came out. "How is that?" asked the green-skinned judge. Sam Bernstein, with a naturally arthritic hand, grappled with a pencil preparing to do his duty. The big moment had arrived, but the judge and defense counsel were not equal to the task, and, besides, Mr. Eno was also speechless.

Our experience did not set new horizons in air law. Neither Columbia nor Harvard Law Review ever referred to the case, and no doctoral student ever read a paper about our trailblazing adventure. But the *Brooklyn Daily Eagle* duly reported the incident and took pictures as we were boarding the plane. Happily for the court and its officers as well as defense counsel, the press was absent when our flight ended. It was in the car rather than in the "clear blue" that the court's official decision was reached.

"Mr. O'Dwyer," said the judge, "your oratory is only surpassed by the clear logic of your position. You have a great future in the law. O'Connell in his heyday could have done no better. All charges against this defendant are dismissed. Let me warn you, however, Counsellor, that if you ever try to talk the Court into engaging in a caper like this, the full contempt power of the Court will come heavily on your head and you will be in much greater need of a lawyer than is this foolish practitioner of an impractical calling."

"And now driver," continued the judge, "proceed to Octjen's Bar with as much dispatch as possible from this more acceptable conveyance and, lest caution gnaw at your vitals, remember that you are carrying the law, or at least the law of Flatbush, whose strong arm is ready to lend you its total protection."

Another personal tragedy struck the O'Dwyer clan in 1926. Jim had stayed late at the firehouse when an alarm came in, and he answered it. At 83rd and West End Avenue the hook-and-ladder truck collided with a motorcycle, and the O'Dwyers lost their counsel, their family worrier, their consolation. Three months afterwards, his only child, Joan O'Dwyer, was born. The remaining brothers, Jack, Frank, Paul and myself, had begun to drift apart. None were married except myself, and we had no children. A small child in the Bronx kept us together.

My relationships at the office continued to be pleasant, and I began to be better acquainted with my associates there. Frank Wing Holmes was a very proper man. His attire suited his court appearance. He belonged to the Crescent Athletic Club on Remsen Street in fashionable Brooklyn Heights.[2] Holmes dined there with judges from the nearby State Supreme Court and the Federal District Court. Mortimer Byers was a United States District Court judge. James C. Cropsy and Norman Dyke were elected to the Supreme Court by the people of Brooklyn. All three were staunch members of the Republican Party in Brooklyn. About this time Charles Dodd, a Democrat, was elected District Attorney, the first Catholic to be so elected. The Jewish population also saw their first representatives elected to the State Supreme Court. Harry Lewis and Meyer Steinbrink, Republicans, and Edward Lazansky and Algeron I. Nova, Democrats, broke precedent and were installed in the prestigious Brooklyn court. Waiting in the aisles were a swarm of Italian, Irish and Jewish judges who had made it to the lower courts—Magistrate's and Municipal. Rufus Perry, the first black lawyer, had hung out his shingle on Hudson Avenue and represented the small black colony which covered a few blocks around Flatbush Avenue Extension. Perry's artful cross examination intrigued the lawyers, and many went to hear him when he performed in jury trials in the County Court. He introduced his audience to a new world, which was soon to be a familiar part of the New York scene.

Neighborhoods were changing, as well, to accommodate new and shifting populations. The Arab colony had settled around Atlantic Avenue, and George Shahady, a well-known detective, spoke for them around election time. Jamie Kelly, Brooklyn historian and County Clerk, acted as spokesman for "our brown brothers," the few hundred Puerto Ricans who were taking root in the slums on Columbia Street, the tenements so recently vacated by Italians who were moving to Bath Beach and Coney Island. The Finns at Sunset Park had brought their knowledge of cooperative apartments to Brooklyn and were 25 years ahead of their time. The neighborhood welcomed the new Scandanavian seamen and ultimately their families, and Brooklyn's Fifth Avenue became known locally as Olsen Avenue. Ebbets Field, home of the Brooklyn Dodgers, was the meeting place for all. It was the great equalizing Brooklyn arena. The Greeks and Armenians and Chinese had remained in Manhattan, and everywhere the old Brooklynites had moved to Queens or to Long Island.

Even the O'Dwyers made a change in residence. As a cop I had lived in a lower-middle class neighborhood, on the second floor of a three-family house. Nineteen twenty-five and 1926 saw some post-war good times, and right from the beginning the decision to leave the police and pursue a law career proved justified. Now, with our new position of relative affluence, Kitty and I decided to move on to the recently-developed upper-middle-class Irish-American colony in Bay Ridge. In

2. The club was then struggling with the application for membership of Judge Edward Byrne, who was otherwise qualified except for his religion. He was a Catholic. Later, the club admitted its first two Jewish members but it had already been wounded by the Depression and eventually passed into oblivion.

time, we bought a house at 449 79th Street, a semi-detached one-family dwelling which was to remain our home until 1946, when I moved to Gracie Mansion.

Although most of my cases brought me to the Magistrate's Court where I could practice the kind of law I knew best, both Oscar Bernstien and I were discontent. He contrived to have me appear in civil cases despite my insecurity about departing from the familiar. "The law is reasonable," Oscar would say. "Use the same reasoning you had when you were a hod carrier, don't let your parchment confuse you. If you use only your common sense, whatever decision you come to, I will show you a case on all fours."

But the Magistrate's Court and the County Court were presided over by a group of judges, each with a special idiosyncracy. One of them, "Old Man Sears," as we called him, had never been a lawyer. He had been a young justice of the peace in the town of Flatbush. He was included with the parcel of cops and political hacks which the city was forced to accept if it wanted political support for the incorporation of Brooklyn into the City of New York in 1898.

George Folwell, another judge, considered himself a linguist, and, if the Italian interpreter was not around, he was delighted to show off before an amazed audience. The non-Italians were amazed at his fluency in Italian, and the Italians didn't understand the gibberish he was emitting. Most of the Italian defendants understood enough to know that the judge thought he could make himself known in their language, and they had enough cunning to show delight and surprise. The law required that each accused at arraignment be instructed on his constitutional rights. Defendants have seldom understood them, even in English. Judge Folwell, in the absence of Joe Fair, the Italian interpreter, attempted to execute this challenging task. The defendant who was not in the cell long enough to hear about the judge's pretentions stood bewildered before the bench. "Sorry, judge, I no understan' so good the Engleesh," he would explain to the embarrassment of the court and the amusement of the court personnel.

The effect of Prohibition on both law and politics was enormous. Prohibition had received New York State approval by the passage of the Mullen Gage Law. The saloon closed the front door and opened the side door, selling inferior booze and "home brew" beer at outrageous prices. The fortunes made in the illegal traffic in alcohol developed a set of gangsters who could not be eradicated after "the noble experiment" was ended by Franklin Roosevelt. The Volstead Act and the Mullen Gage Law presented lawyers with unheard of opportunities, and the lawyer with the right connection would take the United States Commissioner on tour with him through the night after the courts were closed. The

120

Commissioner would set bail and sign the release in front of the lieutenant's desk in the stationhouse, so that the saloon keeper could get back to his customers in time to take the cash register's reading prior to closing up. "Padlock proceedings" were provided as punishment for those caught and prosecuted, whereupon the "speakeasy" owner left the padlock on and contrived to get access to the same premises through another entrance.

A Brooklyn gangster named Frankie Yale decided to enter politics and selected George Joyce's old district, Gowanus, where Paddy Diamond was the district leader. A Yale-backed slate of candidates appeared on the ballot in opposition to the clubhouse slate. It promised to be a rough campaign, but the mob met with Yale and prevailed on him to abandon his project lest Diamond bring down the full power of the law on them. Paddy Diamond was not only the political boss of Gowanus, but also the License Commissioner. Yale gave his excess energy to other pursuits. He built a church in Borough Park, and the blessing of the cornerstone was a great Brooklyn event. Later, when a rival gang rubbed him out, the number of floral wreaths which followed his casket into the church exceeded any tribute ever extended before or since to any Brooklynite. The occasion received more notoriety than the Church was willing to accept, and a new rule came forth from the Diocese of Brooklyn and the Archdiocese of New York: "He who lives by the sword shall not receive a Catholic burial" was an edict which lasted until the old rule, "Judge not lest ye be judged," again took over.

The bulk of gangster cases was divided between two of the most colorful lawyers ever to gain access to our tribunals. Both were well established when I got to the courthouse, and I presented no competition to them. Sam Liebowitz gained his fame from representing Al Capone, and Ed Reilly's greatest hour was in the defense of Bruno Hauptmann, who was tried and convicted in the courthouse in Flemington, New Jersey, of the kidnapping and murder of Charles Lindbergh's child. Liebowitz went on to serve on the County Court bench in Brooklyn, but the Hauptmann case ended Reilly's career. He became mentally ill and was confined to an institution for several years. He still had enough skill left to bring his own action to be discharged, and he convinced the jury he should never have been hospitalized.

In politics, John F. Hylan (Red Mike) was Mayor and soon to be challenged by Jimmy Walker, the dapper Assemblyman from Battery Dan Finn's Irish and Democratic stronghold in Greenwhich Village. Rivalry in the Democratic Party had developed with the new Democratic stronghold in Brooklyn, challenging Tammany Hall for an equal voice in the selection of city-wide candidates. John McCoey was then the Brooklyn Democratic boss, and Irwin Steingut—soon to be the Speaker of the Assembly—controlled the powerful Madison Club. Two of their younger members, Abe Beame and Nat Sobel, were the organization's most effective captains. Beame got into the Budget Director's office, and Sobel became the brains behind the speaker. Pat Lynch, the Brownsville boss, was succeeded by Hyme Schorenstein to accommodate the thousands of Jewish residents who had recently forsaken New York's Lower East Side in search of more room and more comfortable living. The friendly nature of the success was established when Pat's son, John, continued in the same club on a political career which was to carry him to county leadership and ultimately to presidency of the Kings County Trust Company. Meanwhile, Jerry Ambro, a young, aggressive lawyer in the nearby Italian stronghold of Ocean Hill was leading Italian-Americans in their challenge to the Irish/Jewish domination of the Democratic Party.

I was an interested onlooker rather than a participant in these developments in politics. I had become a member of the Mayo Men's Patriotic and Benevolent Society, which began in about 1870 when Irish societies were more benevolent than patriotic and sought to help the new arrival to deal with the overpowering atmosphere of discrimination he would face. But that was long before I had been elected president of the society, which was non-sectarian (with a Catholic chaplain). The society's members were proud to have a lawyer as their president, and an import at that, and they favored me with whatever cases they came across. One Protestant among the membership, a man named George Ormsby, constituted fair proof that those who made up its roster were in no way bigoted. In time George became president, and every honor possible was heaped on his head. Some of us believed it kept him from converting.

During this period, Paul was attending St. John's Law School in Brooklyn, Frank was working as a laborer in the fruit and vegetable business, on the first step in an amazing career in the produce business, and Jack had left the waterfront to manage prizefighters and to open a speakeasy on Broadway. All three brothers thought I had delusions of grandeur when I said I would like to be an assistant district attorney, but conceded that in any case there was no harm in trying. I did try, but I had no political backing and never made it.

Kitty, Frank and I visited Ireland in 1927. My mother, I was told, still sighed now and then about my leaving Salamanca, but with the lapse of years and the favorable developments in my career, the hurt had left her. In its place was a poorly-concealed pride that I had returned a full-fledged lawyer. She was not, however, going to permit any son to show his importance or superiority in her presence. She assumed an authoritative position with little or no provocation. My sisters were concerned lest I take offense, explaining that she had taken on the role of both father and mother after my father's death. It was plain, however, that her sadness over Jimmy's death dampened the great feeling of exhilaration which is always present when the exile returns. The neighbors came to see and enjoy my homecoming, and there was genuine happiness in our village.

Back in New York, matters of income began to concern me. It was an accepted axiom among lawyers that no one accumulates wealth from the practice of law. The most successful ones are those whose clients present them with the opportunity to come into a new business venture, assigning them stock as part payment of their fees or to participate with the client as an investor. "The client will seldom think about it, and you have to suggest it to them," said Walter Hart, lawyer, politician and my confidant. I met few clients with either the capacity or the wish to have me share their fortunes. An enterprising Italian whom I represented was one exception. He was about to buy a new gasoline steam shovel and wanted to make me a partner in the venture. It was a new model and, with the proper management, it held out promise of great success in the construction field. But the idea didn't appeal to me and I passed it up. Another time, the Naples Spaghetti Company was organized by three Neapolitans whom I was fortunate enough to represent. I was offered the opportunity to become associated with them as an investor, with representation on their board of directors, but the idea of being the "Spaghetti King" didn't appeal to me either.

One proposal that came my way, however, did excite my interest. Alfred Cerrillo was an impresario whose recent ventures were less than a howling success, but that in no way dampened his enthusiasm. When he came to the office to discuss a business proposition with me, he looked the very picture of opulence. A heavyset man, six feet in height, he was dressed as befitted a successful manager and promoter in the theater and opera world. His spats were clean, his homburg was set at the correct angle, and he walked with an air of power and dignity. His proposal was not complicated. He planned to promote a concert tour for a now middle-aged woman who had once provided romantic inspiration for many a young Neapolitan blade. The coloratura was known as the "Insuperable Diva." In her earlier years she had been a household name among many of Italy's natives now living in New York. According to Alfred, her popularity had continued even when she should have been past her prime. She was a kind of Italian Mae West with a still-excellent voice. She was sure to attract a tremendous crowd of the Italians who knew her from the concert stage in Naples and Rome. Or so Alfred assured me. The cost was a mere $1,500. I went along with the idea. I borrowed half the money and put up my share of the venture. The diva was scheduled for three appearances in the United States. Alfred made all the arrangements for the concert tour. One of the scheduled appearances was Albany, New York. It was felt that the state capital was a suitable location to attract Italians from Troy, Schenectady, Utica and other mid-state areas. The concert hall was on top of the hill near the Capitol. A wet snow fell that day and the temperature dropped suddenly. Some Italians, with an insatiable love of music and a healthy admiration for a voluptuous woman, climbed the hill, literally, on their hands and knees. But there were not enough of them, and when the expenses were taken out, I was lucky to get back a fraction of my investment. And that was the end of my career as a concert promoter.

My next venture was no more successful, but it was also exciting. There was a Gaelic football team in County Mayo which had just won the championship of the province, and the Gaelic Athletic Association of New York suggested to me that I arrange a tour for the team playing Irish-American teams from San Francisco to New York. My brother, Jack, as a fight promoter of sorts, had met a number of sportswriters, including those from Hearst Publications in New York. Someone came up with the idea that the promotion take place for the benefit of the Milk Fund Drive for Babies, which was under the patronage of Mrs. William Randolph Hearst. It was her favorite charity, and since Hearst Publications at that time owned the *Daily Mirror*, a successful morning paper, and *The Journal American*, a popular evening paper, I was assured of the help of the sports departments of both dailies. Jack brought around such famous sportswriters and cartoonists as Hype Igoe and Burris Jenkins, as well as owners and promoters of the Polo Grounds. With this kind of support and patronage it did not seem possible that we could lose, but I didn't have any money, and I turned to my brother, Frank, who by this time was head of the melon department at the firm of Henry Kelly and Sons, fruit and vegetable merchants. He had no gambling instincts and saved his money week by week. He had accumulated $6,500, with which he had hoped he could open up a small business some day soon. With every assurance that the money would bring him more than its equal, I borrowed the money from Frank and was on my way to be the promoter of an important international athletic event.

The American public had become extremely interested in Gaelic football. Not having the time or the money to make all the arrangements, my brothers Frank and Paul were there to help. Paul, who was new at the law and could afford the time, went back to Mayo to make the arrangements to transport the team to the United States.

The first day's receipts at the Polo Grounds were to go exclusively to the Milk Fund, while the second day's were to take care of my expenses and to reap whatever profits would come from the venture. We had insured both days against rain at a very heavy premium, and there was a tremendous ballyhoo associated with the games. Both Jenkins and Igo were busy cartooning the players as they came from Ireland.

The first day came up sunny and clear, but rain came the second day—not sufficient to warrant collecting from the insurance policy, but enough to dissuade the public from going. I lost Frank's $6,500 and more to boot. Soon the team was on its way back and we were left to pay the bills. This caper ended my career as a sports promoter. But it was not a total loss. I had come in close contact with newspapermen who were pioneers in their craft and who came to us from San Francisco and Chicago, and I had occasion to know Mrs. Hearst, a most gracious lady, the patron of needy children, and a genuine philanthropist. Sometime later, my relationship with her would prove to be invaluable.

CHAPTER 22

MAGISTRATE (1932-1938)

My ambitions, if I had any during the seven years I practiced law, did not lie in the direction of politics. I considered it out of bounds for me. It was the era of the clubhouse, when it was most unlikely that anyone who had neither money, prestige, family connection or clubhouse backing would even consider a political career. Nevertheless, a young lawyer from poorer circumstances had a chance to score success in politics, and it was one of the few avenues available to the children of the poor to break out of their environment, but to do so they had to follow a rather strict ritual.

On Monday and Thursday nights the district leader held court at the club, and the young lawyer was expected to be there to take care of a neighborhood problem or appear in court for a neighbor's child in difficulties with the law. It went without saying that he was to act without fee. The young clubhouse lawyer would also be expected to act as precinct captain and produce the voters of his district at the polls on Primary Day. Election Day was generally left to take care of itself, since the Democratic nomination, in most districts, was assurance of election. For these services, the young lawyer was remembered when the time came for the Mayor or Governor or county-elected officials to fill vacancies for minor offices, or he might even aspire to be secretary to a judge. From that point on, his ability counted, but he was also expected to continue his attendance at the club and through it to serve the public. The young lawyer, in the course of time, might also be expected to be selected as the Democratic candidate for the State Assembly. If the lawyer made good at his legislative post, he could expect, in time, to be nominated for the State Senate, the Board of Aldermen, or even for a judgeship, by the district boss.

It was too late for me to make the start and, truthfully, I doubt if I ever had the patience and the will necessary to score a success in politics through the clubhouse route. So I gave no thought to it, concentrating instead in building a law practice.

But something happened in 1932 which was to rock the foundations of the political machine in New York City. Four years earlier, in 1928, Alfred Emanuel Smith had been nominated by the Democratic Party as its choice for President of the United States, and across the nation he was branded as the vulgar product of Tammany Hall, the New York County Democratic machine. In the Bible Belt, they were more frank, charging Smith with being a Roman Catholic, and he had entered no denial. The Depression followed the stock market crash in 1929, and it appeared unlikely that Herbert Hoover would be re-elected in 1932. Nonetheless, to make sure that no extraneous religious argument would rob the Democratic Party of its special right to take over during a depression, plans got under way early to nominate one who was acceptable to the party but who did not bear the liability of being a Catholic.

An old-line Dutch family from the Hudson Valley had produced a man to fit the occasion. His name was Franklin Delano Roosevelt. He was a patrician who spoke the language of a commoner in a cultured accent. To promote Roosevelt's candidacy, the likeable Jim Farley was impressed into service. He was sent across the country for the purpose of convincing the Irish-Americans who controlled the party in many states that they could lose the Presidential election with Smith at the helm. With Roosevelt's money, prestige and Irish support, the Democratic Party could not lose.

There was one drawback, however. Roosevelt, as Governor of New York, was known to have close ties with some less than reputable leaders of New York City Democrats, and so it was necessary to demonstrate to the rest of the country that he was free from the influence of the disreputable Tammany Hall. Jimmy Walker, a Tammany product, Mayor of New York, was hauled before Governor Roosevelt on charges of malfeasance. He resigned under fire. Roosevelt was nominated for President by acclamation.

With the resignation of Jimmy Walker in September 1932, the president of the Board of Alderman, Joseph V. McKee (Holy Joe), became Mayor. Just before the resignation, the new Polish colony in Brooklyn had produced a lawyer, Bernard Kozicke, who was interested in becoming a judge, and in due course his district leader had recommended him for appointment to John H. McCoey, the county boss. McCoey, in turn, had recommended him to Mayor Walker. Walker had his own troubles and did not get around to making the appointment. The unfinished commitment of Jimmy Walker fell on the shoulders of the new Mayor. McKee found the burden irritating. Besides, the occasion gave him a golden opportunity to establish his independence. He delayed in making the appointment, much to McCoey's annoyance. Still, the incident did not attract much attention, since it was a foregone conclusion in the minds of most politicians that McCoey would have his way or deny McKee the nomination to succeed himself when his term was up.

I had had no interest in the job and it never occurred to me to move in that direction. Then one day in late 1932 I met Kenny Sutherland in the barber shop in Borough Hall, Brooklyn, which lawyers and politicians frequented: the barber doubled as bookmaker. Sutherland, Coney Island Democratic boss, was at odds with Boss McCoey. "There's a vacancy in the Magistrate's Court, Bill," he said to me. "First, do you have any interest in it? And secondly, could you get some independent backing if you were to seek it?"

The idea took me by surprise, and I regarded it as farfetched. "Are you serious?" I asked. "Never more serious in my life," he said. "I can tell you now confidentially that McKee is determined to reject McCoey's choice. You have a lot that might attract McKee for this appointment to a criminal court bench. Ex-cop, lawyer and all that. You ought to think it over. McKee is Ed Flynn's man, but he might just pick a Brooklynite so no one would doubt his challenge to McCoey." "I'll think it over," I said, "and let you know." "You'll need good references," he said.

The idea grew in my mind during the afternoon, and that night I went to Madison Avenue to meet the Bernstiens. Oscar was enthusiastic. "I think it's a great idea," he said, "and let's not let the grass grow under our feet. Besides it's the only way you'll ever make it in politics."

The following day I called Sutherland. "You are at liberty to place my name before the Mayor," I said. "My," he replied, "but aren't you the uppity Mick. You'll need more than that. Who do you know who will urge the Mayor to appoint you?" "Joe Moran, head of the P.B.A.," I said. "Who else?" he asked. "Tom Ford, John C. O'Connor, Sheamus McDermot and Charlie Connolly." "Who the hell are they?" "None other," I said in mock surprise and indignation, "than the owner-publishers of the *Irish World*, the *Irish Advocate*, the *Gaelic American* and the *Irish Echo*, well-known New York weeklies." "Who else," he continued impatiently. "Willie Walsh." "Who?" "Willie Walsh, president of the prestigious Mayo Men's Patriotic and Benevolent Society." "Who else?" This time he seemed to be getting desperate. "Mrs. William Randolph Hearst," I replied with modesty. "Why the hell didn't you say that in the first place," said the impatient political boss with obvious relief. "Get her endorsement and fill in the rest. They couldn't hurt."

Getting editorial support from the four weeklies was no problem. Approaching Mrs. Hearst was not easy for me, but I did it. Soon after, Mayor McKee announced his intention to submit my name to the Brooklyn Bar Association. The clearance should have been pro forma.

I had now practiced law in the Brooklyn courts for seven years, and I expected the appropriate committee to report promptly and favorably on my application. But the committee failed to take action, and the application was pigeonholed until Ed Flynn would return from his European vacation. He would then be expected to have McKee withdraw my appointment.

In American politics when the scene seems too raw, the media can play an important role. The *Brooklyn Daily Eagle* and the *Brooklyn Citizen* began to inquire into what happened to the appointment. The situation became quite embarrassing. The Bar Association was forced to come forth with its approval, and in no time I was raising my hand and was swearing in with the new robe the Mayo Men's Club gave me draped across my back and shoulders.

My appointment caused a rift in the Democratic Party that was to give Fiorello La Guardia a 12-year lease on Gracie Mansion. The party bosses met to select a candidate for Mayor who would be required to run in the 1932 election for the one year left of Jimmy Walker's term. McCoey, smarting from the rebuff caused by my appointment, delivered his punishing blow to the acting Mayor. He was adamant in his refusal to support Joe McKee. In Manhattan, Tammany Hall prevailed on Surrogate John P. O'Brien to resign his post and accept the nomination as the Democratic nominee for Mayor. O'Brien had no trouble in winning the election. As Mayor, he immediately ran into opposition from the bankers, who delivered an ultimatum to him that either he surrender fiscal control to them or they would cut off the city's credit. The result was "the bankers' agreement," which set the rules for tax programs, fiscal spending and social policies for the next decade.

Ed Flynn was furious with the four county leaders who had failed to support Joe McKee, but he held his temper until the following year (1933), when the time came for the leaders to endorse a candidate for Mayor for a full four-year term. It was a foregone conclusion that all Democratic leaders would unite to nominate the Democratic incumbent, O'Brien. Flynn's refusal to go along with the endorsement of O'Brien came as a blow to Democratic unity. Furthermore, Flynn committed the unpardonable offense of starting an independent party, and McKee, with Flynn's blessing and support, became the candidate for Mayor of the newly-created Recovery Party. This maneuver fragmented the Democratic Party.

The Republicans, quick to take advantage of the hopeless split, selected Fiorello La Guardia as their candidate. Fiorello had been first a Socialist and then a Republican. His father was Italian and his mother Jewish, and his stronghold was in the Italian section of the Upper East Side of New York. With the benefit of Sam Seabury, Adolph Berle and similar establishment people, as well as the newly-formed Fusion Party, La Guardia carried the election and remained as the town's Mayor for

12 years.

With no inkling of what the consequence of my appointment might be, I took the City Magistrate's oath of office on December 8, 1932, and I entered into a new phase of my life. That year also marked the beginning of a new era in American history for most Americans. Herbert Hoover was finishing a single term in office which could only be described as disastrous. He had presided over the developing Depression and seemed utterly helpless to halt the impending economic ruin. We were about to witness a revolutionary period in American life, with the political leadership pitted against the economic barons. The change in outlook affected every phase of our existence, both economic and cultural, and evidence of changing attitudes could be found everywhere.

To the world outside the courts, being sworn in as City Magistrate may not have seemed to be an earthshaking event, but to the members of the legal profession, the position was a prestigious one, and it paid $12,000 per annum with some fringe benefits.

It was generally understood that a coveted judgeship in New York had a price tag on it, amounting to one year's salary. In those days the Democratic Party held sway and had been in continuous control in City Hall for over a quarter of a century. Each district leader, with jurisdiction over one assembly district, claimed that a given judgeship was his by virtue of the rule of succession and of the equitable division of the spoils. It was recognized by fellow politicians to be within his exclusive domain to recommend a name to the county leader, who transmitted it to the Mayor for appointment.

In the earlier days when the Democratic Party was struggling for recognition and was champion of the impoverished ghetto, such an appointment was regarded as the reward to a lawyer who had done faithful service to the club and the party. The Harding Administration was merely a reflection of the corruption which prevailed across the nation, and the Democratic Party, too, had suffered from moral deterioration. Now, the most dedicated and experienced clubhouse lawyers often found themselves out-pointed by an ambitious, wealthy father or a very successful lawyer who had made his fortune and craved the outward display of respect from his cohorts at the Bar.

Cliff Evans, then a young *Brooklyn Eagle* reporter with an ear to the ground, heard about the price tags on the judicial robes. He felt that if these rumors were spread without restraint in the places where politicians met around Borough Hall, then committing them to print was merely a way of presenting the naked truth as a good reporter should. "In the bar under the Democratic headquarters," he wrote, "those who are in the know say there were 50,000 reasons" to support the appointment of the most recent addition to the Supreme Court bench. The jurist

130

in question came from banking rather than political circles.

The item was less than startling news in Brooklyn political circles. It was felt that only a banker could afford the price. The rumor, by word of mouth alone, would never have sparked an investigation, but the written story constituted a challenge to the prosecutor that he dared not ignore. A judge was duly assigned to the task, a grand jury was impaneled, and witnesses were called to sift for the truth. The investigation claimed the headlines for a couple of weeks and then died forever. "For the present," Evans wrote, "all parties involved in such transactions shall be on guard henceforth to accept only bills in small denominations." The practice was widespread, and I would venture a rough guess that at least 50 percent of those holding down judgeships found their way to the bench through this corrupt road.

How did they fare afterwards? That all depended on the nature of the man. A confirmed thief would likely follow the same pattern on the bench. Others gained an enviable reputation, wrote learned opinions, and thereafter strictly adhered to the golden rule. And with the passage of time, lawyer and politician, citizen and judge forgot the sordid circumstance which had brought them to the exalted position.

The outlook for Americans was bleak in December of 1932. I had been a successful lawyer by the standards of the early days of the Depression, and, yet, the security of a steady salary was attractive. By 1932 standards, $12,000 per annum was enough to maintain me in comfort. Although Dr. Philip Norman, Dr. George Sheehan, and Dr. Joseph Baldwin, Kitty's physicians, had to be paid, they were, however, more family friends than family physicians and all were generous with their time, and their fees were more than reasonable.

On the national scene, 1933 saw Roosevelt moving into a position of inspired leadership. Banks were closed, farms were subjected to foreclosures, and small farmers, armed with rifles, marched against the nation's banks in order to halt evictions. In the cities, hungry men and women lined up for food, and soon the discontented people began to shout aloud against the misery, hunger and unemployment they experienced and saw all around them. The President protested against the "princes of privilege" and the "robber barons" and reported the state of the country and his plans to the nation over the radio in his "fireside chats." The people believed in the President and took heart. And the labor unions, with new charters of liberty, were forming to counteract those who, in times of distress, were shamelessly exploiting labor.

The Wagner Act, passed in Congress in 1935, and the Little Wagner Act, passed in Albany in 1937, opened the door for an organizing drive which was to increase by leaps and bounds the number of workers who were joining existing old-line unions. But the most spectacular thing of all was the number of new unions which were about to be organized. Socialists, communists, Marxists and radicals joined in the organization drives, working all night to prepare pamphlets and spread them around in the early morning; and when the organization was completed, they were installed as union officers.

People's nerves were frayed and pickets marched peacefully at first, but that did not last long. Then Philip Murray of the Steel Workers, John L. Lewis, head of the Mine Workers, Sidney Hillman, chief of the Amalgamated Clothing Workers, David Dubinsky of the I.L.G.W.U., and Michael J. Quill from the Transport Workers Union started a schism, and the Congress of Industrial Organizations was born from a rib of the American Federation of Labor. They organized one powerful union after another with new and radical concepts.

The struggle of the people for survival was reflected in the Magistrate's Court's docket. It was clear to the constitutional lawyer that the picket sign was the poor man's newspaper and protected by the First Amendment, but the legal maxim was unknown or ignored by many a judge. The educational process began to raise the consciousness of the judges to the true meaning of the Bill of Rights, and criminal lawyers were becoming constitutional experts.

It was my lot to serve in the Brooklyn Magistrate's Court when the Newspaper Guild, recently formed under the guidance of Heywood Broun, called a strike on *The Brooklyn Daily Eagle*. In Brooklyn *The Eagle* was an institution like Borough Hall or Ebbets Field. This well-established newspaper was founded by Henry Cruise Murphy in 1841 as a political weapon to advance his candidacy to various political offices. But in the course of time its original purpose was forgotten, and it remained as the paper the people of Brooklyn invariably read.

The newly-formed Newspaper Guild was suffering from growing pains, and the strike against *The Eagle* was as much an expression of resentment against past wrongs as it was a determined effort to improve the miserable working conditions of its reporters. The other newspapers did what they could to help their distressed sister, and, from many sources, less than subtle pressure was exerted on me to make me see the consequences of Brooklyn without *The Eagle* and the danger inherent in the exorbitant demands on a shaky newspaper.

As some of these cases were appearing on my court calendar, many of the political characters around made it their business to tell me how important it was to continue to be in the good graces of the newspapers, especially *The Eagle*, if I ever contemplated running for higher office. Besides, they said, the strikers were all communists. The police were literally in the pocket of *The Eagle* in more ways than one. An inspector stood by the plant and arrested pickets as they appeared on the sidewalk.

132

The charge was making noise and singing. I discharged them as fast as they came before me. Finally I was reassigned to another court so that I would not be in a position to try any more of *The Eagle* pickets.

Another series of cases that came before me involved May's Department Store on Fulton Street, which was owned and operated by a man who was very well-known and respected, and who had a well-deserved reputation as a generous contributor to local charities. A union organized May's employees and they eventually went on strike. May's lawyer would stand outside with the police sergeant and select the people from the picket line whom the lawyer felt should be arrested. The Police Department dutifully followed orders and brought strikers into Magistrate's Court. Bail, usually set by an accommodating magistrate, would have to be posted at a cost of $25 for each defendant. The unions were in the process of formation at that point and their resources were minimal. The harassment was designed to cripple them.

Several cases of May's pickets were brought before me. Sydney Cohn and Leonard Boudin, then members of one of the earliest labor law firms, Boudin, Cohn & Glickstein, represented most of the labor cases in the Magistrates' Courts. They complained, and with good reason, that the treatment they received in Brooklyn courts was much worse than that meted out in other parts of town. I discussed a plan whereby I would continue to let the same bail be fixed but would take the personal signature of the defendant as his assurance that he would return for trial. In that way there was no cost, no bondsman was enriched, and no union impoverished.

At about this point, disturbances began to occur around welfare offices, and, at first, the police, with no training in how to deal with such a situation, would lock up everybody who was anywhere around the scene. One morning, as I got into the Coney Island court, I found my courtroom lined with policemen. I inquired about the reason and was told that the people arrested were a wild, lawless group of communists, who were making trouble at the local relief station. With the police were a full complement of officers, from the inspector down. I didn't feel there was any reason requiring that kind of display of force and told the inspector I wanted all police removed from the court. The inspector diplomatically reminded me that they had an obligation to watch out for my welfare. "Inspector," I said, "I can always make it to the back window if things get bad." I turned to the crowded courtroom and explained to the assemblage what I had done. "The police are also working for a living," I reminded both pickets and police, and all had similar problems and many common objectives. The crowded courtroom remained calm and for the full day we dealt with each case individually. No unusual or rowdy incident took place.

During industrial disputes the League of Women Shoppers would investigate the circumstances of the strike and, in selected cases, if the facts warranted it, would show up on the picket line in support of the strikers. It was a new phenomenon. Many of these women were well dressed and from prominent families. Joe's Restaurant at Borough Hall was a landmark, and during a strike of the waiters, members of the league appeared on the line. They were locked up with the other pickets and were bailed out in the night court. To my surprise, as I came on to the bench the following morning, I found Becky Bernstien seated among the defendants. I did not know of her new adventures. The women of the league had strenuously objected to the ill-treatment the pickets were receiving, and they learned about it firsthand in the lockup. It was an invariable practice for the police to also incarcerate the bystander who protested against ill-treatment by the police. The league women ran afoul of this time-dishonored policy. When I dismissed the charges, I found a very frightened group of police, including officials. They felt that a lawsuit for false arrest was inevitable.

After the court proceedings were over, I called both the police and the ladies into the chambers and outlined their respective rights, as well as their obligations. From then on things were quiet in front of Joe's. The league and the police engaged in frequent and polite conversation.

When the Mayor decided to put on a drive—and he frequently went crusading—the Magistrate's Court became a beehive of activity. Clerks, using the "hunt and peck" method, tortuously typed out the complaints, while policemen waited for their turn to submit the information they wished to have included on the written charge. The courtroom, the corridors and the clerk's office showed evidence of a sort of hysterical confusion.

Once, after a short period of relative calm in the court, the quiet interlude was interrupted because the Mayor had become annoyed at the musical renditions common to our city streets. Mr. La Guardia's father was a band leader and he was genuinely fond of classical music. Now, part of the New York scene for a century or more was the organ grinder and the monkey with the funny little hat held in place by a chin strap. The music, if one could so describe it, appealed to local taste. "The Sidewalks of New York," "Sweet Rosie O'Grady," and "Alice Blue Gown" were typical of the tunes which came rippling from the metallic strings of the hand organ. This sidewalk contribution to New York's culture was usually manipulated by an Italian immigrant.

The Mayor issued an edict: "No more organ grinding in New York." The people became quite upset. The organ grinder was hurting no one; but the law is the law, and the grinder, the organ, and sometimes the monkey were hauled into the hall of justice, much to the amusement of the crowded courtroom. Often, the decorum was further upset by the antics of the monkey, and the judge would have to call the case out of turn, suspending sentence on the music maker and sending him on his way with dispatch. No New York magistrate could find it in his heart to punish what had become another symbol of "Gotham." Having suffered much frustration from the ineffectiveness of court summonses and summary arrests as a means to ending the nostalgic strains, this approach was abandoned. The police were given the order to take more direct action not contemplated in the penal law, the city ordinances, the police manual or the Bill of Rights. The offending organ grinder was simply banished forever and without benefit of due process.

At other times, the Mayor would chide his Police Commissioner, Lewis J. Valentine, for failing to enforce traffic laws, and the order would come down from the Commissioner through the chain of command. The summons book of each cop would be checked weekly by his superiors to ascertain the number of traffic violators he had tagged. The hour between twelve midnight and one a.m. on the late tour was usually devoted to a lively pursuit of traffic violators. That system left the policeman ample time to while away the loneliest hours of the morning according to his desires.

During the traffic violation drive, the Chief Magistrate kept a watchful eye on his subordinates to see that adequate fines were imposed on the hapless ones who came in the way of the law. "You are handing out an extraordinary number of suspended sentences," warned Judge Jacob Gould Shurman, the Chief Magistrate. "Your rules leave me no alternative," I replied. "You require that I impose a mandatory fine of $5 for everybody. To the rich, this is nothing; to the poor, it may be bread for the family. If I had the discretion to fine $1, $2, $3 or $4, I then could apply the fine as the circumstances warranted." "You have a point there," the chief judge admitted, but the rule continued for a long time thereafter.

Police Commissioner Valentine was a dour man. Earlier in his career, as a district inspector, he had carried out a raid on the clubhouse of the Greenpoint Democratic chieftain, Pete McGuinness. A card game was in progress at the time Valentine's plainclothesmen entered the premises. Judge Seabury, during the famous investigation which bore his name, asked Sheriff McGuinness about the incident. "Is it true," asked the judge, "that when the police arrived at your club, you shouted 'cheese it, the cops'?" "No, Judge," replied the witness, "I said no such thing." "What did you say?" persisted the erudite Seabury. "I said 'Gentlemen, be seated. The cops is here,'" corrected Greenpoint's last sheriff.

Valentine gained no special points with the then-Commissioner,

George V. McLaughlin, because of his foray into Brooklyn's most Democratic stronghold. McLaughlin, a banker, saw no advantage in arousing the ire of so popular a leader as the party boss of the Irish and Polish communities. Inspector Valentine found himself transferred "for the good of the service" to the reduced post of captain of the 68th Precinct in South Brooklyn, where he remained on ice for the balance of the Democratic administration. With the advent of La Guardia, his true worth was recognized and he was promptly rewarded with a summary advancement to the highest post in the department as a symbol of police righteousness.

The pressures put on Valentine by the Mayor were reflected in his attitude towards his men, and he often sought to extend his activities in the direction of the criminal court judges. His method of discharging a cop took the form of a traumatic confrontation. After a police trial, the normally painful duty of advising the policeman that his career was ended had been traditionally handled through teletype orders delivered to the precinct and then to the policeman himself. Valentine departed from this practice. He ordered the cop to be brought before him at police headquarters in the formidable gray stone building with old, massive columns at 240 Centre Street.

He took sadistic delight in having the now-beaten man walk the long distance from the door to his large desk. The convicted policeman walked the "last mile" with fear in his heart, yet with the hope that *maybe*, on this day, the Commissioner might heed his plea. Invariably, the policeman would surrender his last shred of dignity, humbling himself until all the pride was wrung out of him. He would call up the plight of his wife, his children. He would squirm and beg for his job. At the end of this painful and degrading performance, the Commissioner would order the miscreant to stand at attention and salute. "You are dismissed!" Valentine would shout. "You are a bum! You are a disgrace! Take him out of my sight!" he would direct the assistant "executioners." During the Commissioner's term, 109 policemen committed suicide.

Once, on his regular Sunday radio program over WNYC, the city radio station, the Mayor was more belligerent than usual and he directed his remarks publicly to his Police Commissioner, pointing out the failure of the police to arrest lawbreakers. Valentine responded with an order to his men to "go and bring these people in and 'rough 'em up.' " The order has since often been referred to as authority for the contention, frequently expressed by the police, that there is a great deal of law "at the end of the nightstick."

With this direction from the Commissioner's office, the command to "rough 'em up" was taken quite literally by the department. An amazing number of accused people "confessed" to their crimes in the station house. The "third degree" practice finally exploded when a doctor in the Department of Correction in the Raymond Street Jail in Brooklyn became incensed upon finding burn marks deep into one prisoner's wrists. He called Judge Nova, who had charge of the grand jury then in session. The complaint was most embarrassing, but it could not be ignored. Judge Nova directed that the evidence be presented to the grand jury which, in that climate, might have been expected to dismiss the charges.

But the improbable happened. The grand jury took the matter into its own hands. The resulting indictments against the police, including a lieutenant and a sergeant, accused them of tying the prisoner's hands around a hot water pipe in the station house and beating on his body near his kidneys. This treatment was designed, continued the indictment, to inflict extreme pain without leaving marks to prove it. The police had overlooked the effects of extended contact of the tender skin on the inside of the wrists, and it was only by chance that a conscientious doctor reported the incident and brought the matter into the open. Time passed and no action was taken by the District Attorney, and one day County Judge Peter Broncato dismissed the case. The prosecutor did not appeal.

Bookmaking was the bane of every Mayor's existence, and La Guardia provided no exception to the rule. On one occasion he used his Sunday morning air time to advise children who were listening in to please inform the authorities if they discovered their parents placing a bet with the local bookmaker. At various times in his weekly broadcast the Mayor would supply Commissioner Valentine publicly with the exact address where he claimed a bookmaking enterprise was going full blast.

The result was that there would be a deluge of bookmaking cases before the local magistrates during the following week. It was evident that the "rough 'em up" order did not apply to bookmakers. Most of the cases were "accommodation" arrests. The policeman, who had been continually bribed to pay no heed to the bookmaking business in his division, but now faced with pressure from the Commissioner because of the Mayor's public statement, arranged with the bookmaker to have someone "stand in" for the arrest. The evidence invariably was insufficient to warrant holding the accused for trial. But it counted as an arrest on the station house record, and the blame could be charged to the judge for dismissing the case. "We lock them up," police officials would say. "The judge lets them go."

I met Commissioner Valentine one Sunday morning at a Communion breakfast. It was a memorial to Police Captain Kelly of Coney Island, and I was placed at the head table next to the Commissioner. "The Mayor and I have been discussing your handling of bookmaking cases, and the Mayor is not at all pleased," he reported. "I would be glad to discuss the whole business on WNYC," I countered, "at any time the Mayor and you wish to. I think it would be good for the people to know how much police time is taken up with bookmaking." I heard no more from either of them on the subject.

While I was learning about the shortcomings of our criminal justice system in the Magistrate's Court and becoming unhappy with what I saw, the other members of our family were faring reasonably well. Frank, the hardest working and the most industrious of all of us, had won advancement in the fruit and vegetable industry. His upward move was not spectacular but rather earned through complete devotion and back-breaking labor. He had been advanced to the position of buyer in the wholesale fruit and vegetable firm of Henry Kelly & Sons in the Washington Market and was the envy of many who could not find employment, much less advancement. Paul had passed his bar examination and was making some modest gains in the trial courts.

In Ireland, my four sisters who had been trained as teachers in Scotland and in England, were following their profession in Glasgow, Newcastle and Hull. One by one they came back to teach in Ireland as vacancies occurred. Among them they feathered the nest, and in the course of time three of them married and began to raise families.

There was, however, one more tragedy among us. With Prohibition ended, Jack had abandoned his rather unsuccessful career as a prize fight manager and closed the door of his speakeasy on 65th Street and Broadway in Manhattan. With a partner named Andrew Gallagher, he opened up a restaurant in the Borough Hall section of Brooklyn. One night in June 1934 Bill Donnell, a detective friend of Jack's, came to his restaurant at closing time. With two girls, they went to another establishment several blocks away. It was their misfortune that three gunmen at that same time had decided to rob the place. Donnell drew his pistol and fired in their direction. The gunmen returned the fire and Jack was hit in the groin. He died ten days later of streptococcus infection in the Holy Family Hospital.

The tragedy had its effect both in New York and Ireland. Jack had never married and left no widow, but my mother was deeply affected by his death and immediately thereafter began to decline steadily in health. She died six months afterwards at the age of 65. Kitty and I had been to Ireland the year before, and my mother was then in good health, but the death of her son far away in a strange place seemed more tragic than if it had happened at her home.

The holdup men who had been responsible for Jack's death were apprehended and convicted. A hearing was held before Governor Lehman on the question of commutation. It was customary for the victim's

With Paul and Kathleen O'Dwyer, 1939

family to be given an opportunity to oppose commutation, but, after a family conference, we decided not to participate in the hearing. The one who had actually fired the shot was electrocuted. The sentences of the others were commuted to life imprisonment.

Frank and Paul had been living in their own apartment on Plaza Street, Brooklyn, and they gave every indication of becoming permanent Irish bachelors. Kathleen Rohan broke up that combination in 1935, when she and Paul were married at the Polish Church on Green Avenue. Frank carried on the tradition for seven more years at which time he married Mae Sweeney of Bayonne and set up vegetable farming in the Imperial Valley, California, the hottest place in the whole world.

I continued to find the experience as a city magistrate sometimes rewarding, sometimes frustrating. There was some satisfaction in being able to settle some of the squabbling where the poverty and hoplessness of the time were reflected in quarrels over trivia between neighbors. However, there were many inequities which favored the well-heeled miscreant over the impoverished offender. The court personnel, the prosecutor and the judge had grown accustomed to the injustice. It was apparent that in the Magistrate's Court, in the greatest democracy with the finest tradition, there was indeed one law for the rich and another for the poor.

In addition to the frustrations of my professional life, there was also increasing concern at home. By 1937, Kitty's health was deteriorating steadily. The doctors had recommended another operation, medical costs were rising, and the security I thought I had was beginning to vanish. At the fixed salary I was earning, I was bound to end up in financial difficulty. I began to talk to friends about what my chances might be of bettering my position were I to return to the law practice.

CHAPTER 23

COUNTY COURT (1938-1939)

The decision to continue in public service came about in an unexpected way. It could not possibly have been planned, and the people who were responsible for moving me in that direction were neither personal friends nor political associates. During an accidental meeting with John Crews, Brooklyn Republican county leader, he mentioned that he had heard that I was considering retiring from the bench. Of all the people whom I had met in politics, Crews was the only really genuine person whom I had come to know. "I should encourage you to quit, Bill," he said. "If you go, Fiorello owes me this one and I'd probably get your replacement, but I think there is a great future for you in politics. If you quit now, it will either spell the end of your career or set you back several years. I know you couldn't get to first base with McCoey, but McCoey is dead and gone, and Frank Kelly is altogether another kind of man."

"I've met him," I said, "and he seems friendly enough, but I hear Johnston runs the Democratic Party in Brooklyn now." The man to whom I referred was Appellate Division Judge John B. Johnston. "That's not completely true. Kelly relies on Johnston a great deal, but better Johnston than some of the characters who were around McCoey. If you're considering resigning anyway, it could do you no harm to talk to Kelly." I mulled over what Crews had said and decided to take his advice.

To understand Brooklyn politics of the time, it is important to understand its unique character and individuality. Just as Borough Hall stood out as a handsome yet unconventional creation of its kind, easily discernible among its surroundings, so too did Brooklyn politics stand out as a special entity separate from the rest of the city. Brooklyn, in fact, *was* a separate entity for over two centuries, until a bridge, the wonder of the period, brought Brooklyn and Manhattan together. But even after the amalgamation, Brooklyn continued to maintain its separate identity.

Borough Hall, rather than City Hall, became the center of Brooklyn's political and municipal life and claimed the prime attention of the borough's expanding population. Brooklyn commissioners, Brooklyn deputy commissioners and Brooklyn bureau heads were as numerous as the tasks they were designed to perform, and their departments designed to maintain Brooklyn's own political machinery, so that there would be no need for its citizens to cross over to Manhattan, that out-of-the-way territory on the other side of the East River.

Among the constellation of public offices none was more prestigious and none more coveted than the office of public administrator. The fact that the holder of the post did not have to be a lawyer gave it a special appeal. There were so many political openings for which a law degree was required that a non-lawyer in politics suffered a distinct disadvantage. Frank V. Kelly, a power in Brooklyn Democratic politics and the heir apparent to Boss McCoey, the county leader, was not a lawyer, and the public administrator's spot might well have been created with him in mind.

The title gave no clue as to the functions of the office. The public administrator had little to do with the public. Every day in New York several people of means die without having made a will and without known relatives. Relatives eventually show up in most cases, but in the meantime the estate has to be administered. Conducting the affairs of the deceased until relatives appear on the scene is the sole and exclusive function of the public administrator. The appointment was made by the surrogate, who invariably owed his election to the party in power, and it had long been the custom, honored equally by Republicans and Democrats, that the party was given the privilege of recommending the candidate.

George Albert Wingate, a man of respectable WASP background, was the Brooklyn surrogate. Besides appointing the public administrator, the surrogate had the privilege of appointing special guardians to look after infants, unknown heirs and incompetents. These guardians are paid out of the estate, with the surrogate fixing their compensation. From a political point of view, control of the Surrogate's Court was often the deciding factor in keeping the Republicans or the Democrats in control of a county and could keep a county leader of either party invulnerable to attack by any rising ambitious rival.

Wingate's own coronation as surrogate was a tribute to the political skill and acumen of County Boss John McCoey, Frank Kelly's predecessor. After World War I Brooklyn's politics were beginning to reflect the influx of Democrats who left crowded Manhattan to seek refuge around the farmlands of Flatbush. Wingate's law firm was well known and respected in Brooklyn, and it counted among its clients the descen-

dants of the first settlers of the borough. They were Republican, Protestant, respected and well-to-do, in that order. Fame came to George
Albert Wingate on the battlefield in France in World War I, and he was
due to return an Army general and Brooklyn's hero.

At that very time, a vacancy in the Surrogate's Court was looming
on the horizon. The Republican leadership had in mind, in due course,
to offer General Wingate some respectable, lucrative post as would befit
his reputation and prestige. McCoey recognized the value to the Democratic Party of having Wingate on the ticket. He met the general at the
boat and lost no time in explaining his mission. Then and there, McCoey
offered the Surrogate's Court, with all its trappings, to the returning
war hero. Wingate was mildly surprised that fame had preceded him,
flattered by the attention he was receiving, and duly impressed by
McCoey's ingenuity. Wingate's acceptance matched the speed of the
offer, and the Democratic Party had gained a firm and permanent foothold in Brooklyn. The surrogate designee agreed to abide by the party
principles and, most important of all, to honor the sacred rules of patronage. In less than a year after he was elected as surrogate, Wingate
appointed Frank Kelly as public administrator of Brooklyn, and for the
next 16 years the surrogate and the public administrator showed their
devotion to the Democratic Party in every appointment that came within
their jurisdiction.

By the terms of his office, Frank Kelly had control over large sums
of money left by deceased persons, and he had discretion to put it in
whatever bank he chose, there to remain undisturbed until relatives
showed up to prove kinship to the deceased. It was a lucrative piece of
business, and local bankers were well aware of the advantage of being
on the right side of the Democratic Party and of the public administrator.
They usually showed their appreciation by buying tables for the party's
annual fundraising dinner, and they found other ways of easing the
party's financial burden around election time. Kelly, like his predecessors, had a generous number of deputies to look after the belongings
of the unmourned dead, and from this vantage point had ample time
to look to the needs of the Democratic Party. He became a force to be
reckoned with in the county.

Three blocks away, John B. Johnston, in the prestigious chambers
of Associate Judge of the Appellate Division of the Supreme Court, State
of New York, exercised a kind of veto power over all important party
decisions. Surrounded by an array of secretaries, lawyers and clerks,
Johnston found that his performance as a judge in no way hampered
his avocation as kingmaker, patronage dispenser and policy architect for
the county boss. No decision was made to support any candidate, from
the local assemblyman all the way to the President of the United States,

without Johnston's stamp of approval. He was the most powerful single force in the most populous county in the state and the nation. Yet his name never appeared in the papers.

In 1937 I could not tell if Judge Johnston was aware of my existence but I had seen and spoken to Kelly at some public functions. He was not an intimate, but neither was he a stranger to me when I went to visit him that year. His greeting was cordial, as he beckoned me to a seat in front of the large desk which dominated the room he occupied.

"Mr. Kelly," I started, "I've come to talk to you about my own future. I have about concluded that I must move on from the Magistrate's Court, and John Crews suggested I talk to you about it." "It was good that you came, Bill," he replied. "We would have sent for you within the month anyway. You see, I have inherited considerable troubles here. The District Attorney's office is in terrible shape, and La Guardia is only waiting for the next election to move against us, and we have to be extremely careful about our selection two years hence or we will lose the second most important office in the county." (Admittedly, the first was the Surrogate's Court.) "Judge Johnston and I have been discussing this and we will come to a decision soon. We are going over several names, one of which we hope to groom for that position. An independent, these days, seems to have an edge," he said. And then, with a smile, "provided he has organization backing. And I don't mind telling you, you are one of those under consideration."

A week or so later, I received a message in court that Kelly wanted to see me. But this time the meeting place was the rather posh Montauk Club in Park Slope. "That's a good sign," said Eddie Ross, the *Daily News* reporter in the 23rd Street court. "Kelly reserves the Montauk Club for his serious discussions with prospective candidates or appointments. The weeding out process takes place first at the Democratic headquarters or at Johnston's chambers or at Kelly's apartment in The Towers."

"We have a proposal to put to you." It was the Democratic boss in his most serious mood. "I'm sure you will find it attractive." Then he became pompous. "You are our first choice and we have selected you on the basis of your background and record. The people still like the Horatio Alger kind of candidate, and we will need the best. We want you to run for District Attorney with the party's backing two years from now." Now he became patronizing. "But as a magistrate, you lack prestige, no matter what may be your qualifications. As county judge, that's something else. Algernon Nova has been elected to the Supreme Court, and Governor Lehman soon will fill his vacancy. I am recommending several names to the Governor with emphasis on yours. You can then run for election as the sitting judge next year for a 14-year term, but you will have to agree to become a candidate for District Attorney in 1940

With Frank Kelly, Brooklyn Democratic leader, 1941

when Bill Geoghan's term ends." My salary as magistrate was $12,000 per annum, that of county judge would be $25,000, and of District Attorney, $20,000. The advance in salary would be most welcome.

It was now definite that Kitty was required to undergo serious operations in the Polyclinic Hospital, and the expenses at home were running high. "You may want time to think it over," he said, but I wasn't paying much attention to him. The proposal was better than I had hoped. I told him I didn't need time. "In that case, you should go immediately and see Judge Johnston at his home at Prospect Park West." An hour later Johnston repeated the script we were all to follow. "You will be elected county judge at $25,000 per annum for a 14-year term. Do you think you can give that up for a four-year term at $20,000?" "I have already said that I would live up to my bargain," I replied. The judge nodded, and I prepared to leave. "One more thing. Please watch your step. A breath of scandal can ruin all our plans." I knew I was a pawn, but as Oscar Bernstien said, it was the only way for me. Within the week I got a direct call from Governor Lehman appointing me as interim county judge.

Things were different now. No longer was there any hesitancy on the part of the Brooklyn Bar Association at finding me qualified for the post, and they promptly advised Governor Lehman to that effect. As a matter of fact, they requested to be recognized at the induction ceremony and sent Frank Wing Holmes, my old associate, to speak at the occasion on their behalf.

Friends and family were there, and Mitchell May, one of the first crop of Jewish judges to be elected in Brooklyn, administered the oath. Many of the participants spoke about the democracy which permitted the immigrant boy to acquire such a prestigious and important office. The theme of each speaker varied very little until it came time for Frank Holmes to say his piece. He said he had looked into my background and had found that I had come to the United States from an atmosphere of culture, that prior to my landing, I had acquired a secondary education, and that for a considerable period I had attended Salamanca, one of Europe's oldest universities. Those kinds of facts may have been important, but obviously they were not considered newsworthy, and nowhere in the account of the proceedings in *The Brooklyn Daily Eagle* or *The Citizen* was there any mention of Mr. Holmes' revelations. "I hope you don't have Mr. Holmes around at campaign time," admonished Frank Kelly. "That kind of talk could hurt your candidacy." "You don't have to be concerned," I said, "Frank Holmes is a staunch Republican, and it is unlikely that he will repeat any word of praise for me come election time." "That's a relief," said the Brooklyn chieftain.

"I am recommending Fred Loughran, a young lawyer, as your secretary," said Kelly. "And for your lesser assignments, you would do well to listen to Dan Corrigan. John B. thinks very highly of his judgment."

On my first day in office I met Corrigan. He was virtually in charge of all assignments in the county court. A fatherly man, he proceeded to tell me about my surroundings. Then, after a pause, he came to what obviously was to him the most important point in the orientation process. "Mr. Kelly and Judge Johnston," he said, "want to make sure I watch out for you here. Your reputation, Judge, is very important to them. And I hope you won't mind if I speak plainly." "I wouldn't have it any other way." "Well, Judge," he continued, "for a beginning, everybody knows you have a sick wife, and this court is full of gossip. I would get a male rather than a female stenographer/secretary. We have under the title of court attendant a male stenographer who worked for the largest law firms downtown. I'm sure he would be very pleased if he got the chance to hang up his uniform and work for you. His name is Jim Moran." And so my limited staff was rounded out, and I set about the business of trying the felony cases which were assigned to me by the District Attorney's office.

These included highway robbery, burglary, rape and homicide. Even an indictment for riot came before me. I recognized the latter as a further attempt to use the courts as a way of punishing dissenters, and I dismissed it with an opinion in which Oscar Bernstien's fine hand could readily be seen by anybody familiar with his style.

At the Montauk Club I had mentioned to Frank Kelly that, because of my handling of *The Eagle* strikers, my appointment to higher office was not likely to gain the enthusiastic approval of *The Eagle*. "I don't see it as serious," he said. "But I'm glad you mentioned it. Judge Johnston will see to it that you get fair treatment." *The Eagle*'s editorial went further than I had hoped: "Governor Lehman is to be congratulated on his non-political selection to fill the vacancy on the county court bench . . . William O'Dwyer is not a politican in the ordinary sense of the word . . . Magistrate O'Dwyer has made a fine record on the bench." Unless one would come to the conclusion that Kelly and Johnston had suddenly acquired the rank of statesmen, I doubt that there ever was a more political appointment. The grooming process included being named Grand Marshal in the St. Patrick's Day Parade in 1938, and the following year receiving a special award as the number one citizen of Brooklyn.

In the meantime, Miles McDonald, a young politician, managed my 1938 campaign for county judge at the request of Johnston and Kelly. The campaign was not without its difficulties. Louis D. Waldman, a very prominent labor lawyer, had been originally elected to the Assembly way back in 1919 as a Socialist. Because of the hysteria of the time, he was never given his seat in Albany. Now, Waldman was induced by LaGuardia to oppose me. La Guardia promised to get him the Republican and the American Labor Party nominations. A friend of mine, Louis Hamburg, who had been high in the councils of the Republican Party, lent a hand on my behalf. He induced Harold Turk, a Gowanus-Republican leader, to enter the Republican primary against Waldman, and while the Republican county organization dutifully gave its approval to Waldman, the Republican rank and file were not ready to make common cause with someone they considered a downright radical. Turk became the winner and that made the election a three-way contest. It meant my opposition was split in two, and victory in the general election was assured.

Even though the ploy had been successful, Judge Johnston was annoyed. "We have given you the nomination and without a primary," he said. "We stand ready to pay all the campaign expenses, and I have assigned Miles McDonald of one of the oldest political families in Brooklyn to manage your campaign. You would be well advised to leave the political decisions to those who know them best."

It was a firm rebuke, and I knew that sometime in the future a confrontation was in the making. "Hold your temper," said Paul and Oscar, and I did, although one of the two who had offered that sage advice could hardly be considered a successful practitioner of the art.

CHAPTER 24

ELECTION TO DISTRICT ATTORNEY
AND
MURDER, INC. (1940-1941)

From about 1934 to 1939 the scene in New York City had become darkened by the lengthening shadows of Adolf Hitler. His agents or counterparts, admirers or apologists in this city were formed into groups. Many Germans, by birth or extraction, formed into "Bunds" and openly carried Hitler's banner—the Nazi swastika. They were joined by native-born American fascists. Non-German groups also came into being, some out of suspicion or hatred of Great Britain, rather than any affection for the Nazis. It was inevitable, however, that all of them would develop a strong anti-Semitic attitude. Many Americans either friendly to the Nazis or opposed to Great Britain joined an organization known as the Christian Front. Their more militant arm was known as the Christian Mobilizers. In time they began to openly threaten Jewish citizens. Jews on their way to synagogues on Friday nights, particularly in Brooklyn, would go around the block rather than pass the places where the anti-Semites held their meetings.

But even that precaution did not help, as the mob would pursue the worshippers, threatening them and hurling insults in their direction, in what apparently was an attempt to provoke retaliation. A group of Jewish leaders headed by Maximilian Moss recorded the insults and threats and played the recording back for the Mayor. His answer to their protest was unsatisfactory to these leaders, who represented over a million Jewish residents in Brooklyn. It was evident that the Jewish community, and particularly the younger ones, would no longer tolerate these conditions, and not getting any satisfaction from the law or the political leadership, they would undoubtedly go on the attack.

Max Moss, Nathaniel Kaplan and Eddie Silver talked to me about what they knew was brewing. It was evident that a very ugly situation was in the making, and if authority did not intervene, it would be out of the hands of the seasoned and respected Jewish leaders and was sure to wind up in bloodshed.

As an Irish candidate for District Attorney in 1939, I met this issue head on. Cautious campaign advisors warned that an affirmative, aggressive position would antagonize Irish Catholics, who made up the bulk of the Fronters and Mobilizers. I was pleasantly surprised when the vast majority applauded when I said that hooliganism on the streets of Brooklyn would not be tolerated "while I am District Attorney." I had not heard the last of the Christian Front, but I succeeded in separating them from the Irish American community.

Before we knew it, the real campaign was under way. La Guardia took a hand, as Kelly knew he would. He prevailed on the Republicans to nominate Chief Justice of Special Sessions William Bayes, a well-known and respected figure who owed his appointment to the Mayor. Magistrate Charles Solomon became the candidate of the American Labor Party. There was some question as to the propriety of a judge campaigning for a non-judicial office while serving on the bench. But since all three candidates were in the same position, the argument fell of its own weight. It seems if enough people do something questionable, that makes it all right.

The campaign got under way one evening when Judge Bayes and I met at Temple Beth Emeth on Church Avenue. There were not many issues which so deeply affected the Jewish community as the harassment they were being made to endure. My opponents were very unclear in their positions, and I was warmly received as I outlined what I felt was the appropriate thing to do when faced with the possibility of public disorder.

I continued to discuss the actions of the Christian Fronters during the rest of the campaign. Often they would come to heckle, but that always made for an interesting meeting and swelled the attendance, and I began to look forward to their appearance to liven things up a bit.

One night I spoke at the Jesuit Labor School in Crown Heights, at the opening of its labor-management relationship class. I had been invited to visit the home of Judge Nathan Sweedler afterwards. When I arrived, the entire board of Yeshiva College and Maximilian Moss were on hand. Mr. Moss said to me, "Judge, we know of your reputation and have decided not to ask you any questions." "I wish every citizen of Brooklyn who is worried could ask me personally how I feel regarding anything pertinent to the office of District Attorney."

One man said, "Judge, as you are aware, the Jewish people are in serious trouble. What will you do for them if you are selected?" I replied, "If you are disturbed in your rights as citizens, I want you to come to me and state your complaints, and my responsibilities will begin at that point."

Another man asked, "Will you go to see Bishop Molloy on our behalf about these Christian Fronters?" I stated, "No, sir, I am not running for bishop, I am running for District Attorney. If I am leaving your house and someone spits in my face, or otherwise insults me, where should I go for assistance, to the parish priest or to the policeman on the post. I will assume full responsibility on my own without consulting anyone."

Beginning with Columbus Day and ending on the night of November 5, the tempo of the campaign rose sharply and there seemed to be no end to the speeches and campaign oratory. At long last Election Day came, and that night the faithful passed the time at Democratic headquarters at 5 Boerum Place, awaiting the election results. I was in attendance mixing with them. Frank Kelly was in a private room, surrounded by his cohorts, and Judge Johnston was upstairs tabulating. Messengers would come down with little slips of paper, and Kelly was looking pleased. At the local district headquarters, election district captains would come to the clubhouse with figures from the precincts. The district leader would pat the captain on the back, and that reward was sufficient to make the captain feel a kinship to Jefferson, Jackson and Roosevelt and the revered founders of the party. Likewise, a district leader would straggle in from the precinct with small pieces of paper in his hand and the county leader would pat *him* on the back, and the district leader thought of *himself* as an important part of the machinery of the party. I may have been a sort of temporary hero in the street, but at Democratic headquarters that night, I filled a secondary and supporting role. I'm sure they felt I was fortunate to be the man selected by the machine to add to the stature of Kelly, their great leader.

My opponents went through the formality of conceding my election at 10:30 p.m. in a telegram of congratulations. I went home to bed that night exhilarated and at the same time exhausted, but very happy and somewhat frustrated. I felt democracy was generous to winning candidates, but why could it not be accomplished without a county leader and a sinister judge.

When I came home, Kitty was awake and talking to the nurse. She had not gone through her last operation very satisfactorily. Edna Davis, lately of Virginia, who filled the role of friend and companion, was up too, even though the hour was late. Kitty said to me, "I'm glad to see you happy, but I am afraid of it. Are you sure you won't come to any harm?" I gave her all the assurance I could. After a while she calmed down and grew drowsy, and Miss Bergen, the nurse, motioned for me to leave.

In the morning Kitty felt better. She came down to breakfast, and although she was afraid of newspaper cameras because she no longer looked well, she submitted to a barrage of flashbulbs and answered all kinds of questions about her reaction to the election. She had plenty of courage. When she wanted to, she could hold herself in check. Even though suffering from nerves, she was still in control.

Before taking office on January 1, I selected almost all new men. Some of them belonged to the Democratic Party, were active in their local scene, and were recommended by their leaders. There were others similarly recommended who did not measure up to the standards I had set, and I did not appoint them. Some had no affiliation with any political party. A few holdovers were within a year or so of their pensions, and I kept them.

Between November and January, I frequently called Jack Osnato, a detective lieutenant from Brooklyn and a skilled investigator, who gave me the benefit of his tremendous knowledge and experience. I was very much in favor of appointing Osnato, a lifelong friend, as head of the District Attorney's police force. He was intelligent, energetic and loyal, but something that Commissioner Valentine had said about him gave me the impression that there was a personal feud between the two men. Both had done police duty in adjoining precincts in Brooklyn, where Valentine was the captain and Osnato the lieutenant in charge of a formidable detective force. It was very important for me to have Valentine's cooperation, so I did not appoint Osnato.

I had John Gorman assigned to my office. Gorman had been appointed to the police department with me, we went to the Police Academy together, and we had been assigned to the same station house as rookies. I caused John to be transferred to my squad from the Broadway squad, where he had come to know most of the thugs and their haunts. Some of the data he picked up at such places as fight camps became invaluable in important cases.

Jim Furey had gained a reputation for his work on the auto squad. I had him assigned to me and gave him the special job of tracking down stolen cars.

With the approval of La Guardia and Police Commissioner Valentine, I put Captain Frank Bals in charge of detectives and police officers assigned to the District Attorney's office. Often cited for bravery in the performance of duty, Bals had figured in many sensational cases, including the Judd Gray-Ruth Snyder murder. For some time, he had been in charge of the station house covering the Bath Beach section, which was then a hangout for many vicious criminal gang leaders.

The press comments on my election were favorable. Even the *Brooklyn Eagle* had a word of praise: "Judge O'Dwyer has kept his campaign pledge to clean house in the prosecutor's office and to base his appointments on fitness and experience without regard to politics. Up to the moment he announced his new staff yesterday, insiders in the Democratic organization were in the dark about his plans, and many of his selections were complete surprises."

La Guardia, however, lost no time in going on the attack. He was particularly critical of the appointment of Miles McDonald, my campaign manager of a year earlier. "His father, John McDonald," La Guardia charged, "was chief clerk of the Surrogate's Court and a close friend of the late Boss McCoey, 'Grabby' Kelly's predecessor." ("Grabby" was La Guardia's special title for Frank V. Kelly.) La Guardia's abuse was constantly directed at the five Irish county leaders. He cited them by name over and over and over. The citizens could hardly fail to get the message that New York was somehow out of balance.

La Guardia did ask me to get rid of one man, John Harlan Amen, whom Governor Thomas E. Dewey had assigned to Brooklyn as special prosecutor. La Guardia claimed Amen's office cost too much. I said any such move on my part would be misconstrued. "You put him there, it's up to you to take him out. As long as he's there, I'll cooperate with him," I told the Mayor.

The moment I took office I sent a patrol of District Attorney police to check on the sidewalk rowdies, after which they gave me no more trouble. They picked up and left Brooklyn and did not come back. Their spokesman made some statements to the effect that I would receive my punishment in hell for what I had done, and I think they believed it. They continued to operate in Yorkville until our country went into the war.

Another situation that required immediate action was overcrowding at the Raymond Street Jail—two prisoners to a cell where there should have been one. That presented a special problem and one that could have exploded at any time. I immediately set about disposing of the backlog of cases, and, in a few months, the jail population was down to less than one to a cell. During the two and a half years I was District Attorney, with a young and energetic staff, eager to work, we never again let overcrowding at the jail build up.

The Appellate Court had a serious backlog problem. Harry Walsh was an old and experienced lawyer in charge of the appeals division. He was well regarded in the Court of Appeals, and I had retained him. However, I assigned Solomon Asa Klein, a brilliant, young brief writer whom Paul recommended to me, as his assistant. In no time the backlog of appeals disappeared and the appellate calendar was brought up to date.

The highlight of my term of office was our successful war on what was to become known as "Murder, Inc." Murders had become so common during the 1930's that newspapers paid little heed to them. It is not difficult to recognize a gangland killing. The characteristics are the deliberate, cold-blooded, carefully planned execution with every detail considered, with the getaway carefully arranged and stealthily carried out. The unusually large number of unsolved murders in Brooklyn was fair evidence of police incompetence or police corruption. Commissioner Valentine was aware of it and it was embarrassing, yet he was publicly prodded by La Guardia into the pursuit of gambling and prostitution at the expense of the more serious crimes.

These murders were conducted with so much efficiency and secrecy that the police and prosecutors were baffled. Some of the bodies were disposed of a hundred or more miles away under circumstances where it would be difficult to recover or identify the body, and therefore proof of the corpus delecti was made extremely difficult. After a flurry of police activity, followed by no leads, the police would discontinue any further investigation. There might be an occasional arrest, but that was as far as it went.

I asked Valentine to agree that the work of the detective squad in my office would become confidential. The men were to report to me without the usual carbon copies floating through various channels with no protection from police department leaks. With some reluctance, Valentine agreed.

I then directed my staff, which included Captain Bals and about 30 detectives, to break through the curtain that hid the perpetrators of these unsolved murders. My plan was to somehow start at the bottom and go as high up as I could. I directed the squad to spread out a net by rounding up and bringing in some small-time Brooklyn hoods whom we suspected of having knowledge of or complicity in the killings. Twenty-five were caught, and I assigned Kenneth McCabe, then a neophyte, to prosecute them. All were convicted under the vagrancy statutes and given 60 days. The net got us a couple of important fish, including "Happy" Maione and "The Dasher" Abbandando. Now, at least, we had them where we could get them for the next 60 days.

It had been quite a while since Maione had served any time in jail. His status was being threatened, and he railed against the indignity of being convicted of vagrancy. "If O'Dwyer don't stop pushing us around," he confided in a fellow prisoner, "we'll start dropping 'packages' on every lot in Brooklyn. That's going to keep him really busy." A "package" was parlance for the body of a murder victim.

In any prosecutor's office, the mail is a frequent source of information and crime detection. I gave specific instructions as to what to watch for in the mail, and the program soon paid dividends far beyond our expectations. One morning my secretary brought in a penciled note

154

from Rikers Island. Signed by a prisoner named Harry Rudolf, it contained the terse message: "I seen a murder and I want to tell you about it." I had Rudolf brought to my office. He gave information on the murder of Alex "Red" Alpert in 1933, naming Abe Reles, "Bugsy" Goldstein and "Duke" Maffetore as the executioners. All three of them had been in and out of the Raymond Street Jail dozens of times in the seven years that had intervened since Alpert's murder, although Maffetore, the youngest, had never been convicted of any crime.

Knowing that communication among the three would be easy in the jailhouse, I took the precaution of having them assigned to different jails: Maffetore to the Bronx, Goldstein to Staten Island, and Reles to the Tombs in Manhattan. This maneuver caused uneasiness with the mob. Albert Anastasia, Jack Parisi and Tony Romeo temporarily disappeared from New York.

Michael McDermott, an experienced, intelligent policeman, was the Police Department's borough inspector for Brooklyn. He had been placed in this sensitive post by Valentine and La Guardia to watch things and report. After the first arrests, one of his sergeants talked altogether too freely and at a place where the word was carried to Louis Capone, Albert Anastasia's right-hand man. As a result, an indictment in the Alpert case could not possibly end in anything but dismissal. I got accurate information on the matter from my own police squad and had the sergeant transferred. This was the beginning of an open break between McDermott, Valentine and myself.

We were now getting our first inkling of how these murders were arranged and what the *modus operandi* was. It started out with the mob's acquisition of young recruits who served an apprenticeship. These young thugs would be given pinball machine concessions, and that would obligate them to steal automobiles or to drive a getaway car or to dispose of a "package" after a gangland execution. We learned of their preference for special weapons. In addition to the blackjack, baseball bat and lead pipe, the murder weapon was often the sash cord used as a garrote, or the ice pick driven into the lungs or heart.

From the information we were piecing together, we were made aware of a hidden and highly organized syndicate which extended far beyond New York's boundary. We found out that the "combination's" activities in Brooklyn had brought it special notoriety, making its members' services desired in various parts of the U.S., where they were sometimes hired out as special mercenaries. The combination lived off gambling, bookmaking, and prostitution, and they policed these territorial monopolies. Jurisdictional disputes were settled by the top leaders, and no killing was authorized unless it passed through the "court."

The personnel who were charged with carrying out these edicts were a strange assortment of characters who had all come out of New York's slums and had worked their way through its jungle. The two men who had come to leadership and were now directing the affairs of the combination from a safe distance were Albert Anastasia and Louis Capone. Both had graduated from actual participation in the killing. They were now the executioners from afar, giving orders and receiving the reports after the murders had been committed and the bodies disposed of. Capone was closer to the crime, in most cases providing Anastasia an extra layer of insulation.

Better known in the street was Abe Reles, an activist who was seen and heard frequently around gangster haunts. "Pittsburgh" Phil Strauss had earned a reputation as a vicious thug. He was close to Reles and a recognized expert in the use of the garrote. Martin "Bugsy" Goldstein was of equal stature to Strauss as was "Happy" Maione, Seymour "Blue Jaw" Magoon and Charles "the Bug" Workman, who acted as the special representative of Louis "Lepke" Buchalter to the Brooklyn troops.

I directed that the Alpert murder case be presented to the grand jury. Harry Rudolf was not the most impressive witness, but his testimony was sufficient to satisfy the grand jury. It returned an indictment against Maffetore, Reles and Goldstein. There was no provision for bail in a first-degree murder case, so all three were required to remain in jail until trial. The indictment was significant in that it was the first time these hoodlums could be kept in jail for any appreciable length of time, and that fact alone was a signal to the mob that there was trouble brewing.

"Duke" Maffetore was the youngest of the trio and was in every sense an apprentice. I asked Jack Osnato to visit him in the jail. Osnato, known to every gangster in Brooklyn, was both feared and respected by them. It was my hope that he would be successful in getting Maffetore to tell what he knew about Alpert and several other mob killings. Osnato could speak several Italian dialects, including the one "The Duke" knew. Osnato warned him that the mob was getting ready to fix the blame for the Alpert murder on him. The first visit proved unsuccessful but the door was opened, and Osnato kept up his visits.

Harry Rudolf was sent an offer of $5,000 if he would accuse Maffetore and exonerate Reles and Goldstein. This confirmed Osnato's information, and he lost no time in bringing the news to Maffetore. The circumstances of the offer rang true and were sufficient, with some persuading from Osnato, to convince "The Duke" to come forward and give evidence of what he knew, not only about the Alpert murder but all he knew about Reles.

Osnato's visit to my office to inform me of his success marked the turning point in our drive against the gangster world. Yet he made the announcement in a most matter-of-fact way: " 'The Duke' will talk to you," he said, as if what he had done was no great achievement. Soon Maffetore was in my office. "Who worked with you?" I asked him. By now I knew the underlings usually operated in pairs. "I always worked with 'Pretty' Levine," he replied, providing us with another link in the chain. Levine was later to tell us about several murders that were carried out in upstate New York.

By this time we were getting reports from the jail that Abe Reles was showing signs of irritation. Reles was sometimes referred to as "Kid Twist," but the nickname was not used nearly as much as his given name. In Brownsville, just the mention of it was enough to strike fear in the hearts of its victimized citizens.

During Reles' youth, the Shapiro brothers were the ruling mob and controlled every form of vice in the area of Brownsville and East New York. Reles and Goldstein teamed up with the Maione crew and literally wiped out the whole Shapiro mob, sending out word that there had been a change in management, but that business would continue as usual. That took place around the time Prohibition was ending. Among the activities of the new establishment was the "protection" system. Every store in Brownsville was required to pay a given stipend per month or suffer the consequences.

News of the manner in which Reles, Goldstein and Maione carried out their takeover spread quickly, and the new dynasty had little trouble in assuming command of the Shapiro "business" territory. Reles had become better known, and he relished having people quake at the sound of his voice. Once a Negro garage attendant didn't move fast enough to suit Reles and compounded his offense by talking back to the new boss. Reles broke a bottle over the attendant's head. The black man was incensed and could neither be bought nor threatened. With unusual courage, he brought charges and testified against Reles at the trial. Reles was convicted for the first and only time in his life. The judge sentenced him to Elmira Reformatory, where he served three years. Reles learned a lesson from this encounter he would never forget. He was never, thereafter, convicted, although he was arrested frequently.

When the indictment for the murder of Alpert was handed down by the grand jury, Reles showed little sign of fear. He had the benefit of an evaluation of the case from police loose talk, and he therefore knew that Rudolf was not going to be reliable and that his shortcomings would easily be exposed in cross-examination. "I don't need no lawyer to beat this rap," Reles boasted.

As part of the war of nerves, Osnato lost no time in letting it be known that Maffetore was "singing." Reles began to lose his self-assuredness. Rudolf was one thing, but the combination of Rudolf and

Maffetore was something to be reckoned with.

We kept in touch with Rose, Reles' wife. She came from a good, hard-working, decent family who were beside themselves with grief and worry for her. She continued to speak with our detectives, and finally one day she told one of them that Abe wanted to speak to me, but to me alone. It was on the eve of Good Friday when the news came.

To say that there was excitement in the office at this turn of events was to put it mildly. Maffetore and Levine had been helpful, but Reles knew the mob from top to bottom. He was familiar with the minute details of every crime they had planned and committed. Indeed, he had taken part in almost all of them. Cooperation from Reles would mean a sensational breakthrough.

At three in the morning he was brought into my office. He told Detective Boyle that he was hungry. We were cautious lest this announcement be part of a jailbreak plan. I sent out for a sandwich and coffee and watched him as he ate. He really was hungry.

Reles was reluctant to speak at first while others were in the room. "I could tell you plenty," he said. "But what happens to me, and can I trust you?" "You know John McDonough?" I asked. He nodded his head. John was a Brownsville detective who could not be bought, and all the gangsters in that detective division gave him a wide berth. McDonough had never testified to a lie in order to convict any of them, and they trusted his word. "McDonough's working with us," I told him. "I know you have a great deal of information that could be useful to us, and I will see to it that you are given every consideration."

"Look, you got any ideas of the friends the mob has in high places?"

"That makes no difference to me," I replied.

"There ain't a man in the world they can't get if they go after him." He paused, "If I talk, what do you do for me? If I come clean, I mean."

"If you do give me all the information you have without holding back and you are willing to tell it in court, you can rely on me to do the right thing by you." I spent some anxious moments waiting for his reaction. He thought it over. I could see his mind working: "They have me anyhow and, besides, they could double-cross me. I've got no other way out." What came from his lips was something of a surprise.

"If I come clean and you're hurt, what about me? If I play ball, you might not last a week. They'll get you higher up. They have influence all the way to the top, I tell you. And they'll get me, too, even though I'm in the clink. They'll figure out a way to poison me or something."

No one knew better than Reles how far the mobsters would go to get their man. They had disposed of every witness against Louis "Lepke." And they had bought their way out of the Druckman murder case a few years earlier right here in Brooklyn. And, we were to find out a short time later, they had actually plotted to murder Thomas Dewey. For me to be successful, I knew it wasn't enough to protect only Reles. There were other informants who would become valuable witnesses in one or more of the cases. Each of them required full protection. I realized that in jail there were too many ways in which these witnesses could be tampered with or killed.

When I told Reles that he would be kept under heavy guard in the Bossert Hotel, where Dave Martin, the manager, was a friend whom I could trust, the last obstacle was removed. I called in our two stenographers, Frank Maguire and John Canevari. The questioning kept us there till dawn. But we believed him when he told in sordid detail of 85 murders committed by the mob in Brooklyn and in many other places all over the country. Many of the murderers were unknown to the police until Reles told about them. He confessed to participation in many of them. In some cases he was aided by many of the young "troopers," who were paid as little as five or ten dollars for their services.

In the end, I credited Jack Osnato's tenacity in getting Reles to talk and thereby opening up the whole sordid story. When it was all put together, *New York Times* reporter John Popham, in wonderment, exclaimed, "This is really Murder, Inc." and the name stuck.

Thereafter came the exacting job of checking each story, assembling the facts in each of the many cases, presenting the facts to the grand jury and resisting the many attacks on the ensuing indictments by the most able criminal lawyers to be found.

I appointed Burton B. Turkus, a young, ambitious and very able trial lawyer and a friend of Paul, to try the heavy murder cases. Knowing that convictions obtained with the help of co-conspirators would be most carefully scrutinized by the Court of Appeals, I assigned Solomon A. Klein to be the law assistant at the trial. The trials, in many of which Reles played a lead role, stretched out over a period of two years. When all the trials had been completed and the cases finally decided by the higher courts, almost all of the 85 murders had been solved and eight ruthless killers had been executed in Sing Sing Prison.

Reles who starred throughout these sensational trials was still in our custody. He was held under heavy guard at the Half Moon Hotel in Coney Island. One night in November, 1941, his wife, who had been visiting him, left about 11 P.M. One of the detectives guarding him checked on him later. He seemed to have fallen asleep. Another looked in on him at 6:45 A.M. He appeared to be asleep with the radio on. A half hour later he was found dead on an extension to the hotel several floors below his room. He had knotted bedsheets into the form of a rope and added a piece of radio wire. He had tied one end to the radiator in his room and lowered himself out the window, presumably intending to get into the room below. The combination of bedsheets and wire was not fit to bear his weight and he fell to his death. So ended the career of a notorious killer and the most effective informer in the annals of criminal justice, at least in this part of the world.

CHAPTER 25

CAMPAIGN (1941)

In the history of New York, reform regimes have not long endured. La Guardia's proved to be an exception. He was elected in 1933, reelected by a huge majority in 1937, and was a candidate to succeed himself in 1941. Fiorello would give patronage consistently to the local Republican machine. At the same time, he supported the Democratic candidate for President of the United States. With this kind of maneuver, he kept the Democratic chieftains off balance and the Republicans tied to him through the bond of patronage, the strongest cord in the political storehouse.

In the first eight years of his administration, La Guardia kept up a constant attack on the Democratic Party and the five county leaders. The leaders were content if each could guard his territory against the Mayor's intrusion. As a result, the Democrats had failed to develop or produce a single candidate who could be expected to run a respectable race against him.

La Guardia continued to be on good terms with President Roosevelt, and, as a candidate to succeed himself, he was considered invincible. Among the Democratic leaders there was little hope of a victory in 1941, and there was little speculation as to whom the party candidate would be.

Following my successful campaign for District Attorney and the sensational exposure of Murder, Inc., my name was occasionally mentioned as the possible candidate. Brooklyn always had its civic pride, and Brooklynites were quick to point to their numerical strength and to the fact that they had not received favorable recognition in the selection of mayoral candidates for some 20 years. However, my entrance into political life had been less than orthodox. I did not come up through the ranks and was not a pure product of the regular party organization. Its previous support for me was born from the necessity of keeping La Guardia on the west side of the Brooklyn Bridge. I had performed well at the polls, but that did not ensure my entrance into the winner's circle of Democratic leadership. Normally, I would not have been favored by the political leaders as a candidate for Mayor, but the political situation at that time was most unusual.

In addition, my candidacy was not without support. I had been elected District Attorney with the aura of an independent who had organization support, a formidable combination. I had acquired a good record on the magistrate's bench, and my early performance as District Attorney had attracted city-wide attention. It takes almost daily repetition of a name and a picture in the media for a candidate to become "known." That qualification is not easily acquired, but I felt reasonably assured that the massive amount of publicity associated with my work made me a viable candidate.

Another advantage I had was that a prosecutor appears constantly to be a fighter against crime and lawlessness and a champion and protector of public order and safety—in short, a desirable candidate for higher office, irrespective of the qualifications to fill it. On the other hand, my record as a lawyer and candidate was not without its hidden weaknesses. I had been responsible for the prosecution of many murder cases and obtained many first degree convictions resulting in death in the electric chair, yet I was not a believer in capital punishment. Aside from being less than enthusiastic on ethical grounds, I had many doubts as to the effectiveness of the death penalty as a crime deterrent anywhere. I had the feeling that too often it was merely a surrender to the lynch spirit. When I was county judge, I asked the prosecutor not to assign capital cases to me, and I avoided imposing the death sentence during my time on the County Court bench.

There was another drawback. I had no rich friends—not any. La Guardia's reputation as a winner was going to stand him in good stead and discourage anyone from giving money to my campaign.

That meant that I had to rely on the party, but its national head, President Roosevelt, as well as Mrs. Roosevelt, had been supporters of La Guardia. Furthermore, La Guardia was an Episcopalian and had heavy financial support from their circles, and it was unlikely that any of them would desert him for me.

And yet, given the vacuum that existed in the Democratic Party, it was inevitable that I would be considered for the nomination. Speculation about my candidacy began to creep into the political columns of the newspapers. I was invited to be one of the speakers at the Democratic Party's annual Jefferson Day Dinner in 1940, and this helped to affirm the rumor that I was, indeed, a candidate. The *Daily News* of April 5, 1940, was first to put it in print. "If he gets a reasonable number of convictions," they wrote, "in the drive against the mob of alleged cut-rate murderers, O'Dwyer will most likely develop into the logical next

Being congratulated by Governor Herbert H. Lehman at a rally during Bill's first mayoral campaign, 1941

Democratic candidate for Mayor of New York."

Amid alternating moods, hope one day and stark realization of impossibility the next, I decided not to ask anyone to support me nor to make any move to get the nomination.

Nothing happened until mid-July, when I was invited by Ed Flynn, the Bronx county leader, to attend a luncheon at the National Democratic Club in Manhattan. Present at that luncheon were the city's other four county leaders. "We want you to run against La Guardia," Flynn said.

I was impressed by the unanimous vote of the five county leaders, and I was a bit naive. They did not in any way reveal that they had no faith whatever that I could possibly win. I should have known. It was too easy.

Since Flynn was national chairman and, therefore, close to the President, I thought it was appropriate for me to ask, "Will President Roosevelt be with me or against me? I will not get into this race against his wishes." Flynn assured me the President would not take sides. "But," he added, "I'm not too sure that Eleanor Roosevelt won't support La Guardia."

I was still green as to the workings of a politician's mind and took it for granted that Flynn knew what he was talking about and that the President had indeed given assurance of neutrality. Knowing the President's past support of La Guardia, I did not expect an announced repudiation, but if he stayed aloof it could give me a reasonable chance of success. The President had sent a personal spokesman in to speak for La Guardia in the campaign of 1937. Furthermore, La Guardia was sure to be backed openly by the Republican Party, by the Fusion Party, by committees of independent Democrats, and by the American Labor Party (a new party which had been formed by Jim Farley at Roosevelt's behest a few years earlier), which was supported in the main by the powerful Amalgamated Clothing Workers and the I.L.G.W.U.

My record in labor disputes, in civil rights cases, as a magistrate and as District Attorney was well known and popular in the ranks of labor, with liberal groups and with independents. Furthermore, civil servants and transit workers had received some shabby treatment from La Guardia. I believed that it would not have been too difficult for me to obtain considerable support from a very large section of the American Labor Party, particularly when a split between the left and right wings of that party seemed quite probable.

My brother Paul and some of my friends undertook to sound out important members of the American Labor Party who had become annoyed and tired of La Guardia. They agreed to run a candidate against him in their party's primary but wanted our financial help. Kelly and Johnston turned thumbs down on the idea. Had I been wiser in the ways of politics, I would have sought and received the financial support necessary to wage a vigorous campaign against La Guardia. In the relatively close election, it could well have changed the outcome. Ultimately, the heads of many of the trade unions understandably came out for La Guardia, but many of the leaders of locals, including Harry vanArsdale, and a great mass of the rank and file of working men and women gave me active support.

As the campaign got under way, masterminded by Kelly and Johnston, I began to realize that the politicians had very little interest and no hope in the election. The clubhouses, the local symbols of political activity, were closed for the most part. Usually during any election period they are beehives of activity. The interest of the other county political leaders was perfunctory at best. It seemed to me they were willing to let Brooklyn have its fling and wait for better opportunities at a later time.

Other sources of support proved futile. For example, one could always rely on the New York taxi drivers to be opposed to the incumbent Mayor. Talkative, Runyonesque characters, they encourage communication with their passengers and are never loathe to give their opinion. Henry Friedland, my friend and lawyer for the taxi industry, came around to discuss the election with me. He asked me to give him the assessment of my chances of success on Election Day. I did, and that ended what help I might have hoped to get from the taxi industry.

My campaign speeches were prepared for me by Judge Johnston and his staff. They were uninspiring, to say the least, and in many respects, factually erroneous. I began making corrections and some changes. The judge soon got around this bad habit of mine by handing me my speech only five or ten minutes before I went on the air. I was becoming increasingly irritated with him. The climax came when a prepared speech referred to Sam Null as a Communist. Nothing could have been further from the truth. Sam Null was a partner of Markewich and Null, one of the most respected law firms in the city. That year, Sam was a candidate of the Republican and American Labor Parties for Supreme Court judge. The speech had gone to the press before I saw it. I did not deliver it and promptly called Sam Null to apologize.

A campaign is never short of people who volunteer information. News came my way that La Guardia met each evening with Judge Johnston at the Engineer's Club. I found out they were friends of long standing, both having served in Congress together. I must say it did come as a shock to me that the mastermind of my campaign was associating with the opposition on a regular basis and providing him with the contents of the speeches he was preparing for me well before I delivered them. Because of this arrangement, La Guardia was able to reply to any speech I made simultaneously with its delivery. Finally, I discontinued the regular use of written scripts and, if a more formal one was necessary for radio, my brother Paul and Oscar Bernstien prepared it for me.

The responses from the meetings I addressed began to give me great encouragement. I disregarded the indifference of the party leaders and made a direct appeal to the people. I campaigned at schools and street corners, and the crowds began to turn out for the occasions. The lights began to go on in political clubs, and district leaders appeared at our meetings. My own presentation improved, and the public seemed to be enjoying what was turning out to be a real contest. The spirit at headquarters came alive, and we were even getting financial contributions in the mail.

The change showed signs of developing into a ground swell, but the time was growing short. Political reporters and politicians began to express the feeling that the tide was turning in my direction, and La Guardia, for the first time in his political career, was getting irritable, frequently making reckless statements.

Tammany Hall, over the years, had acquired the reputation of being both sinister and corrupt. I had never met the Tammany leaders before my candidacy had received the blessing of the five county chieftains. But La Guardia did not hesitate to put me "in bed" with all of them and to charge that any candidate who accepted their support must suffer from the association. I could not be heard to complain too loudly about that logic. But the La Guardia forces also began to whisper that I was the spokesman for Christian Fronters and Bundists. Fiorello himself also began attacking everything and everyone connected with the New York Democratic Party, at one time calling Governor Lehman a *"gonif"* (Yiddish for thief). At one gathering, the Mayor picked up a head of cabbage. "This," he said, "reminds me of my opponent," a statement that only served to increase public interest in his cabbage-headed opponent, and the La Guardia camp realized they needed help—help that would be effective.

An appeal was made to President Roosevelt. At first, contrary to Flynn's promise, the President had issued a formal endorsement of La Guardia's candidacy. That was now felt to be insufficient. Later, at the urgent behest of Ed Flynn, who I now knew was playing a dual role, Roosevelt made a second statement urging the re-election of La Guardia. Our intelligence had advised us in advance of the imminence of Roosevelt's second endorsement, but we were helpless to do anything about it.

La Guardia won—by only 13,000 votes. It surprised most of the political experts, and I had learned a few lessons about politicians, campaigns and elections. The following morning, I appeared at the District

Attorney's office in the Municipal Building at 9:30 a.m. as usual.

The *Daily News* editorial summarized the warm messages from friends:

> O'Dwyer has been the best District Attorney to function in any borough for years, with the possible exception of Tom Dewey. We're glad that Brooklyn will continue to have his services as District Attorney and we think definitely that O'Dwyer has a political future. Congratulations are due him for the . . . sporting way he accepted defeat.
>

All of these expressions may sound like so many cliches, but, to the defeated candidate, they are a soothing balm for his still-open wounds. The charges of political opponents fade with the passage of time. The scar tissue from double-dealing within one's own camp remain permanent.

The experience must have embittered La Guardia. From that point on, antagonism was to break into hostility. I was beginning to feel it in all of my dealings with Commissioner Valentine. An incident occurred which was soon to bring the fight into the open.

Shortly after the election, I was in La Junta, Colorado, visiting my brother, Frank, when I received a call from my office to return without delay. Back in New York, I had a secret meeting with Deputy Police Commissioner John Ryan, one of the most respected members of the department. Valentine had appointed him to the prestigious post of Chief Inspector, and later, La Guardia promoted him to the post of First Deputy Commissioner. "You're being set up," Ryan told me, "and I could not stand by and see it happen to you."

Ryan had always been an affable fellow, and I had regarded him as a friend, although we had not been close. He unfolded the plot which was designed to pull me down a peg and reduce my political potential. A man named Farley, a nephew of a former Tammany district leader in Manhattan, had been arrested and was in the city prison, charged with the murder of a police officer. La Guardia got the notion that there would be an effort by the Tammany Democratic organization to "fix" the case so that young Farley would go free. The Mayor then caused a rookie cop from the Police Academy to be "convicted" of some offense, and then arranged with his Commissioner of Correction to have this rookie "convict" placed in the cell next to Farley. The "convict" was to learn of any efforts to set Farley free and thus discredit me and destroy the effectiveness of my work and reputation as a prosecutor. The rookie "convict" was promised to be advanced in the department if his work proved helpful, and he was committed to secrecy. Deputy Chief Inspector Reynolds, the Correction Commissioner, Police Commissioner Valentine and La Guardia were all part of the arrangement, although no District Attorney had been consulted in the scheme. They had not taken Ryan into their confidence, but he found out about it from Reynolds.

That afternoon, to the embarrassment of La Guardia and Valentine, I called the rookie before the grand jury, and he told all about the conspiracy. Valentine retaliated by demanding that Police Captain Bals, who had been assigned to the District Attorney's office in Brooklyn, give him a detailed report of all police activities in my office. It had been our understanding from the time I took office that the reports of the police assigned to that office were to be secrets of the District Attorney's office. I reminded Valentine of our agreement, and he responded by transferring Captain Bals from our office. I then called Valentine before the grand jury and personally questioned him about the transfer. Valentine told the truth, and I next arranged to have La Guardia appear to explain his position and participation in the matter. The newspapers got wind of it, and it was shaping up as one of the major political battles of the era. The grand jury was eager to hear La Guardia, and the date was set for the following Monday.

On Sunday, December 7th, the day before the Mayor's appearance, the headlines announced that the Japanese had attacked Pearl Harbor. That same night, I called La Guardia and told him that my investigation was discontinued, as it was hardly the time for political feuding. He seemed relieved. He agreed to allocate enough money to the District Attorney's office to pay a chief investigator. Frank Bals then resigned from the Police Department and was, therefore, no longer under Commissioner Valentine's jurisdiction. I promptly appointed him as chief of the District Attorney's squad on January 2, 1942.

My request for leave of absence to serve in the armed forces was granted in 1942. Thomas Craddock Hughes acted as my successor until my return three and a half years later.

CHAPTER 26

THE ARMY (1941-1944)

December 7, 1941: The Japanese at Pearl Harbor and a declaration of war from the mad butcher who wanted to bring the entire world under his heel.

In that moment I sent a telegram to our Commander in Chief at Washington:

> There is only one thought, one duty and one course confronting Americans in this critical hour. It is to give you as our Commander in Chief our wholehearted and energetic and unreserved support. Please accept my readiness to serve in whatever service your wise leadership may require.

I'm sure the President had more to do than read telegrams such as mine, and I was neither surprised nor disappointed when I received no reply. As the weeks passed by, I became restless and sought out Bill Keary, a friend since boyhood in Bohola and now president of the Empire State Building, and he arranged a meeting with John McCloy, then Assistant Secretary of War.

We met at the Hotel Plaza in January of 1942. I found McCloy very practical but not very encouraging. "How old are you?" he asked. "Fifty-two next birthday," I replied. "In the Army," he said, "you will undoubtedly be commissioned as a major, the lowest rank for your age." "I don't mind that," I said. "That's not all," he said. "The regular Army men will resent your coming. You will probably be given routine assignments and wind up as a glorified watchman of some warehouse right in Brooklyn. I think you would do better in civilian life. We may use you in one way or another as time goes on," he advised. "Anyway, it seems to me you're overweight for the Army. Think it over."

Think it over I did. I set out to reduce my weight, and when I enlisted I tipped the scale at 185 pounds, the lightest I had been in years, but the Army doctors gave me a shock when they reported scar tissue in the left lung. I was permitted to enlist, however, provided I signed a release relieving the government from any liability that might thereafter arise from lung trouble. I was given the rank of major, as John McCloy had said I would.

On my first day in the Army I was assigned to the provost marshal's office on the 15th floor of 90 Church Street, New York City. My job was to make routine investigations into the background of workers in war plants in the area.

The room was almost a block long. Facing north you could see the slums, and to the west the Hudson River and New Jersey. My desk was the eighth in the row on the south side. The civilian investigators came and went, their offices shut off in the westerly part of the floor.

The only friendly face I saw belonged to a boy from Brooklyn who recognized me at once. He passed by my desk many times, each time giving me a look of recognition, but on account of rank, he didn't speak until I spoke to him. Surreptitiously, we got to be good friends. His job was to haul a canvas bag behind him as he moved slowly from desk to desk. Now and then he picked up a useless document and put it in his bag. Security required that these documents be burned; we were terribly careful about leaks.

The major in charge surveyed the whole room from his desk up front. He had been a real estate man in his home town and belonged to the National Guard. He was meticulous in matters of uniform. The Brooklyn boy didn't like him—he told me that one day he was standing before the major and, inadvertently, a button on his tunic was not in place. The major pulled off the button with his hand and said, "You obviously don't need this."

All day long a pot-bellied man in civilian clothes with heavy jowls, his fingers crossed in front of his paunch, rocked gently back and forth, looking at the Hudson River and New Jersey. No one spoke to him, nor did I see him speak to anybody, except once, when he initialed a document that none of the officers in charge seemed to have any idea what to do with.

My interest became aroused in this mysterious man and finally the young lad from Brooklyn told me his story: "I'm allowed to talk to this man because he's not in uniform. It seems he's angry with the Army and especially with old man Rockefeller—the present one's father. He says that when he was a young National Guardsman in Colorado, Rockefeller had trouble with striking miners in the town of Trinidad and got the Governor to send in the Guard. This old man was on the mission. Someone set fire to the tents in which the strikers were living, and when they were all burned down, they found the dead bodies of a woman and 20 children.

"Someone had to be found to admit setting the fire to the tents. The country was up in arms against Rockefeller. This guy claims he knew who did it, and the Guard threatened to pin it on him. He was going to spill the beans and tell who gave the orders, but Rockefeller got the Governor and the Army to make an agreement with the man, so he says. He was to be taken into the Army as a private with the promise he'd eventually be made a captain. He's been in the regular army ever since and still waiting to be made captain so he can retire. He's the only one in the room who knows what to do with official papers. But don't ever sit down with him unless you have plenty of time. He'll talk you to death about the rotten deal he got from old man Rockefeller."

That story brought me back a bit along memory lane. A new generation had grown up which knew nothing of Trinidad or Ludlow, Colorado, and yet it was less than 30 years before that the Colorado Fuel and Iron Mine operators were able to convince the Governor of Colorado that the National Guard should be brought in to bring the striking miners to boot.

In 1914, I had read every account of it with interest. Emissaries were sent to the big cities to speak of the atrocities perpetrated by the National Guard on the strikers, their wives and families. Like most working people around union halls, I had contributed to the relief fund. President Wilson sent an emissary to Rockefeller, Jr., and the emissary was rebuffed. Later, Frank P. Walsh (famous fighting lawyer from St. Louis, who at the age of 74 died on the steps of the New York Federal Courthouse after he had argued his last labor case) was chairman of a federal commission established to investigate the cause of the strike. It emerged that the board of directors of Colorado Fuel and Iron knew nothing of the grievances of the miners. They did know, however, that the company-owned stores earned 20 percent return, and that the saloons on the property, also company-owned, were the most profitable of all. Even teachers and clergy were hired by the mine superintendents and fired if they voiced any criticism. In his masterful way, Frank Walsh elicited the facts detailing the appalling number of miners who were killed at work, and then he read from the company's records the amount of the payments to the injured and bereaved, such as $500 for a crippling broken back to $700 for a life.

Walsh also established that the National Guard had, on orders, fired on and killed many of the miners and burned their tents. When the ruins were cleared, two women and eleven children were found dead from suffocation. Colorado officials were quick to point out that they had not died as a result of rifle bullets.

The usual hue and cry was set up by Colorado Fuel and Iron,

blaming the incident on foreigners, whom they branded as anarchists, and in particular on a Greek, Luis Tikas, who was clubbed and shot several times in the back. The day his funeral procession passed through the town, the Guard had its guns trained on the union hall from the town's rooftops. Tikas' name became revered by the whole labor movement.

Since 1914, a new generation had grown up accustomed to the right to unionize, the right to bargain collectively, and to sit face-to-face with employers to discuss its grievances. And now, in 1942, the momentous event of 1914 had become a distorted tale told by a disappointed and frustrated old man. I doubt if he was aware of the fact that he and his story represented an important phase in our struggle, growth and development. I don't know if he ever became captain. Ten weeks later, when I left that office, he was still sitting in the rocking chair with his fingers joined across his paunch looking westward over the Hudson.

There was one significant event in my political life that occurred in 1942, while I was still assigned to investigations at 90 Church Street. I received an invitation from Judge Johnston to meet him at the Bossert Hotel in Brooklyn. In the past, we had clashed frequently. I felt he was overbearing and pompous, and he, in turn, felt I was an upstart and not from the ranks of the party—not a "regular."

The interview lasted about 25 minutes, and the judge did almost all the talking. He informed me of President Roosevelt's request that the Democratic Party nominate me to run for Governor against Tom Dewey. Over and over again, the judge warned me that I must make no effort to get the nomination. The President had said that if I were nominated, he would relieve me from Army duty. It was plain that the judge felt it was his painful duty to advise me of the plan. He was, however, a strong, disciplined party man and did what Roosevelt felt would be the best. When he finished, I said, "Judge, I don't care to be Governor. I prefer to stay in the Army, and anyway, I'd prefer to hear the message first-hand from the President," an attitude and response that did not help the situation at all.

Shortly thereafter, I was transferred to the Material Command of the Army Air Corps, Eastern Procurement Division. Sometime after that, Colonel Sol Rosenblatt, a noted New York attorney assigned at the time to the office of Judge Robert Patterson, Under Secretary of War, called me to his office and told me Judge Patterson wanted me in Washington to do investigations for him throughout the United States. The nature of the work would be a special investigator dealing with contract procurement for clothing and equipment for the Air Corps.

At my request, Colonel Rosenblatt arranged for the assignment to me of two men I needed for this kind of work, Lieutenant Jerome K.

With niece Joan and wife Kitty during the war

Ohrbach, son of the president of Ohrbach's Department Stores, who was well equipped from his experience to pass on prices and quality, and Lieutenant John M. Murtagh.

I first met John and his twin brother Jim when they were about four years old in the home of a friend of mine, Inspector James McCoey. I had known their father, Bohola-born Tom Murtagh of the New York City Fire Department, who was always the first into a blazing fire until he was seriously burned. His strong heart and mind kept him alive until the twins graduated from Harvard Law School with high honors.

Ohrbach and Murtagh were promoted to captain, I was promoted to lieutenant colonel, and all three of us were transferred to Washington. I had a long talk with Judge Patterson, who explained to me that the Air Corps procurement requirements had jumped from a modest amount to billions of dollars. The procurement headquarters was at Wright Field, in Dayton, Ohio. There had been recurring complaints of shoddy workmanship and the sale of inferior merchandise to the Air Corps. Judge Patterson was afraid that gangsters would climb on board those huge contracts. A man with less understanding and vision would have waited for the scandals to come, perhaps years after the war was over, and let the blame come as it might. But the judge wanted immediate action, preventive measures, strict supervision, and the carrying out of all investigations in quiet, without publicity.

It was his hope that when and if the agents of Senator Truman's Special Committee to Investigate the National Defense Program got around to investigating a specific matter, the record would show that our small force had already discovered the carelessness or wrongdoing and corrected it. All the above constituted my orders.

Following my instructions from Judge Patterson, I sat down with General Oliver Echols, who was in charge of the Material Command. Neither Patterson nor Echols had to demand loyalty. Both men were strong and sincere, each having a clear picture of the objective in his mind. No one could accept a responsibility from them without seeing to it that the best possible job was done.

I found out that I'd be working under Henry Dolan, a former F.B.I. agent, and now the civilian head investigator for the Eastern Procurement District. Dolan was one of the keenest investigators within my experience. His knowledge of the methods of operation placed him in a high position in the command. His staff included Frank Begley, an intelligent young Yale graduate, and James Shields. Since the seat of operations would have to be Wright Field for the time being, Murtagh, Ohrbach and I moved to Dayton.

The Department of Justice assigned George Morris Fay to work with us. If we found any indications of criminal wrongdoing, we were to turn over the information to him. Since part of our job was to ferret out fraud and any suspicion of sabotage that might result in faulty engine parts or slowdowns, we used the same methods that had proved so effective in the Murder, Inc. investigation. This meant speaking with persons who had underworld connections, prospective defendants, defendants or informants, whenever in our judgment the circumstances warranted it.

In my criminal investigative days, the hoodlums who were potential or actual witnesses would get balky with the assistant district attorneys and would demand to see me. I always heard them out, often giving them the assurance that I was aware of the cooperation they were giving and that it was well noted. In the Army things were quite different. Any such formalities took second place to the necessity of getting the job done. I relied greatly on regular police and prosecutorial connections and called on old police friends to help. John Gorman introduced me to a man named Irving Sherman, a garment industry executive, late in 1942. Sherman had come up the hard way in New York, and like everyone else in the Seventh Avenue neighborhood, he knew "Lepke" (Louis Buchalter), Gurrah Shapiro, and all the racketeers who preyed for years on the garment industry. He also seemed to know many people in high places, including Democratic and Republican leaders.

While Sherman lived on the edge of the underworld, he managed to remain within the law, and the Navy found his performance satisfactory. He had a contract with the Navy to supply them with shirts. The contract lasted throughout the war. His workmanship, production and delivery were satisfactory and his prices were all within line.

He briefed me on methods of bidding on military contracts for all kinds of clothing and accessories and warned of chiselers who were trying to muscle their way into military procurement, including those who organized five-percenter corporations to mediate between manufacturers looking for war contracts and the appropriate heads of government agencies.

Armed with the necessary background information and our own investigation, my staff and I soon were familiar with the *modus operandi* of the contractors and some of the civilian help in Wright Field and produced enough evidence for the U.S. District Attorney of Kansas City to obtain several indictments. That was enough to put the fear of God into the personnel at Wright Field. Knowing that gangster participation in contracts was bound to add to costs and diminish quality, we looked for underworld connections whenever that seemed feasible.

One day I received an anonymous letter through the mail about a man named Joe Baker. The letter carried the information that Baker was a contractor fronting for racketeers. There was nothing out of the ordinary about the letter or the accusation, and I turned it over to Henry Dolan for investigation by his men. They learned that Baker had made a call to Wright Field on Frank Costello's private phone. Baker denied making the call or having any association with Costello. A staff member attempted to speak with Costello but was not able to get access to him.

Because of Kitty's health, it was my custom to spend as many weekends at home as I could, and Dolan asked me to try to make an appointment to see Costello while I was in New York. I arranged the appointment, the most convenient time for me being Friday night on my way home. I had no more hesitancy in seeing him than I had with other shady characters or underworld figures during my Army career or previously, when the occasion required it. I visited Costello at his home at 25 Central Park West. I had come directly from Washington and was still in uniform. When I arrived at Costello's apartment, there were several politicians, Republican and Democratic, present, some of whom I knew. They were having drinks before going to a show.

I spoke briefly with the guests, then Costello and I went into another room. He said yes, he knew Baker and admitted that the telephone was his. He said he had loaned Baker money from time to time, but denied with a shrug having had anything to do with Baker's or any other defense contracts. I left less than a quarter of an hour after I had arrived and went home to Bay Ridge content that I had received confirmation of the facts contained in the anonymous letter. When I left Costello's, the political figures were still there, among them Clarence Neal and Bert Stand.

On Monday morning, I took the information to Henry Dolan, who completed the investigative process. Baker's contract was then cancelled, and both he and his assistant were barred from any further contracts at Wright Field.

The incident was a routine one, and with the end of the war, I had no occasion to talk further with Sherman, nor have any kind of contact with Costello. Costello lived in New York City for a long time. He had apparently not had any operation, legal or illegal, in Brooklyn, and in Manhattan, Frank Hogan had him under surveillance for several years. I did not at the time consider the consequences of my association with Sherman during the war years nor my visit to Costello, but given the same facts and knowing the consequences, I still would have had no choice but to do what I did. Several years later, the war behind us, and I in the office of Mayor or Ambassador to Mexico, these incidents were made to take on sinister connotations before the Kefauver committee. But that is a later story.

In the spring of 1943, what appeared at first to be another of our many rather routine investigations brought me into direct confrontation with the Truman committee and particularly Senator Homer Ferguson. The modern Wright Aeronautical Plant in Lockland, Ohio, near Cincinnati, was making engines for Army and Navy planes. The Army corps was screaming for production. The plant was geared to produce a maximum of 3,000 engines a month. The emphasis, up to that time, had been on production.

A government inspector in the plant wrote a letter to Senator Robert A. Taft, who sent it to the Truman committee, complaining that the inspection in the plant was poorly and inadequately carried out. Robert Lovett, the Assistant Secretary of War for Air, agreed with the committee that an investigation should be made to establish the facts, and I was assigned to make the investigation. I had with me Jerry Ohrbach, Jim Shields, John Murtagh and Henry Dolan.

This was an important job which required us to master new technical areas completely out of our usual line. But we all had full confidence working under the direction of the keen-minded Henry Dolan, and thanks to him, and to our own homework, we learned a good deal about the plant itself and about the methods of running a big factory.

There were several ex-hairdressers, ex-barbers, ex-bartenders and one or two ex-shoeshine boys, to give but a few examples of the plant personnel, and yet the precision with which the machine tooling was set up and the ease of operation were almost unbelievable. At the pressing of a button, a part dropped on a belt and was carried to the next stand. All the parts were brought together in one place for assembly. The allowable tolerances in these thousands of parts were small, and it was amazing that the system worked as well as it did. Each engine, after assembly, was placed in a cell with gauges on the outside to show the temperature, speed and all the other required tests. Personnel studied these recorded tests night and day while the engines ran.

What, then, was the cause of complaint? In our estimation, it was simply the low pay of the government inspector who wrote the letter and the high pay of the plant personnel. I presented my report, which stated the facts as I saw them, and sometime later I was questioned on it before the full Truman committee. It was clear to me that some of the Senators were bent on prosecuting the Wright Aeronautical officers for some crime or offense.

At one point during the questioning, Senator Homer Ferguson of Michigan, a former Detroit judge and prosecutor, was more than usually abusive. He said, "You were sent there to whitewash the Air Corps," accusing me of covering up the wrongdoing and thereby endangering the lives of our young men at war. The Senator made this statement under a cloak of immunity, but he wouldn't have dared say it outside.

I responded, "I resent the supposition that I was asked to do anything wrong, or that I did anything wrong," and that started a sharp interchange which might have gotten completely out of hand were it not for the intervention of Senator Truman. I suspected he felt as badly about it as I did. In any event, he did not reprimand me, and I had the feeling he appreciated my reaction.

When I left the committee room, I went to General Echols' office and told him of the committee's hostility and my exchange with Senator Ferguson. In the interest of the service, I suggested to the general that I be transferred to another command. The general replied, "I'll read the record." A few days later he sent for me and said, "It's about time somebody fought back, and since you're willing and able to do it, you ought to have more rank." When I reminded him that under the rules, I wasn't entitled to a promotion for nine months, he replied, "We'll find a way."

Later, Judge Patterson sent for me and said, "You did an excellent job. We are going to promote you. I agree with General Echols that if you have to do this again, you ought to have a rank." General Echols' first recommendation for my promotion was rejected. But the same afternoon, Judge Patterson took action personally, and within a week I was promoted to the rank of colonel.

In the meantime, what happened to the plant in Lockland? Seven F.B.I. agents and two members from the Attorney General's office worked in it for nine months, after which, I was informed, their evidence was presented to a grand jury in Cincinnati. Not a single indictment was returned.

Some time later, we were assigned a case at Wright Field involving a young lieutenant who was about to be courtmartialed for selling a warehouse full of tools "without authorization." The Truman committee was looking into the supposed scandal, the *Detroit Free Press* had blaring headlines about it, and Judge Patterson sent us to Detroit to find out whether, indeed, it was a case of corruption, as the investigative officers of Wright Field had vehemently claimed. Dolan, Shields, Murtagh and I made our own investigation and uncovered a letter authorizing the alleged "corrupt" sale. The general at Wright Field responded to our report with extreme hostility and disbelief. Even after he had seen the evidence and had calmed down somewhat, he still bet me a box of cigars that the F.B.I. would ultimately find corruption. I won the cigars.

Early in 1943, my responsibility was enlarged from contract procurement to cover any activity that might impede production or lower public morale. Wright Field was in good shape and placed in the capable hands of Colonel Edward Cavanaugh, whom I later appointed to office in New York, and who still later became the city's Fire Commissioner. The main labor troubles were located in the New York area. These were under the watchful eye of Julius Kass, a brilliant lawyer and labor management expert. When I became Mayor, I appointed him to my Labor Committee. The Wright Aeronautical plant in New Jersey became the responsibility of Frank Begley.

I got to know Frank Begley very well. He was personable, capable, courageous, and above all, diplomatic. When Trygve Lie asked me later to suggest a security officer to the United Nations, I had only one recommendation. Frank accepted the post, but it was nearly to cost him his life. He was with Count Bernadotte in Palestine when an assassin's bullet killed Bernadotte and wounded him. He performed extremely well in his post and was widely respected by the U.N. representatives.

In September 1943, I was appointed Chief of the Investigation Division of the Office of Legislative Services. My whole team set up headquarters at One Park Avenue, New York City, with Henry Dolan still in charge.

We were ready to move to any part of the country on a telephone call, and several times we had to do this in order to avert a possible uproar. Toward the end of 1943, there was hardly a plant in the country that didn't suffer from personality clashes and anonymous letters. The Fairchild plant near Trenton, New Jersey was one, the Andrew Jackson Higgins plant in New Orleans, which produced outer tips on the C-47 was another, and the Wright Aeronautical B-29 engine program was still another.

There was no danger of an outcry from the Truman committee in the case of Higgins for a simple reason—Hugh Fulton, counsel for the committee, and his young aide, Rudolph Halley, were frequent guests of Higgins.[1] When I arrived in New Orleans, I explained my mission to Higgins, and he immediately contacted Fulton, asking him to direct me to return at once to Washington without making the investigation. I continued with my investigation.

I found the plant a shambles, with tin plates strewn around the floor, and most of the machine tooling altered in such a way as to require expert repair. I reported to General Echols on my return that if production of these parts was necessary, it should be done someplace else.

Still another investigation involved a tragic accident. There had been an exhibition of gliding in St. Louis, which the public was invited to observe. It was well advertised and organized, and the crowd was large. The glider was filled with civilians, among them the mayor of St. Louis. Suddenly, the two wings flew off. The glider nosedived into the ground. Every person in it was killed, their bodies mangled and burned.

1. Halley was made executive assistant for a special investigative committee under the National Defense Program headed by Senator Truman and in 1944 he became chief counsel for the Truman committee.

U.S. District Attorney Blanton was displeased with the Army's explanation. Both he and the grand jury were in an ugly mood. At the same time the grand jury was investigating complaints of faulty shells made in a local factory. I spent three weeks in St. Louis making my own investigation into both matters and consulting with the District Attorney. This was an unusual case in that the shells were for the quartermaster. It rarely happens that one department is represented by personnel of another board.

I finally was called before the grand jury by the District Attorney. I testified twice and explained the remedial measures I had put into effect. I was happy that night to report to Judge Patterson that the grand jury and the District Attorney were satisfied with my explanation and report. There was no indictment in either case.

Often, our headaches involved personnel problems. At one point, General Nichols asked me to intervene in a situation whereby the Northrup Company, working on the then-secret "Flying Wing," had hired a team of experts away from another company, Consolidated, in violation of an Echols rule that, to avoid just such a case of raiding, no important personnel could leave the company. Consolidated, furious, had filed a complaint, and General Nichols, who was leaving for Delhi, left me to sort out a bad situation. At a heated meeting in San Diego, I told the assemblage of angry executives that even though they were technically right, they were pressing a point that would make trouble for General Nichols and, what was worse, tie up the strategically important "Flying Wing." Two of the men jumped all over me, but Tom Girdler, the top man at Consolidated, butted in.

"Keep quiet," he told them. "Either one of his arguments is enough for me. We're licked even though we are right. My hide is full of icepick marks—one more won't make much difference. I've just written one book and after the war I'll write another." He withdrew the complaint then and there.

During the time I was in the Army, politics went on as usual in Brooklyn. After I had left the District Attorney's office to go into the Army, the political opportunists I had left behind felt I would probably never return to it. As time went on, I became aware of undermining at home but at the same time gratifying recognition in Washington.

In the late spring of 1943 the attitude of the leaders of the Democratic Party in Brooklyn was made clear to me when one of them visited me at my home one Sunday afternoon. He called attention to the fact that I had to run again for a full term for District Attorney that November or lose out. Then he listed the number of leaders who would not vote for me because I was in the Army. They felt I should be at home to serve in that capacity if I wanted it.

He ended up by telling me that many of the contractors at Wright Field had friends in Brooklyn political circles, and they felt my investigation was in many respects altogether unfair, and that this attitude was not helping me at home. He hinted darkly that the leaders might select another candidate, and he ended by saying that of course he was warning me about all this as a friend. I thanked him for his interest and then asked him to do another favor—to tell the Democratic leaders that I would first finish all the pending investigations as I promised Judge Patterson I would, and that if I didn't get the renomination, they would have to deal with me after the war was ended.

It is a nice thing on a Sunday afternoon to get a good tip from a reliable source as to what your political enemies are up to. It was also apparent that the gentlemen at Wright Field felt they were dealing with a Brooklyn politician and had reached out to silence him!

I called up Colonel Rosenblatt and gave him the picture, and through him an appointment was made for me to visit Judge Sam Null of the Supreme Court. The judge listened to the story and said, "We will have to do something about this." I also called John Crews, Brooklyn Republican leader, and told him what I was up against. Within a short time I was nominated by the American Labor Party and the Republican Party, and the Democratic Party fell quickly in line.

Before the first of the year, with Judge Patterson's permission, I took time out to be sworn in as District Attorney for another full term.

About Christmas, 1943, Dave Niles, the President's confidant, called on me. "The President sent me to ask you what you know about Spain. He says he believes you went to school there." "That's a long time ago," I said. "Although I haven't been back there recently, I'm sure though I could find my way around, and I know the language. What's on the President's mind?" "The War Refugee Board is not making satisfactory progress. He wants to put you in charge of it," he replied and went on to talk about other things.

The result of the visit became apparent in February, 1944, when the President sent the following memorandum to Under Secretary of War Patterson:

> This is an order to show cause—and you are probably outvoted to start with.
>
> I honestly think that Colonel William O'Dwyer can do relatively a more important job for the War Refugee Board at this time than in any other capacity. I would want him to be under Stettinius and go over to Spain at once. I know no one else could do as good a job.

Two days later, on February 26, Bob Patterson sent the reply:

> In answer to your order to show cause concerning Colonel William O'Dwyer, I submit the following:
>
> Bill O'Dwyer, I firmly believe, has done more than anyone else to prevent fraud and scandal for the Army Air Force.
>
> His work consists of detecting cases of fraud, waste and abuse in production of airplanes and airplane parts.
>
> This work is of the utmost importance, both for production of aircraft and for public morale, and I deem him the best qualified man in the Army for it. We have no one with his special skill to replace him, even temporarily.
>
> In a nation of 135 million why deprive me of Bill O'Dwyer?

Patterson called me in and showed me the exchange of memoranda. That kind of praise was heady wine. It's easy to believe these things when others say them, although I realized after the glow had worn off that my whole group shared in and was responsible for the praise. If our team had worked hard before, after that moment we worked even harder.

The routine became one of solving one headache and barely coming up for air before the next one arrived. Finally, the routine was temporarily broken. In June, in Los Angeles on assignment, I was having lunch with Jack and Margaret Rector when the orders came to report forthwith to Washington.

CHAPTER 27

ALLIED COMMISSION (1944-1945)

The next day I reported to the White House. This might truly be called the biggest day of my life. I found myself standing very stiffly before the President of the United States. He asked me very casually to sit down.

"Bill," he said, "I am sending you to Italy on a special mission for me to do a job that until now has not gone well. We have 24 million people in liberated Italy who are helpless, and we are not helping them. The British and ourselves have a joint operation, but they are in command. I want to know what's wrong, and I want you to do what you can on the spot to improve the conditions of these people. You will need rank. I'll see that you are promoted to brigadier general and that you are given the personal rank of minister in the State Department so that you can report to me confidentially through the pouch anything that should not be sent through Army channels."

Analyzing my own feelings later, looking back over my life in New York from my immigrant days until that moment, I found the most pleasure and the greatest honor I had yet experienced on that one day. What could be a greater moment for any immigrant than to be selected by the wartime President to perform such a confidential and delicate task for him.

My mission was to study the economic situation and the relationship between the Allied Control Commission and the Italian people, to establish policy within the commission itself, and to report to the President in preparation for his September conference with Prime Minister Churchill in Quebec. As brigadier general, a promotion I received on August 3, 1944, I headed the economic section of the Allied Control Commission, a joint command composed of Americans and British. Previous American representatives, outranked by the British, had done little to counter the policies of the British General Henry Maitland Wilson, who was in charge of the joint command.

Murtagh and Ohrbach went with me to Italy. We flew to Casablanca and from there reported to General Charles M. Spofford in Algiers. The next day we flew to Naples and Rome. The three of us were billeted at the Grand Hotel in Rome.

It is difficult for those who have not seen the ravages of war to comprehend the extent of the destruction I observed in Italy in 1944. For almost two years, Italy was one of the principal battlefields of the war. Starting in Sicily, the war moved methodically and slowly up the mainland. The opposing ground forces caused widespread damage and destruction as they proceeded northward. All aspects of the country's economy, including industry, power, transportation and communications were seriously damaged, first by formidable Allied bombings and later by sporadic bombings of the German Luftwaffe. Effective demolition by the retreating Germans and sabotage carried on by the heroic Italian patriots behind the German lines also inflicted severe damage. As Anne O'Hare McCormick, *The New York Times'* distinguished foreign correspondent said: ". . . for total ruin in Italy—nothing equals it, in France, Belgium, Greece or even the Netherlands."

Entire communities were wiped out. Cassino is only the most famous example. It was not unusual to see people living in the one remaining room of a crumbled building or making their homes among the open debris. In September, 1944, a census taken by the Italian Government, at my suggestion, showed that in the 38 provinces then liberated, living quarters which had accommodated over five million people had been destroyed.

The railroad system of the country had been seriously disrupted and disorganized. It was one of the principal targets of attack by both belligerents. The Allied air forces dropped tons of explosives on the railroad beds and on all the principal rail centers. The Germans, as they retreated, ripped up railroad ties, twisted the rails, and carried away movable equipment. In central and southern Italy, the maximum capacity of rolling stock was a small percentage of that available before the war.

To add to the destruction, the enemy in its retreat systematically destroyed every bridge on its course, large and small: not only the bridges on the main roads, but also those on secondary roads, side roads and dirt roads. In large sections of Italy, every bridge and culvert had to be rebuilt.

Italy entered the war with about three and a half million tons of merchant shipping. By 1944, only about 10 percent of the former fleet remained, and of this total the greater portion had been requisitioned by the Allies, leaving only negligible shipping facilities for supplying the country.

As if the unfortunate country had not already suffered sufficient devastation, the German armies also left behind them fields strewn with mines. In the Sangro Valley, 25 percent of the surface was mined. In the province of Littoria, the grain-producing area nearest Rome, a large percent of all productive tilled land had to be abandoned. Casualties were still resulting daily from these mines, and they continued to occur for many years afterwards.

To realize the serious effect of these conditions on the life and health of the Italian people, just compare the birth and death rates in Rome in 1940 and 1944. In 1940 the birth rate was 23 per 1,000 and the death rate 11 per 1,000. By 1944 the birth rate had fallen to 16 per 1,000 and the death rate had risen to 17 per 1,000. Tuberculosis had shown a marked increase, with 21 deaths per 10,000 in 1944 compared with 10 deaths per 10,000 in 1940. Mortality from infectious diseases had risen from 19 per 10,000 in 1940 to 35 per 10,000 in 1944. Infant mortality, one of the best indicators of the general state of health of any population, had shown a steady and steep increase over the previous five years, malnutrition being one of the major causes.

Colonel Charles Poletti, a U.S. Military Government officer, served as liaison between General Sir Harold Alexander, the military governor, and the Italian people, Poletti was in charge, jointly with a Brigadier Lush, a British officer. Lush and Poletti each lived in a villa, as did Captain Ellery Stone, U.S.N.R., our representative. We were offered a villa, but the three of us unanimously decided to remain in the Grand Hotel. I had a feeling that we were being buttered up by the British, who were suspicious from the start.

The President was too specific for me to doubt his intentions, and we were on our guard. I was not there two weeks before Stone showed his teeth. He wrote me a letter one day stating that he had received a complaint from Colonel Poletti and Brigadier Lush to the effect that Rome was not being properly fed and gave me a certain number of days to answer the charge. I called the captain and asked him to wait for my report. While he was talking to me, John Murtagh was on his way down to his office with my answer, which consisted of one sentence: "I demand an inspector general's investigation and report on your whole command." It took at least two weeks for the three gentlemen to cool down. It set the record straight, however, and gave me clearance to do the job for which I was sent. My position was never questioned thereafter.

To accomplish my assignment, I consulted with, from the beginning, many important officials. Michael McWhite, the Irish Ambassador to Italy and former Minister to Washington, was considered the best informed man in Rome. His neutral position gave him the capacity to move around Rome with ease, and he was most helpful to me, particularly during the early part of my time in Rome.

I also consulted with Premier Ivanoe Bonomi, in an attempt to clarify the relationship between Italy and the Allied Control Commission. Prior to my coming, the government of Italy had been in the hands of Premier Pietro Badoglio, and it far from reflected the democratic aspirations of the Italian people. In collaboration with the Allied Control Commission, it had initiated many decrees which were a lot closer to the Fascist policies of Mussolini than to the democratic principles enunciated by the Allies. "Take for example the Labor Decree," said Bonomi. "It is not at all to the liking of the Italian people, and yet the Allied Commission is insisting that our Government enact it into law promptly."

Murtagh, Ohrbach and I immediately set about studying the decree and found it to be as objectionable as Bonomi said it was. Among its more objectionable provisions: any persons organizing labor unions were to immediately submit their names and the names of all prospective members to a government bureau; complete records, including financial records, were to be kept and be open to government inspectors; a daily diary of the union's activities was to be kept and each page initialed by government inspectors; a signed list of names of all union members was to be open to government inspection; all union officers were to have the "status of public officers," acquiring no benefit thereby but subject to a host of restrictions; the government reserved the right in many instances to choose the labor union that would represent all unions in a given industry. Overall, we found, the restrictions were even more severe than those imposed by Mussolini's government.

I again conferred with Premier Bonomi and Giovanni Gronchi, the Minister for Industry, Labor and Commerce. "I have given orders that no further action is to be taken by the Allied Control Commission to have this law enacted," I said. "Labor legislation is a matter to be decided solely by the Italian Government and the Italian people. That is the official position of my Government, and I have been sent here to see to it that there is to be no undue interference with your function in that respect."

"How about other legislative matters?" interposed Sig. Gronchi. "From now on, we take the position that the Italian people are best equipped to handle their own domestic affairs and quite capable of doing it. We shall merely examine legislation to find out if it lies within the terms of the armistice."

"We would, of course, welcome your cooperation," said Gronchi. "That is one of the reasons," I said, "that President Roosevelt sent me here. We shall be happy to advise, cooperate and help, and our function is to see that the Allied Forces are here to assist in every way possible."

Soon after, I received a delegation from the Confederazione Generale del Lavoro, which had enthusiastically received the news of our meeting and pledged its full support and cooperation to us. "This," said the spokesman, "clears the air and gives us courage to go forward with fervor."

The Italian press hailed the pronouncements with enthusiasm. "It is a clear demonstration," wrote a Roman newspaper, "that the principles of American democracy shall be given practical application in Italy."

Having established an effective relationship, we set about working on the myriad problems that needed serious attention. Food was one of the first that confronted us. It was hardly necessary to establish that there was a food shortage. It could be seen everywhere on the streets of Rome. By the time I arrived there, it had already been decided to reduce the bread ration below 300 grams. This figure had been established, I felt, on the basis of very confused and inaccurate statistics. I made a quick survey as to the amount of food that would meet the bare minimums of keeping body and soul together and found it could not be done even at the 300 gram figure. It was therefore a scientific/mathematical conclusion that thousands of Italians would have to die of either malnutrition or starvation.

At this same time, a form was prepared for my signature calling for an even further reduction, on the grounds that the supplies of wheat just were not available. I rejected the recommendation and submitted one of my own, increasing the allotment to meet minimum needs. Later, after I conferred with President Roosevelt, he directed that my recommendation be adopted, that shipping be found to bring in supplies, and that other transportation be made available to facilitate delivery to various parts of Italy.

As for acquiring the necessary food supplies, I found out that General Patch was getting ready in Naples to attack what Sir Winston called the "soft belly"—a misnomer if there ever was one. There were ten carloads of excess potatoes and, under the rule, they belonged to the people and should have gone to Rome. But instead, the British uncoupled the ten cars and sent them to the canning factory to be used as supplies for General Patch's forces. I sent a telegram immediately through channels to President Roosevelt, requesting to be relieved from my assignment. I said, "I have no heart to preside over a national funeral." That afternoon, General Wilson and General Lewis came up from Naples to find out if I was serious.

I said, "Yes." "Of course, it's too bad you're not an Army man—you don't know what discipline is," said General Lewis. I said, "I know what the President of the United States wants me to do." He then asked, "Will you take the equivalent in flour?" "Where is it?" I replied. "Here in Rome," he said.

That afternoon I had a good supply of flour released from a hidden warehouse. I had, of course, no intention of resigning, but the telegram had worked.

In August, I received warm greetings and encouragement from Secretary of the Navy Forrestal, personally and by letter.

My dear O'Dwyer:

I want to repeat what I said to you this morning: that everywhere I went [in Italy] I found the greatest admiration for the competency and sincerity of your efforts. You are carrying out a most difficult and exacting task, and one that calls for courage as well as ability. I gather you have both.

Sincerely
James Forrestal

This was indeed high praise from a man who did not have the reputation of being the easiest one in the world to please.

My next problem involved housing. Meucci Ruini, Minister Without Portfolio, had submitted a plan for the reconstruction of homes. The colonel in charge of public works sharply criticized the plan, and it was subsequently vetoed. After conferring with Ruini, I found there was some basis for the colonel's objections, but that did not necessarily render the plan valueless. I reviewed the situation with Ruini and the colonel and, with some prodding, the colonel found a way out of the difficulty. To save face, I asked Minister Ruini to revise his plans. Within a week the minister returned with his revisions, and some of the building materials, which the colonel had previously reported were unavailable, somehow were found in sufficient quantities to meet the needs.

As a result, within eight months over one hundred million dollars was spent on new housing. Representatives of both the Italian Government and the Allied Commission were present at the ceremonies on March 15, 1945, exactly one year after the bombing of Cassino. It was a symbol of rebirth of war-torn Italy.

The barrage of problems and shortages continued unabated: the lack of medicines, milk for babies, electricity, the list going on and on. The more I got into the middle of each problem, the more I realized that we were merely meeting current needs and warding off immediate and impending catastrophes. If we were to render any permanent effective help to Italy, we would have to survey and understand the problems in more detail. I know a lot has been said about the unnecessary amount of paper used in a war, but no one is quite aware of its real function until there is none available; and if we were to make surveys, we certainly needed a good deal of it. As if Providence were on our side, I discovered 30 tons of paper in a warehouse in Littoria.

I consulted with Bonomi and Gronchi, and we arranged to have a series of accurate studies made of conditions all over Italy. First, a demographic, industrial and agricultural census was undertaken. "The sooner we know what the needs are, the sooner we can do something to fill them," I told the two leaders. "Then you wait and see us in action," replied Gronchi, and in no time at all they had recruited 200 bright, intelligent supervisors, backed up by 5,000 clerks, taken from various government departments. "The restoration of Italy to a place in the family of democratic nations depends on your speed and accuracy," Gronchi told his band, as they scattered out into every town and village in liberated Italy.

The enthusiasm with which they worked was unmatched. They labored as if the fate of their country depended on each person's individual effort. In less than three months an accurate census was completed, a job which would ordinarily have taken at least two years to finish. The following subjects were covered: family food budgets and food prices; family clothing conditions and clothing prices; family housing conditions; transport facilities and transport prices; and the diets and weights of children.

Next, in the industrial area, we uncovered some data in Rome, dated 1938, and using these as a base, we sent out questionnaires. With the help of some of the vast body of Italian unemployed and army microfilm facilities, we established in our second major study an accurate documentation of the destruction and the current requirements needed to restore the country's economy, including precise breakdown of machinery, parts, raw materials and power needs.

The third study was in the field of agriculture. A similar survey was made, but it was limited to war damage to livestock and farm machinery.

When all studies were finished, the census was published. It contained 250 pages, including charts, diagrams, tables and explanatory statements, and was printed in English and Italian. It was the only survey of its type made in any one of the liberated countries.

On a Monday in early September of 1944, I received orders to report on Friday morning directly to the Commander in Chief in Washington, D.C. When it became known that I was about to return to the United States, I received the following letter from the U.S. representative to the Advisory Council for Europe:

Dear General:

Livingood tells me that you may be leaving for Washington,

189

and I cannot refrain from saying that I have been so profoundly impressed by your masterly treatment of the difficult and important problems which have confronted you that I would regard it as a major calamity if anything should transpire which would interrupt for any appreciable time the continuity of your work. After all, it isn't just a local job that is being done in Italy, but a higher obligation is imposed to create and implement here a pattern for the creation of a world order in the American way. So you can see we count so much on you.

Sincerely,
Alexander Kirk

I called Kirk to tell him that my mission was merely to report to the President and return to the job.

In my conference with the President in Washington that Friday, we narrowed down the essential needs of the Italian people to six principal points, which later were submitted in a written report:

1. An increased food supply was necessary.

2. An adequate shipping allocation for the required food should be made immediately.

3. Adequate transportion should be made available to distribute the food throughout Italy.

4. A partial restoration of Italian electric power facilities was necessary.

5. Governmental responsibility in liberated Italy should be placed in the hands of the Italian Government without any major restrictions.

6. The Allied Control Commission in liberated Italy should be abolished and its supply functions placed in the hands of civilian rather than military experts.

Without waiting for the September Quebec Conference with Churchill, President Roosevelt sent a memo to the Secretary of War acknowledging his understanding that the supply situation in Italy was critical and that "The War Department should therefore take immediate action to make available the additional, essential civilian supplies and shipping necessary to remedy the condition."

After the Quebec Conference, Churchill spent some time with Roosevelt in Hyde Park, and on September 26 they issued a joint statement in which they outlined the following plans for aiding the Italian people:

1. An increasing measure of control will be gradually handed over to the Italian administration. To mark this change the Allied Control Commission will be renamed the Allied Commission.

2. The British High Commissioner in Italy will assume the additional title of Ambassador, and the Italian Government will be invited to ap-

point direct representatives to Washington and London.

3. First and immediate considerations in Italy are the relief of hunger, sickness and fear.

4. At the same time, steps should be taken towards the reconstruction of the Italian economy.

At President Roosevelt's suggestion, I conferred with Governor Herbert Lehman, Director General of United Nations Relief and Rehabilitation Administration and, as a direct result, $50 million was appropriated for relief for Italy. Governor Lehman, in addition, directed that $8 million worth of medical supplies be shipped to Italy.

In my final months of service in Italy I saw many of my recommendations beginning to be carried out under President Roosevelt's orders.

In November, 1944, Alexander Kirk was named Ambassador to Italy, and Alberto Tarchiani was named Ambassador to the United States. My own job in Italy ended on January 31, 1945.

I received citations and many letters from Italian officials with whom I had worked. The following is one for which I was humbly grateful.

To Brigadier General William O'Dwyer:

I have the great pleasure of forwarding to you the enclosed decoration of "Grand Officer of the Crown of Italy" bestowed upon you following the proposal of the Minister of Industry and Commerce [Giovanni Gronchi].

Such proposal was made in consideration of the distinguished contribution toward Italy's economic recovery rendered by you in the high capacity in which you served while in my country.

Allow me, my dear General O'Dwyer, to extend to you my personal heartfelt congratulations, and believe me, with every good wish.

Albert Tarchiani
Italian Ambassador to the
United States
Rome, Italy

Back in New York, I kept an interest in the conditions in Italy. John Murtagh returned and kept me informed as to happenings there. Here at home, Jim Murtagh, John's twin brother, as secretary to Senator Jim Mead, stimulated the Senator's interest in the situation, and there was no abatement of activity in carrying out the program.

I was appointed Brooklyn division chairman of the New York National War Fund and as such cooperated with Judge Juvenal Marchisio, chairman of American Relief for Italy. I spoke on radio in this connection and became part of the energetic program initiated by my old friend Generoso Pope, editor of *Il Progresso Italo Americano,* long after the war had ended, when there was the greatest danger that the people's plight would be forgotten.

Soon after, upon the recommendation of the Commander in Chief, I was awarded the following Legion of Merit citation:

William O'Dwyer, 0-464406, Brigadier General, United States Army, Allied Commission (Italy) for exceptionally meritorious services as Vice-President in charge of the Economic Section, Allied Control Commission from the 10th of July, 1944 to the 31st of January, 1945. In this capacity, General O'Dwyer displayed great initiative, marked ability and judgment in making and carrying through to final action, decisions on important problems of military government and relief for the Italian population. He instituted a rapid demographic, industrial and agricultural census of the portion of Italy then liberated. His contribution to the collective work of the Allied Control Commission in obtaining additional imported food supply permitted the increase of the daily bread ration of the Italian people to three hundred grams. His most outstanding contribution was in working out and putting into execution plans for the feeding of Rome during the initial period after liberation.

By performance of duty, marked by extraordinary fidelity and a measure of efficiency, conspicuously above and beyond the usual, Brigadier General O'Dwyer not only contributed greatly to the well-being of the Italian populace, but also to the successful prosecution of the Allied Military effort in Italy. He entered the military service of the United States of America from Brooklyn, New York.

The President had told me previously that he was making the recommendation, but I felt that he was under too many pressures to remember such details. For that reason, it came as a surprise, and of course I was both happy and grateful.

CHAPTER 28

WAR REFUGEE BOARD (1945)

Late in 1944, as I was in the process of closing out my assignment with the Allied Commission, I reported to the President in his office. I will never forget his leaning back in his chair, then pulling himself up quickly, striking the desk with the forefinger on his right hand. "This was a hard job and you have done it well," he said. "Now, tell me what am I going to do with La Guardia?" I said, "Give him a uniform and send him to Italy to give a lesson in New Deal methods." He said, "The army won't have him and he won't go without a uniform." "That's too difficult for me, Mr. President," I said.

A few days later, the President sent for me again and said, "I want you to take over the disposition of war surplus materials overseas. It will be a three-man committee. You'll be chairman." I said, "I have no training for that, Mr. President." "I know you're not a pawnbroker," he observed, "but you can keep it clean."

Within 24 hours, the President officially nominated me for the job. The Judge Advocate advised the President that I would need senatorial approval, that there were literally hundreds of jobs at stake and too many lame ducks on the Hill who were looking for these assignments.

The President was not one to step on Congressional toes unnecessarily. "I have another idea—we can use you somewhere else soon," he said to me.

I did not have long to wait. About the middle of December, Dave Niles phoned. "The President wants to see you. Make it as soon as you can get here." Within the hour I joined Niles in the President's outer office. Presently he was with us, having come away from another meeting. He was obviously becoming weaker in body, but he still had an amazing work capacity, and his mind was as sharp as ever.

"Last spring, I tried to detach you from Patterson for the War Refugee Board, but he wouldn't let you go." He had a way of making you feel your efforts were really important. "Now," he continued, "the need is greater than ever. I want you to be the board's executive director. You may need to go into neutral countries, which means you will have to get out of uniform. I've talked to Morgenthau and Stettinius about it. They will be waiting to hear your decision." It was an order, although it sounded like a citation.

Dave offered me transportation back to my hotel, but I preferred to walk. Out in the street people were hurrying back and forth, lined up for buses or attempting to climb into taxicabs far beyond capacity; it was growing dark and the lights were going on. When I got to the hotel, two visitors from New York with an invitation to dinner were there waiting for me, but I made some excuse and soon I was alone in my room. I found it difficult to fully realize that a few moments ago I had once more received a prized assignment from our great President. My feelings of gratitude and spiritual reward were, if anything, even greater than those I had felt after the first assignment.

I began to think about the task ahead, about those unfortunate victims of a few madmen, of hungry, homeless and helpless unfortunates with hollow cheeks, sunken eyes, vacant stares, distorted bodies, distended bellies. These thoughts were not prompted only by recent sights or experiences. Rather, I found myself thinking back to County Mayo—the battering rams at small thatched cottages, the blight on the fields, the potato stalks brown and withered, people dying and no one to pray over them or bury them, the homeless routed out of homes forever lost, roaming with hungry hearts. . . . Some of the stronger ones drifting to the seaports to the "coffin ships" and others falling by the wayside and dying . . . the survivors yearning to kiss the soil of that new world that has always been the refuge of the oppressed from every land.

Three million Irishmen dead. Three million emigrated to America. Now six millions Jews gassed—human beings kept in cages, exterminated to make soap, lamp shades. Suddenly, fright possessed me. The President had spoken to me as if I were to perform miracles. How could I do it? Should I ask him to find someone else?

These thoughts were interrupted by the telephone. It was Henry Morganthau. He was pleased at my appointment and had not waited to hear from me first. "Meet me tomorrow at ten," he said, and I knew I was ready to take on the task.

Nineteen forty-four had been a fateful year in history. It encompassed the Allied invasion and liberation of western Europe. However, the Allied success only created greater peril for the hundreds of thousands of unfortunates in German concentration camps. Moses Leavitt, secretary of the Joint Distribution Committee, reported on December 10, 1944, as follows:

This year, however, also witnessed a dreadful climax in the German policy of annihilation of the Jews in Europe. When Hungary was taken over by the Gestapo and 800,000 helpless Jews were exposed to the fiendish brutality of the Germans, hundreds of thousands were deported and murdered or placed on slave labor battalions, and as this report is written, the fate of at least 250,000 Hungarian Jews hangs in a precarious balance.

On January 22, 1944, the President created the War Refugee Board by Executive Order 9417. To say that it was an innovation in human undertaking is to understate the case. Here, amid the most ferocious and destructive war in the world's history, President Roosevelt was also concerned with saving and helping those who were in captivity or in hiding behind or within the enemy lines. In the aftermath of the war I have read and heard Roosevelt severely criticized for failure to warn the Nazis of the consequences to them of their barbarism. I think what these critics lost sight of was the futility of threatening the Nazis while they were sweeping all before them. And it seemed to me they were on a winning streak almost until the last year of the war.

Furthermore, any blame leveled at Roosevelt had to be shared with the rest of the world. Our allies always resisted any program that might diminish our total efforts to win the war. Suffice it to say that when the President did move, he put into the project as much of our nation's skills and resources as were needed. He took the same active concern for the victims of Nazi persecution as he had taken for the homeless victims in Italy earlier the same year.

The preamble to the executive order made the President's purpose quite clear: "Whereas it is the policy of this Government to take all measures within its power to rescue the victims of enemy oppression who are in imminent danger of death, and otherwise to afford such victims all possible relief and assistance consistent with the successful prosecution of the war."

The purposes of the board, as outlined in the President's order, were:

1. To save as many refugees from starvation and death as possible;

2. To rescue, transport, and relieve the victims of enemy oppression;

3. To urge the German satellites to abandon cooperation with the Nazis in their policy of extermination and persecution of minorities;

4. To obtain better conditions for the detainees and to try to keep them alive until the armies of liberation came through;

5. To find temporary havens of refuge for escapees and others needing shelter.

The order not only stated the Government's broad and humane policy, but it provided the board with the power and means to carry that policy into effect. The President did not want the board to be circumscribed or tethered by bureaucratic regulations. He therefore stated:

> The Board shall be directly responsible to the President in carrying out the policy of this Government, as stated in the Preamble. And the Board shall report to him at frequent intervals concerning the steps taken for the rescue and relief of War Refugees; and shall make such recommendations as the Board may deem appropriate for further action as to overcome any difficulties encountered in the rescue and relief of War Refugees.

These were the ground rules and they were far-reaching.

In January 1944, John W. Pehle was appointed acting executive director of the board and on March 4th he was appointed as its director. On January 27, 1945 Mr. Pehle resigned.

On January 27, 1945, I was sworn in as executive director of the board and as such was in complete charge of its program. If I were to fail in carrying it out, it could not be said that others were to blame.

In furtherance of the board's stated objectives, I held my first press conference, advocating that the War Crimes Commission prosecute those guilty of atrocities against minorities, even though the minorities be that country's own nationals. There was some question at that time as to whether that particular situation came within the commission's jurisdiction. I felt that in order to protect the lives of those victims still alive, to clarify the President's position, and to ensure the effectiveness of the War Refugee Board it was critical to make the position quite clear.

The board included the Secretaries of War, State and Treasury, whose presence was designed to enlist the active cooperation of these three departments. It also had special representatives in Turkey, Switzerland, Sweden, Portugal, Great Britain, Italy and North Africa, all of whom were given diplomatic status. These men were for the most part professional relief workers, competent and devoted to the task. The Washington staff was composed of about 30 highly trained specialists in relief work, and they in turn utilized the personnel and supplies of the State, Treasury and War Departments.

The following agencies participated in the rescue work with us: the Vaad Hahatzala, the emergency committee of the Union of Orthodox Rabbis; the World Jewish Congress; the Jewish Labor Committee; the American Jewish Committee to Save the Jewish People; the National Refugee Service; the Hebrew Sheltering and Immigrant Aid Society; the

Zionist Organization of America; the Poale Zionist Organization; the American Friends Service Committee; the Unitarian Service Committee; the National Catholic Welfare Council; the American Christian Committee for Refugees; the International Rescue and Relief Committee; the A.F.L. Labor League for Human Rights; the C.I.O. War Welfare Committee; the American Relief for Norway; UNRRA (United Nations Relief and Rehabilitation Administration); and the Red Cross. Many of these agencies rendered invaluable service to the board in developing and financing its plans.

The United States Treasury licensed approximately $20 million in private funds for use abroad. The American Jewish Joint Distribution Committee gave us $15 million, the Vaad Hahatzala contributed $1 million, and the World Jewish Congress $300,000. One hundred thousand dollars was donated by the Hebrew Sheltering and Immigrant Aid Society, and $1 million was allotted from the President's Emergency Fund to cover administration and other expenses, although it was not all used.

Our allies objected to many features of the program, and had we been obliged to subordinate our program to their wishes, a good portion of our efforts would have been completely blocked or sidetracked. For instance, when we licensed the transfer of dollars to be used for rescue, the British Government formally objected on the ground that this gave the enemy foreign exchange for use in the prosecution of the war.

Furthermore, we could not obtain Russian cooperation. That created special problems, since many of the rescued Jews—mostly from Poland—in camps in the area liberated by the Russians were of Orthodox persuasion. The Vaad Hahatzala made an urgent appeal for *schochtim*, scribes and *mohelim*. The *schochtim* were those who were authorized to slaughter animals according to Jewish ritual. The *mohelim* were those authorized to perform circumcisions, and the scribes were those who could declare widows free to marry again after hearing eyewitness testimony as to the death of the spouse.

We also received a number of proposals from Europe. One came just as I took over. Joel Brandt, a Hungarian Jewish leader, had been flown to Hungary by German plane to propose a cessation of the extermination or deportation of Jews from Hungary, in return for 800 tons of coffee, 2 million cakes of soap and 1,000 trucks. Our representative in Turkey, Ira Hirschman,[1] relayed the proposal to us. It was a sadistic proposal and its primary purpose may have been to cause mischief and create discord between the British, the Russians and ourselves. In any event, it required the consent and approval of our allies. The information

1. Hirschman, acting with the cooperation of Lawrence Steinhardt, our Ambassador in Turkey, had been responsible for the rescue of countless refugees.

was sent along to Morganthau. We got no reply.

Other proposals were brought to us by a Swiss subject named Jean Marie Musy, a friend of Himmler. During my first month in office, Musy succeeded in obtaining the release of 1,200 Jews from the Theresienstadt concentration camp. Musy approached a representative of the Vaad Hahatzala with a request of $1 million for favors performed, with the promise of greater things to come. We asked for information and authorized the transfer of the funds to Switzerland, but did not receive authority to pay the ransom. However, these and other negotiations with the Nazis were maintained right up to the end of the war. We did not favor any brusque rejections, lest it cause retaliation against those we were to help.

In April, 1945, our Stockholm representative reported to us that by arrangement, a member of Sweden's Mosaic Society flew to Berlin and met Himmler. The following is the introduction of the reported encounter:

> Himmler arrived at the meeting at 2:30 on April 21, having driven 80 km. from Hitler's birthday party. Probably no more bizarre scene could be staged to record Himmler's unconditional surrender to world opinion—a two-hour drive through wrecked German roads and a conference until dawn with a Jew from Stockholm.

We felt it was important that constant complaints and warnings concerning the treatment of detainees be conveyed to the Nazis, and this was systematically done through Swiss, Swedish, Irish, Portugese and Vatican channels. There is no doubt that the Nazis were beginning to fear reprisals for murder and extermination, but we feared that they would resort to neglect and starvation in the last stages of the war they were now losing. We thereupon urged the State Department to issue a warning on behalf of the United States Government that all groups and individuals in Germany would be held accountable for acts of starvation and neglect, to the same degree as the crime of murder and equally punishable.

Acting on our recommendation, the Governments of the United States, the United Kingdom and Soviet Union on April 23, 1945, formally warned that any maltreatment of detainees or prisoners of war would be "ruthlessly pursued and brought to punishment." This was the last formal warning before the German collapse on May 8, 1945. While these warnings had some effect, the demoralized state of Germany during the last months made the position of the detainees more precarious than ever. The Geneva Prisoner of War Rules did not apply to detainees and denied them benefits that were accorded to prisoners of war. The board, through the Vatican, had made many proposals to the Germans aimed at protecting this group, but they were consistently rejected. During the latter part of 1944, 300,000 Red Cross food parcels were stored in Goteberg, Sweden, but up to February, 1945, only 40,000 of them got through to Germany.

I had a fair idea of what to expect in terms of human destruction, with the German army in a rout. No medium—neither print, nor film, nor drawing—can tell the story or communicate the horror that one feels on actually seeing it with one's own eyes. I had been in Italy and saw and smelled the bodies of men, women and children—hundreds of them—machine-gunned down and sealed in a catacomb.

An American war correspondent, who visited Bergen-Belsen in April, 1945, reported:

> I saw Belsen—its piles of lifeless dead and its aimless swarms of living dead. The great eyes were just animal lights and skin-covered skulls of famine. Some were dying of typhus, some of typhoid, some of tuberculosis, but most were just dying of starvation. Starvation—the flesh on their bodies that fed on itself until there was no flesh left, just skin covering bones and the end of all hope, and nothing left to feed on.

Hunger would not end until the successful armies came, and it was obvious that we could not wait. Some plan had to be devised at least to feed these people and save them during these last desperate months. Shortly before his death, I had outlined a plan to President Roosevelt to get food through to six German camps: Ravensbruck, Neuengamme, Bergen-Belsen, Dachau, Theresienstadt and Mauthausen. The President thought the plan was not feasible, but it received the enthusiastic approval of Henry Morganthau. Notwithstanding the President's doubts, and difficult a plan as it was, we did carry it out successfully, during a period when all efforts were bent on finishing the war as speedily as possible.

The first part fell into place after I had found out that in France there was a supply of oil and gasoline sufficient for our use, and I arranged with the War Department to have it made available. As a result, 2,000 gallons of precious gasoline per week were placed at our disposal, as well as lubricating oil and truck tires. We also found that there were trucks in Switzerland which had been in disuse for many of the war years. We had them put back in operation and Red Cross signs painted on them.

As if Providence were taking a hand, I met Henry Wallace in Washington, who introduced me to his brother-in-law, the Swiss minister. Through him, I was able to enlist the help of Count Folke Bernadotte of Sweden. As a result a Red Cross representative was assigned to each camp to assist, under our supervision, in the proper distribution of food. The trucks, with Red Cross personnel, began to roll out of Switzerland, some carrying extra supplies of gasoline, going north to Lubeck, Germany, where we had delivered the food, which had been stocked in Goteborg, Sweden. Lubeck became the distribution point for the northern camps of Ravensbruck, Neuengamme, Bergen-Belsen and Buchenwald. Other trucks went from Switzerland to the camps at Dachau, Munich, Theresienstadt, and Mauthausen.

We recommended and made arrangements to have the aged and ill transported back to Switzerland. The trucks brought back 1,400 of the worst cases. Our supplies soon gave out, and although we had made arrangements for 300,000 additional food parcels to be delivered through the blockade, it became clear that this shipment could not possibly get through in time. We had to look for other sources. We discovered 206,000 parcels—prisoner of war stockpiles—in Geneva and bought the whole lot, and that guaranteed us a more than adequate food supply. Our effort was accomplished.

In the past, war period stories of unusual and heroic efforts to save refugees from the Nazis have floated around and perhaps the most noted was the amazing accomplishments of a Swede named Raoul Wallenberg whose performance, in the face of constant danger, was responsible for helping so many thousands to get to safety.

The work of the War Refugee Board ended with the collapse of Germany on May 8, after which relief work was in the hands of UNRRA, headed by Governor Lehman. There were, however, some loose ends to be attended to during the summer. This unfinished business was, by order of President Truman, transferred to the Department of the Interior. In August, by virtue of Executive Order 982 refugees were taken to Fort Ontario at Oswego, New York. It was the understanding that after the war they would be returned to their homeland.

In July 1945, the American Jewish Conference reported my position on the subject:

"The disposition of the Oswego refugees is important," General O'Dwyer declared, "as an example to the other United Nations of American treatment of the unsolved problem of stateless persons. To return these people to Italy on the formal consideration that this was the country from which they were shipped . . . would not be in accordance with the President's (Roosevelt's) commitment. Such action would undoubtedly prejudice the action of other countries with large numbers of refugees . . . whom we urged to accept as many as possible while we were at war with Germany."

A congressional sub-committee met at Fort Ontario to inquire as to the fate of these "Oswego refugees," as they were called. I spoke before the committee and recommended that these refugees be permitted to remain. Special legislation followed, permitting them to remain with us. Our example proved of help to many other refugees who were seeking admission to Palestine, which required the approval of the British Government. As a matter of fact, the following year, there was agitation in New York for the admission of refugees to Palestine. Ernest Bevin, the British Foreign Secretary, reasoned, "They do not want too many of them in New York." I was then Mayor of New York, and when the press asked me for comment, I said, "He talks like the rabble-rouser, Joe McWilliams, and he is just as wrong."

My efforts in behalf of the Oswego refugees elicited the following gracious letter from "Old Curmudgeon," Secretary of the Interior Harold L. Ickes:

> With your letter of June 6, you sent me a copy of a memorandum which you presented to the members of the War Refugee Board, setting forth your recommendations concerning the Refugee Shelter at Oswego, New York.
>
> As you know, in view of the impending dissolution of the War Refugee Board, the President has transferred to this Department the responsibilities of that Board for policy guidance with respect to the Oswego project. Accordingly, I have carefully examined the recommendations which you made to the members of the War Refugee Board. As you well know, the successful completion of the fair and humane program which you outline depends upon the agreement and cooperation of other Federal and international agencies and upon the wishes of Congress. But I want you to know that I am in accord with your recommendations, which have as their objective the fair and compassionate treatment of the refugees at Oswego, and the preservation for the United States of the respect of those who are watching our treatment of the unfortunate people at Oswego as a practical test of our benevolence.
>
> On behalf of my staff and myself, I want to express to you our thanks for your splendid cooperation and the excellent work that you have done as Executive Director of the War Refugee Board. Your work and that of the Board have resulted in sal-

vaging the lives of thousands of guiltless political and war refugees in Europe, and you have greatly assisted in outlining the basis for proper handling of the Oswego project. I hope that you will permit me to call upon you for advice as we proceed with our difficult job at Oswego.

Shortly after that came some high compliments from Henry Morgenthau, who in his modesty neglected to mention his own wholehearted and unflagging contributions to the refugee problem and program. At a luncheon at the Hotel Commodore, he made the following comments:

> I think that no agency of the United States government had a tougher or more heartbreaking task to perform than the War Refugee Board. From the beginning it was up against hopeless odds. Its job was to snatch from the hands of ruthless and vindictive enemy men and women who had already been condemned to death. It took patience and prudence and great qualities of determination to carry out this job. Yet, despite these difficulties, the War Refugee Board, created by the warm sympathy of Franklin Delano Roosevelt, managed to save the lives of thousands of helpless men and women.
>
> Among other things, the Board set up a program, financed by emergency funds of the President, to supplement private shipments of food packages from the United States. These packages were destined for the civilian inmates of German concentration camps. Through the services of the American Red Cross some 300,000 packages were shipped in October and November of 1944 and stocked in Sweden and Switzerland. But deliveries to the camps themselves, because of transportation and other difficulties, were very slow. By February of the year only 40,000 of these packages had actually gone to their destination.
>
> The Nazis, as the Board well knew, were choosing to kill their victims by starvation and deliberate neglect. General O'Dwyer tackled what seemed to be an insurmountable situation with characteristic resourcefulness. He came before the Board and presented recommendations for accelerated deliveries to German concentration camps and for removal of the physically unfit to safety in Switzerland. His recommendations found prompt support among the Board members. The War Department instructed General Eisenhower to put essential army transportation equipment in France at the General's disposal. Because of his energy and pertinacity, food at last

reached the starving people in Dachau, Munich, and other German slaughter houses. And some 1400 refugees were brought out to Switzerland in Army trucks.

I was invited to Los Angeles by the United Jewish Appeal to help in their drive on May 1 and 2, 1945. Eddie Cantor was chairman. My talk had to do with the things that I had experienced in the recent past. I felt there was a danger that those who had survived the holocaust might be forgotten and not given a fair chance to live in a free world.

"The emphasis tonight," I told the audience, "must be directed to the task of keeping alive and rehabilitating the saved people. For years, these survivors have lived through torments and agonies that our minds cannot comprehend. Some of them were born in cages and do not yet know that there are in this world people of great hearts and generosity who are ready to bring to them oil for their wounds, food and clothing for their bodies, shelter from the cold, solace for their souls and hope for the future. These helpless ones who, up to now, have attracted the sympathy of the humane world, must not be forgotten in the joy of our imminent complete victory over our common enemy in Europe."

Notwithstanding all the agitation, almost a whole decade passed before those camps were entirely cleared. And as if the suffering were wholly forgotten, other wars and other tensions were in the making.

I urged the erection in New York of a monument to the victims of Nazi persecution, a project that was abandoned after I left the city.

PO'D

It is understandable that Bill O'Dwyer would have been deeply moved when the President appointed him executive director of the War Refugee Board. And what I am about to write in no way diminishes my sense of pride in what my brother accomplished during the crucial months as the Nazis were retreating. I have, however, previously added chapters to this book which are meant to describe the context in which the events Bill recorded took place. In dealing with the war years and the War Refugee Board, I do not wish to leave the impression that the United States and the Allied leaders did all that could have been done and should have been done to prevent the slaughter of millions of Jews and others by the Nazis.

While historians, particularly Jewish historians, continue to carry on a debate on the role of President Roosevelt and the American Jewish leaders in establishing and carrying out policy with regard to the victims of Nazism, the threshold question is a moral one and concerns our Allies but mostly us. What was the obligation of our Government given our most prized traditions? Did we as a people honor the concepts of our founders and those who later sacrificed their lives to keep our traditions intact? We did a fine job of defeating Hitler. We did a poor job of rescuing Hitler's victims.

During the late 30's and before Pearl Harbor Roosevelt had been a source of hope for American Jews. While, by and large, they did not agitate for a declaration of war, Roosevelt's oft-expressed antagonism towards Hitler endeared him to them. His appointments included Jewish leaders like Henry Morgenthau as Secretary of the Treasury and confidants like the most respected and admired Rabbi Stephen Wise. In addition, Dave Nlles had taken up residence in the White House and acted as the President's intimate adviser in Jewish affairs. Ben Cohen of the young team known then as Corcoran & Cohen was a brain resource of the administration. These were but a few of the Roosevelt intimates among the American Jewish community. They were all from the Jewish establishment.

Besides the Jewish advisers and other appointments to high positions in government, Roosevelt had close personal contacts with American Jews in various phases of his life. Trade union leaders, like Sidney Hillman and David Dubinsky, came to his assistance during his Presidential campaigns with the full force of the politically active Amalgamated Clothing Workers Union and International Ladies' Garment Workers Union. Jewish business leaders contributed handsomely each time he was a candidate for public office starting with his quest for the governorship of New York State and Judge Samuel Rosenman was his speechwriter in each campaign for the Presidency.

With the outbreak of the war in 1939 there was a strong feeling throughout the U.S. that we should not be involved in the conflict. Several organizations sprang up aimed at keeping us neutral. Time and time again Roosevelt made it clear where his sentiments lay and much armament was shipped to Great Britain under convoy in answer to Churchill's plea to "give us the tools and we will finish the job" (Feb. 9, 1941). The combination of Midwest isolationism and the suspicion of many Irish Americans who saw our efforts as being helpful to Great Britain made it most unlikely that Roosevelt could have gotten a declaration of war through Congress prior to Peal Harbor. Roosevelt's resolute position in the face of this opposition brought enthusiastic support from the Jewish electorate. Holocaust historian Lucy Dawidowicz described the relationship between Roosevelt and the Jewish community: "American Jews loved him for his good works and ideals but most of all for his hatred of the Nazi regime."

Against that background it may have been difficult for Jewish Americans to believe that Roosevelt was not doing his level best to protect the interest of Jews who had been engulfed by Hitler's plan. If

Acting on behalf of David Ben Gurion, former Secretary of the Treasury Henry Morganthau presents a silver Bible to the Mayor, 1948

Roosevelt viewed his best strategies to be an all-out effort to win the war against Hitler with no deviation, they seem to have accepted his judgment with some misgivings. Dissenters did not agree with the Allies or Roosevelt's position. They felt that with some special effort the tragic happenings in the concentration camps could indeed be avoided, at least in part.

Among the dissenters were Yitshaq Ben-Ami, Peter Bergson and Sam Merlin, who had come to plead for aid and arms for the Irgun, the army fighting for a Jewish state in Palestine. They stayed to plead for six million of their co religionists and an assortment of Jehovah's Witnesses, gypsies and others considered undesirable by the Nazis. Their efforts spawned an organization known as the American League for a Free Palestine made up of Jews and non-Jews, including members of Congress, actors, authors, cartoonists and this writer, and headed by American businessman Henry L. Selden. All of us were convinced that the Irgun had the key to success. All agreed that all pressures should be brought to bear on our Government and our Allies to develop a plan of action.

It was no secret that neither of our two major Allies, Great Britain and Russia, was anxious to become involved in the refugee problem lest it diminish their commitment to the war effort. Many have given this as an excuse for our failure to develop a Jewish dimension in the war aims. As the war dragged on the U.S. was constantly being asked to open a second front. In fact, at any time during the years 1941 to 1944 we were in a dominant position with the Allies and if we had insisted that the Jewish dimension of the war be considered and incorporated in the war effort, our Allies were not in any position to object. It was not done. The excuses that the Russians and the British would not stand for it does not hold water. Besides, we could have accomplished a great deal on our own. We didn't.

Scandalously little was done. In doing the research for this chapter, I learned Hitler's main goal with regard to the Jews was to rid them from his jurisdiction. At least until 1941, he would have let the Jews go if other countries had accepted them. However, no other country would take more than a handful. The limited immigration of Jews to Palestine, which had been designated by the Balfour Declaration as a homeland for the Jews, was reduced. No effort was made to change the quotas to permit "the wretched" refugees inside our borders. In fact, due to increased wartime scrutiny, the number of immigrants from Nazi-held areas was greatly reduced. I remember how my brother had pleaded to get the relatively few Oswego refugees admitted into the U.S. even after the war was over. It seemed so hypocritical for a nation so committed to the destruction of Hitler to be at the same time so insensitive to the plight of Hitler's victims. We who have welcomed literally millions of refugees, who had posted a welcome to the "tempest tossed" at the golden door—how could we do this to the very remnants of the millions doomed to destruction.

As early as 1942, some Americans were aware of mass murders of Jews in Nazi concentration camps and in 1943 the failure of the Bermuda Conference[2] to produce a plan of rescue for the refugees resulted in bitter disappointment. That same year the President received through Secretary of the Treasury Morganthau a memorandum from Jewish leaders who knew what was happening in the concentration camps. The memo charged that the State Department was acquiescent with the mass murders, implying that it was implicated in the plans for annihilation in Hitler's camps. In an accompanying memorandum Morganthau respectfully reminded the President that the task of rescuing Jews from extermination was a task full of difficulties which "only a fervent will to accomplish, backed by persistent and untiring efforts can succeed where time is so precious."

Also in 1943, Senator Guy Gillette of Iowa and Congressman Will Rogers Jr. of Oklahoma, both members of organizations seeking to focus attention on the plight of concentration camp inmates, sponsored a Congressional resolution calling for the establishment of a war refugee board. The resolution passed in December 1943.

Whether it was in response to the Gillette-Rogers Resolution or in response to the Morganthau memo, the President issued the first order appointing the War Refugee Board in January 1944 and he was apparently most anxious to make it a really effective rescue operation. He sent Dave Niles to find out how well acquainted my brother was with Spain. After he got the report from Niles he issued the memorandum to Under Secretary of War Robert Patterson indicating his desire to make Bill the head of the newly formed board. Patterson promptly replied that Bill was indispensible in his current job of detecting fraud, waste and abuse in the production of airplane parts. After Patterson's reply, Roosevelt raised John Pehle from acting executive to full executive and did not come back to get my brother to do the job for a full year.

During that year, the War Refugee Board worked with the Swedish Government which assigned Raoul Wallenberg, that remarkable humanitarian, to the rescue work. In his rescue operation Wallenberg worked through the Swedish Red Cross and as a Swedish diplomat. He and his staff provided appropriate documents to about 25,000 Hungarian Jews. The documents declared them to be under Swedish protection.

2. The Bermuda Conference was a meeting between Anthony Eden and President Roosevelt in June 1943 to discuss the problem of refugees.

The War Refugee Board provided monetary assistance, but it was essentially Wallenberg's skill and daring which was responsible for his remarkable feats. The Swedish Government has established that Wallenberg was responsible for saving the lives of 70,000 by convincing the German military leaders, just before Budapest fell to the Russians, that they would be prosecuted and put to death as war criminals if they allowed Hungarian Nazis to destroy the Budapest ghetto.[3]

Ira Hirschmann was another representative of the War Refugee Board who was responsible for saving tens of thousands of lives. Acting with Lawrence A. Steinhardt, United States Ambassador to Turkey, he got thousands of Jews out of the Balkans. He also helped to save approximately 90,000 in camps in Rumania and Bulgaria who probably would have been killed as the Nazis retreated had he not intervened.

In January 1944, when the board was established, it was already late in the day. In January 1945, when Bill O'Dwyer was appointed its executive director, those left alive in the Nazi human slaughterhouses represented but a fraction of those destroyed.

If Raoul Wallenberg and Ira Hirschmann, with only limited help from the War Refugee Board, could have rescued so many and if Bill O'Dwyer could have accomplished what he did in the short time allotted to him, what might he or any other dedicated and competent executive director, with the power of the United States behind him, have done if the effort had been started in 1942 or even earlier.

3. Wallenberg's career was cut short in January 1945 when Russia overran Hungary. He has not been heard from since and the Russians refuse to account for him.

CHAPTER 29

CAMPAIGN (1945)

In the aftermath of every election, it is to be expected that the defeated candidate shall suffer from a feeling of rejection. But if he is to survive in politics, he must quickly bring his feelings under control and soon put the experience behind him. If the race has been a close one, family and friends and the candidate himself can, and invariably will, find many excuses for losing. Seldom will they look inwardly for the reason for defeat, instead recalling that many friends seemed to lack sufficient enthusiasm about the campaign, and this reaction may develop into a feeling of betrayal. If the candidate and the well-wishers persist in this attitude, the candidate can't help but become an insufferable, complaining bore and is bound to lose whatever followers he had acquired.

In 1941, I had been a comparative neophyte among experienced politicians. The money and the power were on the side of my opponent. Furthermore, a goodly part of the Democratic Party machine was either lackadaisical or disheartened, and President and Mrs. Roosevelt both openly supported La Guardia. Under the circumstances, the results were surprising to Democratic officials. Ultimately, it dawned on our side that getting as far as we did was much more than we ever had a right to expect.

Four action-packed years had now gone by, and in 1945 the scene was altogether different. In the early part of the year, White House confidant Dave Niles called me. "The President has directed me to set an appointment. He wants to see you," he said. And within a few days, I was again with the President. After a few minutes of general conversation, he got to the point. "What are your political plans in New York?" he asked. It was a delicate subject, at least I thought so, but my Commander in Chief showed no hesitancy in making reference to the fact that he had cost me the election in 1941. "I owe a great deal to La Guardia," he said, "and you had him hard-pressed in 1941, when I spoke out in his behalf. But I can assure you of one thing, that if you are a candidate this time, I shall not oppose you, even if Fiorello is running. If he is not, I don't know of anyone else who can ride the three horses in New York." He was referring to the Democratic, the American Labor and the Liberal Parties. It was obvious that he felt La Guardia could not make it again, and he was unwilling to risk the loss of prestige inherent in supporting a loser.

Nineteen forty-five was beginning to shape up well. The war was winding down, and it was only a question of time until Hitler would be defeated and we would be free to marshal all our forces against the Japanese war machine. The disabilities which could account for my loss at the polls in 1941 were now disappearing. The liberal community was satisfied with my war record, thus overcoming its natural opposition to an Irish Catholic candidate, a pheomenon which had developed from the anti-Semitism espoused by Father Charles Coughlin of Michigan and his Eastern cohorts.

Furthermore, the Liberal Party had broken away from the American Labor Party, ending the coalition which Roosevelt, Farley, Flynn and the left-wing labor leaders had forged ten years earlier. A great rivalry had developed between those two factions and it was not very likely that I could, without Roosevelt's help, satisfy both parties. And I believed I could depend on the promised support of the American Labor Party.

I had been speaking with Congressman Vito Marcantonio in Washington, and Paul had kept close contact with the leadership of the American Labor Party during the four intervening years, setting up some appointments for me with its leadership during my trips back to New York from Washington. We had exchanged views as to what kind of America, what kind of New York, and what kind of world we would work for at the end of the war. I believe these talks cleared the air a great deal, and at least for that period of time, gave rise to a feeling of comradeship. I had the assurance of the leadership that it was ready to support me. I had no idea then how important that support was going to be.

As for other sources of support, my relationship with the Jewish community had always been good. It had been enhanced by my service in the war and particularly as head of the War Refugee Board. The Italo-American population had become very sensitive to the criticism sometimes amounting to vilification to which they had been subjected. Anne O'Hare McCormick had written about my activities in Italy for *The New York Times,* and my friend Generoso Pope, editor of the influential New York daily, *Il Progresso,* had also published a full account of my Italian experiences.

It was generally felt that La Guardia would be a candidate to succeed himself for an unprecedented fourth term as Mayor. There was no other Democratic candidate on the horizon who could marshal strong support from various segments of the city.

I received a call from Ed Flynn, Bronx county leader, and met him for dinner. I had no reason to be overly friendly with Flynn. I was aware of the dual role he had played in the 1941 election, and I knew from the Paul Kern incident that he still owed a great deal to La Guardia. As one of La Guardia's commissioners, Kern had insisted on carrying out an investigation into a matter which proved to be very embarrassing to Flynn. La Guardia intervened on Flynn's behalf. When Kern would not lay off, the Mayor summarily discharged his commissioner.

However, I was in no position to turn down an invitation from Flynn, particularly since I was well aware that he was the only New York Democrat with entree to the White House.

"The President wants us to nominate you for Mayor," he said. "If Fiorello is defeated, the President will do something for him. But this time, there is no question that the President wants you elected." I was well aware of the President's wishes on the matter, since he had personally made them known to me a short time earlier.

Soon after my meeting with Flynn, I met Frank Kelly, Brooklyn county leader, at some public function. He pulled me to one side. "Flynn has told me of your talk," he said, "and this time we are sure to win." "How do the other three leaders feel about this?" I asked. "They'll go along," he said with an air of assurance. The other leaders were Ed Loughlin of Manhattan, Jerry Sullivan of Staten Island and Jim Roe of Queens.

It was not very long after these conversations that the President died, and shortly after that, La Guardia announced that he would not seek a fourth term. Both of these significant events had their impact on the plans of the local Democratic leaders, as succeeding events were soon to demonstrate. The first signal I had that something was up happened while I was away from New York.

After a speaking engagement for the United Jewish Appeal in Los Angeles, I was visiting my brother, Frank, in El Centro, when I received word that back in New York Flynn had been taken to Knickerbocker Hospital. It was somewhat of a surprise to hear that on his way into the hospital, in a less-than-guarded and perhaps confused moment, he had issued a statement to the press to the effect that he did not think I would make a good candidate for Mayor. "O'Dwyer is too close to Communism," he said, "and this greatly weakens his chances of getting the Democratic Party nomination or endorsement." It was obviously an unplanned and premature attack, but it put me on notice that the leaders smelled blood and had made another selection. Knowing that my place

211

was in New York, I cut short my visit and immediately returned to Brooklyn and waited.

I soon received a call from Frank Kelly requesting a meeting with him at his apartment at the Towers Hotel on Decoration Day. I went prepared to hear him out.

As always, Kelly was a quiet, gracious host, low-key but effective. He spoke with the self-assurance of one who had it all his own way in his barony and seldom met even a ripple of political opposition. He was available for politics 24 hours a day. The day I was summoned to hear my fate, there was not the slightest evidence of embarrassment in his voice or demeanor as he announced the change in the game plan. He did not delay in coming to the point. He was deciding my fate as if that were clearly his prerogative, and what effect the decision might have on city issues was hardly a subject for thought, much less discussion. The pronouncement was obviously believed by him to have had all the power of an edict from Olympus.

"Bill," he said in a matter-of-fact fashion, "the boys think you would not make a good candidate." There was no attempt to explain the change of position from his statement of a couple of weeks earlier.

"Do the 'boys' include you and Flynn?" I asked. "Yes it does, Bill," he replied. "Dubinsky and the Liberal Party won't back you, and you can't take the American Labor Party—they're too communistic."

"Frank," I replied, "they are the same parties that have consistently supported Roosevelt and every one of our Democratic state candidates."

"Well," he said, "you may have an argument there, but that's the way we see it. I'd like you to see Judge Johnston. He wants to talk to you about it. He's in his chambers. I told him you were coming, and he's waiting for you." I ignored the effrontery and went to see the judge.

It was now clear to me that they had already chosen my successor. With Fiorello out of the way, and without interference from the White House, they could now choose one of their own, whom they could rely on to deal with them to their advantage. So sure were Johnston and Kelly that I would present no opposition to their plans that Johnston had come to his chambers on the holiday especially for this meeting. I had not seen the judge for more than two years, and our parting then had been less than friendly. I went directly to the courthouse and into the judge's chambers.

Johnston wasted no time with preliminaries. "The party can't see you as a candidate this time. However, you can be of invaluable help during the campaign, and your chance will come at a later time. I'm sure you'll agree with me. I've prepared a statement for your signature, and at the appropriate time, we will release it to the press." He handed me the statement. It was to the effect that because of my regard for the

Democratic Party and in the interest of unity, I was withdrawing as a candidate for Mayor.

In his face and demeanor the judge showed how much he relished the moment. It was clear that at last he could put an offending upstart in his place, and he was not at all inclined to soften the blow. I got up and moved in the direction of the door. "You better hold on to that paper, judge," I said, as I was closing the door from his chambers. As I looked back, the judge seemed stunned. I felt a weight lifted off my back. It was a pivotal and liberating moment for me. Finally, I was going to do battle openly with the arrogant bastard.

A few blocks away in the Bossert Hotel, Paul and Oscar Bernstien were waiting for me. We had previously discussed the injudicious statement Flynn had made as he entered the hospital, and we were not unprepared for the Kelly-Johnston tack. We decided any delay in responding to their proposal would be a sign of weakness. Besides, we agreed, I should act while they were still off balance and before they had a chance to recover from the shock. I went back immediately to the Towers Hotel. "Frank," I said, "I met Judge Johnston and my answer is that 'I'm a candidate.' If you and Flynn want to change your position, which you outlined with me a few weeks ago, that's up to you, but, then, you have a primary fight on your hands."

Kelly was stunned. My response was hardly according to his plan. At no time had there been any mention of the arrangement made by Kelly and Flynn with regard to my candidacy before President Roosevelt died and La Guardia decided not to run for a fourth term. They obviously understood that I would be somewhat resentful before and after signing the statement of declination which Johnson had prepared, but a pat on the back and a promise of future recognition would undoubtedly straighten all that out. Dealing with a disappointed candidate was part of their daily routine. My response was a declaration of war on the total machine.

I formally announced my candidacy the following day.

I had no misgivings about the task I had taken on despite the knowledge that I would have a real fight on my hands. Of the leaders in the five boroughs, Kelly and Flynn were strongly entrenched. Jim Roe of Queens was a strong and aggressive Democratic county leader. However, Queens County had been heavily Republican and strongly independent. In a Democratic primary there, the Democratic Party did not measure up in importance to Brooklyn, Manhattan or the Bronx. Staten Island was numerically small, and Tammany Hall, the New York County organization, was totally unreliable. The Tammany membership was in disarray, and many old-time disreputable leaders were still in control.

In Brooklyn, following the death of Boss McCoey in 1934, Frank

Kelly had succeeded to the leadership. He was so far ahead of the other 22 district leaders that no one challenged his position as long as he lived. He spent part of his day at the party headquarters at 4 Court Square, where he dispensed patronage to the faithful, parceled out the minor jobs to the various district leaders, or straightened out their judicial disputes. His apartment at the Towers Hotel was furnished with taste and quiet dignity and gave the impression of comfortable, if not luxurious, living.

While the Montauk Club was the meeting place for dinner conferences with important people on important subjects, Kelly's apartment was reserved for the meetings with Judge Johnston and one or two intimates, with whom he discussed long-range programs and party strategy.

As to Ed Flynn's domain, the Harlem River separates the island of Manhattan from the rest of the upstate area. Bronx County, lying north of the Harlem River, was a Democratic cushion between Manhattan and the rich Republican suburban Westchester County. Bronx County has no wealthy Park Avenue or Fifth Avenue, and the nearest thing to opulence is Riverdale, an isolated area of the well-to-do along the Hudson River. Toward the East Bronx, where I first lived after arriving in New York, were the tenements. Ed Flynn had unchallenged sway over the Democratic Party in the Bronx for many years and at the same time completely controlled the Republican Party in the whole county. For Republican acquiescence, he gave them a share of the patronage, and they were satisfied.

Flynn was a wealthy lawyer, well-read, with unusually fine manners. He was the soul of refinement, lived well, and spent a great deal of his time at his farm where he bred and raised fine horses. He also liked the plush horse-raising lands near Dublin.

Flynn's office was located in mid-Manhattan, though he spent little time there. His firm had an excellent standing, and his partner, Monroe Goldwater, was one of the ablest lawyers in town. While it was true that Flynn's position did not hurt the firm when it came to getting business, the fact was that it could stand on its own feet and did in fact prosper after Flynn's sudden death in a Dublin hotel.

Flynn was the farthest in image from the typical large-city political boss as one could imagine. He looked with disdain or at least stayed aloof from his various district leaders. His habits differed radically from those of Frank Kelly. Unlike Kelly, he had no one to author his book on politics. He kept his own counsel, and it was quite logical that he would be selected as the state's national committeeman. It was just as logical that he would be a confidante of Roosevelt and a friend of La Guardia. Only he could have called La Guardia "New York's finest mayor" with impunity, particularly at a time when La Guardia was to be opposed by a Democrat at the next election. Only once before in his political life had he been frustrated. Roosevelt had nominated him as Ambassador to Australia. It was his great ambition. However, Flynn could not get Senate approval. The senators did not like the idea of an Irish Catholic representing the United States. The excuses they gave for denying him approval were without real substance, but he took his defeat like a gentleman and did not even take time to declare that he knew the real reason.[1]

Outside of that simple setback, life had been tranquil for Ed Flynn. Once he and Kelly had agreed on a program, he never considered the possibility that there could or would be strong opposition to it.

It was not in the script, however, that he would telegraph his surprise punch by an unguarded statement at the hospital door under circumstances which apparently had warped his judgment. It was this error that took the element of surprise from the Kelly-Johnston scenario and gave me time to create a counteroffensive. By now I had the advantage in the game, and while Flynn was still temporarily indisposed, my immediate announcement threw Kelly and Johnston off balance.

I had told Kelly, "You have a primary fight on your hands," but I had said it with more bravado than the facts warranted. Actually it was I who had the fight, and an uphill one, too. A primary fight in New York would be costly. The party machine would go into action for the party's choice. Organizing an independent army of canvassers and poll-watchers in a short space of time would be a most difficult enterprise. Paul and Oscar assured me that there was a young army out there in the new labor unions and the American Labor Party. They felt that the Democrats were unhappy about boss rule and only too willing for just this kind of battle, but I was by no means as sure as they about our capacity to marshal them.

Before the dust settled after my session with Kelly and Johnston, I moved to solidify my position. I told Jim Roe, the Queens leader, of my encounter with Kelly and Johnston. Roe resented the implication that they spoke for him. "I've said on many occasions that you are the logical candidate," he assured me. Roe was big, strong, robust and forceful. He was as tactless as Kelly and Flynn were suave. His listeners may not have agreed with him, but they were never in doubt where he stood. He ruled a tempestuous county and mirrored the political turmoil that seemed to infect the area. "Is it a fact that Dubinsky will not go for

1. Times changed radically from that time to 1950, when my name as Ambassador to Mexico came before the Senate. Only two persons spoke before the Senate Foreign Relations Committee against my appointment. One was a Republican candidate for Congress from New York.

you?" he asked. "I believe they are right in that," I replied. "Dubinsky feels that my brother is too close to his archenemies, the American Labor Party." "That's too bad," Roe replied. "Can you rely on the American Labor Party?" "We can put more workers in the field than Kelly and Flynn, and the C.I.O. unions will follow the American Labor Party." Roe slapped his knee. "That's all I want to know," he said. "Flynn and Kelly better know that a primary is no idle threat. How does Loughlin stand?" I asked. "I'll let you know," he said.

Ed Loughlin was a quiet, well-meaning man who sat on the powder keg called Tammany Hall. It had seen no real peace in the decades since Charlie Murphy was its leader. The failure to find a leader of stature to take Boss Murphy's place caused Jimmy Walker to remark, "The brains of Tammany Hall is in Calvary Cemetery." Loughlin was trying to do his best with an impossible situation, but the party's worst elements were forever running away with the ball. His New York County organization could not be depended upon for an hour. Clarence Neal, a shrewd and wily politician from East Harlem, was a thorn in Loughlin's side. I would have to take a hand twice within the next two weeks to stop chicanery initiated by Neal. These problems notwithstanding, Ed Loughlin lined up with Roe, and that left only Jerry Sullivan.

Sullivan was the leader of the island which Giovanni da Verrazano and Henry Hudson saw over on their left side as they entered the harbor nearly four centuries ago. Originally settled and named by the Dutch, Staten Island was sparsely populated. Subsequent settlers sought to call it after the Earl of Richmond, and in official documents it is referred to as the County and Borough of Richmond, but the Dutch name clung to it, and the people always refer to it as Staten Island. Once Sullivan knew that Roe and Loughlin had lined up with me, he followed suit, and that's how things stood for several meetings of the county leaders at the National Democratic Club in mid-Manhattan.

Public interest in the selection process had become heightened, and the press was watching for the smoke signals. Flynn and Kelly tried to convince the other leaders to reject me, but Roe, enjoying his new role as the sponsor in the primary contest, was adamant. For once he had the upper hand over what would normally be considered an unbeatable combination. As a last resort Kelly made a personal appeal to me. "Bill, in the interest of party harmony, why don't you withdraw your name?" he asked. "Party harmony will come," I replied, "when you and Flynn join the majority."

Finally, they capitulated, and I became the nominee of the Democratic Party. The approval of the American Labor Party followed almost immediately. But that was not the end of it. The city-wide ticket encompasses the Mayor, the Comptroller, and the President of the City Coun-

216

cil. It had long been the custom for the head of the ticket to be consulted about his running mates. However, Kelly and Flynn allowed Loughlin to select the candidate for President of the City Council, and that moved Loughlin to cast his lot with them. The party leaders showed their complete disdain by ignoring me completely as to the rest of the ticket. They nominated running mates whom I had never met. Kelly and Flynn with a flourish announced that Lawrence Gerosa, a Bronx contractor with no experience in municipal government, would be the candidate for Comptroller, and a Manhattan lawyer would be the candidate for President of the City Council. Neither candidate contacted me before he was nominated, or after. I did not know their views on the many problems that were then besetting the city. Each city-wide office holder had an equal number of votes in the Board of Estimate meeting and could jointly play havoc with any program I would sponsor. It was obvious that the leaders were going to box me in and the outlook for the years ahead was looking dim.

Therefore, when their selections were announced, I sent the following telegram to the five county leaders:

It is more important now than ever before that we deal courageously and progressively with the great and perplexing problems confronting the people. They are concerned, among other things, with civil rights, housing, jobs, inflation and special problems affecting veterans. This City ranks second only to the Federal Government, itself, in the variety of its affairs and the size of its budget. Never before in the history of the City have the people stood in greater need of public officials to whom they can look with confidence. Under the great leadership of the late President Roosevelt, this country and its Allies have successfully concluded the first phase of the war. But we are still in it, and under President Truman's capable guidance, we are on the road to final victory. To strengthen the forces of democracy we here in the City need public officials of proven experience and ability and so known to the people.

Without impunging the honesty or integrity of the gentlemen you designated as candidates for Comptroller and President of the City Council, they do not in my opinion measure up to the expectations or hopes of the people. As the Democratic designee for Mayor, I cannot in good conscience lend support to their candidacy. Will you please reconvene at once and designate candidates for these offices who will justify the enthusiastic support of the people. I will be glad to confer with you.

Consternation prevailed, and the town was enjoying the spectacle of this uneven fight, with David, for the moment at least, maintaining the upper hand against Goliath.

A few days later the leaders responded with an invitation to join them "at a conference called at your suggestion for Monday, June 11th at 12 o'clock noon at the National Democratic Club."

That was more like it. The meeting produced two other candidates, both of whom I had known previously. Lazarus Josephs, a State Senator from the Bronx, whose outstanding record as a liberal was well known, was nominated as Comptroller. Vincent Impellitteri, who was counsel in the famous Rubel Ice holdup case, which had been tried before me when I was county judge, was nominated for President of the City Council. In the intervening period, I had received the assurance from the American Labor Party that they would support my running mates. However, I took the precaution of having Paul check out the names before I approved them. The city-wide slate of candidates was complete. I promptly issued the following statement to the press:

> I have known both of my splendid colleagues for many years. My relations with them over this long period have been close and what pleases me most of all is that they stand for things I stand for and for which I have fought all my life. After we take office on January 1st next, we three will work together in harmony for a common purpose, to give to our City an Administration that will fulfill the hopes of the people.

Capitulation to my wishes put me in temporary control of the situation, but it was not long before another serious problem crashed onto the stage.

When Thomas E. Dewey had left to become New York's Governor in 1942, John Mullen, a judge in the Court of General Sessions and an old Tammany wheelhorse, arranged with the Tammany leaders to nominate Frank Hogan to succeed Dewey as Manhattan's District Attorney.

By coincidences easy to understand, important cases with news value and those wherein a desirable outcome were likely to enhance the prestige of the District Attorney were found to be scheduled before Judge Mullen.

In spite of the political maneuvering which catapulted him into the office of District Attorney and his background as a Tammany precinct captain, Hogan had, as an assistant district attorney, sat at the counsel table and assisted Dewey in the prosecution of Jimmy Hines, an influential Tammany boss and a close friend of President Roosevelt. Notwithstanding his link to Tammany politics, Hogan had become an energetic and able prosecutor.

A few years earlier, Hogan had tapped Frank Costello's telephone and accidentally intercepted a converation between Costello and a candidate for a Supreme Court vacancy. The conversation established that Costello was an influential voice in naming Supreme Court judges in New York County. Exposure of the conversation drew wide publicity. The judge in question was a good friend of Clarence Neal and Bert Stand, who then dominated the Tammany organization.

When it came time for renomination to the District Attorney's office in 1945, Neal and Stand had their revenge. They broke with Mullen, Tammany's judicial political advisor, and nominated Edward Ennis for the post. The decision was well thought out. In naming Ennis, the Tammany sachems selected an independent Democrat, a man with a fine liberal record, one that would ensure him the endorsement of the American Labor Party and perhaps the Liberal Party as well.

This move was intended to be sufficient lesson to any ambitious prosecutor who might in the future seek to upset the political plans of the Tammany leaders. It would also establish Frank Costello as a real power in New York politics.

Hogan called me before the news appeared in the press.

"This is Tammany's way of getting even with me for exposing the wiretaps," he said. I told Hogan to stand by for my phone call. Within half an hour I was talking to the leader of Tammany. "Call the county executives together," I said, "and nominate Hogan." "We can't do that now," he replied. "Had we known before how you felt about it, we might. . . ." I interrupted, "Then face a primary fight. I'm supporting Hogan." I called Hogan to tell him that I was going to insist on his nomination and support him in the primary.

A few days later Ed Ennis called to see me. After the interview I released the following statement:

I have informed Mr. Ennis that if he remained in the race, I would support Mr. Hogan in the primary against him. I have great admiration for Mr. Ennis. He has a fine reputation and I am convinced that had he spoken to me, he would not have accepted the candidacy against Mr. Hogan. I have reason to believe that an important decision will be made by Mr. Ennis later this afternoon.

Two important decisions were made that afternoon—Ennis withdrew as a candidate for District Attorney, and Tammany grudgingly nominated Hogan.

"Thanks, Bill," said Hogan later that evening. "Frank," I said, "I'm almost sorry they capitulated so easily. I would have rather enjoyed letting the Democratic voters of New York County pass on that issue. I know Tammany would not stand a chance."

In May, 1945, the *Daily News* had conducted a preferential poll for the office of Mayor. Jimmy Walker led it by a very comfortable margin. He pulled 38% of the votes to 30% for me, 25% for La Guardia, and 7% for others. It was New Yorkers' way of saying they felt that Walker had been treated badly and that they were sorry. The news of his high score was hailed everywhere, and there was little doubt that had he been in good health and in a position to run, he would have defeated all contenders hands down. The press inquired about his intentions, and he emphatically denied any intention of becoming a candidate.

A reporter asked Walker whom he favored for mayor. He said he held O'Dwyer in high regard. I had never met Walker up to that time, and "Broadway" Johnny O'Connor, a well-regarded journalist, felt I should pay him a courtesy visit at his home on East End Avenue.

Walker apparently had not been feeling well. He greeted us in his pajamas and complained of having a cold. "We should go into Betty's room," he said, leading the way. Betty Compton, a one-time actress, had been married to Jimmy. After they divorced she married again. Betty had died the year before. Now Jimmy, Betty's second husband, and Betty's dog occupied the apartment.

"Good luck to you, Bill," Walker said. "You have a hard act to follow." Jimmy and La Guardia had been on the best of terms. Jimmy had been away in Europe for a year after his trial. When he returned, La Guardia got him a job paying $20,000 per year as an arbitrator in the clothing field. His advice to me was not to appear to be so close to Michael Quill and, if I could avoid having my brother, Paul, around the campaign too much, it would be a help.

It was obvious that he was going downhill, but the *Daily News* poll gave him new life, and he felt it was his hour of vindication. We made arrangements to have him visit Gracie Mansion in the event of my election. He never made it. Death came too soon.

As the campaign got underway, things seemed to be shaping up well for me. The Republican and Liberal Parties got together that year, although it was no great principle that brought about that coalition. The Republicans had been branding the Liberal Party as communistic ever since its birth, and the Liberal Party had been equally vociferous in denouncing the Republicans as reactionaries. But it has often been said, "Politics makes strange bedfellows," and there was none more strange than the combination who opposed me. To confuse the picture more, they selected as their mayoral candidate a stalwart of Tammany Hall, General Sessions Judge Jonah Goldstein, who previously had been a magistrate, appointed by Jimmy Walker. He had been very active in Jewish charities and was extremely popular.

In the meantime, La Guardia had become angry at both his Republican friends and Liberal Party adherents for failing to consult him about their selection. He denounced the arrangement as a "deal" and decided to teach his "friends" a lesson. He formed a new party, calling it the No Deal Party, and nominated Newbold Morris as its candidate for Mayor. It was not that La Guardia loved me the more, but after 12 years as Mayor, he felt betrayed. In selecting Morris, he divided my opposition into two camps, and that made my election inevitable. If La Guardia's efforts were to show the Liberal Party and the Republicans how unimportant they were without him, he succeeded with a vengeance.

Political campaigns in our nation have more often than not been bizarre performances, in which exaggeration, distortion and downright falsehood too often become the weapons of the contest. Frequently the attack is on the character of the opponent and seldom on the principles he or she espouses or the program presented. It is a primitive appeal to the emotions, rather than the reason, of the voter.

The fact that such an approach has seldom been successful never seems to dampen the ardor of the next set of contenders.

These circumstances have been responsible for the intrusion of image-building public relations firms and agents into political campaigns. They do raise issues, but their prime objective is to make their candidate attractive. It has been charged that the make-up man in the Nixon-Kennedy debate was responsible for the Nixon defeat in one of the closest races in American history.

I believe most candidates start out with a firm resolve to keep the campaign on a high level. I know I wanted to conduct a campaign in which the people could and would hear a discussion of the problems ahead. I knew the city, and I knew what the post-war period had in store for us, and I was hopeful that we would get to a substantive discussion of New York and its people, as we went into the transition from a wartime economy to peacetime programs. I bravely faced my first audience with this in mind.

> We New Yorkers are justifiably proud of our great city. There is no place like it anywhere else in the world. Its material wealth is beyond measure. But its greatest treasure lies in its seven and a half million people. Its population is drawn from the four corners of the world.
>
> Each group of our people contributes its culture, its energies, its skills. Nowhere has the composite result been finer. From each of you, of whatever background, this city draws its

store of wealth, its stamina and its growth. For each of you, the city must provide, in equal measure, opportunities for livelihood, security, education and health.

Progressive forces throughout the nation are fighting to preserve and enlarge the opportunities for a good life for all of our people. These progressive forces are lined up behind the program described by the late President Roosevelt as a "second Bill of Rights under which a new basis of security and prosperity can be established for all, regardless of station, race or creed."

The program calls for the right to useful and well-paid jobs; the right to a decent home; the right to adequate medical care; the right to be protected from the fears of sickness, unemployment and insecurity in old age; the right to a good education; the right of every businessman, large or small, to work in an atmosphere of freedom and opportunity—in short, the right to all the benefits of the American way of life.

This was President Roosevelt's program. President Truman had made it the keystone of his Administration.

I know our city. It has been my school where I have learned the meaning of American democracy. It has strengthened my faith in democracy and has made me keenly appreciate its blessings. I have worked in this city as a laborer. I have patrolled its streets and waterfronts.

I have lived in its tenements, and have come to know the problems of slums, of poverty, of social conflicts, of labor and industry. As a policeman, judge and district attorney, I learned the problems of law enforcement. No one need tell me how intimate is the connection between honest government and the happiness of our citizens.

I am the candidate of the Democratic Party and of the American Labor Party. I am honored by their nominations. If elected, I shall be the mayor of all the people. I shall be under obligation only to the people and responsible only to them. My administration will be governed by that principle. My appointments will be determined by myself. I will select honest men and women on the basis of merit and fitness alone. This is my pledge to you, the people of the City of New York.

However, discussion of the city and its problems took a back seat in the campaign. Instead, a personal attack on the frontrunner took its place. It seemed that the only hope of defeating me lay in that course. My single encounter with Frank Costello in 1941 in the course of my Army duties was now made a campaign issue. With great fanfare, Goldstein and the Republican machine made it appear that Costello and I were close friends and that I would be obedient to his influence if I were elected Mayor.

I had made one bad tactical error early on in the campaign process, and now I was to pay dearly for the mistake—both during the campaign and after. In the event of my election as Mayor, Governor Dewey would fill the vacancy in my office as District Attorney in Brooklyn, and his choice would undoubtedly be a Republican. If I continued to hold office until January 1, my successor would then hold office for a full year.

In the summer of 1945, when my election seemed assured, Frank Kelly asked to see me at the Montauk Club. "Bill," he said, "you would do us a great favor if you resigned in time for your successor to be elected this year rather than next. There is a Democratic landslide in the air, and we don't want to give the Republicans a chance to capture this office for a whole year or maybe more."

"Who is to be my successor?" I asked.

"I plan to nominate Miles McDonald," he replied. McDonald had been a protege of both Kelly and Johnston, and I had appointed him assistant district attorney on their recommendation. Nevertheless, I had no reason to complain about his performance. He worked hard at his job, and I was pleased about his nomination to this prestigious post.

Without thinking it through, I decided to grant Kelly's request. On August 2, 1945, I filed my resignation as District Attorney. That decision permitted Dewey to appoint a successor, George Beldock, who immediately became the Republican candidate against McDonald. Beldock made every use of his new office to tear down the reputation I had painstakingly built up over years, and while it did not help him, his effort provided plenty of material for criticism in later attacks on me.

Beldock promptly began to investigate all of my cases and everything I had done. He looked for errors and shortcomings and found them, and those became my record, instead of the 85 murders I had solved. Beldock promptly convened a grand jury and called witnesses to establish that my office had not been at all what it was supposed to be.

He called me before the grand jury to tell all about the cases pending in the District Attorney's office when I entered the Army, and he caused grand jury presentments critical of my administration of that office to be publicized, by arranging for radio time to coincide with the signing of the presentments, and then making them the subject of his radio talk.

The presentments were later expunged from the record, but by that time the election was over and nobody cared. Not even Beldock. They attempted to break down the record I had built up in the prosecution of Murder, Inc. They omitted mentioning the long list of killers, includ-

223

ing Lepke, who had been convicted, but instead picked on our failure to convict Anastasia. By the time the campaign was over, Beldock, Goldstein and the full force of their public relations staff made it appear that my time in Brooklyn, the many sleepless nights, had been spent not in solving all those murders, but in protecting one notorious murderer. They uttered not one word about the future of the city or the people's needs.

It is difficult for a candidate to assess the effect on the public of charges and denials. With the space given to the charges in the newspapers and the time allotted on radio, the people could hardly have missed them. Yet in the end, the people gave me the largest majority ever given to a mayoralty candidate up to that time.[2]

After the election, Judge Franklyn Taylor, the Brooklyn county judge in charge of the grand jury, took action. He was known for his zealous concern for the dignity of the court and the grand jury process, and he was furious that it had been prostituted. He expunged the two grand jury presentments, making plain reference to the circumstances under which they were made. "The Presentment of October 19, 1945," he said, "was used by that candidate [Beldock] in radio broadcasts for his own election and for the defeat of his predecessor in office, Honorable William O'Dwyer, as candidate for Mayor. . . . Both presentments violated the Penal and Criminal Statutes of the State of New York. . . . The offending documents cannot be tolerated on the court records."

Beldock, defeated by Miles McDonald by a very large majority and now back in private practice, took no umbrage at the action or language of the court. He took no proceeding to have Judge Taylor's order revised or the biting criticism expunged. Two years later, I was requested to officiate at the dedication of the Veteran's Hospital in the Bronx. George Beldock was there to introduce me at the dedication ceremonies. He made the following introduction:

I am an active member of the Republican Party and in 1945 served as Republican Party District Attorney of Kings County. That year I was a candidate for election for a four-year term as District Attorney and my predecessor in that office was the Democratic candidate for Mayor. Well, during political campaigns many heated and intemperate statements are made and many remarks during the campaign are exchanged. In fact, I conducted an inquiry of my predecessor's administration of that office and on this occasion, I am indeed happy to say that

2. But that did not end the charges and the accusations. I was to hear them all again at the Kefauver hearings in 1950, except that on that occasion there was no jury, and no Election Day for vindication.

during that inquiry I never found anything that reflected in any way upon the personal integrity and honesty of the man I am about to introduce. I wish to present to this audience William O'Dwyer, Mayor of the City of New York.

So it was with politics and politicians in the 40's and I rather think it was ever thus.

But then a voice from above the battle was heard. Eleanor Roosevelt, in her daily column on the eve of Election Day wrote:

> My own reaction to the accusations that have been made during the past few days is that they have been largely political accusations. They are perhaps not entirely untrue, but put in their proper context and with all the circumstances out in the open, they would present a different picture to the public eye. General O'Dwyer knows his enemies and the enemies of good government well, and I think the future will prove that he knows how to fight them.

McDonald, on the occasion of his induction in December, 1945, told the assembly of judges and lawyers, "Five years as prosecutor under General O'Dwyer have taught me that a large part of the success that comes in that particular field of endeavor depends upon the ability and integrity of the law enforcement agencies." He mailed me a copy of the proceedings, which bore an equally complimentary legend above his signature: "To Honorable William O'Dwyer, my preceptor in the ways of prosecution, and a better never lived."

The grand jury investigation, of course, was hardly our only preoccupation during the campaign, though it did succeed in keeping me somewhat off-balance through much of it. Wayne Johnson, a prominent tax lawyer, was my campaign manager, and he enjoyed the excitement of the contest. Ben Fielding, whom I later appointed Commissioner of Licenses, acted as liaison between campaign headquarters at the Commodore Hotel and the American Labor Party.

Like all campaigns, it had its moments of humor. One day, one of our officials complained to me that a "spy" from the opposing camp had come with the proposal that he could deliver our opponents' speeches ahead of time. Sean Keating, later to be one of my commissioners, and who had served with the Irish Republican Army in 1919, threw him out. "An informer is an informer," he protested, "and if he works for us, it does not make him clean."

During the height of the campaign, an important lady publisher of great charm, who was very much committed to Newbold Morris' side, made a speech to a ladies' club on Park Avenue on his behalf. A reporter later that night stopped me on my way into one of the school meetings and called for my reaction to her statement that Mr. Morris' drawing room manners were much superior to mine. He grinned. "Would you like to comment?"

Reluctantly, I conceded that the lady had made a point. "But the lady well knows," I argued, "that there are more rooms in a home than the living room."

Before the evening was finished, a reporter from the lady's paper had me in tow. "Sir," she said, "did you have any particular room in mind?" "I did indeed." Finding my wisecrack getting me into deep water, I said, "The kitchen, of course."

The campaign, as already suggested, got completely out of hand. Reckless charges were made each night, and by the time our headquarters had an answer ready, a new set was already in print. It was quite difficult to keep temper under those circumstances, but it apparently heightened interest in the outcome, and on election night, Goldstein and Morris conceded my election by 9:30 p.m.

Calls and telegrams came pouring into headquarters, but I did not stay there long. I went home to Kitty. She looked at me with what looked like pity. We had coffee by the fireplace, listening awhile to other election returns, and retired for the night.

The following day I received an encouraging telegram:

Heartiest congratulations. I feel the cause of good government has been vindicated by your sweeping majority and predict for you a successful administration.

Harry S. Truman

With President Harry S. Truman in the White House, 1945

CHAPTER 30

MAYOR

"Patience and fortitude" was La Guardia's slogan. He used it frequently and always ended his speeches with it. It also became his goodbye. New Yorkers often used it, too, while he was Mayor. No one ever questioned Fiorello's fortitude, but patience was another thing. When the election was over and he was finishing his term, I came to pay him a visit. "Patience and fortitude, Bill," he said, "and you'll need a great deal of both." He was a consummate actor and one who knew how to get his message across, and the press loved his antics. When the press joined us, he got up from the Mayor's chair. "Sit down," he said, indicating with a gesture that I should occupy the chair. I accommodated. "Now," he said, "you have inherited a perpetual headache." Everyone laughed, and I did, too, because I didn't believe it. I had no idea what a headache it really was and how perpetual it was going to be.

It had been 16 years since a Democrat sat in that chair, and the interim took in the Depression and the war years. John P. O'Brien was the last Democratic Mayor. He had left the Surrogate's Court, where he earned a reputation as an honest and capable judge, to assume the Mayor's chair, and the changeover brought him into a totally unfamiliar atmosphere. The Depression was in full swing, and the city's treasury was empty. When O'Brien said so, no one believed him, because every Mayor coming into office complained about a bare cupboard. But the banks knew, and they told Mayor O'Brien if he wanted money, there was only one way it could be arranged: he must put up the city for security. John O'Brien was a quiet man, and experienced, and he knew enough not to resist. He signed on the dotted line. History calls the document the Bankers Agreement, but it could better be described as the city's surrender. From that point until the war came, bankers ran the town.

With the war clouds coming, the economy picked up, but building and other materials were unavailable, so there was little or no new construction, while older buildings were generally dilapidated. Not a single hospital had seen a paint brush in the 16 years prior to my swearing-in ceremonies. In the meantime, the city's population had increased by a million residents, and each department was woefully undermanned. The smoke was choking New Yorkers, and the raw sewage had long ago discouraged fish in the bay or the North River and had rendered our beaches dangerous for bathing.

The city's piers, once a main source of revenue, were now rotting, and trucks delivering cargo were constantly breaking through the rotting boards. It was not profitable for private builders to erect middle-class or low-income housing, and the veterans were returning in droves with no place to live. There was a smelly slaughterhouse at the site where the United Nations now stands, and that brand-new organization was in search of a home, with many eager cities vying for the privilege. Old labor unions, subdued by the Depression, were once again on the march, and militant ones like the Transport Workers Union were the result of the aggressive Congress of Industrial Organizations, which was formed during the Depression. The rapid transit system, once our pride and joy, was falling apart and badly in need of equipment and repair.

Solving any one of these problems would take time, energy and massive amounts of money and human resources. Our expense budget was about to reach $1 billion, and I was trying to keep it below that figure. It meant we would have to do much with little money, and it was apparent that my work was cut out for me.

The official swearing-in ritual took place in Rockaway in the home of Molly Lenihan, a cousin of Kitty, where we were temporarily staying. It was an accommodation to Kitty, since she wouldn't have been able to stand the excitement of a public ceremony at City Hall.

"Do you have anyone specially in mind to deliver the invocation?" asked my brother, Paul, and a mutual friend, Sean Keating, sometime prior to the ceremony. Their interest in the invocation, of all things, was a bit surprising. "Hadn't given it a thought," I said. "Would you have any objection to Sean Reid?" one of them asked. "I think it would be nice," I replied, "to have a Carmelite." Sean Reid was a young and lovable member of the Carmelite Order whose parish was beside Bellevue Hospital. They were chaplains to the hospital and the patients. But more than that, the Carmelites were beloved by the Irish community for having braved the condemnation of the archdiocese in 1919, when they openly aided and abetted the Irish Republican Army in its fight against the Black and Tans in Ireland's War of Independence. I thought it was a good idea to have Sean Reid deliver the prayer. I had no idea he would slip in some of the propaganda of his sponsors into the middle of the invocation.

It started reasonably enough by imploring God to bless me and give me strength, but then the clergyman, I thought, departed from his function and began to wax eloquent with a political and social philosophy somewhat alien to the Roman Church in New York at the year of 1946. "Mr. Mayor," he said, reading aloud from a prepared text. "I have just prayed that God will give you guidance to help you solve the many problems that face you in your new task. These problems are complex, but they can be solved. To do so will take courage and resignation.

"Much will be written and said about the problem of the subways, of Idlewild, of arterial highways and of adequate parking space; but, Mr. Mayor, they are really minor problems. The *real* problems that confront you are how you can bring about better conditions for the poor, the humble, the lowly and underprivileged. There are two other problems, Mr. Mayor, that must be faced. As an aftermath of the late war and partly as a result of the poisonous propaganda of hate that blanketed the world prior to it, there exist in this and every other city, great racial animosities. They must be eliminated.

"Then there is the Negro problem which can no longer be ignored. We cannot have two sects in this city—one discriminated against and the other discriminating.

"The emancipation of the Negro is a meaningless thing if we continue to hold them in almost literal slavery. They must be given an equal opportunity to use their talents for the betterment of themselves, the city, the state and the nation.

"These are your pressing and immediate problems, Mr. Mayor. They must be solved without thought of political future, without yielding to pressure, without concern for the criticism and calumny that solving them will evoke. May God strengthen your hand."

As he finished I looked in the direction of Paul and Keating. Their eyes did not meet mine directly, but their faces betrayed a sense of satisfaction similar to that displayed by the cat who has recently disposed of the canary.

Negroes at that time constituted about ten percent of the population but less than four percent of the voters. I can't say that the invocation started any immediate chain reaction. We had grown up in our own smug, segregated way around New York and occasionally bemoaned the fate of the Southern Negro. It was apparent that there was a problem, and it was like Marley's chain: we had forged it, inch by inch and yard by yard. It was of our own making. We had established a democracy. We had made New York the cultural head of it. We had preached equality and equal opportunity, and we continued the first- and second-class citizenship idea. Sometimes we were surprised and annoyed because the disinherited took our pious declarations literally. We just had not given thought to the full consequences of the musical phrases: "We hold

230

Mayor Fiorello LaGuardia leading the Mayor-elect to the "hot seat," 1945

these truths to be self-evident, that all men. . . ." Equality where? and how? In the right to work? The right to educate one's children? The right to a decent home in any part of free America? I would surely have to face up to these inconsistencies, but other things claimed my immediate attention and consigned the problem of democracy to the back burner. The first of these other problems was our city's antiquated mass transit system.

CHAPTER 31

TRANSPORTATION: THE TRANSIT SYSTEM

On January 1, 1946, I became the head of the largest passenger railroad in the world. Up to that time my association with railroading was confined to an ill-fated experience with the industry during my first year in this part of the world. My 1911 job as a Newark trolley conductor had lasted only three weeks. I returned to New York and made no attempt thereafter to return to railroading. Thirty-five years afterwards I found myself virtually in charge of some 32,000 underpaid employees who operated an obsolete and decrepit railroad.

I was alarmed at what might happen in the event of a crash at rush hour. On January 3, 1946, the *World-Telegram* reported my concern and my plan to avert a catastrophe:

MAYOR'S FIRST IS FIRST

When Mayor O'Dwyer sees rehabilitation of the City's dangerously rundown subways as the most important job of his administration, he sees straight and true. He is also right in putting the potential period which "might cause many deaths in two minutes" ahead of the comforts. Mayor O'Dwyer makes an excellent start by promptly putting his eye and mind on the present disgrace and danger of the City's subways. He could have picked no better or more urgent First.

New Yorkers have always felt unhappy about their subway system, but at the same time maintain a strong proprietary feeling about it. In 1904, Mayor George McClellan initiated the long, underground railroad which started at City Hall and ended at 145th Street and Broadway. It was a proud day for New Yorkers and especially for the Mayor. He was not content to don the motorman's cap and pose beside the expert. Before astonished passengers and a thoroughly frightened motorman, the Mayor occupied the motorman's cabin, manned the driving devices, and operated the train until it came to a safe landing at the last stop.

The subway, analogous to the Thames in London, is ugly and unclean, but there would be no New York without it. The initial Broadway line was patterned after a London subway that was put into operation in 1863. There had been numerous attempts to provide the city with a subway system from 1863 on, but all had been thwarted by private, greedy, and corrupting interests, which recognized that passenger railroading in New York City was a veritable gold mind.

From the Civil War period up to the end of the 19th century, political shenanigans, financial maneuverings and stock manipulations were the familiar weapons used in Albany and on Wall Street to bar the attempts of equally corrupt rivals from establishing an underground transit railroad. The primitive and bloody competition, the greed and the corruption that had marked the establishment of the cross-country railroads paled by comparison to the savage rivalry for control of New York City passenger roads, even while plans to create them were yet before the State Legislature.

The cast of characters who had their fingers in the pie (the Whitneys, the Goulds, the Tweeds, the Ryans and the Astors) was responsible for delaying the establishment of cheap transportation by almost half a century, and thereby delaying New York's growth. Were it not for the fact that the people took the subway out of private hands, they might have succeeded in doing irreparable damage.

On the plaque in the pavement at the entrance to City Hall, the name of the subway contractor is listed as John B. McDonald, and the name of his financial sponsor, August Belmont. The curt account emblazoned on the brass plate, over which thousands of New Yorkers walk daily, is a rather deceptive description of our town's experiment in railroading.

Messrs. McDonald and Belmont were merely copying the engineering genius of a man named A.P. Robinson, who planned that road in 1864, and the management skills of a man named Hugh Wilson, who witnessed the London subway being constructed and put into operation in 1863. In 1864, spurred on by the enthusiasm of Robinson and Wilson, New York City attempted to get its Albany legislators to authorize a rapid transit system, only to be thwarted at the state capital by the apostles of the free enterprise system.

A young and persistent genius, however, appeared on the scene and took the law into his own hands. His name—Alfred Ely Beach. He had been a journalist at 19, and a prestigious inventor at 21. At 22 he was a publisher of the *Sun*. His ambition was to build a subway in lower Manhattan, but Tweed and the others blocked his way. Beach devised a plan to overcome these difficulties. Using a retail clothing store at

Broadway and Murray Street to cloak his excavation and construction activities, he burrowed uptown under Broadway several hundred feet, removing the earth at night under cover of darkness. He built the walls, the roof and the bed with no outward sign that there was any construction in progress. He laid down tracks, put a railroad car on them and then announced his feat to New York. It was the surprise of the century and an immediate success. New Yorkers were pleased with their new plaything—that is, all New Yorkers except William Marcy Tweed and Jay Gould. The Governor was Tweed's man, and Beach was denied a franchise.

John Jacob Astor helped to scuttle Beach's attempt to obtain financing for the venture with the pronouncement that the Broadway buildings along the route would cave in if Beach were permitted to continue with his foolish adventure. Astor's statement was without any foundation, but it was enough to discourage investors. It killed the plan, but worse than that, it also spelled the end of one of our brightest and most enterprising New Yorkers. Some time later the Brooklyn-Manhattan Transit Company, which had been developed in Brooklyn, joined up with the line which Mr. Beach had created nearly half a century earlier. They found it in perfect condition, none the worse for four decades of neglect.

Schemes to merge all railroads brought Russell Sage and Jay Gould into the picture, and the stockholders' losses from that manipulation were substantial. After Gould's death, William Whitney and Thomas Fortune Ryan took their turns at city railroading, got controlling interest in several branches, and made millions on merger manipulation. Millions were lost by gullible stockholders and made by the stock gamblers.

But all that was behind us and forgotten in 1930. It was interesting as history, but nothing more. The railroad employees were, for the most part, Irish immigrants, and their attempt to form a union was beaten back. A strike in 1927 had ended in complete failure. Dishonest leaders got paid off, and the honest ones were weeded out and banished from the road. The Interborough Rapid Transit Company imported gangsters from Chicago, known as "DeVito's men," to break the strike, making arrangements to house those hoods in the car barns here.

In 1935, the Congress of Industrial Organizations was formed. The revolution in Ireland, which had ended in 1922 in a civil war, had resulted in thousands of emigres coming here in the middle twenties. They were by no means as docile as their predecessors, and many of them had taken part in the war against the Black and Tans. Radicalized by their early experience, they formulated the Transport Workers Union, which soon became a part of the militant, newly-formed C.I.O. The demand for higher wages had to be met, and this did not help the two

New York City subway companies' balance sheets.

The newly-organized union and a brand new collective bargaining agreement were enough to raise the question as to whether the companies had a bright financial future. The IRT notes were offered at ten cents on the dollar with no takers. The stock of the BMT was greatly depressed and selling for about $6 per share with a par value of $100, and the bonds of the BMT were presented for sale for 33 cents on the face of each dollar. The IRT was in the bankruptcy court and in the hands of a receiver, and the BMT was about to achieve the same status. The total asking price of the stock of both companies on the street was set at about $139 million. There was no trading in either stock.

Under these grim circumstances, New York City looked like the only likely contender for the privilege of paying good money for a bankrupt operation. In 1936, Mayor La Guardia appointed Samuel Seabury, who had been hailed or condemned as the Father of Reform, and Adolph Berle, Jr., who was then the city chamberlain, to study the oft-proposed "unification" of all the inner-city railroads. They came up with a proposal whereby the city would buy the two systems for $436 million. There was an immediate adverse public reaction to this scheme, and it was then withdrawn. Later, La Guardia appointed Newbold Morris to head another committee to develop still another plan for "unification." Morris' committee proposed that the city buy the lines for $326 million. This plan met with the approval of the Mayor and the Board of Estimate.

The price of the stock among speculators on Wall Street jumped from $139 million to $248 million. The day the deal was closed was a great day for the Wall Street manipulators. The stock by that time was worth $436 million and the killing was even greater. It was never disclosed who profited from the deal. It was reported that a famous international figure, one Serge Rubenstein, who apparently found out when to buy, made a million or two on the trade.

In 1946, I was required to include as part of the debt service for this deal the sum of $70 million annually during each succeeding budget year I held office to pay for the maneuver which made so many manipulators rich. I also included $212 million for rehabilitation of old cars and buses, power plant modernization, platform repairs, and some replacements.

At that moment, I would gladly have given both systems to the Port of New York Authority, or to anybody else who would take them. Our subway system had also suffered from the Bankers Agreement and the war years. In addition to being run down, it was dirty and its equipment badly aged and worn, but I could not let it get any worse.

If there was any bright spot in this otherwise dismal railroad picture, it was the fact that the system owned and operated its own power plants and could supply most of the current needed in the operation, while at the same time providing a basis of comparison for the cost of electricity. All in all, the power plants represented a valuable asset, and I considered it a necessary adjunct to the railroad system, one that gives it a measure of independence.

But even in this area, I was about to run into serious problems. For years, the plants had been coveted by the Consolidated Edison Company, which knew that with such an acquisition came a built-in reliable customer. I felt I was stuck with the transit system, but to sell the power-producing machinery necessary to operate it made no sense at all.

Yet that is exactly the proposal put forward by the president of the transit system, one General Charles Gross, fresh out of the Army, an appointee whom I inherited and whom I was stuck with for much of my first term. I was very much opposed to Gross' plan, and so was Mike Quill, international president of the Transport Workers' Union, the New York State vice-chairman of the CIO, and labor's most effective and colorful leader. Quill saw in the proposed transfer the loss of dues-paying members, who would become employees of Con Edison, under the jurisdiction of another union. Quill and Gross got into a bitter argument over the issue, and the Transport Workers Union threatened to strike if such a transfer were effected. I was getting some benefit from the aggressiveness of the T.W.U. and intervened to guarantee that any such transfer would have to have the people's approval in a referendum, ending for the time being, at least, both the transfer and the strike.

As an aftermath of the controversy, however, I was to have serious labor troubles. The workers in the industry had long been underpaid, and under General Gross' regime, their problems had been met with arrogance and a lack of understanding. These were the ingredients of a full-scale strike, and the signs had frequently been in evidence.

Within a month after settling the power plant controversy, Quill demanded a huge wage increase under threat of a strike, which would have really shut down New York. I was a new mayor and I was being tested by the wily labor leader. I called Philip Murray, national president of the Congress of Industrial Organizations. I had known Murray from my days in Washington during the war, when I was investigating defense plants. I felt he would talk to Quill and avert a strike. I did not want to go over Quill's head, but I either had to surrender to unreasonable demands in my first weeks in office or go through a crippling strike. All attempts to work a railroad during a strike in New York had been disastrous. Every mayor is told of the Malvern Street wreck, a railroad catastrophe in Brooklyn that resulted from replacing striking motormen with green operators, causing much loss of life. Murray's intervention was successful.

The end of the conflict brought me some very favorable editorials, but the abuse on Michael Quill was a negative. I knew he would remember the castigation he received when the next contract time rolled around and would then be that much more difficult to deal with. The editorial comments were typified by one carried on February 27, 1946, by the *Herald Tribune:*

MR. QUILL'S DEBACLE

On at least two counts New Yorkers can rejoice that the threat of a transit strike has been withdrawn—one, that the appalling hardships in prospect have been averted, and two, that the settlement appears to be a very definite defeat for the egregious Mr. Quill, indicating his complete deflation. The Mayor, to be sure, has accomplished this happy result with the valuable aid of Mr. Philip Murray, President of the Congress of Industrial Organizations, to which the Quill union belongs. But that seems to us to detract no whit from the tribute that should be Mayor O'Dwyer's for the victory he has won. . . .

© 1946 / International Herald Tribune

But the threatened T.W.U. strike was only one of three serious labor situations I had to deal with during my first weeks in office, any one of which could have critically affected the city, its essential services, or its economy.

The second labor crisis was a strike by fuel oil deliverers. In fact, I was hardly comfortable in my office when all deliveries came to a grinding halt. I quickly convened an emergency group and began to close down what I felt were non-essential services. Some felt I handled the situation poorly. There was a difference of opinion between the people who were inconvenienced and the more thoughtful editorial writers as to the measures which I had adopted:

The New York Times - February 9, 1946

MR. O'DWYER AND THE STRIKE

The City now faces a situation that can very easily develop into a major disaster resulting in death, starvation and great property damage. It is to the credit of Mayor O'Dwyer, however, that he recognized immediately the extent of this danger, laid his plans with foresight and wisdom, carried them out to the extent necessary, worked incessantly along with his labor advisor to avert and then to settle the dispute and in everything he did, lived up to his responsibilities as Mayor and his military reputation as general.

But the working press, representing the complaining public, saw it differently. It was somewhat of an exaggeration to say I closed down the town, but that's the way City Hall reporters presented it and later put it to song at the annual "Inner Circle" show. While I felt it came under the heading of overreacting, I knew I should henceforth give greater heed to trying to settle strikes before lines became hardened.

Finally, during the same period, I had to deal with the tugboat workers' stoppage.

These three events, all taking place during the first few months in office, constituted a fair sample of the troubles that lay ahead for me. Each of the situations was different, but each presented a challenge to authority and jeopardized public health or safety, and I came to see the need to establish more effective means of dealing with them.

After nine months in office, I knew just how difficult it could be to handle strikes and to defend against them, and so in September of 1946, to guard against strikes in either the public or private sector that could seriously injure our economy, I established the Division of Labor Relations, a labor committee consisting of Theodore Kheel, Julius Kass and Edward Maguire. Its job was to birddog potential strikes, to flush them out, and make sure that a work stoppage did not take place. Maguire was a seasoned labor lawyer who knew the labor leaders well. I had known Julius Kass in the Army, and Ted Kheel had been with the War Labor Board and was recommended to me by labor lawyer Sidney Elliot Cohn. The media recognized what I was attempting to do. Typical was the following appraisal in the middle-of-the-road *New York Times*:

THE CITY'S LABOR DIVISION

It is intolerable that every labor dispute involving an essential industry here should be dumped directly into the Mayor's lap for solution. His normal duties call for all the energy and devotion any one man can muster. When he has to endure the long hours and strain imposed on him during the trucking strike, the Mayor suffers, the city suffers and the civic machine slows down. The Division of Labor Relations will relieve Mr. O'Dwyer of some of that strain, and in many cases, we hope, prevent the necessity of it.

The *Daily Mirror* and the *New York Post*, political opposites, ran editorials expressing similar views.

It seems that all things come to those who wait. The following year, I was able to make the changes in transportation management I had wanted to make for a year and a half. First, I appointed Sidney Bingham to a vacancy on the Board of Transportation. Bingham was an unusually brilliant transportation engineer, whom I had first heard about in Italy. He had designed General Eisenhower's armored train and the army hospital trains.

Six months later, with a sigh of relief, I accepted the resignation of General Gross and appointed William Reid as Chairman of the Board of Transportation. Reid was an unusually capable public servant. The *Herald Tribune* described him as "a level-headed, hard-working career man who has served the city well for 34 years."

A few months later, during the early part of 1948, I again had to deal with Mike Quill and the T.W.U. The transit labor contract signed in 1946 was for two years, and I was more seasoned and in a better position in 1948 to deal with the proposed renewal. I let it be known early on that while I would negotiate I did not believe government employees, whether working for the city, the state or the nation, had a right to strike. I usually welcomed editorial approval of plans or performance, but occasionally editorials involving sensitive labor leaders and delicate disputes can cause mischief. Those published on this issue did nothing to calm the feelings of the trade unionist, who was in a position to make life difficult for us.

The New York Times - April 15, 1948

MR. O'DWYER TO MR. QUILL

Mayor O'Dwyer has promptly and properly pointed out to City Councilman Michael J. Quill, top officer of the Transport Workers Union, that the city cannot tolerate a strike against itself. There is a significant distinction between a strike against privately operated bus lines—which would be serious enough—and a strike against the city-owned transit system, which would be illegal.

However, a development within the union itself made it necessary for me to take a different attitude toward Quill and the union. Many Communists had been among the T.W.U.'s founders and were elected on the basis of their efforts to alleviate the very poor conditions under which its members were employed. In spite of their political views, they had strong support among the Irish subway workers, particularly because of their capacity to spend long hours on the job, their continual educational campaign, and their constant and militant demands for higher wages and improved working conditions. They had, however, made a fatal error. Ideologically, they accepted the Communist Party position in opposition to increasing the fare from five to ten cents. Every transit worker, however, realized that a raise in fare was a necessary prelude to a raise in his own wages. Quill decided to break with the Communist leadership, who had been his most faithful supporters and undertook a campaign to oust them from leadership. I was satisfied that for the sake of future stability it would be a development devoutly to be wished and agreed to a very substantial raise, which would be of great assistance to Quill in his campaign.

After a particularly acrimonious contest, the leadership was ousted and replaced by Quill's selectees. Quill emerged as the undisputed leader of the Transport Workers Union across the country. His enemies were purged, and he was in sole control of its destiny. As a result, wages were increased substantially, necessitating abandonment of the traditional five-cent fare. I raised it to ten cents.

And so in the space of two years, I was able to bring a sense of reasonableness to both sides of the bargaining table and to add capable railroaders and experienced executives to deal with our most important function; and the public accepted the rise in fare as a practical necessity and indeed as inevitable. It was not the political end of the Mayor who would tamper with the five-cent fare, as sages had predicted. Every newspaper supported the move, as did a strike-weary public.

CHAPTER 32

TRANSPORTATION: IDLEWILD, THE NEW YORK THRUWAY AND CITY TRAFFIC

A second critical transportation concern also had its roots in the previous administration. Fiorello La Guardia was one of the nation's early aviation enthusiasts. He was a pilot in World War I and survived a plane crack-up over Italy. He continued his interest as Mayor and was responsible for turning a swampy area in Flushing Bay into an airport that was named after him. Towards the end of his administration, with Eddie Rickenbacker and other airline representatives, he developed plans for the establishment of another airfield, and millions of tons of sand were pumped from the Jamaica Bay wetlands on the south side of Queens County at a cost to the New York taxpayers of over $61 million. The area now consisted of 5,000 acres of dry land. It was named Idlewild Airport, and, by the time I was preparing to take office, the plans called for the expenditure by the city of huge sums of additional money for capital construction.

However, we needed very substantial money to catch up with the lag in construction. All programs had been virtually halted because of the Bankers Agreement, which had put both Mayors O'Brien and La Guardia into a strait jacket. At about the time the Bankers Agreement was terminated, action on the crying need for schools and hospitals, hospital repairs and housing had to be again postponed during the war years because of lack of construction materials and skilled labor. I realized that the city could not finance its own airport and tend to those other needs as well.

The decision not to go it alone with Idlewild brought me into immediate conflict with my predecessor. Every mayor has certain projects which he favors and yet are impossible to complete within his term. A great deal of frustration and bitterness ensues when the new mayor develops ideas at variance with his predecessor.

In the last days of his administration, in preparation for this possible turn of events, La Guardia and Comptroller McGoldrick sought to have the City Council approve an expenditure of $45 million for Idlewild Airport. As the incoming Mayor, I consulted with Robert Moses, already appointed as coordinator of all building construction; George Spargo, his deputy; Bill Reid, an experienced administrator in city affairs, whom I would later appoint as Board of Transportation chairman; and Assistant Corporation Counsels Charles Preusse and W. Bernard Richland. I then had talks with the City Council leaders who would soon be called upon to approve these capital expenditures. The council eliminated from the capital budget the $45 million for Idlewild, as well as $10 million for a proposed new vegetable market, and approved the rest of the capital program.

La Guardia became enraged. His performance on the air was somewhat hysterical. "Don't do it, Bill. Don't do it, Bill," he fairly shouted into the microphone. "I will call a meeting of the Board of Estimate tomorrow and, if you approve of it, we can call a special meeting of the City Council and put back these items in the budget."

He then directed the full force of his attack on Moses and at a press conference told the newspaper men, "I recognized the fine Italian hand of Obermeister Moses." I could no longer avoid an open disagreement with La Guardia.

I called a press conference. "I shall not be drawn into a last minute controversy with the Mayor," I said. "His administration on the whole has been successful, but it has been unfortunately marked by an increasing tendency to denounce, ridicule and vilify those who do not happen to share all its views and prejudices. I will not be swayed by radio blasts and hysterics over WNYC or any other station. We simply cannot afford another $130 million hole in the diminishing balance of capital funds for this one project in the face of the other dire needs of the city. The decision of the Council is, in my opinion, in the best interest of New York, and in so far as I am concerned, it will not be changed." I was thinking of the overcrowded classrooms and hospital wards bulging far beyond capacity.

I then set to work to determine my administration's position on the Idlewild construction. The contracts with the airlines and oil companies had been signed by Comptroller McGoldrick but not by La Guardia, for reasons which were never explained. It was clear to Moses, Richland, Preusse and myself that to meet competition and keep New York in a preeminent position, we needed an airport of a size New York could not then afford to construct.

To further complicate matters, I found out that La Guardia Field had been poorly constructed. The field would soon be under water unless massive construction to halt the deterioration was commenced without delay. The administration building had to be done over completely. If we were to try to meet all our construction needs and build two airports, the city would surely be in financial difficulty for many years to come.

I felt I had to get out of the contracts that had been arranged with the airlines. I invited management of all of them to a meeting to explain that the city was unable to finance the construction of Idlewild. Captain Eddie Rickenbacker, spokesman for Eastern, became enraged, declaring that he was moving his company to New Jersey, and the meeting at Gracie Mansion became quite acrimonious.

"This city," I said, "was here before us, and its greatness is due to no one in this room. If you find you must go to New Jersey, there will be others to take your place." Pan American's Juan Trippe suggested we meet again to discuss it further. Since my mind was made up and any attempt at further consideration would only give the wrong impression to the airlines, I discouraged the idea.

In the meantime, I contacted the legislative leaders with a proposal to establish the New York Airport Authority. Recognizing that I needed Governor Dewey's approval, I called in Harry Guggenheimer, Lawrence Rockefeller and General Jimmy Doolittle to help. Guggenheimer, like La Guardia, a World War I aviator, and head of the Daniel Guggenheimer Fund for the Promotion of Aeronautics, was to act as chairman. The three agreed to promote the authority idea, and I floated the plan to the public. The reaction from the Port Authority was not altogether unexpected. Having long lusted for both airports and our waterfront, it now presented a plan through which it would gain full title to all the lands at Idlewild and La Guardia forever. The proposal also provided that the Port Authority literally would have a monopoly on our air travel for all time, in return for which it would relieve the city of the burden of construction costs. It would then agree to provide a first class airport into the indefinite future.

New York City has always managed to hold on to almost all its commercial waterfront, and I was not enthusiastic about dishonoring this tradition. I rejected the proposal. The Port Authority then went to the newspapers, successfully convincing several publishers that theirs was the only feasible plan, and soon I was daily subjected to severe criticism, along with the gloomy foreboding that unless the Port Authority got its way, we would have a fourth-rate airport and New York would lose its importance. And I was subjected to pressures from every direction. These editorial comments were not without reason. But I was determined nevertheless to hold on to title to the land.

When it was plain I was not being moved in the direction of the Port Authority, I was invited to lunch with Eugene Black, who was later to take over the World Bank, and Winthrop Aldridge of Chase National

Bank. They explained how important it was for the city's industry and commerce that the Port Authority proposal be accepted. They reminded me that the Chase was the holder of $2.8 billion of the city's bonds and that I would need its help in the years ahead. Further, they said that notwithstanding the prestigious names attached to the New York City Airport Authority, Guggenheimer, Rockefeller and Doolittle might find funding difficult without approval of Chase's board.

They hinted darkly about the Bankers Agreement during the O'Brien-La Guardia days, and said that Chase had no wish for a like condition during my regime. "You have already antagonized the airlines, and they may leave the city if you persist. And the newspapers will continue to attack you," Black said.

"I will not bind this city forever," I replied, "and I will not give up an inch of it," and the conversation ended. He was right about the newspapers. They did keep up the pressure. I heard no more from the Port Authority for about a month. In the meantime, we were indeed experiencing difficulty in financing the New York City Airport Authority, and its prospects were not bright. Then Black broke the silence. "Bill, if you give up the idea of a New York City Airport Authority, we can probably satisfy you. I think the authority could agree to a 99-year lease. It will spend $300 million, which you cannot now undertake, and besides, we will arrange to pay a rental to the city." I replied, "I see no magic in the figure 99, but, if you talk about 50, that's different." Negotiations were resumed.

We kept the idea of the New York City Airport Authority alive and a threat until we got the terms we wanted. We finally wound up with a first-class airport, with no capital expenditure by the city and a provision providing for a return of the airport intact at the end of 50 years. At least one newspaper editor expressed his personal approval. *Herald Tribune* editor Geoffrey Parsons telegraphed: "My hearty congratulations on a fine job done for the city. Without your patience, judgment and resolve this happy solution would have been impossible. We owe you a great debt."

The solution was a triumph over the arrogance and tremendous power of the Port Authority. Without my Army experience, the efforts of Moses, Guggenheimer, Rockefeller and Doolittle, the backing of the Legislature, and Governor Dewey's neutrality, I could not have successfully resisted.

On July 31, 1948, Idlewild was officially opened with a great deal of fanfare. I asked President Truman to come and he was on hand, as well as various foreign dignitaries and thousands of other spectators. The latest in aircraft was displayed and the day was hot and the speeches were long.

Elaborate preparations had been made by Grover Whelan, who served as unpaid host to important visitors to the city. With gusto and great pride he outlined his plans to us at City Hall. The seats had been arranged for countless thousands and all preparedness had been made for their comfort and enjoyment. There was, however, one serious omission.

My executive press secretary, Bill Donohue, was looking over the blueprints. "Grover," he said, "you seem to have overlooked one small item. Where are the toilets? A red-faced Grover acknowledged the oversight, but he was equal to the occasion. "Mr. Mayor," he said, "I did not intend to start a back to the sea movement of all that sand that was pumped in from the ocean bed. We will meet the emergency."

At the last minute we had our trouble with protocol. The nine-day air show at Idlewild was part of the golden anniversary of the establishment of Greater New York. This was the Presidential election year. A Democratic Mayor is not expected to overlook these things when inviting guests to celebrations such as this. Obviously, New York's Republican Governor, Tom Dewey, would be on hand as would Republican Governor Driscoll of New Jersey.

As early as December, 1946, I had been in touch with Mr. Truman about appearing for the dedication services. He not only came but also brought a number of his cabinet. The Saturday morning before the show was to go on, Grover Whelan came to Gracie Mansion with one of his customary insoluble problems. "I have spoken to Major O'Hara of Governors Island," he said, "and he is quite prepared to arrange for the gun salutes for the President, but he is hesitant about a gun salute for the Governor."

"The major is undoubtedly of Democratic extraction, Grover," I said. "This is a serious matter," replied Grover, "and Howard Cullman is considerably irked. He is in charge of the Governor's reception."

Cullman, the head of the Port Authority, and myself never did see eye to eye, not only during the course of the Idlewild argument, but later when he sought to gain control of all our city-owned waterfront piers. "Grover," I said, "you had better tell Cullman to bring his own gun, but make sure where he's aiming it."

As they sat on the stand, Truman shook hands with Dewey for the benefit of the press. "I hope you like the White House," Truman said to him in an aside which surprised the few within earshot. Later that day, during a lull, I complimented the President on the remark. "That was a generous thing you did today, Mr. President," I said.

"It wasn't as generous as you think, Bill," he snapped. "He's going to be a loser soon and he may as well enjoy these few short months." He knew, even then, what no one else did.

246

My own relationship with Tom Dewey during the previous three years always had to be defined within the basic understanding of how subservient a mayor must be to the governor and to the State Legislature if he wishes to be able to get some meaningful assistance for the city.

The state is the parent of New York City. The city has no powers not granted by the state and must ask permission even for the privilege of taxing itself. The majority of the State Legislature are drawn from rural and suburban areas of New York. They have always found it difficult to understand this lively, vibrant city and are generally unsympathetic to its problems and hostile to its requests for help.

In my time as Mayor, the State Assembly and the State Senate were under Republican control (and therefore under Dewey's control), and a brave minority of Democrats in both houses had to be content with making the voice of the minorities heard on issues on which the parties differed. It was to be hoped by Paul Fitzpatrick, the state Democratic Party chairman, and the minority leaders that I would be a voice to support them in their moral indignation and in exposing the nefarious behavior of that other party.

But when I got into office, I realized that if I were to play that political role, I would undoubtedly find myself quickly at odds with the Governor and the State Legislature, and I was not likely to gain very much help I so badly needed for the city. Very early on, I made it known to the Governor that I wished to have his cooperation rather than enmity, and that I saw no reason to inject myself into the Senate and Assembly squabbles. Over the years, Dewey supported many of our needs, and I had an opportunity to return that support on one of the Governor's biggest and most valued projects.

I found out a plan for the creation of a massive thruway from New York to Buffalo was approved by the State Legislature in May of 1942 during the administration of Governor Herbert H. Lehman, but did not get very far. Dewey revived the plan giving it his name. That was enough to warrant the opposition by the Democrats in the State Legislature. They condemned the project as a waste of public funds. The Democrats were in the minority in the State Legislature and Dewey was in control there but the Democrats knew that Dewey needed my help to provide for the approaches into the city which would ensure the free flow of traffic through the city lines. Without appropriate connecting links the traffic bottlenecks would have made the thruway unworkable. The frustrated Democratic legislators, at odds with Dewey in Albany, wanted me to scuttle the whole plan. Paul Fitzpatrick, state Democratic chairman, was their spokesman.

I had the same relationship with the Board of Estimate and the City Council that Dewey had with the State Legislature. The choice was clear enough. I could give my cooperation and gain Dewey's support for New York City projects I wished to advance, or honor the Democratic legislators' request and see all of our ambitious plans for the city die on the vine.

The agreement was reached early but was made public during my second term. I gave notice of my complete approval of the thruway and for a cooperative plan which would prepare the roads of the city for easy access. The Thomas E. Dewey Thruway became a reality and the relationship between the city and state continued to be cordial and cooperative. *The Times* and the *News* summed up the situation in the following editorials:

The New York Times - March 13, 1950

THE CITY AND ALBANY

It is a pleasure to observe that working relations between the New York administration and the State during this legislative session seem to have taken a considerable turn for the better. A number of reasons may account for this. But whatever is mainly responsible, the result is that for the first time in recent years the city administration has presented its requests with dignity and without partisan bombast, and because it refrained from extravagant demands for the sake of making a political show, has not suffered the humiliation of being turned down. That this attitude has not endeared Mayor O'Dwyer to the Democratic leaders in the Legislature is obvious. The displeasure of some leaders became acute when the Mayor, after his only visit to Albany this session, gave his hearty endorsement to the Thruway and the Dewey method of financing it.

We believe Mr. O'Dwyer deserves warm tribute for the nonpolitical fashion in which he conducted himself on that trip.

Daily News - March 8, 1950

THRUWAY DETOURS POLITICS

The long discussed State Thruway, or express highway between New York City and Buffalo, got a surprise boost day before yesterday when Mayor O'Dwyer came out flatly for Governor Dewey's plans for carrying the project through. . . . Now that Mayor O'Dwyer has acted like a statesman instead of a politican, why should the Legislature hesitate?

Meeting with Governor Thomas E. Dewey soon after being elected Mayor, 1945

However, the Democratic legislative leaders' unhappiness grew. It was galling to them that a thruway going all the way from New York to Buffalo would be named after the Governor who had brushed aside their every wish. They were giving him all kinds of problems with respect to it, and I was also to suffer the loss of their friendship. But the Governor had already earned my support through his assistance in housing and in a variety of other ways.

There had to be a give and take in my relationship with the Governor. I did not feel that I was giving away too much when I arranged to give New Yorkers the opportunity to get on to a thruway that would bring them upstate easily and would also facilitate visitors coming to our town. I thought I had made a reasonably good bargain. In addition, by way of bonus, I was assigned the privilege of naming an old friend, David Martin, an engineer, as one of the members of the Thruway Commission.

Closer to home, there was another less tractable set of problems relating to the movement of vehicles, and that was the ever-worsening traffic in Manhattan. Notwithstanding the various attempts to solve the problem, there was little material change in traffic conditions over the years of my administrations. The more we eased the midtown jam, the more automobiles were made in Michigan and the more they were induced into the city by our greater accommodation to them.

Early in 1946, I did manage to get some expert advice by asking the newshawks in "Room 9" at City Hall who they felt was best equipped to deal with our deteriorating traffic situation. The *Times'* Paul Crowell and several others felt the most reliable expert in zoning matters was Frank Bloustein, who had been secretary to Mayor La Guardia and now was secretary of the Planning Commission. Bloustein's understanding of the problems—the inadequacy of parking facilities and parking spaces, the ineffective job being done by the Board of Standards and Appeals—was remarkable, and I realized he would be a valuable asset to my administration. Over partisan protests, I soon asked him to take the place of Newbold Morris, who was about to retire from the Planning Commission at the end of his term. Bloustein became the most valuable member of the commission after that and continued to advise me about traffic management, among other matters.

But the problems were not to be so easily alleviated. Early in 1949 I reorganized and centralized the city's Department of Traffic, and for the job of commissioner I sought out the best the nation could offer. The *Times* commented on the new appointment I made in a vain attempt to ease the situation:

The New York Times - February 2, 1949

TRAFFIC ENGINEER

We welcome Mayor O'Dwyer's choice of T.T. Wiley of Detroit for the post of executive director of New York's Traffic Commission. Mr. Wiley is a trained engineer, with broad exprience.

Notwithstanding the finest in personnel and management, things did not seem to improve, and editorials do not solve traffic jams. I sought to shake up the Traffic Commission, and I'm sure it did its best, but the easier it became for an automobile to travel in New York, the more came. A year later, both the *Times* and the *Tribune* recognized my predicament:

The New York Times - March 4, 1950

CRACKING DOWN ON TRAFFIC

Mayor O'Dwyer laid down the law to his Traffic Commission yesterday. He expressed himself as thoroughly dissatisfied with the progress being made and intimated that a "czar" for traffic relief might be in the offing. In the meantime, it is reassuring that the Mayor is thoroughly aroused about the failure to get anywhere on traffic reforms.

Herald Tribune - March 6, 1950

AND HIGH TIME, TOO

We are delighted that Mayor O'Dwyer has got around to the traffic mess. The sight of a city official in eruption is always stimulating. . . . Mayor O'Dwyer is disgusted with the City Traffic Commission for failing to solve the traffic outrage. . . . And now Mayor O'Dwyer, angry at general failure, has yanked the rug from under.

Three months later, I appointed Lloyd Reid, former Highway Commissioner of the State of Michigan, to head the Department of Traffic, but on the day I left office, the problems were as bad as the day I'd begun.

CHAPTER 33

HOUSING

When I took office in 1946, the acute shortage of housing made it obligatory that rent control not be abandoned, otherwise the law of supply and demand would drive rentals far beyond the reach of most New Yorkers, leaving them at the mercy of the landlords. Yet, people were weary of forced controls and, against their own interests, wished to have them discontinued. Also, the Federal government was about to relax its controls. I immediately stepped into the breach to make certain we had a bill passed into law, even before Albany got around to considering one. I had doubts of our legal capacity to do so, and I needed—and received—support from Governor Dewey to proceed.

I established the first local rent control programs and appointed Paul Ross to supervise them. Paul had a distinguished record as the New York head of the Office of Price Administration and had done a fine job of policing a very difficult situation here during the war years.[1]

Time was of utmost importance in all our housing efforts. We hoped to have the United Nations in New York permanently, which meant we had to deal with the housing problems of all its representatives. And beyond that, there were a number of other critical human needs brought on by the war's end which had to be dealt with quickly. Housing, particularly for veterans and their families, was high on the list of challenges to be faced immediately and which would require considerable time and attention.

Housing meant city involvement in construction, and invariably in the past, city contracts had been accompanied by corruption. Some of the culprits had been caught and prosecuted over the years. The chances were, however, that many met with success in cheating the city out of

---

1. Soon after he started his new job with me, I received a visit from the F.B.I., informing me that they had every reason to believe Ross was a Communist. We were then in the height of the anti-Red hysteria, and their action was not unusual. I told the agents that I found his work satisfactory and could find no logical reason to justify discharging him, as they suggested. Later on, Ross resigned, explaining that he could not accept being part of an administration that had raised the subway fare from five cents to a dime.

exorbitant sums of money. To guard against this happening in my administration, I appointed as building coordinator a man who had not supported me in the election, Robert Moses. Since the days when Governor Alfred E. Smith recognized his genius and started him on his career, Moses had acquired an enviable reputation as a man who could get things done—impatiently, sometimes ruthlessly, but with competence and decisiveness.

A commission of inquiry I appointed before actually taking office indicated we needed to house 360,000 families. Most of those were now living in crowded conditions, having doubled up with relatives or friends.

I realized we needed the help of both state and Federal government on any projected construction, and I kept up pressure on both groups. As a result, I was able to get Quonset huts and barracks, 7,000 units in all, which the city then constructed at a cost of $10 million. It was not much, but many veterans, recently returned and married, were glad to have them, and I knew it was a start.

Early in 1946, the Taft-Ellender-Wagner Housing Bill was introduced into Congress. Its purpose was to relieve the housing pressure, and since its authors were among the most prestigious public figures in the country, it seemed that a measure of relief was at hand. But the real estate lobby effectively resisted, and the fight for its passage was to last for more than three years. In the meantime, I had hoped we could get some help in Albany. On February 27, 1946, I sent the following telegram to Governor Dewey:

> Senate Introductory 502 Print 1271, providing for the Temporary Housing Program for New York City has passed both houses and is now before you for executive action. I urge you to sign it immediately.
>
> The Board of Estimate meets tomorrow and will have on its agenda resolutions to condemn land necessary for our temporary housing. The condemnation of such land is conditioned on the enactment of the Temporary Housing Bill and the board will be unable to adopt such resolutions tomorrow unless the bill is law at that time.
>
> The Temporary Housing Program must be put into effect promptly so as to provide shelter for veterans and their families. The city has made arrangements with the federal government to provide seven thousand dwelling units. The sites for these units must be prepared quickly.

At the same time, we were having trouble at home. Moses was

impatient with our lack of progress in the construction of the Bruckner Houses in the Bronx because of a dispute between the plumbers and the hod carriers. Each claimed jurisdiction over the distance between the sewer and the building line. It concerned only a half dozen men, but the whole job was held up. I sent a telegram to William Green, president of the A.F. of L., stating:

> This is a deplorable situation for which I see no justification and I earnestly request, in behalf of our veterans and our city, that instructions be immediately issued which will enable us to man the job with plumbers and complete this most essential work.

I got quick action on that one, but soon the same thing occurred at the Castle Hill housing project in the Bronx, and there the strike dragged on.

Also, on the local front, Moses was in a temperamental mood over clashes with Hugo Rogers, Manhattan Borough President. He had two votes on the Board of Estimate and fancied himself as an expert in housing, and Robert Moses, who dashed off a letter with each irritation, large or small, let me know his feelings. The formality of the opening words gave every warning that my coordinator was about to quit, even in the opening salutation:

> Dear General:
> We are having plenty of difficulties in expediting the various housing projects for veterans emergency public housing and redevelopment housing.
> A new problem which has been added has been the effort of Hugo Rogers to upset existing contracts in order to advance ideas of his own as to planning and layouts. This kind of thing has got to stop if we wish to make progress.

It was signed "Cordially, Bob," although it was difficult to discern much cordiality in the body of the letter. Making progress was indeed important, and if a mayor wishes to make progress, he is required to spend at least half his time settling quarrels and catering to personality clashes among his subordinates. It took all my skills to get Rogers and Moses to agree. They did so begrudgingly.

In July, prior to the anticipated Congressional vote on the Federal Taft-Ellender-Wagner Housing Bill, I communicated with Representative John McCormack and received a discouraging response from him:

A number of members of the Committee on Banking and Currency are opposed to the bill. A minority, but a substantial one. They are using all their parliamentary tactics, in an effort to prevent this bill from coming up before adjournment takes place.

Later in the month, the Congressional hearings were closed on the bill, and I was requested to make sure all New York Congressmen attended the appropriate Monday morning session for the vote.

On July 29, I got the following telegram:

Taft-Ellender-Wagner Bill was considered by House Banking & Currency Committee today. Chairman Spence said no action was taken thereon because any motion to report the bill favorably would be defeated or tabled. The predominant sentiment is against the bill. I see no clearance for it.

Congressman Emanuel Celler

And the bill died in 1946.

Nevertheless, during that year we started eight housing projects; the construction unions were at peace with their employers and with each other, and there was hope of future accomplishment. The feeling was short-lived; soon hopes were dashed by a trucking strike which did as much damage as the failure of Congress to pass the housing bill. It brought construction to a complete halt.

Early in 1947, we tried to implement the Veterans' Emergency Housing program, which was tied to Federal public housing legislation planned before the war, but before we could get on with it, we needed to get Congressional approval to meet the increased costs brought on by the war. In desperation, I appealed to President Truman and Senator Styles Bridges about it.

The President had the matter studied and prodded the Congress to live up to the Government's commitments:

March 20, 1947

My dear Mayor O'Dwyer:

This will refer to your letter of February 5, 1947, concerning the need of additional funds for the completion of the Veterans' Emergency Housing program authorized by title V of the Hanham Act.

The developments in connection with the program caused

me some concern, and I recently requested appropriate officials to review the matter so that such relief as may be proper could be provided as quickly as possible. As a result of their study, I am convinced that the Federal Government must carry out contractual obligations accepted in good faith by educational institutions, municipalities and other local bodies. Accordingly, on February 28, 1947, I forwarded a message to the Congress recommending a further appropriation of $50,000,000 in order that the Government may meet its contractual obligations and that this phase of our continuing program of aid to veterans may be carried out.

Sincerely yours,
Harry S. Truman

The Taft-Ellender-Wagner Bill was again introduced in 1947, and I wrote to Taft urging its passage. On June 24, after an increasingly frustrating series of referrals to other federal officials, I sent a telegram to Jesse P. Wolcott, chairman of the House Banking and Currency Committee, outlining the desperate condition we were in:

The housing situation remains critical. It jeopardizes the health and family life of many of our citizens, particularly veterans. Action by private enterprise and government are both necessary. New York City and New York State have taken steps to help solve the serious situation by means of public housing and offering inducements and encouragement to private enterprise to build houses. Private enterprise, however, is not able to provide for the entire range of housing needs in the community nor are there any reasonable prospects of its being able to do so in the near future. Additional aid which can only be furnished by the Federal Government must be given. The Taft-Ellender-Wagner Bill seeks to accomplish this purpose in giving further aid and impetus to help solve this most pressing problem. Its basic purpose is to assure the construction of adequate shelter for all sections of the population. The bill is concerned not only with the construction of public housing but goes far towards encouraging private building. Your committee is urgently requested to report out favorably the Taft-Ellender-Wagner Bill without further delay.

His reply the following day left us with no hope for quick passage of the bill since Wolcott could not even indicate when his committee would hold hearings on it.

Donal O'Toole, Congressman from my home district in Bay Ridge, Brooklyn, wrote to me in September, 1947. His explanation of the machinations of the real estate lobby was not surprising. "The Taft-Ellender-Wagner Bill," he wrote, "has been buried in Committee as a result of the most vicious and powerful lobby that I have ever encountered in Washington."

In May of 1947, I selected General Thomas Farrell to head up the Housing Authority and a well-known banker, Tom Shanahan, to work with him. Farrell had a fine war record and was recommended to me by Dewey, Lehman and Stichman.

Even in spite of what President Truman called the "Do-Nothing Congress," the strides we made were impressive. On August 5, 1947, Moses sent me a progress report which provided some consolation:

> Ninety-two thousand five hundred people are actually living in homes completed since you took office. This includes veterans' emergency housing, permanent public housing, redevelopment company housing and private or speculative housing, a good deal of it stimulated and guaranteed by the F.H.A.
>
> This represents an exceptional local effort in the face of limiting conditions such as material and labor shortages, steel and coal shortages, steel and coal strikes, exorbitantly high prices, and other factors, many of them beyond the City's control.
>
> In addition to units so far provided, we have a large City program under way which will be completed this Fall and in 1948 and 1949. This program is estimated to accommodate 279,000 more people in new housing under the various types of sponsorship. In view of the failure of enactment of national housing legislation, it does not include any further federally-financed housing.

Moving into 1948, there was very little change in the housing situation. One hundred thousand veterans had now filed applications for any available kind of housing. We tried to meet the demand, but it was a losing battle. We had contributed to the establishment of the temporary Quonset huts but could not get our share of the rents from the government, and that held up our plans for further relief for the veterans.

For the third year in succession, the Taft-Ellender-Wagner Bill was filed. This year, there was a new voice to be heard from:

March 17, 1948

Dear Mayor O'Dwyer:

Because of the importance of your stand on the housing question, I have taken the liberty of inserting your letter to me in the Congressional Record of March 15th, a marked copy of which I am enclosing for your attention.

Again, let me thank you in behalf of the veterans of the country for your expression of keen interest in the passage of the Taft-Ellender-Wagner Bill.

Best kind regards, I am

John F. Kennedy

In May, I wrote to Senator Tobey in an attempt to get the Senate Banking and Currency Committee moving. On June 4, 1948, I got what seemed to be another run-around:

Once again I wish to assure you that it certainly seems to be the sentiment of this Committee that the problem of temporary war housing disposal to municipalities be considered immediately at the beginning of the 81st Congress. If it is handled thoroughly and expeditiously at that time, there will be ample opportunity to pass legislation before the termination of present statutes relating to the subject of war housing.

Sincerely yours,
Charles W. Tobey
Chairman

When the House Committee again failed to act, I urged the Congressmen to attempt to discharge it by petition. It was an act of desperation, but we *were* desperate in New York. Finally, there came a ray of hope. The Taft-Ellender-Wagner Bill passed the Senate in May. I called in Congressmen Rooney and Keogh of Brooklyn, by this time two of the most influential members of Congress. They pledged their support to get the bill passed by the House, as well.

I began to get some helpful responses. First, there was Congressman Javits' on May 3:

Thank you for your letter of April 28th. I am delighted that you are so actively supporting S. 866 which I am sponsoring in the House. The tempo of the fight for this housing legislation is increasing daily and I feel confident that with the support of persons like you we cannot lose.

And then on June 14, upon hearing from Congressman Abe Multer, our hopes began to run high: "After tough fight finally got a public housing and slum clearance bill out of Banking and Currency Committee by vote of fourteen to thirteen." However, our hopes were dashed two days later by another telegram from Congressman Multer: "Rules Committee by Republican six to Democrats two, voted to table housing bill."

Three years of fighting for what seemed to have been the very minimum consideration for the needs of the American people brought one disappointment after another. We had no hesitancy in appropriating money and more money for war, but we seemed to be unable to cope with a condition of post-war peace.

It was difficult to understand, and the only explanation, at least as of early 1949, was that the Congress regarded President Truman as a lame duck and would not cooperate. In any case, it was difficult to understand how the Congress could turn its back on the veterans returning from service to their country. Its action on this and other bills also indicated that it was in no mood to help the cities.

Meanwhile, the lack of Federal help during the previous years put a damper on our housing plans. Yet, even with no new Federal legislation, the city undertook to start at least one public housing project a month. In many cases we were required to destroy old tenements which had become fire traps and were disease-ridden. By 1949, there were 42 new projects completed or well under way. With Federal aid attached to only one, but with state aid to several others, the city spent over $410 million on new housing. In addition, the unions began to take a hand in sponsoring several projects, and with the city's help or tax abatement, $26 million was spent on construction in that category. These expenditures should have been undertaken by the Federal government as part of the war costs. Indeed, much of the city's money was spent to try to provide minimum shelter for returning veterans, but New York had really never received an equitable share of its contribution to the national treasury. It was adding insult to injury to make the city pay for what was so clearly a Federal obligation.

As 1948 progressed, Paul Betters, executive director of the United States Conference of Mayors, kept me informed on matters which needed my attention. In preparation for the first Congressional session of 1949, a new, revised Taft-Ellender-Wagner Bill was being introduced:

November 18, 1948

Dear Mayor:

Just this note so that you are informed as to all developments. The old Taft-Ellender-Wagner Bill is being revised and redrafted.

It looks now as if the new bill will contain two major sections—one dealing with slum clearance and the other with public housing.

Every effort will be made to get prompt consideration without lengthy hearings when the new Congress convenes. This, on the basis that voluminous testimony and evidence has already been presented.

When the preliminary draft is completed, I shall see that a copy is gotten to you immediately.

Yours sincerely,
Paul V. Betters
Executive Director

In November, events took a turn. Harry S. Truman was elected President, as he predicted he would be. Truman had been a severe critic of the 80th Congress and the real estate interests that a majority of them represented. He had made their conduct a campaign issue, and his election was a defeat for them.

George Welsh, Mayor of Grand Rapids, was president of the United States Conference of Mayors. He, David Lawrence, Mayor of Pittsburgh, and I asked for an appointment to explain our plight. The President was at his best—peppery and lighthearted. I left with a better feeling about housing and just about everything else in the nation. It was so easy to share his hope for the future of America and the world.

In July, 1949, the long awaited Housing Act was passed. It was the last year of my four-year term, and I was grateful and relieved that this piece of legislation had finally passed while I was still in office.

All in all, even in spite of the handicaps, the record of three and a half years recorded a major start in establishing housing for all New Yorkers, and the *World-Telegram* took note of it in an editorial on August 25, 1949:

PUBLIC HOUSING REPORT

The New York City Housing Authority has just reported to Mayor William O'Dwyer the city's accomplishments in providing and planning public housing from January 1946 to June 30, 1949.

In the 42-month period, 47,600 apartments were provided by projects built or under construction in 42 wisely chosen localities throughout the city. Forty-nine neighborhoods, most of them in slum districts, have been approved tentatively as possible sites for 80,000 additional apartments with state and federal aid.

. . . Politics aside, the Mayor and the members of the Housing Authority should have the city's gratitude for doing a hard job well.

My appointment of Robert Moses had worked out well. He had kept everyone on their toes, and his conceded expertise in cutting through red tape was enough reward for the many hours I had to spend in applying liniment to the bruised feelings of elected officials and bureaucrats. Because Moses loved to battle, his style almost invariably demanded a violent response. It was the price one had to pay to have him supervise a project. His reputation for honesty discouraged any venality, and we were to come through the entire, monumental construction program, probably for the first time in the City of New York, without a breath of scandal. Among other contributions, Moses was also an integral part of the team that helped me establish New York as the permanent home of the United Nations.

CHAPTER 34

THE UNITED NATIONS

The East and West Sides of Manhattan developed somewhat differently. When Giovanni da Verrazano and Henry Hudson first came into the harbor, they discovered that the flow on the North River (running along the west side of Manhattan) was sluggish and the tide effective all the way to Albany. The current on the river flowing east of the island gave them the impression of a fast-flowing river, and therefore they discouraged the use of that side of Manhattan for shipping. On the other hand, the North (Hudson) River, from the day the very first Dutch settlers set foot here, was a suitable place for trade.

As the island developed, the waterfront on the West Side contained warehouses and commercial buildings suitable to transportation, and the busy waterfront gave rise to many related business ventures. On the East Side, without the same stimulus, older buildings began to decay over time, and many areas developed into slums. When I took office, the drive along the East Side, F.D.R. Drive, included any number of unsightly conditions that attracted one's appalled eye, and they were not just limited to the Harlem area. One encountered several dilapidated factories built more than a hundred years earlier, and the area north of 42nd Street, at a site exposed to the visitor travelling into the city from New England, was about the worst of all, containing as it did a slaughterhouse. I was all too familiar with its smell and appearance as I passed it twice a day on the drive to and from City Hall. The slaughterhouse and the smell of death emanating from it made the area one of the most undesirable in town. It was one of my hopes to be rid of it before my term expired, and it came about in a way I had not planned.

The experience of the League of Nations, its lack of power and its failure to take action against Mussolini when he invaded Ethiopia, became an object lesson for the various countries which had suffered so much during the war. There was a general feeling that a new organization must be created which would have the support of the major powers and would be committed to take more positive steps to prevent future aggression. In 1945, representatives of many nations met in San Francisco and formed the framework of the United Nations Organization. Because of my own wartime position and experiences, I was familiar with the benefits which could flow to mankind from an international body whose members could surrender some of their nationalism. I was sympathetic to the need for such an organization to succeed, and I also believed it could best succeed in the enlightened atmosphere which New York could provide. My motives were not completely unselfish. I wanted New York to be the home of the United Nations.

I could not afford to wait until I was inducted into the office of Mayor before contacting representatives of the new body. Immediately after the election, I invited the organization to make its permanent headquarters here. It was not a bit too soon. Other American cities, including Boston, Philadelphia and San Francisco, put on vigorous campaigns to get the U.N. Geneva and other European cities were also campaigning to be chosen. A committee of the United Nations came to talk with us, and after the first encounter, I felt that our chances of getting it were poor. I clashed almost immediately with the committee chairman, a Yugoslavian named Dr. Stoyan Gavrilovic, whose attitude was so arrogant and demanding that it was almost impossible to deal with him.

In an effort to be helpful, I asked him, "How many persons must be housed and how much office space will you require?" "That information," he said sharply, "does not lie within my frame of reference." It was typical of his attitude. He demanded 50,000 square feet of choice office space in Rockefeller Center, and he also demanded that we commandeer the Waldorf Astoria for the living accommodations. The demands would have been impossible any time, but with the tremendous and acute housing shortage at that moment it did not look as though we would be able to accommodate the extensive needs of the prestigious body.

But good fortune was on the side of New York. Dr. Gavrilovic was removed from his post, and a big, affable, charming Scandinavian, Trygve Lie (who became secretary-general in 1946), replaced him. A personal, friendly relationship developed between the two of us, which was accurately described by the *New Yorker* magazine's Phil Hamburger in his book *The Oblong Blur*:

> "I have met many important men during the past few years," Lie is fond of saying, "and I would rank Mr. O'Dwyer among the top twelve. When that man gives his word, he sticks to it. I can look him in the eye. How many men *can* you look in the eye?"

Mayor O'Dwyer is just as extravagant about Lie. In the

year and a half of their official association, the Mayor has become Lie's most unbridled booster. "On my way through life I have observed many men—men in exalted positions and men in humble ranks—and I would place Trygve Lie high on the list of *men* . . . His face is open, he has the facts and figures, he states his needs, he knows what he wants and when. Poor fellow, he's a fine stabilizing influence, but what a burden he carries, dealing with the 57 varieties!"

I felt that nothing less than a carefully planned campaign would be able to satisfy the idiosyncracies of the various delegations. We started out with the advantage of having Lie personally disposed to me and I could not totally delegate so important a job, so Robert Moses, Wallace Harrison, Andrew Cordier, Warren Austin (United States Ambassador to the United Nations) and I met religiously every Tuesday at 8 a.m. at Gracie Mansion to discuss the many problems which the United Nations would encounter in its formative stages and, of course, to induce the organization to stay here permanently. Our first decision was the temporary site of the Security Council.

The United States Navy was ending its tenancy of the Bronx campus of Hunter College in March 1946. Since Hunter was part of the New York City university system, we made it available to the Security Council, but not without objections and demonstrations from students clamoring to have their campus returned to them. Hunter's president, who had been preparing to take back the campus, was also vociferous in his opposition, and pickets were around City Hall for weeks. Despite this activity, it was prepared by Moses and his staff and made ready for the first meeting of the Security Council on January 12, 1946.

The Sperry Plant at Lake Success was cutting down on its activities because of the war's end, and we obtained its use for the United Nations Secretariat in the fall of 1946. We suggested, as a permanent site for the United Nations, the World's Fair Municipal Auditorium in Flushing, about a half hour by train from Times Square. The United Nations committee found it unsuitable as permanent headquarters.

It was at this time that a combination of Nelson Rockefeller, Robert Moses, Wally Harrison and myself finally selected the site on which the United Nations now stands. It was the slaughterhouse at 42nd Street and the East River. A prominent real estate company had taken an option to buy the area in question, and I talked to Moses about it. He proceeded to get the Rockefeller brothers to pick up the option, buy the land for $8 million, and turn it over as a gift to the United Nations. I prevailed on the United States Government to put $65 million into the deal.

It was then up to the city to do its part. I directed Jerry Finkelstein, chairman of the Planning Commission, to develop a plan to create suitable approaches to the proposed United Nations building and to present it to the Board of Estimate without delay. The editorial in the *Herald Tribune* of April 23, 1947, helped me to convince the Board that the city investment of $45 million was sound:

> Mayor O'Dwyer has sent to Jerry Finkelstein, chairman of the City Planning Commission, a reasoned and eloquent plea for replanning the area around the United Nations headquarters. The City's plans, he wrote, "must embrace the vision of the world capitol in the heart of our metropolis for many years to come."
>
> This mark of the Mayor's interest promises that the City Planning Commission is at long last to be entrusted with the job outlined for it in the City Charter. And that is a most happy and hopeful prospect in this era of rapid growth and change.
>
> © 1947 / *International Herald Tribune*

Even with such newspaper approval, I still had an obstacle to overcome. The proposal called for the expenditure of a great deal of money. The real estate investors in the neighborhood, out to make a killing, became very obstructive, in the hope of gaining exorbitant profits from the sale of their property. Were it not for the rather aggressive support from Robert Moses, the plan would not have gotten off the ground. The *Eagle* editorial of August 31, 1947, gave a fair analysis of the situation:

ACTION WELL TAKEN

> The Board of Estimate has approved the project of the City Planning Commission to improve the approaches to the United Nations site in midtown Manhattan, at a probable cost of $18,000,000. So the acrimonious give and take which led to an attack on City Construction Co-ordinator Robert Moses by the president of a real estate firm may be considered so much heat gone up the chimney.
>
> On the other hand, Mayor O'Dwyer's refusal to condone the condemnation of property for resale to private interests is so right as to admit of no debate. . . .

In addition, the city agreed to make the United Nations extraterritorial, which action immediately took it off our tax rolls at a continuing cost to the taxpayers. We more than got our money back, because immediately property values on the East Side went through an unprecedented rise, and the city has reaped tremendous tax benefits ever since that time.

Looking back on our endeavors, I feel that the warm atmosphere that prevailed at our meetings at Gracie Mansion had a lot to do with our ultimate success. It was there we were able to make the most persuasive arguments in favor of our city and compare our assets to those of the other competing cities. And I believe that the atmosphere helped convince the United Nations officials that New York was not a distant, impersonal metropolis, and not, as our rivals would have it, too big, cold and inconsiderate.

CHAPTER 35

GRACIE MANSION

As for my own feelings about Gracie Mansion, which of course served as my home as well as the scene of important events and meetings such as the United Nations negotiations, it was the source of great pride and also of great sadness, for reasons soon to be explained. Certainly I was not unhappy over the "fringe benefits" that came with the mansion.

Perhaps it was Fiorello La Guardia's long association with a vigorous trade union movement which made him aware of the value of fringe benefits. In Mayor La Guardia's case, the "fringe" changed his whole mode of living, and that of all the mayors to follow. It gave him trained and experienced butlers to tend to his needs; engineers, paid by the Parks Department, to tend to the heating of Gracie Mansion in the winter and to the cooling system in the summer; a chef to prepare meals to suit the palate of the most fastidious gourmet; painters to examine every foot of the house, inside and out, and insure the elegance of the structure; handymen ever present to correct any neglect while it was still controllable. The lawn looking out over the East River had shrubs planted here and there to suit the season, with some along the iron fence to hide the occupants from the prying eyes of strollers in the adjoining Carl Schurz Park. And all service personnel were paid for out of the city treasury.

When the mansion was first being prepared for the Mayor's use, a parcel of land had been cut off and separated from the rest of Carl Schurz Park by a six-foot iron rail fence. Within the compound, henceforth, important visitors would be entertained. Otherwise, it was to be used exclusively as the Mayor's home, where he would eat, sleep and relax.

This plan was wrought through the proposal of Fiorello's faithful friend and companion, Newbold Morris. Fiorello promptly moved in on May 14, 1942. If Jimmy Walker or his predecessor, John F. Hyland, had suggested appropriating a museum in Carl Schurz Park to provide living quarters for the Mayor, there probably would have been a full-scale investigation. Because La Guardia made the move, it seemed like the appropriate thing to do.

Whether it was correct or not, no one since that time has suggested surrendering the privileges which are now firmly attached to the office of Mayor, and certainly I, as the holder of that office, wouldn't have thought of changing a custom which established, more than anything else, the importance of the building and the status of the occupant.

Gracie Mansion was built by a Scotsman named Archibald Gracie in 1799, and no more delightful location could have been selected. The easterly porch commanded a view of the East River and Hell Gate and Astoria, on the western end of Long Island. The environment has suffered much since Gracie's time. In colonial days, slaves were smuggled to freedom out of Pot Cove on the Astoria side of the river, which was then unencumbered by bridges or ugly flashing neon lights screaming out from across the water.

But even in spite of the changed surroundings, Gracie Mansion continued to be a home that reflected its proud origins and provided New Yorkers with a symbol of pride and beauty. I used it as a showpiece, but also as New York's home. It stands as evidence of the grandeur which once was New York. Its stairways, balconies and surroundings are in period style, and the architecture is there to remind us that another generation of New Yorkers valued spirit and beauty in their homes and did not regard the cost as extravagant.

Most New Yorkers have a sense of pride in Gracie Mansion and few begrudge the Mayor his use of it. No matter how badly the city is faring, they want this official home to remain elaborate and gracious. La Guardia used to provide himself and Marie with the privacy to which he was entitled, and it was seldom used for ceremonial purposes. I did not crave privacy and used it constantly for social events, parties for foreign dignitaries, Board of Estimate meetings, and a variety of uses associated with city affairs.

Kitty was never really a part of Gracie Mansion. For so many years prior to my election, her health had been steadily worsening, and she was sensitive about it. When I lost the election in 1941, she had said there was a consolation to it: she would not have to move into what she called the "museum."

After my election years later, we made preparation for Kitty's coming to Gracie Mansion. None of the skilled physicians who were now available to her could stem the ravages of Parkinson's disease, from which she had begun to suffer a few years earlier. It dominated all her other previous afflictions.

Knowing that she would have great difficulty negotiating the stairway, I had a small elevator installed, although it was never used. The atmosphere depressed her from the beginning. The lonely sounds from the river, the foghorns, and the bells on the buoys kept her awake and made her conscious of her condition. Old wooden structures have a habit of making creaking noises, and these were most disturbing to her. She would have been more content to stay in our semi-detached, red brick house in Bay Ridge, from which she could go unnoticed to a car at the curb and have someone take her for a ride. At Gracie Mansion it was different for her, and she had no wish to leave the grounds.

Her short stay brought Kitty neither contentment nor happiness. The interesting events and visitors meant nothing to her, and she was not equal to being any part of the life around her. She got around upstairs only through the use of a wheelchair. It was a sadness that she, who had been part of my earliest struggle, was robbed of the enjoyment a wife is entitled to when the family's situation changes for the better. Her only diversions had been music and drama, but by this time she had lost these interests as well. Visitors sometimes went up to see her, and friends came to celebrate such things as anniversaries. But mostly she was ill-at-ease with any but a few old, faithful friends, and we did not encourage visitors.

She was pleased with her nurses, Florence Pugh and Frances McGuinnes, but her most faithful friend and companion, and mine as well, was Edna Davis who had been part of our household since she came as a child from the South.

On October 12, 1946, the family was called together. My brothers Frank and Paul and my niece Joan, of whom Kitty was fond, came to the mansion. Sean Reid, a family friend whom Kitty liked and who had delivered the invocation at my inauguration, was called to perform the last rites and an end came to her suffering.

The wake was held in a midtown funeral home. On the night before the funeral, the body was moved into Gracie Mansion, where the family kept vigil. The mass was arranged with the pastor of the local church, but Cardinal Spellman would not hear of it. Mass was said at St. Patrick's Cathedral with all the pomp and ceremony which only the Catholic Church can put together. Burial was in old St. Mary's Cemetery in Staten Island, where my two brothers, Jim and Jack, are buried.

I returned to Gracie Mansion with a feeling of emptiness, as if the soul of the house were missing. As days passed, I came to know that this sick woman had been a much greater part of my life than I had realized. Soon I left with my brother Frank to visit with him at his farm in El Centro. The change and the rest were badly needed.

The first year as Mayor, with all its difficulties, and the personal tragedy of Kitty's hopeless sickness had been a physical and emotional strain on me. But the complete change, Frank's sense of humor, and his wife May's patient understanding of my needs helped me over the difficult period. After a while I felt equal to returning to New York.

I was soon to complete one year in office, at which time I was rewarded with the following commentary by *The New York Times*: January 1, 1947

New York's City Hall is a rugged testing ground for the man who sits in the Mayor's chair. William O'Dwyer has stood up well, in general, to the trial of his first year in office, a year which in some respects offered unusual difficulties. His administration has been devoid of scandal, achieved a reputation for honesty, and given the impression of serious-minded effort to govern well and humanely.

CHAPTER 36

POLICE

My career in the New York City Police Department had ended in 1924, before liquor gangsters had perfected their murderous bootleg organizations. My observations from that time until the Eighteenth Amendment was repealed in 1933 were from the outside and from afar. But even at a distance, it was easy to see the extent to which Prohibition had corrupted the department on almost every level. Every mayor and every prosecutor was aware of it. Yet, each feared that a full-scale outside investigation might mean wholesale suspensions and firings, leading to a breakdown in morale and an adverse effect on the detection and prosecution of crime.

Mayors and prosecutors invariably preferred to cast the burden of investigation on the Police Commissioner in the hope that he would be able to contain corruption and gradually beat it back. Mayor La Guardia publicly rode herd on Commissioner Valentine. On his Sunday radio program, he would tell Valentine that there was a bookmaking establishment at such and such address. A telephone call might seem to have been a more appropriate manner of communication, but the radio announcement was meant to be a deterrent to erring cops and a grim reminder to Valentine that the Mayor knew things that he did not. In effect he was saying, "Your cops are on the take, Commissioner, and I know it."

This attitude of caution lest the army be rendered impotent was prevalent when Thomas E. Dewey was elected District Attorney of New York County in the late thirties. Soon after his election, Dewey let it be known that he would no longer tolerate the corruption, formerly Prohibition-related and now centered on the various forms of gambling. He had not consulted with Lieutenant Barney Dowd about his announced intention. Dowd was the head of the special police squad working out of the District Attorney's office. When the lieutenant heard of his boss's decision, he came into Dewey's office with his shield and a letter of resignation in his hand. "Mr. Dewey," he said, "what you are about to do would render it impossible for me to function. I could no longer get the cooperation going in the station house I need if I can be of service to you." "Hold your shield a while and we will think it over," said Dewey. A few days later he quietly dropped any investigation into police corruption.

My own relationship with the Police Department was cordial, but my performance on the Magistrate's Court, from the department's standpoint, was disappointing. At the beginning, it was expected that as "one of their own," I could be relied upon to see truth in the policeman's testimony. As time went on, that attitude ended, because I had come to believe that in most cases coming before me, particularly gambling cases, the appropriate arrangement had been made with the arresting officer. Dismissals and acquittals, and they were frequent, did not make me popular with the department, especially in labor cases where I had reason to believe that the actions of the police were motivated by the employer in the form of a suitable reward for police diligence and efficiency.

As District Attorney, I made sure that my squad reported to me and to me alone and not to inspectors or superiors in the Police Department. The rule was invoked after I heard that prospective defendants were tipped off as to what we had in mind, and in a very important case the defense counsel was secretly given an evaluation of the prosecution case.

Commissioner Lewis Valentine and I had many disagreements that would have broken into the open if Pearl Harbor had not intervened. During the war years, I had no right to be in the District Attorney's office, and I never interfered with Thomas Craddock Hughes, the Acting District Attorney. Even if I were permitted to and had wanted to do so, I had no time.

Between November and December, after my election as Mayor, I had to select some key cabinet appointments, and one of the most sensitive and important was the much-coveted position of Police Commissioner. The term was for five years, and because of his tenure, which frequently brought him past the Mayor's term and tended to make him independent of politics, the position also conferred power. Invariably, the commissioner had exclusive control over all his men, brooking no interference from anyone. I knew I was going to be judged by my choice, and I also knew I did not want to reappoint Valentine. At the same time, I was concerned that a sudden change in the top echelon would encourage the venal elements both within the department and outside it to take courage. Therefore, I reluctantly decided that the best course was to ask Valentine to stay on. Before I got around to asking him, however, La Guardia took a hand, and his call was a most welcome intrusion.

"Valentine feels it is time for him to quit," said the Mayor, "and I would like to talk to you about his successor." "I'd be pleased to hear whom you have in mind," I cautiously replied. "I like Arthur Wallander," he replied, "but if you are going to let him go on January 1, I would not appoint him." A couple of days following, I gave the Mayor my answer. "Wallander taught us in the Police Academy. I know his background. If you appoint him now he can stay. I won't replace him." Wallander did stay for several years, and his appointment was an unexpected benefit. Unwittingly, La Guardia had taken care of my dilemma, and we went into the new year with at least the outward manifestation that crime and corruption were getting an early priority. I was under no illusions that the conditions in the department would change miraculously under Wallander, but I knew that he was a thoroughly honest and respected cop and that he would do everything in his power to keep things under control. Besides, he was Scandinavian, and New Yorkers attributed a kind of hard-nosed, conservative honesty to the tribe I had come to know and respect in my old Bay Ridge neighborhood. As long as Wallander was in charge of our police force, an atmosphere of respectability and an aura of honesty prevailed. We had a few problems under his tenure, and it wasn't until he left and a new commissioner was appointed that things began to slip badly and my troubles began.

At the beginning of my term, the greatly-increased civilian population demanded an enlarged police force. The department was undermanned and badly in need of new station houses, new equipment and facilities. We worked out a $10,466,141 program to provide, as rapidly as possible: 11 new precinct station houses; alterations and improvements to others; a central motor and stanchion repair shop building in Queens; new precinct garages; a new stable for housing police horses; two police launches; $3 million worth of traffic signals and other traffic devices and appurtenances, including a communication system in all boroughs; ultra-high-frequency radio telephone equipment for mobile units in all boroughs; and police laboratory equipment. At least now we could be in competition with the many police units across the country.

We kept a careful watch on all personnel and kept them on their toes. Wallander switched them around and spent a great deal of time in trying to keep them honest. But old habits were soon to re-emerge. In June, we received word that some of our detectives were receiving "rake-offs" from bookmakers, and I called on Wallander to attend to this rising police scandal.

Commissioner Wallander could not have been ignorant of the effects of horse betting on men under his command. Constant arrests for bookmaking all over the city were sufficient evidence that the department had failed to curb the illegal practice. Still, it was his hope, however unrealistic, that he had it under control.

When I saw no obvious results, I turned the matter over to the Commissioner of Investigation, with the objective of keeping the police—and the Commissioner—on their toes. A *Times* editorial described the chronology of events, as well as my intentions:

August 28, 1946

MR. O'DWYER AND THE POLICE

The Mayor is jealous of the good reputation of New York's finest and he wants to keep it good. He knows that in a department of thousands of men some will go wrong. Last June, after reports that detectives were getting a "rake-off" from bookmakers, he announced that the Commissioner of Investigation would make an inquiry. Three hours later he changed his mind on the petition of Mr. Wallander and decided to give the police a chance to clean their own house. Now, apparently, Mr. Wallander is not satisfied with this housecleaning, and the Mayor has told Commissioner Murtagh to go ahead. "This check-up will continue through the balance of my administration," the Mayor says.

The laws on betting on horse races are full of contradictions, and many upright people differ on the right and wrong of gambling. But there can be no question about the necessity of keeping the police free of corruption. We suspect that it was an unpleasant course that the Mayor and the Police Commissioner were forced to take yesterday in admitting that a cleanup from within had not wholly succeeded. We commended them for their determination to see it through for the good of the Department and the City.

Towards the end of my first year, we launched another shake-up. The *New York Post* editorial reported the gist of what we sought to accomplish:

December 13, 1946

THE BIG POLICE SHAKE-UP

The Police Department is shaking up. And that tells us that

Mayor O'Dwyer and Commissioner Wallander are doing their job faithfully and honestly.

For one of the best measures of the integrity and independence of a city administration is the management of its Police Department. You don't get police shake-ups in bossed cities. It's a case of "influence" at Headquarters; of racketeering winked at and accommodated to, because the bosses running the town have a working arrangement with the chiselers and gunmen; so much protection for so much graft and/or help on election day.

O'Dwyer deserves particular kudos because as a rule Democratic Mayors in New York don't go in for police reform.

By my second year in office, crime was beginning to show an increase in spots, and I was worried about so many young men returning from the war with nothing to do. I provided for more police:

The New York Times - June 18, 1947

MORE POLICE NEEDED

Last month the Police Department revealed that major crime in this city has been steadily rising for the past three years. Because the increase over last year was almost 12 percent, Commissioner Wallander hit on the expedient of night patrols by volunteer members of his force. It will be a relief to troubled citizens, therefore, to find Mayor O'Dwyer getting down to cases and discussing a police force really large enough to deal with our complex local crime problems. The Mayor suggests not only staffing the department up to its full authorization but perhaps even expanding that figure if it is found necessary.

About halfway through my term, I spoke again to Wallander of the necessity of shaking up the department, so that we did not let the police get too comfortable or the bookmakers too brazen. On August 5, 1947, the *Daily News*, in a policy position, took the view that bookmaking could not be suppressed: ". . . New York's estimated 30,000 illegal bookies . . . will probably continue to be bookies until we Americans lose our zest for betting, or until betting is legalized." The *Journal American* was more encouraging: "Commissioner Wallander, in full concurrence with Mayor O'Dwyer, has acted with exemplary promptness in response to charges of police-protected gambling . . . the Commissioner has issued clearcut orders to commanders to jail or oust the bookies, and has spanned all five boroughs in a shakeup of the higher police echelons."

In May of 1949, Arthur Wallander resigned to take a position with the Con Edison Company. The *Brooklyn Eagle* reflected the regard New Yorkers felt for him:

> Mayor O'Dwyer is thoroughly competent, conscientious and hard working. His appointments have generally been fine. Indeed, he has surrounded himself with many unusually able men. . . . Arthur Wallander · was one of the best police commissioners in the history of the city. Not a scandal has marred the record in this department, the conduct of which has been the downfall of many previous administrations.

Wallander's resignation was a great loss to my administration. I sought to find the same type of career policeman. William O'Brien seemed to fit that bill admirably. The *Herald Tribune* concurred, stating on February 3: "Mayor O'Dwyer has chosen well. Again a lifetime policeman, up from the ranks, heads the Police Department. The excellent tradition carried on."

Bookmaking had always been the bane of the existence of the county prosecutors. It was their fond hope that they could chase the headquarters out of their county. None of them had the illusion that they could eradicate it. No police commissioner or district attorney would publicly admit that he was aware that every bookmaker was a prime source of graft for members of the force. Yet, privately each would admit it constitutes a real headache. Each of them was conscious of the fact that many young patrolmen assigned to plainclothes duty all too often became engulfed in the criminal system even though they may have previously determined to have none of it.

While bookmaking was primarily a police problem, the District Attorney in each of the five counties making up New York City realized that failure to keep it in check was a reflection on him.

The most successful District Attorneys in New York City's history were Sam Foley of the Bronx and his successor, Sylvester Ryan. They had gained enviable national reputations for preventing gambling syndicates from conducting business within the confines of the Bronx. Tom Dewey, during his comparatively short tenure as New York District Attorney, ran them a close second, and in Brooklyn when I left the District Attorney's office to go into the armed services in 1942 there were no syndicates in operation in that county. That did not mean that gambling was eliminated in any of the counties. It meant that ingenious gamblers got around the difficulty by the use of telephone lines from locations outside the city to points within its boundaries.

Betting at the racetracks had become legal. I had often spoken about the inconsistency of permitting betting at the racetracks but prohibiting it outside those favored areas. Our puritanism, however, was so deeply ingrained in our society that it took us 150 years to get Sunday blue laws amended so as to permit baseball games on Sunday, and another 25 years to permit betting at the racetracks. A complete change in the betting laws was an idea whose time had come. Yet, the legislature was not courageous enough to propose decriminalizing horse betting outside the track, even though the change would have provided a source of revenue instead of suffering the continued corruption.[1]

In Brooklyn in 1949 my successor, Miles McDonald, discovered that under his nose a new syndicate had come to fill the vacuum. It had operated for two years without his knowledge. The same old methods of corrupting members of the Police Department were used by the syndicate, which was quite extensive and was headed by a man named Harry Gross. Mr. McDonald asked me to provide money to conduct an investigation. I recommended it to the Board of Estimate. They approved the allocation of what monies were adequate for the job. The Police Commissioner provided Mr. McDonald with several young policemen from the Police Academy who would not yet have been subjected to temptation.

It is important that investigations of this kind be conducted with as little publicity as possible. The great majority of police have always been straightforward and honest, otherwise law enforcement would come to a halt. The Brooklyn investigation was accompanied by much publicity and the Commissioner complained to me that many of his men were unduly harrassed. The news spread through the department and policemen who had never condoned dishonesty were being subjected to ridicule and their children reported about remarks being passed by students at school about "the crooked cops." The extent of the resentment was demonstrated when a young police captain against whom no charge was made was called before the grand jury. He was emotionally disturbed by the experience and the attendant notice. He committed suicide.

The Police Commissioner felt the morale of the Police Department had been seriously affected by the suicide, and 6,000 policemen showed up at the funeral. Commissioner O'Brien advised me that a word of appreciation to the department would help. The appearance of an elected official at the funeral of a policeman or fireman killed in action was usual, but this was different. The young captain was not killed in action.

1. The Off-Track Betting Corporation was established in 1971 by the New York State Legislature for the purpose of operating a system of pari-mutuel off-track betting within the City of New York for the benefit of the city and state. (PO'D)

I attended the funeral and to my own subsequent regret I went further.

At the end of the funeral services the press asked me for my reaction. I said that the investigation had been turned into a "witch-hunt" and had hurt the families of policemen who were in no way involved in bookmaking. It may have been a justifiable label, but it was not good politics to say so, and I paid the price for the rash statement. I was severely criticized in many quarters. Psychologically, it placed me in the position of downgrading the efforts of my Brooklyn successor. Irrespective of how bookmaking came to reach such proportions in his county, he was then in the process of pursuing it, and any word of discouragement was bound to be most unpopular. It was not that New Yorkers were much concerned about bookmaking. Indeed, they regarded the law which prohibited it as akin to the Volstead Act which had outlawed liquor. But the idea of police graft did disturb them greatly.

The revelations which came out of the investigation in 1949 created sensational press headlines. One hundred fifty frightened policemen resigned or retired from the force. Harry Gross, who headed the bookmaking operation, at first cooperated with the investigation, but soon he had a change of heart and refused to testify for the prosecution further. As a result, the charges fizzled out. No policeman was convicted.

I had, with poor wit, placed myself in the position of being about the only casualty of the investigation. The articles on the subject which appeared in the newspapers did great damage to my standing in the city. Up to that time my record had made me invulnerable to attack from any political opponents. What all of them had failed to do to me during campaign time, I did to myself. It became clear to me that no man in public life is completely secure. The use of an unfortunate phrase at an unthinking moment or a rash reaction in temper can lead to an immediate change in public attitude.

CHAPTER 37

TAMMANY

Tammany Hall, headed by Ed Loughlin, was populated by a group of the most disreputable parasites our town had ever known. Among its activities it was common gossip in the best-informed political circles that there was a price tag of $50,000 on every Supreme Court judgeship. It was impossible to prove. One man paid the money for the nomination, but the election went against him. He approached the man to whom he had given the bribe to get it back. He was reminded that if word got out he would also lose his "parchment." There was only one thing that I could do to show my opposition to Tammany Hall. I would ignore its recommendations for appointive positions and let that fact be known.

Patronage was the lifeblood of Tammany and the only thing which was then keeping it together. At one time it had the partially redeeming feature of being the only reliable service organization where the poor could get redress. But new social programs, first in New York State and then the nation, made Tammany Hall unnecessary, and, therefore, its only usefulness to the party faithful was in the parceling out of the much-coveted judicial robes at so much a robe, as well as any other appointments it was able to recommend to the Mayor or the Governor or the Presidential pork barrel.

With the news that it was out forever at City Hall, the subleaders questioned their right to be leaders any longer, and the subtle battle to clean out Tammany Hall was on. It worked reasonably well, and Tammany was under control for a while. The change was noted, if not hailed, by the editorial writers, who had doubted that it could be done. First in 1946 it was the *World Telegram*, the New York Scripps-Howard newspaper.

June 21, 1946

FIRST TEST FOR NEW TAMMANY LEADERS

All minor revolts and rows in the Wigwam pale in the

present prospect that the Loughlin-Neal-Stand regime, with its sinister Marcantonio and Costello tieups, will be ousted and replaced by an entirely new Tammany leadership backed by Mayor O'Dwyer.

This should mean not only brighter days for a Tammany now in imminent danger of total disintegration, but also better political going for the whole Democratic party in city and state.

A few months later Mr. Loughlin's political career came to an end

Herald Tribune - March 4, 1947

CONGRATULATIONS TO MAYOR O'DWYER

Another leader of Tammany Hall has walked the plank. Edward V. Loughlin turned in his resignation yesterday without waiting for the formality of an elective ouster by the district leaders.

Mayor O'Dwyer is to be congratulated on his victory. Tammany Hall has been around a long time, and presumably he is under no illusions that reform is an overnight matter. But Mr. O'Dwyer deliberately chose to make a fight on his own issue of cleaning up the Democratic party and is off to a good start. We hope he keeps fighting.

But all that was in 1946 and 1947. In 1948, the most lucrative piece of patronage was on the horizon—the Surrogate's Court vacancy.

It was one situation above all others which would call attention to the rotten state of Tammany politics. A cabal of Tammany leaders was determined to control that post with all of its inherent patronage. It could be forced on the new leadership for the reason that the surrogate was selected first at the Democratic Party primaries, and money could be raised for any faithful and willing candidate with a good personality and absolute adherence to the party.

The cabal began its work at the prestigious National Democratic Club on Madison Avenue, to which many fine people belonged. But it had been utilized, of more recent date, by people who had met there to carry out nefarious deals that really had nothing to do with the regular Democratic organizations in the five boroughs, nor with the elected leaders to public positions of trust. There, this sinister group, made up mostly of those who had lost prestige, began to manipulate the organization and in due time plotted to take over the Surrogate's Court.

I had no power over the surrogate's job as such. It was beyond my jurisdiction. But I had heard of the plans to capture it, and I felt that, as leader of the city, I could not shut my eyes to what was going on.

Before the vacancy was to occur in 1948, I publicly exposed the plans to take over the court, referring to the National Democratic Club as a cesspool. As a result, the first deal fell through, but a second one came into being, whereby the Tammany organization put forward John Mullen, a Tammany wheelhorse and a judge of the Court of General Sessions, as its candidate. The election was confined to New York County, the home of Tammany Hall.

The Republicans took courage and put up a man of excellent reputation named George Frankenthaler. Even in spite of the fact that New York County was a Democratic stronghold, Frankenthaler won, and Tammany Hall lost the Surrogate's Court for the next 14 years. I earned myself the emnity of Judge Mullen, a friend of District Attorney Hogan, who was in charge of various prosecutions, and two years later he was in charge of the grand jury at the time I was called before it. I was then truly to pay the price for my activities against the Tammany organization.

If I earned the emnity of Judge Mullen, the Court of General Sessions and Tammany Hall in 1948, I also earned a certain amount of approval:

Herald Tribune - July 2, 1948

MR. O'DWYER CHOOSES TO FIGHT

The big news in New York is that Mr. O'Dwyer, as the No. 1 Democrat in this city and state, has declared open and full war on Tammany Hall. From his position of power and prestige, he has dramatically stated the issue against the curious lot of Tammany district leaders, and the masters behind them, in their persistent efforts to annex the Surrogate's Court. It is, as Mayor O'Dwyer says, a plundering "political conspiracy" of the rawest sort, a drive to collect a patronage tax from widows and orphans for the benefit of a discredited political organization trying to slink back into the juicy areas of control and profit.

World Telegram - July 2, 1948

MAYOR O'DWYER INTO BATTLE!

Mayor Bill O'Dwyer has taken on the biggest, toughest and bitterest fight of his embattled career.

No decent citizen or politician can stomach that present

group of district leaders who have no qualms about trafficking with vice, and gambling, and domination of the Surrogate's Court, that last line of defense of widows and orphans.

Having helped deprive Tammany Hall of access to the coffers of the families of the deceased in 1948, my opposition continued in 1949. The customary annual county dinner of the Tammany organization took place in May that year. But a new group of insurgent young men and women, headed by Justin Feldman and others calling themselves the Fair Deal Democrats, chose to have a meeting on the same night as the regular, impressive and expensive county dinner. I chose to ignore the dinner to which the heavyweights, public figures not only of this city but of other areas as well, were invited.

The *Herald Tribune* of May 4 decribed the continuing differences between Tammany Hall and myself:

O'DWYER AND TAMMANY

Tammany Hall charged $50 a plate for the 150th anniversary dinner at the Waldorf, which is entirely too much for filet mignon and champagne, especially when the city's leading Democrat is absent. Mayor O'Dwyer chose to visit a little meeting of insurgents who call themselves the Fair Deal Democrats, where he returned to an old and favorite subject—the politician's responsibility to the people. For all his studied generality the Mayor, by his timing, was telling Tammany off. And despite the impressive gathering of politicos at the Waldorf, where everybody from Jake Arvey to Governor Dever of Massachusetts gathered to hear Hugo Rogers again on the defensive, the absence of one man spoiled the party. . . .

Whatever Mr. O'Dwyer's plans as he picks his way toward the future, we enjoy the sight of New York's chief Democrat returned to the job of kicking Tammany around.

© 1948 / International Herald Tribune

But Tammany Hall would have its day, and it came about through the Kefauver hearings, at which the very forces I had deposed from leadership in the party found their way to the hearings and were used to describe my presence many years before in Frank Costello's apartment during the course of an official Army investigation. The witnesses were two Tammany leaders I had toppled, Clarence Neal and Bert Stand.

The attack by the Fair Deal Democrats on the old-line organization was not successful. However, ten years later, the young people whom I had encouraged, with the help of Eleanor Roosevelt, Governor Herbert

Lehman and my brother Paul, formed the Committee for Democratic Voters and began a grassroots reform movement which was successful in bringing to an end one-man boss control in Manhattan and a very ugly condition within the party.

CHAPTER 38

CITY HALL: THE BUILDING

City Hall was, of course, the place from which I governed New York City, and I never failed to be aware of its history and traditions.

Local government in New England and in the Southern colonies was generally established as a result of noisy discussion among the colonists. The town meeting presented the opportunity to the citizen to be heard, and governmental machinery was a logical consequence.

New Amersterdam, on the other hand, from its very inception followed the form of government of its sponsor. From the moment in 1625 when the Dutch West India Company set down the first colonists, a governing body was established as part of Dutch life in the New World. When the colonists on Manhattan numbered but a few hundred, the Stadt Huys on Pearl Street served as a makeshift tavern, hotel, courthouse, jail and town hall. With the issuance of the first charter in 1653, the Stadt Huys was continued as the official seat of government. As the town extended northward, a new City Hall was established uptown at Wall Street, and the bricks from the wall, which was earlier built to protect the Europeans from their Indian neighbors to the north, were used to construct the new edifice which in 1699 cost $3,000.

That building served as the government center for New Yorkers for another century. The earliest days of our national existence are closely linked with that New York City Hall. It served as our country's Capitol while we were discussing our future plans. The second City Hall could not boast of being a very sturdy structure. In 1812 it was auctioned off and "knocked down" to the highest bidder who took title to it for $425.

In about 1804 the Common Council did not seem to be impressed with the historic nature of its official home. It decided to abandon the building and move further uptown, and the records indicate that payment to the contractors was made out of current revenues—no bonds, no notes, no debentures. The public advertisement offered $350 to the architects whose drawings for the new City Hall would be accepted. The contract was awarded to a Scot named John McComb, Jr., and a

Frenchman, Joseph F. Mangin, who also became the contractors.

The new building faced southward towards the town. The contractors were given instructions that brownstone, instead of marble, would be acceptable for use on the back of the building facing north, since few would be looking at City Hall from that direction. The brownstone came from quarries in Newark, and the marble for the front of the building was specially selected from quarries in Stockbridge, Massachusetts, because it was considered the finest quality available.

Construction problems were revealed when the amount of money advanced to the contractors far exceeded the value of the rock supplied to the site. The contractors were in debt to the city for several thousand dollars. Even with council supervision, it was discovered that one of the stonecutting contractors had substituted an unskilled boy for an experienced artisan and had sought to charge the city for a journeyman's wages.

Eventually, a durable building was constructed. It took nine years to complete it. It was still intact when I took office, and barring an earthquake, I should think it will last for all time as a tribute to the Common Council and the inspiration of the early days of New York. However, during the latter half of the 19th century, the building had been allowed to become rundown and suggestions were made that it be demolished and rebuilt in another part of the city. Extensive renovations took place from 1906 to about 1920, much of it with private funds, most notably from Mrs. Russell Sage.

The interior of the building was most impressive. From the beginning, the Common Council devoted time and attention to it, and we know that the council contracted with the most famous artists of its day, and, by virtue of its foresight, priceless pieces of art by renowned painters and sculptors still adorn City Hall.

Before construction of the present building got underway, the American Academy of Arts put in its bid for a room in the new building. The bid received immediate acceptance, and this early association has been taken by its successor, the Municipal Art Commission, as proof of its proprietory interest in the city. The Charter of 1898 firmly established the commission as the sole judge of the type of architecture to be used in all public buildings and of all works of art to be displayed in City Hall.

I had hardly come to City Hall when George J. Lober, the commission's executive director, made his presence known and dramatically conveyed his fears that the three million dollars worth of art in the building was in the process of deterioration, even disintegration. I asked Mr. Lober, who had been appointed by La Guardia some years before, why he had not made his request before the paintings had reached their present perilous state. "I raised the question several times," he replied, "but the money was tight here."

For the next few years, City Hall became a sort of paintings repair show. Wilford Conrow, an acknowledged expert, was selected by the Art Commission to painstakingly restore these paintings to their former splendor, and another artisan went to work in putting the frames in shape. In the process, it was discovered that a painting attributed to one artist, was, in fact, the work of another more prestigious one, making the painting much more valuable. The discovery more than paid the total cost of reconstruction. In the meantime, the City Council, the Board of Estimate and the Mayor were all getting a liberal education in the arts, and the experience was to stand me in good stead later, when I had to step into a dispute over a portrait of La Guardia.

In December, 1945, the City Council and the Board of Estimate were under Democratic control, and the reform administration was coming to an end. A proposal was made by Mayor La Guardia's friends that the Board of Estimate approve a contract to pay an artist $2,500 to paint a portrait of the Mayor. The Democrats insisted on a "package deal," and a contract to paint portraits of Jimmy Walker and John P. O'Brien was offered. Each artist selected was to receive $2,500 for his work.

In due course each committed to canvas his respective subject. But when the artists' names were made known, the wisdom of paying such a sum to the painter of the La Guardia portrait was sharply questioned by some leaders in the field of art. When the portrait was completed, it was submitted to the Art Commission which promptly refused to approve it or to permit it to occupy a place of honor at City Hall. The rejection became a controversy that lasted a couple of years, but in the end the portrait was exiled to Brooklyn College and a new artist commissioned.

In the case of John O'Brien, a difference of opinion arose between the artist and Judge O'Brien, who was irritated by the tedious hours the artist required in order to capture the spirit and personality of her subject. When he finally saw the completed portrait, the judge proclaimed that the artist had captured the immediate mood of her subject, rather than his soul, and he was therefore displeased with the result. The Art Commission held to a different view and accepted the portrait. Judge O'Brien forbade it to be exhibited. After his death, it was exhumed from the Archives and placed on the wall at the entrance to the Mayor's office. O'Brien's family got word of it and again raised objections, and the offending portrait was consigned to the Archives forever.

Neither Walker nor La Guardia lived long enough to see their portraits unveiled. Both had died within the first two years of my taking office. Even though their characters and personalities differed radically—as a matter of fact, they might be regarded as direct opposites—they were both typical New Yorkers, and each in his own way portrayed the best of the city. Each represented a distinct period of New York life. Walker, gay, witty, kindly, fun-loving, represented the 20's and La Guardia, serious, hard-working, irascible, abusive, dogmatic, was the type of mayor that a disappointed, critical, and hungry people of the Depression years wanted as their leader.

When the Walker canvas was ready to be unveiled, I made arrangements for the ceremony, which attracted a large number of Jimmy's personal friends and members of his family. My talk at the ceremony conveyed the deep affection New Yorkers felt for him.

> As Mayor of this City, this is one of the happiest moments in the turbulent two years that I have been at City Hall. I am the medium through which the City receives Jimmy Walker back to City Hall. This time for ever and ever. Those of us who knew him had a privilege that shall be missed by future generations. Posterity will see this picture, will gather an impression as to his physical appearance. But will they get the grace, will they get the warmth of his heart? Will they know, as they look over these portraits of the Mayors of this City, how much this one, above all the others, loved his fellow man? Will they know that there was no hurt in him? Will they know that there was a deep and abiding affection in him; will they know of his graciousness; will they know that his ready wit and gift of speech was never used to hurt? Will they know how much New York loved him and how much they mourned at his passing? Even this artist's great talent cannot completely capture the real, true Jimmy Walker. As Mayor I speak for seven million New Yorkers. On their behalf as well as my own I welcome Jimmy back.

Due to the Art Commission's rejection of the La Guardia portrait, the planned unveiling ceremony did not take place. I had wanted to pay him an equally personal tribute. My relationship with La Guardia had never been friendly, and on public matters, we continued to be partisan and hostile towards each other. Yet as time went on, we became closer and closer. As my problems in office increased, I could understand Fiorello better, and our relationship became more cordial.

His passing brought sorrow to the city he had served. The proclamation I issued was a real expression of how New Yorkers felt:

WHEREAS Fiorello H. LaGuardia, as Mayor of the City of New York, established a brilliant record of public service and enjoyed the affection and admiration of our citizens, and

WHEREAS his death has brought deep sorrow to the people of this City, and

WHEREAS our citizens will desire to pay their last respects to the memory of an outstanding American citizen and a great public servant whose life was a shining example of unselfish devotion to his fellow citizens,

NOW, THEREFORE, I, William O'Dwyer, Mayor of the City of New York, do hereby proclaim Monday, September 22, 1947, a day of mourning in memory of the Honorable Fiorello H. La Guardia, and I hereby direct that flags on all public buildings fly at half-mast for a thirty-day period. I also ask our people to offer their prayers for his eternal peace.

CHAPTER 39

CITY HALL: CEREMONIAL OCCASIONS

City Hall has also been the scene of many historic happenings. Both Lincoln's and Grant's bodies lay in state there to be viewed by the public before being finally laid to rest. In 1858 City Hall became the scene of a famous auction, at which all of its furniture and belongings were sold to the highest bidder to pay a judgment obtained against the city by a Wall Street broker named Robert Lowber. It seems that Lowber had sold land to the city at an exorbitant price, and the new reform Mayor, Daniel Tieman, refused to pay for it. Lowber got a judgment against the city and had the sheriff execute against the city's belongings at City Hall. The sole bidder was Tieman's agent, who returned the property to the city without profit.

The ticker-tape parade, including a welcome at City Hall, has long been a part of our history, the early honorees ranging from the Marquis de Lafayette to Henry Clay. In the 1920's, Mayor Jimmy Walker was not content to wait until Queen Marie of Rumania arrived at City Hall. He accompanied her up Broadway from the Battery. Bystanders along the way good-naturedly urged their dapper chief magistrate to show his welcome appropriately to the royal visitor by making love to her.

It seemed to me that every high potentate or distinguished visitor who received an invitation to visit our nation's capital felt that his or her sojourn would be less than satisfying if it didn't also include the opportunity of being officially greeted by New York's Mayor. We have always been flattered that our city is found attractive to renowned strangers. The State Department, however, was often concerned that somehow we lacked the tact to deal with delicate situations without the risk of causing an international incident.

There was the time when we were about to receive guests from the Republic of Mexico. For the occasion we arranged for the attendance of the Army, Navy and Marine bands. At the last minute, I spoke to Bill Donoghue, my press secretary, about a haunting fear that surfaced in my mind. "Find out what the bands intend to play," I said. "They will start off with the 'Marine Hymn'," he said. "Say no more, Bill," I replied. "Explain that the State Department does not wish reference made to our armed forces' experience at the Halls of Montezuma while the Mexicans are in our city."

Receiving representatives of European nations at City Hall was a particularly rewarding duty. Representatives of France, Holland, Belgium, England, West Germany and the Union of Soviet Socialist Republics were all greeted, and we had the opportunity to reflect back on the war, its implications, its brutality, and to reflect on how close the world had come to being ruled by a madman. I developed a good understanding with the Russian diplomatic corps in this city, and they were frequent visitors to Gracie Mansion.

However, I would have gladly surrendered to the State Department the pleasure of receiving the most prominent of all the visitors to come to New York during my term in office. In January, 1946, I received the following letter:

Dear Mr. Mayor:

The other night when I met Mr. Churchill as he was passing through New York, he asked me to present his compliments to you and to say that, on his return, he hopes to have the pleasure of calling on you.

Sincerely yours,
Bernard Baruch

A few days after I received a personal visit from a representative of the State Department. He did his best not to be patronizing. "Mr. Mayor," he said, "the State Department is of course quite anxious that Sir Winston Churchill will receive all the public honors which I know this generous city of yours has bestowed upon other distinguished visitors over a long period of time." "I have not been honored with a personal visit from the State Department as a prelude to the reception of other prestigious visitors," I said, and the representative showed ever so slightly that he was ill-at-ease. "What makes you feel there shall be any exception in Sir Winston's case?"

The State Department man fumbled awkwardly. He was obviously told that under no circumstances was he to express the department's reason for its misgivings. "You may report to your superiors," I continued, "that this city has always behaved in an honorable and straightforward fashion and in the best tradition of the founders of our nation." I don't believe my visitor felt as assured as he would have liked. The reference to our "founders" and the use of the word "straightforward"

During the City Hall ceremony welcoming Winston Churchill to New York, 1946

did make him wince slightly.

A subsequent request from representatives of Irish societies justified the State Department's misgivings. A few days later, John Wrynn, the detective who for years manned the gate, announced their presence. I didn't need to be told why they had come, and I was sure that they would be a lot more forthright than the visitor from the State Department. They handed me a letter which recounted all that Churchill had done to thwart the Irish Freedom Movement, and the letter charged him with being mainly responsible for the Black and Tan atrocities some 25 years earlier. I knew most of the members of the delegation well and was on a first name basis with many of them. Today was different, and their disappointment, if not their hostility, was apparent. "Mr. Mayor," the chief spokesman started, "we are disturbed by news stories that this city . . ."

"Let me interrupt you, gentlemen," I said. "Today I would feel a lot more comfortable as one of your delegation than I do receiving you. When one accepts the position of Mayor, he surrenders many personal privileges. New York is as important as Washington, and the Mayor may not permit himself the luxury of receiving one visitor and denying to another the hospitality of the town. I have been requested by the leaders of our nation to extend our courtesies to Winston Churchill and have assured them that I would." The delegation were polite but disappointed. As I walked with them to the door, a few held back. "Bill," one said plaintively, "will you be pinning a medal on him?" "I'm new here, John, but I assume the reception could take that form." "Then, Bill," he replied, "so this visit is not a complete loss, will you stab him with it as you put it on? You can explain to the State Department that your finger slipped."

Two days before St. Patrick's Day, 1946, as the Mayor of the city, I presented a citation to Sir Winston Churchill for his "distinguished and exceptional service for his public benefactions as wartime Prime Minister of England, when he inspired his nation out of the depths of Dunkirk and led it to victory over the destructive terror of fascism." It was with a sigh of relief that I delivered Sir Winston to the State Department. I did not mention a word about the Black and Tans, and I didn't stab Sir Winston, and I believe I was equally entitled to a citation for unusual forbearance.

Other official ceremonies had far less weighty problems. One of them occurred during the Golden Jubilee celebration to mark the 50th year of the existence of Greater New York, which took place towards the end of my first term. Although I had worked hard to use the event to create interest and discussion about atomic energy, I had to surrender the serious side of things to a plan which Grover Whalen had up his sleeve.

Grover was a familiar figure at City Hall, a strong, blustery man with the mustache of a British sergeant major, at home in a top hat and morning coat, who served a number of preceding mayors as unpaid host to important visitors. He was a real showman, and for the Golden Jubilee ceremony, he unearthed an antique tallyho from its resting place in some museum. Grover had been Police Commissioner and so he obtained the services of a mounted policeman named Burke to drive the coach. I was to sit beside the coachman on the top of the tallyho, which was to lead a massive parade. The choice of Burke left a lot to be desired. He was familiar with the habits of the well-trained police horses, but the animals hitched to the tallyho were not police horses. I had some intuitive misgivings about my role in the first place but received Grover's assurance that I was quite safe aloft. As we started off, Burke seemed to handle the reins deftly enough and I began to feel secure, but my anxiety soon returned.

The photographers came in front of the horses to get their shots. The flashbulbs fairly frightened the animals and they began to bolt. The tallyho began to sway from side to side. Many things entered my mind, such as the age and condition of the vehicle, but Grover caught my attention. He lunged for the bridle and checked the horses as they were about to take off. He looked at me sheepishly, and only his act of bravery saved him. "It won't happen again," he said with assurance. Self-preservation, nature's first edict, commanded me to abandon this adventure and to seek the reassuring arms of mother earth, but the politician's fear of being branded a coward provided an antidote. The battle within my conscious mind was finally resolved. Concern for my public image soundly defeated the more natural instinct to be safe.

We had traversed about ten blocks without incident when a German band again frightened the horses. This time the passengers, actors dressed to represent the mayors of New York's cities and towns at its unification in 1898, decided they had lived dangerously all too long and fled in the direction of a Third Avenue bar to replenish their courage. When we came to a downgrade, my fears again proved justified when it became apparent that the brakes were not working. The horses were pushed forward and again we were careening. An intrepid, nameless New Yorker, who obviously knew something about horses, saved the life of the town's chief executive. We ended the trip with sweaty, skittish horses, an embarrassed horse cop, and a Mayor with all the red blood corpuscles withdrawn from any proximity to the outer skin.

Grover Whelan's next extravaganza was to have much greater sig-nifcance for me. The event was the Educational Exhibition at Grand Central, designed to show "New York at Work," and it utilized the talents of the fashion industry. Grand Central Palace was dimly lit as the models came in to display New York fashions.

"This reminds me of speakeasy days," said one model to another, her back to me, but within earshot. "You're much too young to know about speakeasies," I said, and she turned to answer me, somewhat embarrassed. She was beautiful. I invited the whole group to come to Gracie Mansion after the show, and Sloane Simpson rode with me in the car.

Since Kitty's death, my family had urged me to remarry, but I had resisted the idea. Any widower, especially one who also carries a title of importance, will discover that his name is linked romantically with eligible women. I proved to be no exception. But no one whom I had met in the interim period had affected me as did this charming and attractive young woman.

I had been having a very undisciplined life for the year since Kitty's death. The days were full of official obligations and the evenings often taken up with charity or social functions. I enjoyed the Harold Rosses (Harold was the founder and editor of *The New Yorker*) and the Bernstiens; show people like Ethel Merman and her husband Bob Leavitt, Ella Logan and Fred Finklehoffer; or newspaper people and writers whom I had known. But these moments were intermittent, and there was little in Gracie Mansion to break the monotony, and most of the time, after 10:30 or so, it became a lonely place. Nobody could imagine the life of the Mayor of New York being monotonous, but at times it was.

It was not merely my family who urged me to marry again. I was being constantly introduced to attractive women by well-meaning friends. Once Billy Rose and Eleanor Holm were at Gracie Mansion at a cocktail party. I was very fond of Eleanor. There was an attractive woman there who was quite wealthy. When she left the room Eleanor took me to one side. "Bill," she said, "there's a gal that's got money. You have everything else but, and she is attractive. If you want me to, I will arrange for a private party." "Leave it alone, Eleanor," I said, "I don't think I'll ever marry again."

But after seeing Sloane Simpson for some time, I began to feel differently. Besides her natural good looks, she was both educated and cultured. Her father, Colonel Sloan Simpson, had been with Teddy Roosevelt at San Juan Hill, and her grandfather, Colonel John Simpson, was a cattleman in Texas, where Sloane was born. She had been educated in the Sacred Heart School in Torresdale, Pennsylvania, and Stevens College in Columbia, Missouri. She was 27 years younger than I. It was obvious that the age difference would act as a discouragement, but just thinking about marriage indicated we were moving in that direction.

Receiving an award from the United Jewish Appeal presented by Rabbi Stephen
Wise and former Governor Herbert H. Lehman, 1948

With Dwight D. Eisenhower, then president of Columbia University, 1948

Greeting Indian Prime Minister Jawaharlal Nehrú, 1949

Welcoming Dr. Ralph Bunche, U.N. Acting Mediator for Palestine, to City Hall, 1949 (J. Raymond Jones, Harlem political leader, at left)

Photo courtesy of Brooklyn Public Library/Brooklyn Eagle Collection
International News Photo

At a testimonial dinner in Bill's honor with (left to right) Secretary of the Navy James Forrestal; Paul Fitzpatrick, Democratic state chairman; U.S. Attorney General Tom Clark; and Secretary of Commerce W. Averell Harriman, 1947

CHAPTER 40

SNOW, SEWAGE, WASTE & SMOKE

In addition to the problems of transportation, housing, crime and corruption, it seemed there was always a crisis relating to the environment New Yorkers lived in, whether it be sewage, waste disposal, air pollution, or, in winter, crippling snowstorms.

In earlier times, the snow was removed by men hired at the local sanitation office as soon as the snowfall made travel difficult. The horse and wagon came under contract and teamsters were paid for each load collected and dumped. The crooked tallyman often counted the same load twice, and in that free enterprise atmosphere great trucking fortunes came into being. In those early days, snow was an annoyance for most people and a source of corruption for others. It nevertheless constituted life-giving patronage for the Democratic district leader and a measure of work relief for the unemployed. It seemed that people at that time complained less about the inconvenience caused by the snow than they do now, when the snow-removing equipment opens up the main thoroughfares within a matter of hours.

A sudden snowstorm can make matters extremely difficult in the life of a New York mayor. Winters are seldom without snow for the whole winter, and the mayor hopes it will hold off until February, when the days are longer and the sun stronger, so that nature can then lend a helping hand in getting snow off the streets.

After the heavy city snowfall, we can anticipate a number of problems, such as our older citizens falling on the icy sidewalks. Such a fall often results in a fractured hip, and our hospitals expect many such cases after each storm. It also means commuter traffic will be tied up, as well as commercial traffic, and the inconveniences to passenger car drivers are enormous.

People in the outlying areas of the boroughs become irritated if the city does not do something about removing the snow from in front of their driveways. There is an ordinance which requires landlords to clean off the sidewalks in front of their property, and this works reasonably well in tenanted areas, but where properties are vacant, the snow can pile up and remain on the sidewalks from the middle of December until the first of April.

The law allows a mere 48 hours to get the sidewalks cleaned so that the people can walk on them with safety and, if their slippery condition exists after that time, the city, rather than the adjoining property owner, is liable in damages to one who slips on the icy sidewalk. The real estate lobby has been successful in defeating all legislation which would place the burden equally on the city and the adjoining landowner, whose property receives its value in the first instance because the adjoining street has been paved at city expense.

At the end of my second year in office, the city was free of snow as I presided over the Christmas tree lighting ritual at City Hall. My nephew, Rory O'Dwyer, threw the light switch, and the look on his young face reminded me of the way millions of kids everywhere enjoy the season.

It had been a difficult time for me, and I was run down and exhausted. So I headed out to visit my brother Frank in El Centro. The day after Christmas I got out on the golf course. Before commencing the game, I called New York. Deputy Mayor John Bennett said it was snowing lightly around City Hall. I called a few hours later. Bennett reported it was snowing, but it was still manageable. I called a little later and received the news that commuters were snowbound in New York City and were being put up in the armories. Twenty-four inches of snow had fallen, the city was in a mess, and La Guardia Airport was closed. I knew that New Yorkers like their Mayor to suffer with them during storms of all kinds. It eases the pain. "Clear one strip, John," I commanded. "I'm on my way back."

When I arrived in Buffalo, the pilot balked at taking me any further. Under great pressure, he landed precariously on the only runway opened at La Guardia, and I immediately took charge of the emergency effort. Of course we were short of snow-clearing equipment, and to make matters worse, a heavy ice was forming on the snow. The infamous storm of '47 cost the city $8.6 million, but by the end of the year we had the removal operations well in hand. All over the city everyone cooperated, and we had a minimum of complaints. New Yorkers worked together on the problem as only New Yorkers can:

World-Telegram - December 30, 1947

BIG EMERGENCY WELL MET

New Yorkers, wriggling from under their 99,000,000 ton

snow blanket, owe their thanks to the 23,000 workers who are making swift progress in their huge removal job. . . .

There may be lessons to be learned about future preparedness for big snows. But in this instance, it seems to us the city and workers, from Mayor O'Dwyer down, together with others supplying quick and generous aid, have so far met a big emergency in a way that all New York citizens can applaud.

We learned many lessons from that storm and soon after sought out the best snow-removing equipment we could find, eventually buying it for $7 million in Montreal. The following year there was a 19-inch snowstorm, but with the heavy equipment, we brought it under control in 48 hours:

Brooklyn Eagle - December 22, 1948

Last year's snowstorm extraordinary that sealed up the city for days will be remembered for a generation or two. And so will this year's, but for different reasons. When the snow came down inch by inch the day after Christmas, 1947, and made the streets impassable for weeks, the city, and particularly that part of it that is Brooklyn, found it extremely depressing. Today we have something of great importance to rejoice about at Christmastime. Brooklyn streets are no longer neglected.

Thank you, Mr. Mayor, and bravo!

A fringe benefit of the 1947 snowstorm was a copious supply of water in our watershed, and drought was no threat to us for a long time after. Drought in New York can cause inconveniences to the suburbanites, who must witness their nice, green lawns literally turn to dust, and to the city dweller, who must forego the bath and use the shower instead; but to the mayor of a city the size of New York, drought must be considered in relationship to a possible outbreak of disease. If our sewage system fails to perform for lack of sufficient water, or any other reason, the results could be catastrophic.

Through the years, we have gone through occasional droughts, and each time it has been a scary experience. It means that the water, delivered free of charge to residents, is now in such short supply that we are never sure we have enough to take care of the basic needs of wasteful New Yorkers. However, New Yorkers respond well to a common problem, and with humor. "Take a shower with a friend" was the slogan they invented during one period when our supply was threatened.

With each new convenience designed to make life in a large city more bearable, there is a price we must pay. There are no political speeches made during a mayoralty campaign about the tons of human waste which the city must dispose of each day. The subject is still regarded as too indelicate for frank, public discussion. But my Commissioner of Public Works, Fred Zermulian, gave me the facts. One billion gallons of water and fecal matter passed through our sewage system each 24 hours in 1946, when I took office. For the most part, it flowed right into the harbor. We have had sewage plants of one kind or another, beginning with an effort by the Dutch West India Company, but it was not until Jimmy Walker's term in office that a sewage treatment plan was devised. For a quarter of a century before that there had been warnings of the dire consequence of our failure in this respect. I asked Dr. Harry Mustard, my Health Commissioner, to study the condition of the waters around New York. His report was alarming. We had been so reckless in our determination to enjoy our indoor comforts that several of the city's beaches had become so ridden with bacteria as to be unsafe for human use.

Nothing less than a comprehensive plan would suffice to render harmless the billion gallons of bacteria-laden liquid which made the harbor an extension of our sewer system. Inasmuch as our problems also affected New Jersey and Connecticut, we entered into a joint agreement in 1949 to set up a ten-year program to accomplish the goal of a clean harbor.

I ran into trouble with the first project. The plans to establish a sewage treatment plant are always met with opposition from people in the designated neighborhood. People want the plant, but, invariably, somewhere else. Our engineers felt that the best place to start would be in Brooklyn, where my home was. But they further advised me that the best place in Brooklyn was the Owls Head area in Bay Ridge, the very neighborhood from which I had been elected Mayor. It came as a shock to my neighbors that I would do this to them. It was necessary for me to personally crusade to have it established in that neighborhood. I spoke to neighborhood councils to advise that there would be no malodors, and my engineers explained in detail how it would work. By May of 1950, treatment plants in Owls Head, Brooklyn, and Hunts Point in the Bronx were under construction. We had allocated $45 million for both plants.

The waste which goes through our sewers is not the only potential health hazard with which a mayor must be concerned. The Industrial Revolution and subsequent technology gave us every imaginable kind of paper product: hats, plates, cups, containers, towels and newspaper. Because paper is comparatively cheap, available for so many uses, and "disposable," manufacturers and users invariably leave to the city the burden of carting the soiled and used paper which they have found so convenient. To add to the problem, New Yorkers are given to discarding newspapers and other rubbish in our gutters, giving the city an unkempt look and requiring our Sanitation Department to collect it. My predecessor often took the citizens to task for their slovenliness. But to no avail.

Modern technology also has given us the convenience of cheap glass and metal containers. The labor costs of returning them to the factory were too great and they, too, became industry's gift to our Department of Sanitation. Add to that problem the endless disputes between tenants and landlords as to who should be obligated to place trash at the sidewalks, and one could begin to understand why the filth became strewn through the streets and vacant lots.

Before a Supreme Court decision in 1934 put an end to the practice, it was customary for the city to dump the garbage ten miles out to sea. The current and tide helped its homing tendency and it invariably made the return trip and decorated our shoreline and our sandy beaches.

The argument about the disposal of our garbage was a frequent topic of discussion at our Board of Estimate meetings. The Board was made up of our five Borough Presidents, the Mayor, the President of the City Council and the Comptroller. The public meetings held every other week were designed after the old town meeting and gave the people an opportunity to be heard on the matters on that day's calendar. I seldom missed a meeting of the Board of Estimate. It was there I learned that things were not quite as placid as my staff seemed to tell me they were.

The voting strength of the various localities, or lack of it, too often was the final determining factor as to where garbage was to be dumped, and Staten Island, sparsely populated and with little voting strength, became one of the likely spots. Bob Moses wanted it dumped on wetlands, where new parks could be created, but naturalists quarreled with his interference with nature, since the wetlands were the natural breeding beds for wildlife. The people in the surrounding neighborhoods had violent objections to the malodor from the decaying garbage. Myra Barnes, a resident of Staten Island and a frequent protestor before the Board on matters concerning Staten Island, made the point at one meeting that the trumpet swans had left their natural breeding area because of the proximity of the foul-smelling garbage in decay. The inconvenience caused to the swans was treated humorously, with James Lyons, Bronx Borough President, assuring Mrs. Barnes that the swans had moved to the Bronx and were alive and well.

Not long after the protest from Staten Island, Lyons announced that natural gas was discovered in Bronx garbage heaps. It was plain that

Moses had moved the garbage disposal to the Bronx when opposition from Staten Island had developed local strength. Jim Lyons, who had found so much that was humorous in Myra Barnes' plea for the trumpet swans, now found the shoe on the other foot. Irate citizens from the Bronx told about sending a pipe a few feet into the ground and lighting a match to find a full flame burning from the gas pockets created in the decomposing waste.

In the process, much new park land had been created by Robert Moses, then Park Commissioner, among other titles. He brooked no opposition to any plan he developed, and it became the Mayor's job to come into the breach and justify his policy, if not his behavior. After one of those particularly noisy meetings in the Board of Estimate, I called in Moses and George Spargo, his deputy. "These people seem to me," I said, "to be required to suffer for the convenience of others, and if the atmosphere under which they are now compelled to live is anything like they describe, it is unjust. Besides, if they take the city to court, I believe the garbage disposal practice will be halted by mandate. You must find another means," I said to Moses. "Lyons is no crank."

I heard no more from irate Bronxites, and Lyons became reasonably quiet. Then one day, some time after, I had occasion to visit the south shore of Queens County with Moses and his faithful friend Spargo. As we were riding out along the parkway at one point, a number of seagulls seemed to be congregating in one area. I made mention of it to Moses. "Bill," he said, "they are not seagulls. It is an altogether different species of wild bird, which lives half on land and half on sea, and natives down here can predict the weather from their behavior. This formation indicates a storm at their natural habitat." I wondered at the knowledge of my companion and reflected on how lucky we were to have men with so much useful knowledge about so many things.

It was a couple of months after this ride that the irate citizens of Queens came before the Board of Estimate to complain of garbage dumping on the south shore. I sent for my park builders. "What did you say the name of those wild birds were, that to the unsuspecting eye looked like seagulls at a garbage dump?" I asked. "Just a little while longer, Bill," said Moses, "and I promise you the finest, greenest park this side of Ireland." "Fully equipped with a full supply of malodorous gasses, I suppose," I replied. "We have the phenomenon conquered," Spargo claimed. "We can complete the project with another month's garbage."

The parks are green and they are smooth, and if one does not kick up the sod, they smell all right, but time had come for another method of garbage disposal. Besides, we were subjected to lawsuits and proposed state legislation, and it was obvious the people did not share Mr. Moses' theory that if they could only stand the smell, they would inherit the earth, all green and nice.

We had to turn to burning garbage as a last resort and that was not the perfect solution, since the chimneys of the incinerators were not high enough to prevent the smoke on a calm day from descending on the city, like a cloud, fouling the air New Yorkers breathe. Yet, there was no other way, and we launched a plan to build five new incinerators as well as to revamp older ones. The total cost was $71 million, and the plans we initiated, with the passage of time, would mean no more garbage dumping anywhere.

Engineers were then working on a way to properly use the combustible garbage so that it could in turn provide energy which we were going to find in short supply. Other plans were to compress the garbage and place within the layers some chemical which would insure fast decomposition. The end product could then be used as fertilizer.

In my time, the lack of rain caused no end of complications related to accumulated garbage in the streets. One summer, with a prolonged drought having begun to cause havoc, the rainmaker came among us. He had a plan for seeding the clouds, if he could find clouds. And in desperation I hired him. The experiment was not universally hailed as a bit of mayoral genius. No rain fell in New York City, but by accident or otherwise, torrents came down in the farm regions upstate. As a result, various farmers and merchants in that area began to sue us for what they said we had done by interfering with nature, bringing a deluge down on top of their crops and ruining their business.

I never was really proud of my performance with the rainmaker and when anybody brought the subject up, I did my best to change it.

My war on air pollution came about at the beginning of my second term after a meeting with a man named Hugh Holohan, who had fought in Dublin in 1916, and who had lately written a series of articles in the *World-Telegram* about the foul condition of the city's air. Holohan came to me as a representative of the anthracite coal industry, which was not getting its share of coal sales in the city. He claimed that bituminous coal was poisoning the lungs of New Yorkers and depositing a layer of partially-burned coal dust on the furniture of every home. Anthracite, he said, threw off little or no smoke and gave much better heat.

I could hardly deny the fact that our air was polluted and that housewives were, indeed, complaining about the coal deposit in their apartments, but I still didn't understand what my visitor was getting at. Finally, he came to the point: "All the plans to sell anthracite have been frustrated by the Consolidated Edison Company, and even though your administration has passed ordinances to deal with air pollution, the Con

Edison people have gotten around the rules, and now it's impossible to summon them, no matter how their stacks belch smoke into the ozone. As you may know, the rules provide that the inspector must view the smoke emitting from the chimney at a distance of closer than 200 feet. The Edison stacks are higher than that, which makes them immune from prosecution."

Holohan's story as to the extent of influence of the Edison Company in city government under my very nose was revealing. I checked it out and found it to be accurate.

"Find out," I said to Bill Donohue, "who is the outstanding authority in this country on air pollution. The smokiest city used to be Pittsburgh." In a few days Donohue was back to me. "Pittsburgh was the worst in the nation," said Donohue, "but a fellow by the name of Raymond Tucker cleaned it up." I called John Bennett, the Deputy Mayor, and told him to make arrangements to hire Tucker and put him in charge of smoke control. In no time at all, he was working for the City of New York. The coming of Raymond Tucker made all the difference in the world, and the *Times'* editorial proved to be the signal which was needed to make it clear that cleaner air was going to take on importance in my administration:

June 27, 1950

MOVING IN ON SMOKE

Mayor O'Dwyer's announcement yesterday that the City called in Raymond R. Tucker of St. Louis as a consultant drafting anti-smoke rules is news of the first importance for residents who have grown increasingly impatient for action. Professor Tucker, who is head of the Department of Mechanical Engineering of Washington University in St. Louis, served as Smoke Commissioner of that City from 1937 to 1942. He helped draft the laws that are generally credited with working a great improvement in St. Louis. Many other cities have borrowed his methods or his services, among these Pittsburgh, Los Angeles and Syracuse.

The employment of Professor Tucker is a good sign and city acceptance of the type of regulations that emerge from his study will be the critical test.

A *Times* editorial of three weeks later tells the story of the new rules:

July 17, 1950

TOUGHER SMOKE RULES

The Board of Smoke Control has come up with a third set of rules and regulations to enforce smoke abatement in the city, but this time the surrounding circumstances are different. It is not surprising that Mayor O'Dwyer was regarded as "not entirely satisfied" with the earlier drafts of these rules. Many of their provisions were half-hearted and left loopholes, suggesting a fear of stepping on somebody's toes.

. . .Now, apparently prodded by the Mayor to "get tough and stay tough," the Board, advised by the consultant summoned by Mr. O'Dwyer from St. Louis, Prof. Raymond R. Tucker, has offered revisions to its rules and regulations that put new punch into the proposed controls over smoke emissions, fuels and heating equipment. © *1950 / The New York Times Company*

The amount of bituminous coal used was diminished and the use of anthracite increased, and there was, for the time being, a change for the better in the air quality in New York. But automobiles and buses continued to emit poisons which were equally injurious to human health. It became obvious that the whole area of pollution needed a thorough overhaul. It could not be dealt with by one city or one state alone, and it was no respecter of state or county lines.

CHAPTER 41

PEOPLE

New York City has always had more than its share of larger-than-life personalities, and one of the most fascinating was Francis Joseph Cardinal Spellman.

During the course of one of our labor negotiations, I called in Mike Quill to discuss the current problem. It was at a time when the Cemetery Workers Union had called a strike for better wages and working conditions. One of the employers was the Roman Catholic Archdiocese of New York, and Cardinal Spellman, the powerful Archbishop of New York since 1939, was personally conducting the management side of the dispute. In dealing with this sensitive situation, no one was more arrogant than the Cardinal. He would not negotiate, and as the hearses pulled up at the cemetery gate, he called on the young postulants at Dunwoodie Seminary to bury the dead. It was one of the corporal works of mercy, as the archdiocese saw it. The union called it strikebreaking, and one of the neophyte priests was the son of a striker. It was a test of his obedience to the Holy Mother Church.

The day Quill called at City Hall, a picture appeared in the *Daily News* showing the Cardinal with his foot on a spade in the act of digging. Beside him was a coffin ready for burial. The weather was bitter cold and the ground fozen solid for two feet down. Newsmen were taking their pictures from the sides of the holy statues, from a crotch in a nearby tree, on the ground, from a kneeling position, looking down from the roof of a nearby crypt, and from every other possible vantage point. After all, it is not every day the Cardinal, himself, is leader of this kind of adventure. I showed the picture to Quill. "What do you think?" I asked. The Irish rebel before me surveyed the scene, taking in each detail. "I think," he said, "that poor bastard is not going down very far."

Francis Cardinal Spellman was an extraordinary man who conducted his rather substantial empire with the advice of the most talented industrialists and with the aid of men like John A. Coleman, the most powerful figure on Wall Street and president of the Stock Exchange. The Cardinal was a man of unyielding convictions. When he came to New York as the spiritual leader of its millions of Catholics, each parish priest had been accustomed to conducting the affairs of his own parish with local autonomy and little interference from the Cardinal. When the parish priest believed a school should be built, he raised the money to start it, arranged a loan with the bank, and hired a contractor to build it.

Contractors were known to have taken advantage of the local shepherds, and the banks charged the maximum interest. The gross indebtedness of the archdiocese to the various banks was in staggering figures, and the interest was a heavy drain on church resources. Cardinal Spellman issued an order to all the pastors that all business transactions henceforth would be carried out from the Chancery Office, which conducts the church's temporal affairs. Located at the back of St. Patrick's Cathedral, it was known among Catholics as the "Power House." He called on the banks and advised them that all future loans and renewals would be arranged through his office and guaranteed by the archdiocese, but the rate on each loan and renewal on every school or church in the archdiocese would be reduced by one half of one percent.

The first bank whose loan became due resisted the attempt to lower the interest rate. The Cardinal entered into no negotiations with the bank. Instead, he promptly paid the mortgage off. The other bankers got the message. One by one they fell in line. They acceded to the Cardinal's terms without a whimper.

A joke going the rounds at the time depicted the Cardinal at the Pearly Gates. "What was your business down below?" asked St. Peter. "I was the Cardinal of New York," the new arrival from New York answered. The Keeper of the Gates turned to his books. "Cardinal, Cardinal," he muttered, half to himself. Finally he looked over his glasses and said, "I don't find you listed." "That's preposterous," said the Cardinal. "I don't understand it at all. I served the Lord well on a most difficult assignment. I was given high praise by everybody in New York. I even got a favorable editorial in *The New York Times*. And, St. Peter," here the Cardinal paused for emphasis, "you know how difficult that is for an Irish Catholic." "Give me an example," demanded the still skeptical Keeper of the Great Gates, "of some outstanding performance which merited you such fulsome praise."

"Well, for one thing, I outwitted the New York bankers at their own game—in the Lord's behalf, of course. You see," he continued, "they held the mortgages on all of God's houses of worship and were extracting what I considered to be usurious interest rates." The Keeper remembered the argument about Caesar and God and the coin. He seemed pleased and bent again to his research. Soon he lifted his head

President Miguel Alemán welcomes Bill on his arrival in Mexico City on vacation, 1949

with obvious satisfaction. "Oh, you're down here all right," said the Lord's first Pope. "Sorry for the inconvenience. We had you listed under Real Estate."

Cardinal Spellman clashed frequently with those whose views he opposed. He watched the legislative halls for any enactments which would in any way hamper the teachings of the church or would seem to encroach upon what he regarded as the exclusive domain of the church or tamper with its temporal welfare. One such piece of legislation was introduced in Congress by Congressman Barden and passed by him and his colleagues. It considered parochial schools as private institutions, and its children were not provided with any of the benefits given to non-sectarian organizations. It sought to solidify the doctrine of separation of church and state and was meant to block the tendency towards providing private schools with assistance from the public treasury.

The Cardinal condemned the bill in no uncertain language, while in her syndicated column, "My Day," Eleanor Roosevelt praised it. The following day, the Cardinal had some uncomplimentary things to say about Mrs. Roosevelt. It looked like the first round of a Hatfield-McCoy war. The disagreement had been accompanied with personal abuse on the part of the Cardinal, and Mrs. Roosevelt was not one to back away, no matter how long the encounter might last.

I felt I should try to prevent the situation from getting out of hand. I called three people closer to the participants than I: Ed Flynn, Anna Rosenberg and Governor Lehman. All were reluctant to get in the middle of the controversy, although I impressed on them how injurious this situation could be to the city. Everywhere there were discussions about this clash, and arguments were beginning to get heated. In the meantime, the press sought my reaction. My reply: "I think it is most regrettable. I have a very high regard for Mrs. Roosevelt. By the very nature of the controversy, a great deal of emotion has been engendered, and when things cool off, I'm sure you would find the Cardinal shares that opinion."

Finally, I decided to speak to the principals myself. I called Mrs. Roosevelt first and spoke to her at great length. She was a sincere, fairminded and kindly person, and quite hurt. I said I felt that there were two parts to the controversy. One had to do with aid for school construction and pay for teachers and the other with feeding hungry children. Knowing Mrs. Roosevelt's record, I felt sure she would not oppose legislation which would make sure that children, otherwise deprived, would eat at least one hot meal a day. Her response was what I thought it would be. "What I oppose," she said, "is the maintenance of any private or parochial school by the government. It would be contrary to the Constitution. Separation of church and state has been with us a long time. It has served us well and it should be jealously guarded. However, I am in favor of feeding hungry children, wherever they are found."

"There does not seem to be a very fundamental difference between the Cardinal's view and yours," I said, and she seemed to agree. I called the Cardinal, and he was pleased. Having gotten both of them to calm down sufficiently, I suggested that they issue a joint statement on which they could both agree. That same evening, Mrs. Roosevelt called the Cardinal on the telephone. Later, Al Parks of the Associated Press called to go over the statement with me. It was issued the same day. Shortly afterward, on his way upstate, the Cardinal stopped off at Hyde Park to see Mrs. Roosevelt. They had tea on the veranda. The media just happened along, and that ended the controversy. New Yorkers breathed a sigh of relief.

Robert Moses was another extraordinary achiever, against whom one only reluctantly did battle.

One of the least known eruptions in the personal history of "Moses the Doer" took place when the great constructor ran afoul of the city historians.

The War of 1812 saw our nation's Capitol and White House burned. At the same time, our city was poorly defended. The government had plans to build forts hereabouts but had no money to build them. The Mayor was De Witt Clinton, and under his influence the City Council loaned $1 million to the government to meet the defense costs. The fort located in the harbor about one hundred feet from the tip of Manhattan, was called West Battery. After the war it was renamed Castle Clinton which was little enough honor to give a Mayor who loaned city taxpayers' dollars to a government in need.

In the intervening 134 years, the fort had its ups and downs. It was a concert hall known as Castle Garden, and "Diamond" Jim Brady was once its stage-door Johnny. The Swedish Nightingale, Jenny Lind, was one of the many prestigious artists to perform there. At one time it became the Immigrant Landing Depot, and literally millions of immigrants came through it on their first stop to the coal fields or the blast furnaces or the sheep they were to herd in the western country. Their first impression of the New World came from their temporary stay in the military-like structure. From 1896 to 1941 it was the New York Aquarium.

Now it experienced its first and only battle—a war for its own survival. It stood in the way of progress, at least that's the way Moses saw it. He had played a supervisor's role in the Brooklyn-Battery Tunnel construction, and now he had plans for the development of Battery Park. But with the excavation of cellars and subways, the land between the fort and the mainland was filled, and the fort blocked a planned promenade. With a gesture of contempt, Moses pointed out that there was never a hostile shot fired from Castle Clinton. "It was of no use to the city or the country ever," he said, "and age did not improve its condition. In its best day, it could not have withstood an artillery attack, and any big gun would have demolished it, and that's all there is to it."

But historians are a strange lot. They saw things about Castle Clinton that the indomitable Moses didn't. They saw it as part of our heritage and of an era long gone and unfortunately forgotten, even by a smart man like Moses. It was built during the lifetime of those who fought for our independence, of those who were part of our struggle, and by those who proclaimed the Bill of Rights. Surely, they argued, no man respectful of our proud heritage would dare push a wrecker's ball against this pride of our city.

To the forefront of these and other scholarly arguments, which Moses may have known but had not regarded as important, came Mrs. Iphigene Sulzberger, on behalf of the Park Society, and George McInenny, venerable and articulate spokesman for the New York Historical Society.

"It will be an eyesore in the middle of the park," said Moses, feeling that was the argument which should drown out all opposition. I thought our historical and park representatives would have apoplexy. The insult was more than they could take, and their strong reaction only served to make matters worse. "Any further discussion would be useless," said McInenny. "Mr. Mayor, it is now up to you."

Even at the risk of having Moses quit, I sided with history. "If there were only two bricks which remind us of the thinking of the people at a time when the concept of democracy was in danger, I favor preserving it." I knew of Moses' staying power, and, even after I had made my views well known, I feared he would find some way of wiping our Castle Clinton, if not by earthquake then by a bulldozer gone out of control. That night I called Congressman Sol Bloom and Senator Robert F. Wagner and explained my predicament. They immediately initiated legislation to have Castle Clinton made part of an historic monument and taken over by the National Parks Service.

John L. Lewis and his brother, Denny, were powerful men who misjudged New York. In 1949, District 50 of the United Mine Workers, a catch-all union, attempted to organize the taxi cab drivers of the City of New York. There had been various attempts to do it previously and one by Michael Quill only a few years earlier ended in failure.

John L. Lewis was then probably the most powerful labor leader in America. When I was in Washington, Lewis was a permanent fixture in his corner of the Hay Adams Hotel's dining room, where he could be easily seen by those who wished to be impressed by Washington personalities. In the previous election, peeved with President Roosevelt, he had attempted to turn his whole trade union against the President. And now his brother Dennis, better known as Denny, came to New York to organize our taxi drivers. I received information from the Police Department that Denny had come to town with a contingent of organizers. The police described them as "strong-arm goons."

Denny Lewis and his group gave immediate notice to the taxi owners that District 50 of the United Mine Workers Union represented the majority of the drivers and that the leadership was ready to negotiate a contract. The industry responded that it would only recognize a bargaining agent after it had been certified by the appropriate government agencies.

Fearing a repetition of the violence which had accompanied a previous attempt to organize cab drivers in the La Guardia administration, I issued a statement of policy explaining to the District 50 leadership that they were free to organize if they wished, but that violence would not be allowed and rowdies would be prosecuted. I had found out that there was no attempt made to organize and that the committee supposedly representing the drivers was from Pittsburgh.

My statement was ignored, and the drivers who did not want District 50 were fearful of driving through the streets. I agreed with the police plan to lay out certain routes with police protection for cabs to operate. A few days later one of Lewis' men came to see me at City Hall and told me rather bluntly, "We don't like your regulations." I asked him to repeat what he said. He simply looked me coldly in the eye and said that there would be bloodshed if they did not get a free hand in organizing according to the traditional way of mine workers. I replied, "If there is a drop of blood spilled in New York, you and your group will not see Pittsburgh for long and many a day." I directed Detective Joe Boyle to escort the emissary to the street. Within a week, Denny Lewis and his group packed up and left, abandoning any further attempt to organize taxi men in New York.

The *Daily Mirror* summed up the situation:

> The Lewis brothers, John and Denny, have seldom taken such a licking, from Bill O'Dwyer down to the newest rookie on emergency twelve hours duty. The City handled the Lewis threat admirably.

Some of my favorite personalities were not so well known. One such person presented himself at the annual presentation of the budget to the Council of the Board of Estimate, a ritual which had long since lost its original meaning. The Board listens to a number of proponents and opponents, those who are disappointed at not being properly protected. Taxpayers, real estate interests, representatives of the city employees, and various agencies are heard from, and few, if any, changes are brought about by the annual display of oratory.

One night, at the end of this tedious meeting, a large man with a heavy mustache asked permission to be heard, identifying himself as David Owens, the leader of the Watchmen's Union. He wished, he said, to dispel the notion that his union had any political power. "We have no voting strength," he said. "We are only 75 in number. I am addressing you on their behalf, an honor for which I am grateful, with no hope of receiving assistance. I have one request, however, which would cost no money, and that is to tell our supervisor to have a heart. Our lives are dull and hard, and he makes them harder.

"A case in point: One of our members is a great musician, who taught official bands in and out of the services, and he led them, as well. This man is no second-rater. He is a man of universal musical talents. Our supervisor assigned him to a warehouse out by a graveyard that had machinery stored in it . . . the smallest piece weighed 50 tons. It is lonesome, gentlemen, in the middle of the night out by a graveyard. He amused himself between rounds [at this point, Owens took a handkerchief out of his pocket, put it over his left shoulder and set an imaginary violin under his chin] by playing his fiddle. The supervisor caught him at three o'clock one morning and moved him up to the Bronx. I don't know what you can do to help get this man back where he can appease his soul without causing annoyance or discomfort to any living creature. I know that the injury to an artist of such talent and beauty is little by comparison to the important things you have to deal with.

"Gentlemen, I thank you for your patience."

I sent an aide to find out more about the musician, but indeed I was more interested in David Owens. We helped his friend, and I heard regularly from David and wrote to him thereafter. After I had left New York, I received frequent postal cards, clippings and notes from him, and I have never returned to New York that he didn't come to see me. But the letters stopped coming. Shortly after one of my visits to the city, he died.

CHAPTER 42

MINORITIES

At my induction ceremony in January of 1946, Sean Reid had said that the *"real* problems" that would confront me were "how you can bring about better conditions for the poor, the humble, the lowly and the underprivileged," and that racism and discrimination had poisoned our city. His words stayed with me throughout my term of office.

It became clear to me right from the beginning that we had been carrying on an official policy of discrimination. The days of public housing on a large scale had not yet come. Private industry was not meeting the crying need, and life insurance companies were looking toward the creation of semi-public housing projects. Metropolitan Life, under the leadership of Fred Ecker, was the first to pioneer in this direction. Under La Guardia's administration, in Manhattan great areas of slums were cleared by the city and the vacant land turned over to the Metropolitan, which erected two extensive housing projects, Stuyvesant Town and Peter Cooper Village. The law which created those projects gave no protection or promise to Negro taxpayers who paid part of the construction costs. Nothing was done to give them a share in the advantages to be gained from these new developments.

Paul was the attorney for a number of people who raised the issue, but the highest courts held against him on the ground that the original contract between Metropolitan and the city, entered into before the war, gave no guarantee that the projects would be available to Negroes. The Metropolitan readily admitted that it had a policy barring Negroes, pointing out, however, that the law did not prohibit it from doing so.

When this situation came to my attention early in my administration, I had a local law prepared which forbade any discrimination in public housing. While this would seem now to be but a minimum of fairness, it was then considered a real innovation and a victory for liberalism.

Housing was a real problem for everyone, but for Negroes, who were given no freedom of choice as to where they could live, the problem was greatly aggravated. They were relegated to live in ghetto slums that New York created and maintained, not, as in the South, by a legislative fiat, but segregated and overcrowded nonetheless. As a factual matter, they were no better off in New York City than in the deep South. If there was any area in which they needed some measure of protection, it was in housing.

In the course of the campaign I had met Ray Jones, Harlem political leader. In the early days, when Negroes moved from the South, they became Republicans. They had no reason to hold with the principles of the Democratic Party they had known. To them the Republican Party was the party of Lincoln, of Emancipation, of the Reconstruction. Later, young men began to turn the tide in favor of Democrats, began to preach that the Republican Party had abandoned that fight and had become the party of privilege. Jones was one of those who convinced his adherents that their best interests lay with the Democratic Party, even in spite of Dixiecrats.

I had seen Jones as he worked around Harlem and I had come to regard him as one of the smartest and most astute politicans in New York. He spoke with the musical cadence of his native St. Thomas, but softened by exposure to his Harlem constituency. I had never seen him angry.

I appointed Ray Jones to be Deputy Housing Commissioner. He grew with his job and became totally dedicated to it. Without neglecting the rest of the city, he considered Harlem his proving ground. He knew I had appointed him to his position not merely to give token recognition to the many Negro citizens who lived among us, but rather to be of significant service to the people and combat the particular problems of Harlem.

One morning soon after his appointment, he appeared at Gracie Mansion, just as the housekeeper Mary Brady was serving coffee in the little alcove overlooking Carl Schurz Park and fashionable East End Avenue.

"Good morning, Mr. Mayor," greeted my new commissioner. "What's on your mind this morning, Ray?" I asked, as I saw he was anxious to get onto something. "How's your stomach, Mr. Mayor?" "Over the years," I replied, "I have developed a number of cultural fads, Ray, but my stomach remains in a reasonably good state of repair."

"I'm glad of that, Mr. Mayor," he said, as he produced pictures of rats running through apartments in Harlem, right under the gaze of horrified adults, and frightened children. "Five babies bitten this morning," he said. I'm afraid my stomach was not as peasant-like as I had imagined. "You told me to go out and do a job," he said, "and this is the beginning." Soon after, the Housing Department, operating with an inadequate staff, started a campaign, but neither my commissioner nor I was content, so I asked him to come before the Board of Estimate. We had no difficulty in the establishment of a new Rodent Control Unit, and this action let loose the full force of building inspectors and police, who served summonses wholesale until a real effort was made to contain these disease-breeding creatures.

Jones continued to serve the people of Harlem faithfully. "How are things in Harlem these days, Ray?" I asked one morning, as we rode together down to City Hall. "I know you're a busy man, Mr. Mayor," he started, and I knew there was something coming. "But," he continued, "every morning when Barney Collins or Jim Furey drives out the gate, you always direct them to drive south to City Hall. It must be dull and monotonous. Why not change the direction just once?" "Ray, " I said, "will you stop beating about the bush. You want me to drive through Harlem. Now, what good would that do without you? Rich people from Westchester and Connecticut do that twice a day and never see anything wrong. How about you and I making the tour together, and whatever is amiss, I can depend on you to show it to me."

As we drove through Harlem the next morning, the streets were filthy, and the backyards and vacant lots were filled with refuse and looked and smelled of neglect. The kids played in the streets among the cans, refuse and waste of all kinds. "Do you wonder that we have the highest rate of T.B. and child mortality anywhere?" Jones asked. I did not wonder, and said so. "We also have the highest rate of unemployment," he continued. "Even during labor shortages, we have difficulty in getting our people placed."

This was indeed a black eye to our democracy. First things first. "How much would it take to clean those lots up so the kids can play in them?" I asked. "If the question comes from you officially, Mr. Mayor, I can get it done by volunteer work on a block-to-block basis, but we will need some money for cartage." By that evening I had received assurance from John Burke of B. Altman's department store that I would have the funds available from the Friedsam Foundation he headed. The new plan worked well, and the cooperation of the private sector, the community, and the city brought a change in some drab surroundings.

In 1946, we were accustomed to reading about hoodlums who lynched people, and Josh White was singing "Strange Fruit" and being accused of being a Communist because of it. During that year, I proclaimed an "End Lynching Day," expressing belief in the proclamation "that it will focus attention of all true Americans on a cruel and murderous cancer which, in sporadic outbreaks, shocks and horrifies the nation, and holds us up to the world as a people who advocate equality and justice for all but often fail in the application of these precepts."

Similar proclamations declared a day in honor of Booker T. Washington and another in honor of George Washington Carver. These proclamations were more of symbolic than practical value, but I felt it was important for New York to maintain its leadership in progressive thinking.

Later, in 1947, I received a letter regarding Sydenham Hospital:

October 29, 1947

Dear Mr. O'Dwyer:

I am writing to you because I feel you are as interested as I am in Sydenham Hospital, the first interracial hospital, giving Negroes scientific opportunities equal to those of white citizens.

I hope you will want to join me and others who wish to help this hospital to become a genuinely effective institution.

Edward R. Murrow

I was still somewhat shocked to know that opportunities for scientific research were not available to Negroes—in this land where the people owed so much to the generosity of a slave named George Washington Carver.

Sydenham Hospital was so badly in need of money that it was impossible for it to be maintained any longer by private funds. I arranged for this pioneer institution to be taken over by the city, so that it could continue in its great tradition.[1]

Still later, I urged the passage of the Fair Employment Practice Act in Albany, but I was disappointed in the final result. I don't believe the law made any great contribution to the solution of the problem. Laws are often necessary to curb excesses, but they need to be augmented by a campaign of education. The unfortunate part of this particular law was that it almost ended the public campaign to educate, a campaign which would have opened up many doors to Negroes. But for all of its shortcomings, New York did lead the way in at least its approach to the constitutional guarantees to our citizens.

It was clear to me, however, that my small efforts were far from adequate, and that ultimately my most important contribution would be to use my office to spotlight the festering sore until enlightenment broke through the horror of ignorance and bigotry. I felt that the Negro community would need encouragement and greater educational opportunities to make the leaders of tomorrow, and that it was the bright, young Negro students of New York who would come forward and from

1. In late 1980 Sydenham Hospital was closed as part of a city effort to cut medical costs and streamline health care services. (PO'D)

their own talents win out over the forces of intolerance. And it was also clear that the time was long past due when they should have representation on the Board of Education to hasten that day. I was proud to have had the privilege of appointing Rev. John M. Coleman as the first Negro member of the Board of Higher Education and delighted that the gesture did not pass unnoticed.

World-Telegram - March 8, 1946

A STEP FORWARD

The naming of Rev. John M. Coleman of Brooklyn to the City Board of Higher Education gives that governing body its first Negro member. By this appointment, Mayor O'Dwyer not only has chosen an exceptionally able man but has made a real contribution to the cause of education—a cause that should recognize no creed or color.

And from the *Times*, March 6, 1946: "His presence also makes the administration of our schools more truly representative of the democracy of equal opportunity which we teach and believe in."

I appointed Negroes to the bench, the Fire Department, the Civil Service Commission, the City Parole Board and other city departments, but the ones I regarded as most significant were the sensitive positions in housing and education.

Only a few short years have passed since these kinds of efforts were necessary in the City of New York. By recognizing the need and doing something to focus public attention on conditions, we received reciprocal acknowledgment from the Harlem community that it was getting as close to fair play as it was possible for the city to give it in order to catch up with centuries of discrimination.

In 1946 the town was made up of literally hundreds of minorities, but it seems to have been that way from the beginning. Historically, in New York City, a minority would come to occupy a poorer area, then, in the course of time, improve its position, moving out of the ghetto and on to greener pastures.

At the end of World War II, Spanish-speaking Americans had become a new phenomenon in New York and began arriving from Puerto Rico in increasingly large numbers. They were beginning to displace the Italian colony in East Harlem and along the Brooklyn docks. But there was a difference between the new arrivals and their predecessors. Al-

321

though they spoke a foreign tongue, they had been Americans for two or three generations.

The Spanish-American War was one of our nation's less than honorable adventures. It has become generally accepted that the war was the result of agitation conducted by the most influential publisher in America. William Randolph Hearst was the owner of a nationwide chain of newspapers and was also a power in politics. As a matter of fact, old-time Democratic politicians believed that he was once elected Governor of New York. They said the election had been stolen from him by Tammany chieftain, Charles Murphy, the most able and cunning of all Democratic leaders since the forming of Tammany Hall soon after the Revolution.

No matter how despotic Spain had been in dealing with its remaining possessions, it is difficult to believe that the advancement of the cause of liberty was the motivating reason for our involvement in the war which so increased the circulation of the Hearst newspapers and made Teddy Roosevelt a national hero. The end of that war, if one could call it a war, placed our nation in a dominant position in Cuba, and our flag was raised over Puerto Rico and the Philippines. We had come a full circle and were now in every sense a colonial power, somewhat more benign than our own oppressors, but colonial nonetheless.

Our sugar merchants were happy to have a product which could be delivered at such a cheap cost, and to show our appreciation we sent an army general into Puerto Rico for the purpose of bringing "the blessings of democracy" to the island. For about fifteen years we sought to Anglicize Puerto Rico and, having failed miserably, we gave up the experiment entirely. Instead, we presented the Puerto Rican people with the option to become American citizens, and we began to refer to them in terms of affection. We said they were our "brown brothers." The fraternal feeling, however, was not recognized at the Federal courthouse or by the Justice Department, which continued to prosecute Puerto Rican seamen whose curiosity about their new country caused them in increasing numbers to sign off the ships that had brought them to the mainland paradise. It seemed obvious we liked our "brown brothers" best in their native sugar fields.

With the coming of Franklin Delano Roosevelt, a "Good Neighbor" policy was proclaimed, if not really adopted, towards Latin America. Knowing that our sincerity would be seriously questioned were we to continue to mistreat Puerto Ricans, we radically changed our attitude towards the islanders during the early part of the Roosevelt years.

In 1934 we abandoned the policy of requiring them to speak, read and write English, adopting instead a bilingual approach in the primary and secondary schools. Prosecutions ended and the small colony of

With Eleanor Roosevelt, 1949

Photo courtesy of New York City Archives

Cubans occupying a section of East Harlem found the ranks of the Spanish-speaking barrio swelling with new migrants from Puerto Rico. Columbia Street in Brooklyn had an impoverished Puerto Rican colony and Jamie Kelly, Brooklyn historian, became its only patron. In New York City, a Dr. Cistero was for many years the colony's sole spokesman. These Puerto Ricans were, for the most part, unregistered and poor. Our educational policy in their island home had left them illiterate in both English and Spanish. Our literacy laws deprived them of the right of franchise, which they had enjoyed at their point of origin. Congressman Vito Marcantonio came manfully and unselfishly to their defense and in turn was blamed for their coming to New York in such large numbers.

I realized that here we had a new type of problem—a minority of American citizens with a literacy and a language barrier. I set up a special committee to act as liaison between the city government and the Puerto Rican community, and in June 1948 I spent a few days in Puerto Rico talking with the Mayor of San Juan, Felica Rincon de Gautier, and with the soon-to-be-elected Governor, Luis Muñoz Marín. A special office was set up in New York for the Commonwealth of Puerto Rico, and its leader, Manuel Cabranes, was in constant touch with me. Another committee I set up to help Puerto Ricans in employment, housing and other essential services was expanded later to include all minorities and became known as the New York City Human Rights Commission. I learned that having a Spanish-speaking Mayor in City Hall tended to make the new arrivals feel more at home, but that was a far cry from solving their psychological, social and economic difficulties.

In retrospect, I believe it was a mistake to have dealt with the Puerto Rican problem, which was unique and massive, in conjunction with the difficulties which other minorities were encountering.

By the end of my administration, I felt I had accomplished some good, in that there were tangible signs of progress, that our town's minorities were getting along better than they had in the past, and that there were no harmful and destructive riots, such as those that took place during my predecessor's term. For that, of course, I was deeply grateful.

CHAPTER 43

HEALTH

The care of the sick has been the concern for all civilizations, and the custom came to New York on the very first ship to land its precious store in 1624 at Fort Orange, now called Albany. The "comforter of the sick" was assigned by the Dutch government to look after any colonist who might be stricken with illness of any kind. He was an important official, and since no clergyman was sent with the first settlers, the comforter of the sick also led the early burghers of New Amsterdam in prayer.

By 1946, health stations and hospitals were in profusion all over the city. Hospitals were divided into three general categories: voluntary hospitals, like St. Vincent's, Mt. Sinai, and Lutheran; privately-owned hospitals, usually in the hands of doctors and meant to suit their business and professional convenience; and finally, the New York City hospital system, which catered to those who were financially incapable of buying their way into better health.

After my first year in office, I was beginning to feel very proud of our health and our hospital service. New Yorkers have always demanded the best, and while there were some complaints of hospital overcrowding and about the food, they were not too numerous. Our Hospital Commissioner, Dr. Edward Bernecker, was a frequent social visitor at Gracie Mansion, and I was in constant touch with him on city hospital matters. On Palm Sunday, 1947, I was at Gracie Mansion when Commissioner Bernecker, accompanied by Police Commissioner Wallander and Commissioner Weinstein of the Health Department, came to see me, all three in a high state of agitation. They told me that a man named Eugene LaBar had come from Mexico and had died in the Willard Park Hospital of smallpox. Overly secure in our feeling that with our system of vaccinations no harm could come to us, we had forgotten what *could* happen to a city stricken with a foul communicable disease like smallpox.

The visitors to Gracie Mansion were close to panic. No one knew how LaBar had traveled from Mexico, whom he had been in contact with along the way, what form of transportation he used, or where his fellow passengers went. There already had been 12 death reports, and we could not afford the time to investigate the patterns. What transpired thereafter was a massive and gigantic New York effort. We called on the town's citizens to make sure that everyone was vaccinated. I was photographed getting my innoculation, and President Truman, who was coming to New York to greet President Miguel Alemán of Mexico, was photographed getting his vaccination—as was Alemán. All Broadway musical productions had their chorus lines photographed getting innoculated on their bare buttocks. These efforts succeeded in alerting the people, but the program was on the brink of failure for another reason—we ran out of serum. With long lines forming at our makeshift innoculation centers—station houses, firehouses, and other central places—we were faced with panic.

Fortuitously, we discovered a batch of serum in a warehouse in Jersey City, and with the cooperation of that city's police, we went after it and again had a supply that would keep the operation going. By that time, we had also invoked the aid of all the pharmaceutical firms in New York, and they jointly supplied us with all the serum we needed. At the end of a two-week period, we began to breathe a sigh of relief. Up to that time we did not dare think of the consequences which the spread of this dread disease would have caused. It would have meant closing all schools and colleges, shutting down all transportation systems, and quarantining the harbor. It would have meant a call for volunteers to bury the dead and to tend to the dying. Dr. Bernecker said that advanced as the town was, it could not have coped with such a situation, and we had come close to losing control. In the end, we had vaccinated six and a half million New Yorkers, a massive cooperative undertaking.

Nineteen forty-seven was a year of new leadership in the city administration, and I had little trouble in getting the best in the country. I had waited for an opportunity to get Dr. Harry Mustard on our team as Health Commissioner, and towards the end of the year, I was able to appoint him. The *Herald-Tribune* was unusually loud in its praise of the appointment:

November 5, 1947

A SPLENDID APPOINTMENT

Mayor O'Dwyer, now engaged in a reorganization of city Departments, has enlisted Dr. Harry S. Mustard, director of Columbia University's School of Public Health, to head the City Health Department. The appointment brings to the city's service, and to one of the most important public health posts in the country, a nationally known expert. It would be hard to think of a man better fitted for the post by training, experience and standing in his profession.

If I was feeling good about the city's health services, I was somewhat less sanguine about myself. After two years or so in office, the constant grind was beginning to wear me down. I had not been feeling well of late. One day, after what might be considered a collapse, I was taken to Bellevue Hospital where both my own doctor, Phillip Norman, and Dr. Bernecker reported that I had "a coronary heart condition" and was "physically depleted and worn out from overwork." Truly, I was not aware that I had been so run-down, and reading the news that I had suffered a slight heart attack came as a surprise to me. I spent three weeks in Bellevue. During the time I was in the hospital, *The New York Times*, often sparing in its praise of my work, and at times begrudging, became somewhat more generous:

February 23, 1948

THE MAYOR'S BURDEN

Nobody ever worked harder in office than Mayor O'Dwyer.
Nobody not trained to the tough routine of a working cop could have stood it. Now he is in the hospital hoping through rest to escape the penalty of his labors. Every voter in Bagdad-on-the-Hudson wishes him a quick recovery . . . Mayor O'Dwyer is a brave man and a willing one, but what New York really needs is two Mayors to spell each other off.

I was able to see at firsthand the scientific effort put into the care of a hospital patient. I wondered if every citizen got the same careful treatment. From the hospital bed, I was in a good position to observe the needs of our hospitals, and nurses and doctors were only too anxious to talk to me about them. Overcrowding was the chief complaint and lack of help was next in importance. We could not compete for competent nurses. Our wage rate left us understaffed, and what staff we had were disgruntled. "In your capital budget you have too much money for highways," an alert doctor told me. I found out the criticism was justified and had $20 million taken out of the highway budget and transferred to hospitals, schools and libraries. The money went to rehabilitation and equipment. Two programs we initiated, the Out-Patient Program and the Home Care Program, cut the hospital population substantially. I also soon arranged with Drs. Bernecker and Mustard to have our hospital diagnostic services made available to private physicians, a minimal effort that was met with opposition and suspicion.

By the end of my term, we had constructed in whole or in part $38 million worth of new facilities or improvements. Painting the hospital walls had top priority. They showed positive signs of 15 years of neglect.

In December, 1949, I was ill but still felt obliged to attend the funeral of my friend, Bill Robinson, the great Negro entertainer. He was a real New Yorker and his passing was universally mourned. I got home from the funeral in a state of collapse and was taken again to Bellevue. They diagnosed my condition as thyroid (although subsequently a Mexican doctor assured me it was hepatitis). I was ordered confined to the room with no visitors, and Detective Joe Boyle, my bodyguard, let no one pass through. Downstairs, newsmen had heard that I was dying, and the media were anxious to get some visual evidence of my condition. However, no one was able to break through the cordon downstairs or to pass Detective Boyle, with a lone exception. One woman, on in years, slipped by him as Joe Boyle turned his back. She came into the room without approval. Before Joe could block her way, she was on her knees beside my bed.

"Bill," she asked, "are you all right?" "Yes," I said, "I'm all right." "Could you write your name?" she insisted. I explained that if it became necessary I could just about do it. "Then," she pleaded, "tell Joe Boyle to bring up my nephew, Elmer. You know, Bill, you promised to make him a magistrate and I know you are as good as your word." "Can't that wait?" I asked, and I knew I could not have looked too good when she simply said, "I don't know, Bill, anything can happen." I'm afraid Elmer never did make it to the bench, but it was not for want of an aunt's noble efforts to get in ahead of the grim reaper.

Reluctantly I came to the conclusion I had had about enough of the office of Mayor, a decision in which each member of my family concurred. It had been a grueling task, and I finally announced that I would not be a candidate to succeed myself. I had not always been on good terms with *The New York Times*, but I understood them and sought to let the *Times* and all the media know what I was attempting to accomplish. In an editorial the day after I made it known that I would not seek reelection, the *Times* evaluated my three and a half years in office:

May 27, 1949

MAYOR O'DWYER'S DECISION

. . . We regret this decision by the Mayor not to seek re-

328

election. He seems to us to be head and shoulders above the likely candidates from official circles who are mentioned as his successor to the Democratic nomination. Starting from the ranks of common labor, he worked to educate himself, and through diligence and ability rose to what is, perhaps, the second highest administrative office in American public life. He has worked hard at the job of being Mayor. He made his mistakes, and he has been subjected to considerable criticism from time to time. We have contributed no small amount of this criticism, and we must say that the Mayor has stood up to it like a man. Furthermore, he has often responded to this criticism with a change of course. . . .

First of all, in importance, he broke with the old five-cent fare political fetish. He put under way major rehabilitation of the transit system, and has made headway in stabilizing transit labor relations. He has greatly improved our public school plant, with the building of about fifty new schools and the renovation of others. Hospital conditions are better, and a further building program of $150,000,000 or more is in prospect because of his initiative. He has worked steadily and effectively for more housing, both subsidized and unsubsidized; the accomplishments in this field are outstanding. He cleared the way for Port Authority erection of the Union Bus Terminal, and has made other constructive beginnings toward traffic amelioration. He removed the burden of airport development from the city's capital budget, and at the same time assured adequate aviation facilities.

He has given the city's civil service employees as generous treatment as financial conditions permitted, he strengthened the police force and Fire Department. He has an anti-smoke program under way. He endorsed a study for wiser zoning, looking to land use for industry. Health services have been notably broadened. . . Programs for garbage incineration and the cleaning up of polluted waters on our beaches are begun. The Welfare and Marine and Aviation Departments underwent reorganization and are better equipped. A considerable number of emergencies, some manmade and some a visitation of nature, were dealt with, most of them capably.

The *Times* followed up with a second editorial two weeks later:

June 10, 1949

. . . The Mayor of the City of New York carries a heavy burden and it grows heavier every year. Although an able Mayor had preceded him, Mr. O'Dwyer on taking office in January, 1946, inherited grave problems, some dating back to depression days and others to the war. So, in addition to the normal strains of administering a city of 8,000,000 people, Mayor O'Dwyer had the task of attempting to rebuild with limited funds a governmental plant that was at best shabby and, at the worst, in ruins. Hospitals, schools and especially the transit system were in a painfully run-down condition. At the same time an abnormally high birth rate, after the war, made even more pressing the housing and school problems.

To these unusual tasks and many others Mr. O'Dwyer addressed himself with vigor, and his record has, on net balance, been good. On many occasions we have commended his accomplishments, and on others criticised his mistakes and his omissions. The many warm expressions of regret that he was stepping down at the end of 1949 may be accepted by the Mayor as the public's thanks for what he has done to try to make New York a better place to live in.

The *Herald-Tribune* also summarized what it felt were the most significant accomplishments of my administration:

May 27, 1949

THE MAYOR WITHDRAWS

Mayor O'Dwyer's announcement that he will not run for re-election heralds the close of what has been an eventful and, on the whole, a successful administration. The Mayor has been faced during his term of office by a series of crises, ranging from record snowstorms to recurrent threats of strikes in vital areas of the city's life. He has met these with calmness and efficiency, benefiting from an instinctive ability to handle men. In getting away from the five-cent fare, long a bogy even to reform administrations, he showed as much courage as realism. Co-ordination of the airports around New York and the establishment here of permanent headquarters for the United Nations, both accomplished during his term, will long stand as landmarks in the city's development . . .

And as customary, the *Daily News* editorial was direct and blunt:

June 11, 1949

O'DWYER OPTS OUT

. . . We're sorry to see this development because we think Mr. O'Dwyer has been a hardworking conscientious and 100% honest Mayor, and has made an excellent start at cleaning up the confusions and inefficiencies he inherited from the La Guardia Administration, which got scatterbrained in its last years . . .

And finally, the *Brooklyn Eagle* summed it up for the city's largest borough:

May 27, 1949

MAYOR'S REFUSAL TO RUN AGAIN
SURPRISE AND DISAPPOINTMENT

Mayor O'Dwyer's surprise announcement that he would not be a candidate for re-election has got the whole town talking. It was a surprise not only to the plain citizens but also the politicians, even to top-flight municipal leaders.

It took us by surprise, too, but our principal reaction was one of intense disappointment. For Mr. O'Dwyer has made a splendid record as Mayor, and his departure from City Hall would be a real loss to the city.

CHAPTER 44

REMARRIAGE AND REELECTION

The announcement of my intention not to seek reelection brought a number of candidates into the field. Frank Hogan asked if I would support him, and I thought it would be good if he were elected Mayor. He had made a fine record as District Attorney, and he carried with him the support of Governor Dewey, who had been his party's choice for President of the United States. I found out, however, that the county leaders were divided on Hogan's candidacy.

One day I met with all the county leaders. Ed Flynn pleaded that if I didn't run to succeed myself, there would surely be a primary battle, and with his bad heart condition he could not possibly withstand the rigors of a primary campaign. John Cashmore, Brooklyn leader, was even more emphatic about the result of such a contest on his own health. Furthermore, they argued, things had stabilized, the various ethnic groups had been getting along without riots or disturbance, and they would want it continued for another four years.

The health problems of John Cashmore or Ed Flynn were not a persuasive argument, since my own health had to be considered as a higher priority, and there was strong opposition to my continuing in office from Paul and Sloane. But, in fact, the aftermath of the decision left me with rather mixed feelings. Good judgment and concern for health and well being were struggling against the knowledge that I had loved every minute in City Hall and Gracie Mansion, and I knew I would miss all that they had come to mean to me. In further meetings with the Democratic leaders they became aware of my feelings, and I was urged to reconsider. They again emphasized the need for continued tranquility and pointed out the projects I had started that needed to be effectively continued.

I must have shown a weakness in my resolve. Paul and Kathleen got in touch with Frank. Many times since Kitty's death he had urged me to take a less onerous assignment, easily available to a former Mayor. He came from El Centro to help the rest of the family argue for maintaining my first decision. He was in Gracie Mansion when Flynn and Cashmore called on me for a final session. After several hours I agreed to announce that I had changed my plans. Frank was deeply disappointed in the decision; Paul, who was no admirer of the county Democratic leaders, was angered; and Sloane was saddened. She left for Europe after the decision.

The press and the political reporters felt they had been misled by me and implied that I had never really intended to retire from the race.

The campaign which followed was rigorous, but the result was never in doubt. Newbold Morris was again my Republican opponent. The American Labor Party nominated Congressman Vito Marcantonio. It started out as a simple campaign with little chance of my being defeated, but soon it became evident that Marcantonio was waging a very energetic campaign. He had no chance of winning, but his heavy support in the Italo-American sections of town would normally have gone to the Democratic candidate. Our information was that Marcantonio was running neck and neck with Morris, making it anybody's race. It was clear we could not afford to ignore Marcantonio.

And so for the last month of the campaign, in a strategy worked out between Paul and Generoso Pope, we concentrated our efforts on the Italian sections of the town. Pope's newspaper, *Il Progresso*, featured my record in Italy during the war and gave wide publicity to the recognition I had received from the Italian government for my help to the Italian people during the war. On Election night the tally showed that I had received 1,266,000 votes to 956,000 for Morris, and 356,000 for Marcantonio.

Throughout my first term, until its last months, I had been well able to cope with the most serious crises confronting me. I felt secure in the knowledge that I had the capacity to deal with every eventuality. That feeling of self-assurance had infected the members of the Board of Estimate, which gave me enthusiastic cooperation, as did the City Council and my commissioners. It was a term, despite all the problems, with a large measure of fulfillment and gratification.

But the end of 1949 found me peevish with the press and irritated by any sign of imperfection in subordinates. Mixed feelings as to my future with Sloane didn't help. I knew I had fallen in love with her, and I was supremely happy and content while we were together. She had made no demands on my time, accepting the life she knew the wife of a mayor would have to lead. I wanted very much to marry her, and yet, misgivings about a May-December marriage continued to haunt me, and all of Sloane's assurances did not diminish vague forebodings.

I was also in poor health the last six months or so of my term, and how much of my disturbed feelings were due to hepatitis, I can now only hazard a guess. Its effects on the nervous system were not generally known at that time. In any case, my restlessness and display of bad temper were ascribed to an old thyroid condition, the diagnosis of hepatitis coming much later. Had the true nature of the disability been properly diagnosed, I probably would have been in a better position to cope with my personal problems and the pressures of office.

Looking back, I realize that my reaction to and behavior regarding the Brooklyn District Attorney's investigation into bookmaking was an early indication of my health problems.

My state of irritation expressed itself also in my relationship with the working press. I had always been on cordial terms with them and had taken the trouble to take the editorial boards into my confidence. I would brief them on many of the things I believed they should know about in more detail. Now, they irritated me. For one thing, they were constantly badgering Sloane and me about our intentions.

Shortly after the election, Sloane and I left for Saratoga, New York, to spend a few days with the Martin Sweeneys, old friends of mine, who managed the Gideon Putnam Hotel. When we arrived there, reporters and photographers were everywhere. I railed at them publicly for invasion of privacy. That of course merely whetted their appetites, and they kept up the inquiry as to whether we were being married that weekend.

So I was back in Bellevue Hospital. New Yorkers were understanding and sympathetic, but I had worked hard at the job and it was frustrating to be making decisions from Bellevue Hospital. I decided to take a vacation in Florida. The *Times* described it as a "breakdown," and I was loath to admit it, although, in retrospect, that was a reasonably accurate description:

December 12, 1949

MAYOR O'DWYER'S VACATION

Leaving the gray city of New York yesterday in search of Florida sunshine, Mayor O'Dwyer described himself as a "refugee from a hospital." He is, in fact, a victim of one of the world's hardest jobs. His most active political opponents would never deny that he works at the job with a soldierly devotion to duty and gives it the last ounce of his strength. Before his breakdown, he gave it more than he had to spend.

A few days in Florida did much for me. I was in touch with Sloane each day. We arranged to get married in Florida before my return, and

Attending the theater with Sloane Simpson shortly before their marriage, 1949

she came down to join me. It seemed appropriate that she stay away from the villa in Hobe Sound where I was staying, and so she cruised the inland waterways on a small boat with its owners, Dr. and Mrs. Edward Bernecker, and their daughter, Alma, arriving at the villa only the night before our marriage. In the meantime, I had made arrangements with Father Timothy Geary, pastor of the church in Stuart. Even though the atmosphere was quieter than it would have been in New York, the local press was delighted, and the pastor, whose chapel had not previously received much attention, was not displeased. The Berneckers were the witnesses, and we spent our honeymoon in Hobe Sound.

The new year brought no surprises to City Hall. Most of the team that had worked so hard were retained. An exception was the Commissioner of Investigation. Early in my first term I had discovered insubordination in the Marine and Aviation Department, where my rule that piers were not to be rented to stevedoring firms but rather to responsible shipping firms had been violated. In May 1947, I put Joseph Minetti in the job with a "scrubbing brush, some soap and a pail of water."

Otherwise, I had survived four years without any breath of scandal, and the beginning of my second four years was hailed by the media:

Herald-Tribune - January 2, 1950

THE CITY'S NEXT FOUR YEARS

Mayor O'Dwyer's second term will be officially launched when old and new appointees are sworn in at City Hall this morning. . . The appointments reflect, it seems to us, a renewal of the Mayor's earnest intention to give the City sound and forward-looking government. There are not too many changes. Good men, like Bob Moses, have either been continued in their jobs, or, like former Transportation Chairman, now Deputy Mayor William Reid, given new and greater responsibility.

The New York Times - January 2, 1950

MR. O'DWYER'S SECOND TERM

William O'Dwyer began yesterday his second four-year term as the one hundredth Mayor of the City of New York. . . . The tasks that lie ahead are imposingly large, but in some respects simplified as compared with the first four years. The Mayor brings to his responsibility far better equipment personally. He has experience behind him that embraced coping with almost every form of emergency that could present itself. He is surrounded by a team of officials, also experienced.

In Gracie Mansion things began to change and Sloane soon put a sense of order into everything. Calls were screened and meals were regular. However, the daily grind again began to wear me down. Dr. Clarence de la Chapelle, Dr. Bernecker and Dr. Elaine Rawli insisted that I take time out again in Florida. For a Mayor of New York it is unthinkable that he be basking in the sun while a snowstorm cripples the town or a strike is in progress. I could not have done much about the snow but the citizens who were inconvenienced didn't see it that way. As for strikes, I had met with a great deal of cooperation in settling them in the past, and my absence would have been inexcusable.

My condition was not improved any by the appearance one morning at 6 a.m. of a young stranger in my bedroom in Gracie Mansion. It was indeed a rude awakening. "Are you O'Dwyer?" he asked. "No," I said, "but I'll take you to him." I wondered how he got past the security at the gate, and the fear that he had done in Joe Previtel gave me cause for alarm. I took him down to the kitchen and pressed the buzzer which connected with the police booth. I was ever so relieved, for the sake of the police guard as well as myself, when they immediately responded. It turned out that the young man had somehow gotten over the high iron fence, had come in through a back entrance, and wandered through an empty Gracie Mansion until he came to my bedroom. As he was being taken to Bellevue Psychiatric Ward, he protested: "I only wanted to talk to him for a few minutes." "What about?" asked a curious cop. "I wanted to discuss juvenile delinquency with him," said the young man.

A few months after my election, I was not feeling any better, and I somehow felt things getting away from me.

One evening, I found myself seated next to Dean Acheson at a dinner. I took advantage of the occasion to discuss with him a wish which I had previously broached with him. I made known to him again that I would like to serve in some mission, as an ambassador or otherwise, in some Latin American country. I explained that as Mayor, I had developed a very good relationship with the Latin American republics and heads of state and that my Spanish was again fluent. I had read a great deal about South and Central America and was familiar with the history, background and culture of all the important countries. I told Acheson that Dr. de la Chapelle had warned me of trying to continue to the end of my new term as Mayor.

Acheson seemed enthusiastic about the prospect and promised to talk to the President about it. Later I spoke to Ed Flynn. I told him what my doctors had said and urged him to speak to the President. Soon President Truman sent for me. Walter Thurston, a career Ambassador to Mexico, was resigning, and Truman felt I could do a good job there.

The following day, August 16, 1950, *The New York Times* commented on my decision:

> We did not support Mr. O'Dwyer for reelection, but we believe we can say without inconsistency that we regret his decision now to leave office. While we have written a day-to-day record of disagreement with and criticism of him on a number of matters, we have also found much that was good in his program for the city. We lose an experienced executive who had a close knowledge of municipal affairs . . . Mayor O'Dwyer at the age of 60 will be embarking on a new career. While the field of international diplomacy is somewhat, if not entirely, new to him, his personal charm, his knowledge of languages, and the friendships he already has below the border will serve him well. He has done many good things for New York City. His warm sympathies for the underprivileged and the sick will not be forgotten. His concern for his health, which although good recently is certainly a major factor in his decision, will be understood by those who are familiar with the exhausting and nerve racking job that goes with being the Mayor of New York City. We wish the Mayor well.
>
> © 1950 / The New York Times Company

On August 30, I received an encouraging note from the President, the first addressed to me as "Ambassador:"

Dear Mr. Ambassador:

> I appreciated very much your letter of the twenty-fourth and we shall proceed with the necessary arrangements for your tour of duty to Mexico.
> I am sure you will like the assignment and I am also sure you will do an excellent job there.
>
> Sincerely yours,
> Harry Truman

Mexico would have been my first choice. Besides the fact that it rated in importance second only to the Court of St. James, I had, as the *Times* reported, developed the friendliest relationship with Fernando

Photo courtesy of Brooklyn Public Library/Brooklyn Eagle Collection

Receiving congratulations from Brooklyn Borough President John Cashmore on election night, 1949. Onlookers include (left to right) Captain Frank Bals, Walter S. Hart, Hyman Schorenstein, Miles McDonald and John McGrath.

Casas Alemán, Governor of the Federal District of Mexico. I had also developed a close relationship with Miguel Alemán, the President of the republic. Both were extremely pleased with the choice and let it be known promptly that they would be very happy to welcome me as the new United States representative. I resigned as Mayor on September 2, 1950, and waited for the Senate to approve the nomination.

On an extremely hot day I took my leave of the city I dearly loved. I knew my going would be likely to extend my life, but I was leaving so many friends behind and a city which had been the epitome of all things warm, sincere, friendly and generous. If it had shortcomings, I didn't notice them that day.

It took some time for the Senate to schedule hearings on my nomination. Two witnesses appeared to oppose it. Neither of them was prestigious nor well-known, and the approval came through without difficulty. After the customary briefing by the State Department, Sloane and I set out on a new adventure in Mexico, where, with a mild climate and a more relaxed atmosphere, my health began the slow process of improvement. Representing our great nation became a challenge, and I bent my efforts to justify the faith that the President, the Senate and the people had placed in me. My ambition was to become the best Ambassador the United States had ever sent to our nearest neighbor to the south.

CHAPTER 45

MEXICO

We arrived in Mexico in November, 1950, and were delivered in style directly to the residence of the Ambassador, a beautiful home with old-time elegance, its long terrace looking out on a large garden patio as green as springtime. Notwithstanding the season, there were still some leaves on several of the old trees. It was a solid, one-story building, with fireplaces in most of the rooms. The house contained a large reception room, dining room, an extensive terrace, five bedrooms, a kitchen and an office. Without furniture it looked dreary to me, but Sloane's first remark was, "How beautiful!"

I soon presented my credentials to President Alemán and was struck by the sincerity with which he conveyed his greetings to President Truman. I quickly fell into the daily routine of office work and my other duties as Ambassador, leaning heavily on Paul Culbertson, the minister counsel, and a wonderful secretary, Bernie Witfield.

Sloane also kept busy. She conducted square dances on the lawn of the patio to help the Leper Hospital in Mexico City, in which our friend and physician, Dr. Roberto Lebrija, had a special interest. She used the embassy to help the Benjamin Franklin Library and the nursing school at the American-British Cowdray Hospital. There were television programs, and she was constantly being interviewed on cultural affairs and charities.

With the help of my staff, I planned extensive visits to the various states, arranging to meet with the governors, presidents of the municipalities, senators and other high officials.

On my tour, the dedication of the Yaqui Dam in Sonora by President Alemán and a visit to the Yaqui Indian town of Vicam brought me in contact with Mexican Indians, who had resisted European culture and kept their own customs intact, stubbornly remaining aloof from their Mexican neighbors. The citizens of La Paz, an interesting town in the lower tip of Baja California had never before seen an American ambassador, and curiosity overcame their resistance to speak with a stranger.

In the state of Oaxaca, Sloane and I had promised the state's Governor we would attend the opening of the Frank Peters School in the isolated town of Loma Bonita. From what we were told, we gathered that Peters, a North American, was a pioneer in the growing of pineapples, on which the town's economy depended. We had visions of Peters as a man of spirit, daring and vision and greatly looked forward to the ceremony.

Once in Loma Bonita, we were driven to the home of the superintendent of the pineapple canneries. There was a vacant chair across from me held in readiness for the guest of honor, who had not shown up. Someone suggested sending a messenger to the barber shop, where Peters was known to spend his spare time. About an hour later, a little man in his seventies, displaying but two teeth, a battered hat, wrinkled pants, an old pair of shoes run down at the heel, entered, and everyone stood up. The guest of honor turned out to be a hard of hearing, petulant and quite incoherent old man who kept insisting that the pineapple company had taken away his acres of land years ago and never gave it back. Nothing I could say would convince him he was the town's most honored man.

Back at work in Mexico City, my Mexican and American associates and I made an attempt to improve the living conditions and pay of the braceros, those intrepid Mexicans who worked across the border, from the Imperial Valley to Los Banos or from the Gila Bend to Casa Grande and Eloy, and many other parts of the Southwest. It is stoop labor in the fields, performed under the burning sun. I have never seen any volunteers for this work from the locals.

Up to that time, the Mexican farm hands entered the United States surreptitiously. Sometimes their entry was winked at because of the great need, and sometimes Immigration got active, arresting and herding the braceros into camps to be carried across the frontier, where they were left to shift for themselves. The farmers treated them badly, paid them as little as they could, gave no attention to their housing or food or health. Nothing could be more inhumane than their treatment.

Manuel Tello, the brilliant Secretary of Foreign Affairs, and I, with the aid of Licenciado Miguel Calderón and some members of our State Department, concluded the first international agreement to provide protection for the braceros from these outrages.

The establishment of a limited Point Four program in Mexico was completed about that time, by which the United States provided scientific and technical assistance to Mexico and many other underdeveloped countries.

After some time in Mexico, I discovered that all too many Americans visiting on official mission had not taken the trouble to learn the language, the history, or the customs of their nearest neighbor to the south. It seemed to me that a brief account of its history would be a sine qua non for anyone attempting to come to Mexico and engage in business or diplomacy in that unusual country. I was fortunate in that I had long known its history, having studied it in Salamanca as a boy, and in later years visitors to New York from Mexico had kept green the memory of what I had learned. Briefings with the State Department were helpful refreshers. But even with that background I really could not say that I knew Mexico or Mexicans as well as I would have liked to.

Being of the Catholic faith was both an advantage and a disadvantage. Ninety-five percent of the people in the towns and cities were Catholic, and on Sunday the churches were filled. But the Catholicism of Mexico differed from the rigid Catholicism which had infected the Irish, who had come under the influence of European Jansenism. The Penal Laws in Ireland required students for the priesthood to get their education and training on the European continent. They returned to Ireland more Catholic than the Pope.

In Mexican Catholicism, the strong prohibition against eating meat on Friday, so prevalent in the American and Irish churches, was totally absent. As a matter of fact, an attempt to make Mexico conform to that Catholic prohibition met with a determined outcry from the people, who had great pride in their exemption. It was a token of gratitude for Spanish assistance to the Crusades.

The great mass of Mexican Catholics wholeheartedly approved of the complete separation of church and state, and the tradition was strongest among church-going people. Thus, neither nun, nor monk, nor priest could wear religious garb in public, and this law was obeyed to the letter. The young bishop who occasionally accompanied me to the bullfights on Sundays did not object in any way to the regulation. He found, before Pope John relaxed the rules of dress, that being at the bullring without the garb of a bishop gave him much greater freedom. But the old archbishop was not at all enthused about having to come to embassy functions with an attaché case in which he carried the robes of his office. We provided him with a place to change, and when it was time to go, he would again change into ordinary clothes.

The changes brought about by the revolution not only wiped out the power of the Catholic Church in matters of state but it also wiped out seminaries. As time went on, however, the institutions for the training of young priests were called by other names, and so a reasonable supply were educated and ordained, but no bishop or other clergy appeared at presidential inaugurations or other such functions. The new custom was a far cry from the time before the revolution when the church and the priest held so much power over the people and the government.

To some, my appointment as a Catholic was regarded as a long overdue acknowledgment by the United States of Mexico's culture, customs and religion. At the same time, it was at first feared that I might seek to restore the church to its former power in Mexico. When I refrained from any such interference, that suspicion evaporated, and after a short time my religion became irrelevant. But the fact that I was of Irish extraction was regarded favorably. It seems that in the 1846-1848 war between the United States and Mexico, Irish soldiers in the American army deserted to the Mexican side. They were well known as the "San Patricio Batallion." Their reasons for changing sides appear in the history books as it struck the prejudices of the individual historian. The batallion fought bravely against the undefeated North Carolina regiment at the battle of Churabusco. Of those captured, many were hanged and the remainder were branded on the forehead. Their contribution to the battle was significant, and they earned the eternal gratitude of the Mexicans.

For centuries Mexico was one of the most harassed countries in the world. The conquest by Cortés and a handful of men in 1519 was dramatic. His arrest of Montezuma, the fury of the Aztecs who drove him out, his return with his hand-hewn boats that were used to cut off food supplies, and his capture of the young Cuauhtémoc gave him control of a wonderful world. He received for his effort no great honor in Spain except to be made a marquis and the undying hatred of Mexico. I don't believe that there is a statue of Cortés in all the republic.

The foreign interests of every kind following in his footsteps robbed the natives' and the nation's richness. With political and religious control in the hands of foreigners, there was no freedom left to this amazing people. The conquistadores brought with them the unmatched cruelty of the Inquisition, during which humans became so warped as to pray calmly for the soul of the wretched victim of torture while they enjoyed their lunches from a basket brought from their homes so as not to miss the disgusting spectacle.

In 1810 a native parish priest, Father Miguel Hidalgo y Costilla, rang his church bell at 11 o'clock in the evening with a cry, "Viva Mexico," and the first major rising began. Father Hidalgo led his peasants triumphantly up to Cuajimalpa, on the outskirts of Mexico City. He returned to continue fighting in the interior, but lacking money, he turned north in an effort to reach the border and seek aid from the U.S. He was captured, however, at Acatita de Bajan, Chihuahua, both court-martialed and sentenced by the church tribunal, and shot to death in 1811.

Father José María Morelos y Pavón was in charge of the revolution in the south. His military genius had astonished the Spanish govern-

Being sworn in as Ambassador to Mexico; Secretary of State Dean Acheson and Sloane look on, 1950

ment. In the midst of his activities, he had gathered in Chilpancingo the first body of legislators for the rebels, which under his leadership produced the first constitution at Apatzingan, Michoacan. (It seems the legislators followed him around wherever he went.) In 1815, like Hidalgo, he was court-martialed, sentenced by the church tribunal, and shot.

This was only the beginning. In 1820, when the foreign powers were driven out of Mexico, one of the first acts was to prohibit any of the cruel forms of the Inquisition. The shrieks of the victims had gone higher than the prayers of the onlookers.

From this period onward, for more than one hundred years, the relationship between our country and Mexico was not always a happy one. I had recognized from my arrival in 1950 that although one could find a generally friendly attitude on the part of Mexican people on all levels of its society, there was at the same time a pervasive suspicion of the United States. In my early months in Mexico, I pursued in some depth the reasons for this antagonism. The story, beginning in Texas in the early 19th century, was not to our credit.

In 1821 Moses Austin secured a grant from the local Spanish authorities to bring American settlers into Texas. Austin died shortly thereafter but in 1823 the new revolutionary Mexican Government renewed the grant to his son Stephen F. Austin. Arguments occurred between other American settlers headed by Haden Edwards, who had sought to take land away from Mexican settlers. Edwards with a small band in 1826 started what was known as the "Fredonian Rebellion." Stephen Austin would not lend his support to Edwards and the revolt fizzled. Later, the Mexican Government sent a large security force into Texas. The Americans became alarmed and another revolt started. On March 2, 1836, Texas declared its independence. Mexican General Antonio López de Santa Anna moved against the rebels and was defeated by Sam Houston on April 21, 1836. The Mexicans regarded the Americans as betrayers of their trust and invaders of their country.

The Republic of Texas was established. Sam Houston tried to have his friend President Andrew Jackson accept Texas into the Union, but Jackson, afraid to offend Mexico, put it off. Texas finally became the 28th state to enter the Union in 1845.

In the 1846-1848 war between the United States and Mexico, in President Polk's time, our armed forces, under Generals Zachary Taylor and Winfield Scott, marauded a number of Mexican cities and finally were found tramping the streets of Mexico City in a march against the fortress at Chapultepec. Rather than surrender, nine boys and their commanding officer guarding the fort jumped over the cliff to their death holding their country's flag. Known as *Niños Héroes*, they still live in the hearts of all Mexicans, a reminder of a war denounced by Lincoln, Calhoun, Clay and Daniel Webster as unjust.

When the smoke of the war had cleared away, the Treaty of Guadalupe Hidalgo awarded half of Mexico's territory to the United States. It established the Rio Grande as the boundary between the two countries, recognized Texas as part of the United States, and ceded New Mexico and California to us in return for a payment of $15 million.

Ten years later, in 1858, Juarez was elected president, but the old greedy hands in Mexico City would not give up the power. He was in hiding in Vera Cruz. Buchanan wrote him a letter and offered him the help of our armies, provided he ceded the state of Chihuahua to the United States. Juarez proudly refused.

For a time following the election of Abraham Lincoln, Mexico had full confidence in our government. Lincoln, among other friendly acts, had returned to Mexico former mission lands, with their rich herds of cattle, that local politicians and strong arms had taken over after 1821. A great friendship existed between Lincoln and Juarez, and Lincoln's assassination was a severe blow to the Mexican president.

Then followed the benign dictatorship of Porfirio Díaz (1877-80 and 1884-1911). In 1910, a revolution originating in the northern part of Mexico spread southward under the leadership of Francisco Madero. The names of Mexican revolutionaries became everyday words in the United States: Carranza, Villa, Zapata, Obregón and many more. Madero found himself in trouble with General Victoriano Huerta, the provisional president, in Mexico City. At that time our ambassador was Henry Lane Wilson. Wilson handed Madero over to his enemy Huerta, and Madero was shot on the eastern side of the old penitentiary of Mexico City. Wilson's letters to the State Department are now public property, and another outrage against Mexico by an officer of the United States found its way into books and the public press.

Some of the worst anti-American sentiment also began around this time and involved Mexico and American oil companies. I had heard about the Mexican expropriation of the oil companies and was anxious to find out what the facts were, especially since some claims remained and were causing continued difficulties. I had an obligation to honor the country I represented, and I knew that President Truman wanted his administration to mark a new and honest relationship with Mexico.

Some time before the turn of the century, in the period of Porfirio Díaz, the oil companies from Europe and the United States got a foothold in Mexico. The Rockefeller Group of the United States and the Aguila Group from England were the most powerful. They made discoveries of great deposits and they operated with great energy. There are legends of their methods of operation but few historical facts.

It was said at one time that the oil companies had 3,500 men under arms employed as guards to protect the wells and the "payrolls." They were never known to contribute to the building of a school or a hospital or a factory. They went from place to place leaving behind them nothing more than nine-hole golf courses. The legend also says that the bribery of public officials was brazen and not uncommon. These outrages created a strong ill-feeling against them, so perhaps they needed the 3,500 men under arms.

In 1917 at Queretaro the new constitution was adopted. It followed generally the lines of our Constitution. One outstanding difference was that oil in Mexico became the property of the people. The revolution did not settle down too early. There were still disturbances, but by 1938 President Cárdenas had things well in hand. The workers at the wells were not being paid a living wage. The Mexican Federal Labor and Arbitration Board decreed that the workers' salaries should be increased and their working conditions improved to the extent of 26 million pesos per year. The oil companies refused, and President Cárdenas brought together both sides at a hearing in March of 1938. The chairman was Gustavo Corona, a brilliant attorney, who in 1959, for the purposes of this book, described what happened at the hearing. (His letter has been translated from the Spanish.)

The fact is that a few days before the expropriation was decreed by the President of the Republic, Gen. Lázaro Cárdenas, in March of 1938, a meeting was held at his office in the National Palace attended by representatives of the oil companies who had been sentenced by the Labor and Arbitration Board, in a judgment handed down in December 1937, to increase the salaries and improve working conditions of the industry's workers to the extent of 26 million pesos.

The purpose of the meeting was to convince the companies to abide by the judgment handed down by the board, which they had been refusing to do, arguing that their economic situation did not allow them to increase their expenses for labor in the amount ordered by the board. They had appealed the judgment before the Supreme Court of Justice of the nation.

It was forcefully pointed out to them that the Supreme Court had already handed down a decision confirming the judgment, that this decision was final and there was no legal recourse to call on, and that there was nothing else for them to do but comply.

In replying, the companies repeated over and over again the same thing. They could not comply because their economic situation did not allow them to do so. Their economic condition had not been properly taken into account by the board, and as a consequence the sum of 26 million pesos per year was in excess of their economic capabilities.

I was present at the meeting as president of the Federal Labor and Arbitration Board which had handed down the decision and I explained briefly how the board based its judgment on the study and conclusions prepared by the Committee of Experts, appointed for this purpose by law, to determine the economic situation of the companies as well as the possibilities of granting increases to their workers.

The companies replied by returning to the same argument: their economic situation prevented them from complying with the increase ordered by the board. They further argued that once the increases were put into effect, the sum total would exceed the 26 million pesos because, they repeated, the estimates made by the board had not been calculated accurately.

To this latter argument I replied that the estimates had been calculated with due care and accuracy and there was no reason to assume that the judgment would exceed 26 million pesos upon application.

Then President Cárdenas intervened and told the representatives of the companies that they had heard my statement—by the president of the board—to the effect that there was no danger that the sum of 26 million pesos would be surpassed on complying with the decision. This being the situation, what was their determination?

The companies then asked who would guarantee that, as the president of the board states, the sum of 26 million pesos will not be surpassed in practice?

Then President Cárdenas replied with emphasis: I guarantee it as President of the Republic.

There was a brief, expectant pause, and then the companies declared through the representative of the "El Aguila", whom all the other representatives had appointed as spokesman, that despite this they still could not abide by the judgment.

President Cárdenas then asked them if they had given careful consideration to the consequences of their reply and they answered yes.

Still President Cárdenas asked them: Is this your final word? They again replied: Yes.

He then said: In view of your reply, there is no purpose in continuing this discussion. And he broke up the meeting.

Thus ended what to my mind was the last attempt to convince the companies to abide by the decision of the Mexican courts. At least I am not aware that any other attempt was made later.

The arrogance of the oil companies in their refusal to obey the laws of the country in which they enjoyed the privilege of doing business and their contempt for the edict of the Mexican courts made President Cárdenas' decision to expropriate extremely popular in Mexico. Mexican politicians were well aware of the fact that Cárdenas acted only after consultation with and the consent of the P.R.I., the dominant political party in Mexico.

Home in the United States we were still in the throes of the Depression. Even if Roosevelt had wanted any aggressive action to be taken against Mexico on an oil issue, he would have been likely to encounter more trouble than he bargained for.

The expropriation took place at a time when President Roosevelt was proclaiming a new and more civil approach to our Latin American neighbors. The President's Good Neighbor policy got off to a poor start. In 1933, soon after his inauguration, the President appointed Josephus Daniels as our Ambassador to Mexico. The new representative was unfamiliar with the Spanish language. Lack of knowledge of the country's idiom is not a complete bar to success, but it is a definite disadvantage. There were other factors in Ambassador Daniels' background which added to his difficulties. He had served in the cabinet of President Woodrow Wilson, at a time when the Democratic wartime President proclaimed the rights of less powerful nations to remain free from interference from powerful neighbors. President Wilson's performance in Mexico was hardly consistent with that lofty pronouncement. While Daniels was Secretary of the Navy, the United States Marines landed in Vera Cruz, and the incident awakened in every household in Mexico memories of past injustices suffered at our hands.

These memories were just beginning to fade when the unfortunate appointment of Mr. Daniels revived it. President Roosevelt did not have long to wait for a reaction. The windows on the train carrying our Ambassador to Mexico City were smashed with bricks and stones. Notwithstanding those many handicaps, Daniels stayed long enough and applied himself to his task well enough to be finally regarded as a good Ambassador by both countries.

But the oil companies did not accept Mexico's decision to take over its oil. They made every effort to stir up sentiment against Mexico in the United States, seeking to create the impression of having been unfairly treated by an irresponsible and dictatorial government. The

Depression and the new spirit of liberalism which prevailed in the thirties gave them little chance to incite our country on their behalf. In this respect one could properly say of our Depression, "It is an ill wind which blows no good."

But in Mexico, the oil companies threw every stumbling block in the way of the government's effort to operate its own resources. They attempted to create doubt as to Mexico's ability to produce her own oil. They sat like vultures on the frontier, hoping for Pemex (the Mexican Government Oil Authority) to fail. They missed no opportunity to make it difficult for the Mexican government to obtain credit.

That campaign had not yet spent its force by the time I reached Mexico. Immediately prior to my arrival, they successfully blocked a United States government loan to Pemex, lest it be a recognition of Mexico's right to her own "black gold." The law firm of Sullivan and Cromwell, representing the Rockefeller interests, had one of its men in the State Department in charge of Latin America who successfully opposed the loan to Pemex.

The oil companies feared that the Mexican example might be followed in other oil producing areas, such as Venezuela. Claims against Pemex were made by these companies running into millions of dollars, and after an adverse decision in the highest court in the land, they turned to our State Department to require our Ambassadors to bring pressure on the Mexican government to settle the rejected claims.

One of my predecessors wrote to the Foreign Office that failure to settle certain claims of an American oil interest against the Mexican government (in face of the Mexican court decision) might cause bad relations between the two countries. His effort was renewed when I came to office. A letter, again pressing the claims, was being transmitted from the State Department to the President of Mexico, and the letter invoked the name of President Truman. I called the State Department and asked if it was serious about what it proposed to do. The answer was yes. "Then," I said, "I am coming up to Washington to explain the case to President Truman, to find out if his name is being used with his knowledge, and to acquaint him with the true facts of the case." As a result of my action, the letter was withdrawn.

In spite of everything the oil companies did or tried to do to thwart the production of oil in Mexico, Pemex succeeded in getting a direct loan of many millions from European sources. Towards the end of my term, the oil companies, finding no comfort from President Truman, finally gave up the battle, and a new loan was extended to Pemex by a consortium, of which the Chase National Bank was a partner.

I kept in close touch with President Truman and kept him informed about events in Mexico. He obviously had a most friendly interest in the country. On August 25, 1951, I received a note from him stating, "I am highly pleased with the manner in which you are handling our relations with Mexico and I am glad to tell you about it."

President Truman's reputation for honesty of purpose at home travelled across the border and was verified by his determination not to permit the interests of American business institutions to worsen our relationship with our Latin American neighbors. The day will long be remembered in Mexico when Truman himself placed a wreath of flowers before the monument of *Niños Héroes*. His gesture was a silent apology for the War of 1848.

My term proceeded rewardingly. There was a major and traumatic interruption in my ambassadorial duties: my appearance before the Kefauver committee and other investigative bodies in New York in 1951. I got my share of abuse after the Kefauver hearings, and demands were made for my resignation. When the pressures were on the Senate to recall me, the President said, "He won't quit, he's a fighter like me. . . . He was a fine Mayor, a great soldier, the best-ever Ambassador, a credit to America and Ireland."

The President, who always supported me completely, had been in touch with me personally on numerous problems which arose. He did not trust the regular State Department channels, and he often sent his personal representative, David Stowe, to see me about matters of concern. Whenever I found out that the State Department policy was at variance with what I thought would be the President's wishes, I sent word to the President, an arrangement that pleased him. As an example, President Truman was very proud of his Point Four program which would make our technology available for underdeveloped countries. But the State Department attempted to extract a commitment from the receiving countries that they would support us in any war in which we might become engaged. Manuel Tello, Secretary of Foreign Affairs, refused to sign the document. When I heard it was not being signed, I knew there was something amiss. I called on Señor Tello. American Ambassadors did not do that, but, on the contrary, insisted ministers come to their offices. "The Point Four program has a joker in it, Mr. Ambassador," Tello said. "It calls for our commitment to join you in your military or other adventures." I replied, "That is not our President's policy. Change it any way you want it, and I will straighten it out with the State Department and the President." He crossed out the offending paragraph, and the program went into effect.

One other event, this time in Mexico, marred the end of my term there. I had always tried to maintain a good relationship with the working press and while I could not feel happy about the constant repetition of what I regarded as unfair or snide comments, I was able to quickly shake off the unpleasant feelings they engendered. There was one occasion, however, when a story which emanated from the head of the United Press hurt deeply.

About the time that I was winding up my affairs as Ambassador, I received an early morning call from Paul from New York. "The story originating with the United Press reports that you are giving up your American citizenship. It's hit every paper." Paul had tried to spare me from adverse press stories. I knew when he called he felt as I did that this story had to be answered in no uncertain terms. I called on the press to come to the embassy residence.

Nothing that had been previously written cut more deeply than the charge that I was giving up my citizenship. I mulled it over awhile and tried to convince myself that it was just an extension of, and on a par with, other critical and unfair stories about me which had been common at that time. I wasn't very successful in my attempt to brush the accusation aside. The foreign correspondents and the Mexican press went into the living room. Mr. Prescott, the newspaperman whom I had identified as having filed the story, was among them. In the presence of all his colleagues I called Prescott a "lying bastard." The denial made the headlines and the story was never again repeated.

In the fall of 1952, I went to Los Angeles for a checkup at a Beverly Hills clinic. The daily dose of hormones I had been taking for the thyroid for the last three years was found to be inappropriate, and the doctors ordered me to stop taking them. My thyroid condition was diagnosed as normal, and the change in my disposition, they felt, could have come from hepatitis, which they believed I had been suffering from right along. From that point there was a steady improvement in my health.

I visited my brother Frank and his family at El Centro and drove back with him and a few friends to Mexico City.

It was obvious at that time that General Eisenhower would win the election in November, which meant that the time had come to submit my resignation.

At the termination of my service in the State Department, my financial circumstances made it imperative for me to carefully consider my future from every viewpoint. It narrowed itself down to one of two choices: remain in Mexico or return to New York. The beauties of Mexico, its delightful people, its unmatched climate, its progressive outlook and its innumerable business opportunities seemed to me to be an inducement. The atmosphere at home was difficult for me to accept. To live there would be frustrating.

By November 1, Sloane, who had visited her mother back home, had returned. Differences had arisen between us and we discussed our future plans. My future was not particularly bright. I had a genuine affection for Mexico. I was on my way to recovering my health in this even climate. Sloane had her own ideas of what her future should be. As a result of our conversations, there was only one solution, and that was to go our separate ways as friends. We received from the Catholic Church the right to separation and the following June obtained a civil divorce.

Sloane left Mexico for New York. I moved into the Prince Hotel in Mexico City, and it became my home for a long time thereafter.

Harry Hershfield came down to see me and so did Walter Hart. They talked about the fact that it would be good to get back to New York and they wanted to see me back there. There was no reason, they said, why I couldn't obtain some job as the advisor or the arbitrator in any one of a number of industries. La Guardia had done so for Jimmy Walker, and certainly there were a number of people indebted to me in one form or another. I would have no difficulty, they suggested, in picking up the phone and having one of them assign me to something. I turned the idea down. Paul and Oscar agreed with me that I had come so far without obligation to anyone and ought to continue in the same way. They felt certain we could manage quite well together, either in New York or Mexico or in both places.

It was then we decided to set up the law firm of O'Dwyer, Bernstien & Correa. I was given permission by the Mexican Government to serve as counsellor to the law firm, which included George Correa, a member of one of the most distinguished families in Mexico.

I had not seen President Truman since I left office. Paul made arrangements for us to call on the man for whom I had developed deep admiration and profound respect. The President invited us to lunch with him at the Muehleback Hotel in Kansas City. Mr. Truman liked to talk about his campaigns, and the exciting 1948 campaign in New York was the subject of much discussion. When I told him that I felt content to remain in Mexico and view the political struggles of New York objectively, he laughed at this. "A New York Irishman," he said, "who went as far as you did, will never be content with merely an objective view. I don't believe a word you say."

President Truman was partially right. Often I found myself reaching for every scrap of news of New York State. When Walter Hart or Nick Petti, New York judges, or other close friends of mine came to visit me, there was the same impatience that gave such zest to my life in New York. Come hell or high water, I was determined I must not stay away from home for too long a period.

I had returned to New York for the Kefauver hearings, but otherwise I did not get back to New York again until 1954. I had determined to come to New York while Thomas E. Dewey was still Governor and while the Republicans were in charge of the national government, lest it be said I was deliberately postponing my return until the Republicans left office.

By 1954 my health had greatly improved. At the invitation of the Hilling committee, a Congressional committee of inquiry into the extent of communism in Latin America, I testified at its hearings in Los Angeles and then came back to New York.

During my visit I attended a football game in the Polo Grounds, stopped off to see an old friend, financier Bernard Baruch, and attended a luncheon arranged for me by 250 labor leaders whom I had known well. The reception was enthusiastic at the Polo Grounds and heart-warming at the Roosevelt Hotel luncheon. These appearances were well attended by the media and were meant to be a clear answer to those who had inferred that I was fearful of returning to New York, but they didn't accomplish what I had hoped. Comedians and newsmen, careless of the truth, continued to remark that I was avoiding the consequence of my return, and such treatment did not let up even after I had returned to New York permanently, many years later.

After the 1954 visit, I continued to return to New York periodically. In 1956 as the "fall guy" at the Circus Saints and Sinners Club, I appeared at the Waldorf, and in 1958 at a dinner for my very good friend Maxi-millian Moss of Brooklyn.

In Mexico I had not been lacking in visitors. I think almost every New Yorker who visited Mexico called at the Prince Hotel where I was staying, and I enjoyed them all. The American newspaper reporters and Pepe Romero of the Mexican *Daily News* were in constant touch, and I was deeply interested in the always intriguing Mexican politics. Show people and artists would drop in. Dolores del Rio and other Mexican performers, like songwriter Augustin Lara, were frequent visitors. Harry Hershfield, Ella Logan, Barry Fitzgerald were some of the many show business people who came by and, with no shortage of female visitors to enliven my life, Mexico was never dull.

When I had to undergo a prostate operation, Paul and Oscar wanted me to have it done in New York, as did the Perusquias, my closest friends in Mexico, who came to convince me, but I overruled all of them as I had great faith in Mexican doctors, particularly my friend, Dr. Roberto Lebrija. Everything worked out well in the Mexican hospital.

With the passage of time, however, I had been getting lonesome for New York, and after this episode, Oscar and Paul insisted I get back and join them in the law practice. With their urging and my own wishes, I returned to the town I really never could get fully out of my system, no matter how warm, friendly and attractive Mexico had been. In the meantime, Sloane, whom I had seen frequently, after trying her hand at show business, decided to come to live permanently in Acapulco. That was in December, 1960.

PO'D

Bill's 1954 return to New York City was marked by fear and hostility, the Democrats fearful of how the Republicans might exploit his appearance. In fact, his return brought no reaction from the Republicans. Their highest command had by this time exhausted its investigation, and their hopes that the Internal Revenue Service, after years, would have found something on which to charge or even criticize had discouraged any further harassment. But his return did cause some uneasiness in the Democratic Party. Averell Harriman was the candidate for Governor and Franklin Delano Roosevelt, Jr. the candidate for State Attorney General that year, but Carmine De Sapio was, however, the power in the party in New York State.

When word came that Bill was returning to New York from California, I received a call from David Martin, a Thruway commissioner. Martin and Bill had been like brothers, but his term as commissioner was expiring, his health was poor, and he would be in difficult financial circumstances were he to lose his position. His reappointment was dependent upon a Democratic victory. De Sapio was aware of the close relationship between Bill and Martin.

By prearrangement I met Martin at the Biltmore Bar. "Paul," he said, "I want to warn you about what will happen if Bill sets foot in New York. The Republicans will use his return as a way of trying to embarrass the Democrats. I know Herbert Brownell, the United States attorney. He is calling the shots for the Republicans here now. He is a cold WASP and would indict his own mother. I know him personally and I can tell you that he will serve a subpoena on Bill at the airport." "What's the charge, Dave?" I asked. "You know, Paul, when they make up their minds, they will find something to charge him with, and they don't have to bring it to court until after the election." There was something about Dave's manner which made me feel that he was an emissary of De Sapio. I was stunned. I couldn't believe that Martin would do it. I suggested that nothing short of fear of losing his job would have made him behave that way. "What will your answer be, Paul?" he asked, as we prepared to break it up. "If they had any reason to charge Bill with wrongdoing, they would have done it long ago. Brownell would not need to wait at the airport. The subpoena on an American citizen is effective in any part of the world. And certainly in California, where Bill has been on several occasions during the past few years." Martin seemed crestfallen. "Please, Paul, think it over," he said. Somehow, I felt I was no longer talking to a friend.

At Senate confirmation hearings with Senator Tom Connally, chairman of the Senate Foreign Relations Committee, and Senator Walter F. George, 1950

I did not have long to wait for verification. My friend Sean Keating called on me. He said De Sapio had called him to say that the candidates would take a dim view of Bill's return before the election and would denounce him when he landed as a precaution against having him tied to the campaign. "Sean," I said, "I don't want those who sent you to later claim you were never authorized. I want to meet Harriman, Roosevelt and De Sapio and let them tell me."

The following day I received a call from De Sapio asking me to meet him in the Biltmore. At that time De Sapio was the national committeeman from the state of New York to the national Democratic Party. He was consulted on every decision of the party, and in New York State he was the most powerful leader since Jim Farley's term. He had a suite of rooms on the 16th floor of the Biltmore where the most important and confidential business was transacted. We met the following night. "Paul," he said, "the boys don't want Bill to return here at this time. It is upsetting and I told Sean Keating they say they would have no choice if he were to come here but to publicly repudiate him. The Republicans would claim that he is returning to take part in the campaign." "Carmine," I said, "I would like to know to whom do you refer when you mention 'the boys.' " "The candidates and their advisors." "Carmine, do you mean Harriman and Roosevelt?" "Well, yes, that's right," replied De Sapio. "I'd like to hear that message from each of them," I said. "That's not possible," said the leader. "They have delegated me to give the message." "Then," I said, "you might carry a message back. Bill will be here to visit. He has no desire to return to New York politics, but I promise your candidates, if either one of them utters a single derogatory word about my brother, I will buy time on radio and will personally work for their defeat. I have the time, the money and the ability and we have as many friends in New York as Harriman and Roosevelt put together. And Carmine," I said, "the last time I heard that threat, it had another messenger but the message was essentially the same." When Bill arrived there was no word or comment from the state Democratic candidates.

Harriman squeaked through and Roosevelt was defeated. If Harriman had made the blunder, he would also have gone down to defeat. I knew that my own relationship to the party leaders was at an end, and the Herbert Lehman/Eleanor Roosevelt movement in 1958 had an immediate adherent.

CHAPTER 46

THE KEFAUVER COMMITTEE HEARINGS

I first met Senator Estes Kefauver in Washington in 1950. George M. Fay was then the United States Attorney for the District of Columbia, and a more brilliant prosecutor never lived. I had worked with him while investigating the suppliers of material to the Army Air Forces during the war. The Senate Special Committee to Investigate Organized Crime in Interstate Commerce, headed by Kefauver, had been established but had not been able to get started, and the chairman had difficulty in selecting knowledgeable counsel. He turned to Fay for help. After an initial meeting with Fay, Kefauver expressed a desire to see me, and Fay arranged the appointment. We met at the Carlton Hotel, where I outlined what I had learned about crime conditions in the large centers of population throughout the country. Kefauver asked if I could give some time to his counsel at a later date, and I promised to do so.

My experience with Congressional committees was limited to the one encounter I had had while still a lieutenant colonel. The chairman of that committee was the rough, energetic, conscientious and most politically-wise Senator from Missouri, and I have since learned to regard Harry Truman as my favorite American of all time. At that time, his committee, performing essentially the same work as I was doing, kept me and my investigators hopping.

Roosevelt had reached for the indefatigable Bob Patterson as his Assistant Secretary of War, and Patterson in turn, reached for me. Patterson did not want to have one exposure after another of shoddy material being supplied to the soldiers by unscrupulous suppliers or careless inspection by Army personnel. My job, as I previously described it in this book, was to get in there and ferret out whatever was wrong, to eliminate the offending practice and, if need be, transmit to the local prosecutor any evidence of crime. Sometimes we got to the scene before the Truman committee investigator, and before long I found myself in frequent clashes with the committee and its counsel, Hugh Fulton, and his successor, the assistant counsel, Rudolf Halley.

After my meeting with Kefauver in Washington I did not hear from him for several months. The Senator called me at City Hall, reminding me of my promise to him, and arranged for Halley to see me. Notwithstanding our clashes before the Truman committee and our differences of opinion on the Higgins contracts in New Orleans, I did not believe that there was any residue of acrimony between us. I assigned Police Sergeant Maguire to Halley to assist him in his inquiry. Maguire was highly recommended to me by Police Commissioner Wallander as a young, intelligent and experienced investigator, and Halley was very satisfied with him. Maguire had full access to all the police records, and he furnished all the information Halley requested. Maguire compiled a dossier on all known criminals in New York, including those who had Florida connections, and Halley put it to great use. When the committee started out, it was necessary to establish that criminals operate across state lines, otherwise prospective witnesses might successfully challenge the committee's jurisdiction. Halley came to see me at City Hall on several occasions, and both he and Kefauver thanked me for helping them get started.

Later, when I had been nominated as Ambassador to Mexico, I was required to go before the Senate Foreign Relations Committee for confirmation. There were only two witnesses in opposition to my appointment, one of them a Republican candidate for Congress from the New York region. My confirmation came through without any trouble, Kefauver voting in my favor.

The job of being Ambassador to Mexico is an exacting one. It is our most important embassy in the Americas. Not only for my own sake, but for the sake of the President who appointed me, and for the sake of my friends, and in the interest of the Republic that had honored me, I wanted to make good. With the help of a most loyal and devoted staff, I set out to create and establish a tide of good will toward this country. I knew there had existed considerable ill will and suspicion between the two countries, and I was determined to overcome these problems of our past.

As a result, I had little time to follow events of the Kefauver committee or the happenings in New York. Paul kept me somewhat informed from time to time, and the information I received was annoying, though not disturbing. The election of Vincent Impellitteri as Mayor left a vacancy for the President of the City Council, and Halley, being a New Yorker, had his eye on it. I learned he was going to use his committee position to catapult himself into office. Furthermore, it seemed as if the hearings were to also provide Chairman Kefauver with a springboard for the Presidency. The methods they were using to promote themselves through national television were producing nothing which had not been already known by the New York prosecutors. But the rehash had caught the fancy of the American public, who always felt that New York was a sinful place, and now could see it plainly on television.

In the midst of these disquieting reports, I learned from Paul that the committee desired to send a representative to Mexico to see whether I had any further information of value, with the suggestion that he would later talk to me about coming up to testify. From such a distance and in the midst of many important official assignments, I was unaware that the spotlight was turned on me. Every charge leveled at me during my political campaigns, each of which had been discussed at length and judged by the electorate, was now being revived and given new, nationwide publicity. The outstanding accomplishments in the Brooklyn District Attorney's office were being distorted and an effort made to charge me instead with dereliction of duty in that office.

Had I been conscious of the sinister about-face which the chairman and the counsel had executed since the time I had supplied them with the necessary information to get them on the road, I would not have agreed to be interviewed by their representative. Their emissary to Mexico was Louis Yavner, a former Commissioner of Investigation of the City of New York under Mayor La Guardia and now Halley's assistant. Yavner was no stranger to me. As Mayor, I had called on him to look into some Department of Education problems, and he did an excellent job.

I welcomed his visit. I could not conceive of Louis Yavner doing anything dishonorable, and Paul told me that Yavner was assigned to make the trip because both Kefauver and Halley knew of my high opinion of him. I believe now, as I believed then, that Yavner is a man of integrity.

He stayed at the embassy as my guest and accompanied me on my routine activities from morning to night. Our conversations were mostly in the embassy car, or late at night at the great colonial edifice that served as my dwelling place, rather than the office of the American Embassy.

Yavner made notes of what I had learned about gangland activities, and later we talked about the personalities on the committee. I found it difficult to understand their seeming hostility and speculated that it might have been generated by Senator Herbert R. O'Conor of Maryland. He had written to me when I was Mayor asking me to intercede for one of his friends who had submitted a bid for a city contracting job. I had turned the supervision of all contracts over to Robert Moses on the first day of my administration, wanting no scandal or favoritism to attach to any contracts with the city. All similar pieces of correspondence, including O'Conor's letter, went to Moses. I did not inquire as to the reply

O'Conor received, but I know how brusque Moses could be. I shared my misgivings with Yavner, but he did not seem to think there was substance to them.

As far as the other members of the committee were concerned, Senators Alexander Wiley and Lester C. Hunt seemed to be on the sidelines, enjoying the performance. They were fair-minded men, and neither one had any ambitions to seek higher office. Senator Charles Tobey of New Hampshire was loud and clownish and inclined to cry out in great moral indignation.

Yavner went over most of the material that I had previously discussed with Halley and Kefauver. He suggested that I might be questioned about some items that involved my personal honesty and integrity, and I told him I didn't mind. The matters he mentioned had been fully explored over and over again by political opponents during my two mayoralty election campaigns.

Yavner returned to New York, and later the committee invited me to appear before it.

The invitation came at a time when I had been down with the flu and a return of hepatitis. Leonard Lyons, the newspaper columnist, published the fact and hazarded the prediction that because of my ill health, I would not be able to attend. Halley, a close friend of Lyons, was aware of my state of health. Paul called my doctor and, on his advice, said he would arrange for a postponement of my appearance for a week or so to give me a chance to get on my feet.

Meanwhile, Mexican government officials and some Mexican newspapers took offense at what they considered harassment of their Ambassador and a slight to their country. They felt that the hearings tended to diminish the stature of an Ambassador who had been known in Mexican circles as a friend. To establish where Mexico stood, President Alemán sent word that he wished to see me. "You would do Mexico an honor if you would permit us to demonstrate our affection for you and our satisfaction with the work you have done since you have come to Mexico," was the way he put it. "I am placing the Presidential plane, pilots and crew at your disposal to take you to New York and to return you to your post." I declined his invitation, but I knew the gesture was a genuine one, typical of the people I had learned to love. Whatever my state of health, the nobility of the country gave me courage and assurance, which, at that hour, I needed.

At Idlewild Airport newsmen, radio reporters and television cameras were there in force. Paul had made arrangements for an orderly press conference in a room inside the building. The day I had left for Mexico to serve as Ambassador, New York put on a parade and ceremonies for me. Crowds had lined the streets downtown and there was an atmosphere of genuine friendship. Now, when I returned to testify, few people showed up at the airport outside of my family. It was a blow. One lone figure from my political past stood out in the crowd, Supreme Court Justice Walter Hart. Otherwise the feelings of warmth and applause with which I had left New York were now replaced by the unsmiling faces of the newsmen, all of them a bit tense, as if they had an unpleasant task to perform and were determined to do it well.

A couple of days later I worked my way through the crowded chamber in which the hearing was taking place. I went alone, so that there would be no appearance of counsel in the room. There seemed to be no room for anyone else to squeeze in. Each Senator and Halley had reserved tickets for their friends. There was noise and confusion everywhere, and the noisiest claque was that which had come as Senator Tobey's guests. The television lights were many, glaring and hot, and I was suffering from a high temperature, a combination designed to make me most uncomfortable. Wiping the perspiration off my face was to be avoided, lest it give the impression that it was the subject matter rather than the heat causing the discomfort. At least that was my intention. I now can't say with what success I carried it out.

There was little new in the questioning. For the most part it was a rehash of the campaign charges of 1945. There was no attempt to elicit from me what knowledge I had about the extent and nature of crime in New York and its links with other states. At the end of the session, Tobey said he believed Abe Reles was thrown out the window of the Half Moon Hotel in Coney Island, and that remark set in motion a full-scale inquiry by the District Attorney's office in Brooklyn. Two assistant district attorneys were assigned to the job, as well as a full complement of police and county detectives. All the physical evidence which the F.B.I. labs had tested at the time of Reles' death was still intact. Over 200 witnesses were called to the grand jury rerun. I was one of those who gave testimony on a matter which had been thoroughly investigated years before, when the facts were fresh in everybody's minds.

Senator Tobey was called to come to Brooklyn and declined. In the end, the Brooklyn grand jury filed a written report. Its conclusions paralleled the grand jury report at the end of the first hearing shortly after Reles' death. Both grand juries concluded that Reles sought to escape his captors from where he had been confined at the Half Moon Hotel, that the sheets and wire he used to attempt his escape were incapable of supporting his weight, and that he fell to his death. No notice was paid to the grand jury findings.

Another situation from the past that now confronted me involved James Moran, who had been the chief clerk of the District Attorney's office in Brooklyn, and whom I appointed to the post of Deputy Fire

Commissioner. The Commissioner, Frank Quayle, had been in the typewriter business until he was appointed the postmaster in Brooklyn. He served in that post for many years and had an enviable reputation.

It was revealed in a subsequent investigation that for about 20 years before I came to the office of Mayor any contractor seeking to install an oil burner in the street invariably paid a gratuity to the inspectors to facilitate the application and get his application processed through the bureaucratic red tape. If he failed to honor the custom, the contractor ran the risk of having his crew stand idly by awaiting approval. The cost had been $15 per application. No contractors complained, and the evil the custom engendered never came to public attention either in my time or during the tenure of my predecessor.

When James Moran got to the Fire Department, he apparently became aware of the racket. He upped the price and, with the help of the civil servants who had been part of it, he took over the collections. I'm certain that if Frank Quayle had known about it, he would have called it to my attention. In the whole of my administration, this was the only incident where any of my commissioners or deputy commissioners had been charged with any official misconduct. I was questioned sharply about Moran by the committee. It was plain they were trying to infer that I was aware of what he was doing.

The major "bombshell" of the hearings was the accusation that John Crane, president of the United Fireman's Association, had illegally given me $10,000 in cash at Gracie Mansion as a contribution to my 1949 campaign. I had received no such contribution then or at any time and said so, but this particular accusation would prove the cause of much grief for years to come.

Almost immediately after my appearance before the committee, I received a call from a Mr. Kennedy, who headed the Intelligence Unit of the Internal Revenue Service at 253 Broadway, requesting my appearance at his office. The function of this unit was to investigate a target with a view towards prosecution if a violation of the law were established. The unit is in no way involved in, nor has it any jurisdiction over, auditing tax returns. I was feeling pretty groggy at that time, much more so than when I left Mexico, but I wished to offer no excuse, least of all poor health. The Internal Revenue Service agents could have arranged an appointment at my hotel or some other place, as they frequently did, but I realized they wanted it known that I was being investigated. I was sure of it when they suggested to me that I use the freight elevator to get to their office. I declined the offer.

I had the feeling that were I to use the back entrance and the freight elevator, the press would have been on hand as I came off the elevator. The office is across the street from City Hall. As it was, the news of my

Testifying before the Kefauver committee, 1951

appearance was leaked to the papers shortly after I left the Internal Revenue office.

I went to the meeting alone. There were five agents present, and again, I was asked about Crane's story and reiterated the denial I expressed at the Kefauver hearings. I was asked to furnish a statement of my "net worth." No one is required, nor can he be compelled, to submit such a statement, which can leave the giver open to perjury charges. The detailed statement of assets and liabilities also supplies the Intelligence Unit with many leads and facilitates the enlargement of the inquiry. If the statement contains any falsehoods, an indictment for perjury or for income tax violation will surely follow. I recognized my legal rights but also my moral obligation to the United States and President Truman. I did not want it said, as I returned to Mexico, that I had failed to answer any questions or failed to submit even a most detailed account of what assets I possessed.

The statement I filed showed that aside from my interest in the City Pension Fund, my net worth (total assets over liabilities) amounted to $14,096. It did not change materially during the years that followed. I believe that figure represented a record: I had less of the world's goods than any mayor since the first Dutch burgomaster took office over three centuries ago. I'm certain I had less to my name than any United States ambassador anywhere. However, I did not consider myself poor. I had many friends and had been favored by people and Presidents, and to me that represented more than wealth.

The Internal Revenue Service agents conducted a preliminary inquiry which they typed up and sent to me a few days later at University Hospital to sign. They were to continue the investigation after I returned to Mexico.

Next, I received calls for other appearances—one from my former assistants, Miles McDonald and Julius Helfand, requesting me to appear before the Kings County grand jury in Brooklyn. Dr. Bernecker, the Commissioner of Hospitals who had examined me, urged me to postpone my appearance before the investigating bodies in favor of a stay in the hospital to convalesce. I felt that I must reject his advice regardless of how I felt.

My former protégés in the Brooklyn District Attorney's office requested me to sign a waiver of immunity. Feeling that was the right thing to do under the circumstances, I signed it. The request is clear indication that the witness is indeed a target of the inquiry. Thereafter, I testified extensively as to all matters in which the prosecutor and the grand jury were interested. I was asked there also to submit a "net worth" statement, which I did, giving it to the grand jury and the prosecutor. I was then presented with a questionnaire requiring much

Photo courtesy of Brooklyn Public Library/Brooklyn Eagle Collection
International News Photo

Leaving University Hospital with Paul's wife Kathleen, 1951

more detailed information concerning every item of income I had received and every item of expense I had incurred for several years prior to my appearance. To be certain it was accurate, I took some time to gather all the information, then signed and presented it to the several prosecuting agencies.

Frank Hogan, District Attorney of New York County, had suffered some disappointment at not being nominated for mayor by the local Democratic Party after I resigned. I had promised to support him, but he blamed me for not getting the five Democratic leaders to accept him. He, too, requested me to appear to talk about Mr. Moran, as well as other matters, including Crane's story. Once again, I signed a similar waiver of immunity before testifying before the New York County grand jury.

To show the seriousness of the inquiry, Hogan himself conducted the proceedings. He had seldom done so, previously leaving such matters to subordinates. I answered under oath all questions I was asked. In New York County, the inquiry was as extensive as it was in Brooklyn.

After all the inquiries were completed, I signed in again at University Hospital. Exhaustion had taken over and it took several days of isolation before I was on my feet again. If the news from the city I loved was crushing, the news from Mexico was heartening. Its people, government, President and press all came vigorously to my defense. The Mexican presidential plane arrived a few days later, and I returned to my duties at the embassy.

The Kefauver interview and final reports came through in due course. They contributed a devastating assessment of my time as District Attorney and Mayor. In a few paragraphs, they had distorted a lifetime of accomplishment in the public domain. It was a crushing blow. But there still remained the President of the United States, who had expressed his faith in me, and the government and the people of Mexico, who were unaffected by the abuse. I settled down to continue to try to do the best job ever performed by an American ambassador.

As a final note in my story, I'd like to share an article by Bill Corum, a New York sports columnist. Charles Guptil, Associated Press correspondent in Mexico City, handed it to me on an August afternoon in 1953.

Journal–American—August 12, 1953

This is one fellow's idea and opinion, mine. Nobody suggested that I write this. If they had, I probably wouldn't be writing it. If the man about whom it is written ever reads it, he is likely to be the most surprised of all that it was written by me and appeared here.

Bill O'Dwyer, former mayor of this city, and I were never intimates, as I was intimate with Jimmy Walker. We were nodding acquaintances and no more than that.

Mr. O'Dwyer never did me a favor, or vice versa. I am not and never have been remotely connected with politics. Hallelujah in the mawnin!

When, during his term as Mayor, O'Dwyer slapped a 5 percent tax on racing, I thought he was wrong, and said so, because it seemed to me to be a discriminatory levy. And I thought he was doubly wrong when he did it, took the money for the city treasury and continued to knock racing at the same time.

The sports of other countries do not come in my province and are not among my preoccupations. But if the killing of bulls, the cutting off of their bloody ears as trophies and if dolls waving red capes in front of bewildered heifers to make pictures for newspapers, is a sport, then perhaps, thoroughbred horse racing isn't too bad. And if the excuse in Mexico and Spain is that the people like bullfighting, the fact that our people like racing should be an equally valid excuse.

So I thought badly of O'Dwyer's attitude toward racing in N.Y. and, I repeat, said so on several occasions.

There is, therefore, only one possible reason for me to say what I'm going to now.

That is that the arch, the keystone, the fundamental factor, in sports, is sportsmanship.

And that I believe that O'Dwyer is being treated as unfairly, with as little sportsmanship and decency and common fairness in this city, for which he did so much, as ever I have known a man to be treated in this country.

There's Something in a Book About It:

Now, if O'Dwyer has committed some crime, if he has done something that a sports writer in his insulated little world, wouldn't know about, then, of course, he should be charged and tried for that crime—even as you and as I.

Never have I seen that he has been charged with a crime, unless, perchance, it is that I would call the 'decent crime' of loyalty, however misplaced the loyalty.

I say that I did not know O'Dwyer really. Yet I knew a thing or two about him.

369

I knew and know, that no official of this wonderful and magnificent city ever had a deeper concern about the 'stick-ball kids' who play in its streets than Bill O'Dwyer.

Surely that couldn't have been wrong.

I know, too, almost by accident, that there was a sad man who walked out of a patrolman's job in Brooklyn into, in succession, a judgeship, the D.A.'s office, the office of Mayor, and an Ambassadorship.

That I know because City Editor Paul Schoenstein once assigned me to do an interview with him shortly after he became Mayor. The result was no great shakes of an interview or story, either. But in it, I wrote a line that said approximately, this man strikes me as a sad man; as one who is carrying a load that perhaps only he knows about.

At the time, I knew nothing about him having an invalid wife. Nothing whatever about his personal affairs.

It was something that I felt about him, as he answered the casual and unimportant questions that I asked him. I also would have long since forgotten that I wrote it, except that I never talked to O'Dwyer after that without his mentioning the fact. 'How did you guess that about me in such a short time?' he always asked.

But it isn't of O'Dwyer I'd been thinking exactly. It's about us, here in the city that was his city. If he has done no great wrong, and nobody has said so, then what of us?

Have We Been Fair?

What sort of neighbors and friends and people are we? Yesterday it was published in the papers that his lady had divorced him in a civil action. It was news, I suppose, even though it was well known that she had gone elsewhere some time ago. Her business and his, at any rate, not mine and yours. Any man that has a lady of his choice to walk with him in the years that go down the hill to the lonesome time, has something going for him, even though the breakfast dishes play spin-the-plate when the toast is burned.

It may be that I've used too many words to say that here is one citizen of this city that once acclaimed him, who is sorry for Bill O'Dwyer. Who thinks, on all the evidence that he has heard, that we have given the man a shabby deal.

And who, although no reader of The Book, he regrets to say, thinks he still remembers a line his grandmother sometimes read to him on peaceful and happy evenings long ago, maybe from Matthew, although I'm not sure . . .

Returning to New York from Mexico accompanied by Paul and his family and niece Joan, 1954

A line that began: 'Therefore all things whatsoever ye would that men should do to you . . .'
'Do Ye Even So To Them . . .':

I hope that I have the words right. And the spirit. I'm sure. and I think the time has come for N.Y.C. and its people to be, at least, commonly decent to former Mayor O'Dwyer, who did a very great deal for N.Y.C.

And somewhere in that same Book that I've been mentioning, there is something about the casting of a stone.

One of the few things that life has taught me is, that those who know all about what everybody else is doing, or has done, have almost no time left to find out what they are doing.

To finish the quote from Matthew, as I remember it, it goes:

'. . . do ye even so to them.' "

Corum's column was published in 1953, and there were many more miles of life's road to travel before I returned permanently to live out my life in the city that produced a hundred Bill Corums for every ambitious revenue agent.

CHAPTER 47

COUNSEL FOR THE DEFENSE

PO'D

"He who is his own lawyer has a fool for a client." It is a very old saying with much wisdom in it, and yet it was imperative that I take on my brother's case—in all its detail. I had spent a lifetime in the courtrooms or on the platform and I had experienced injustice in every level of the courts, particularly in political cases. I could see the wisdom of getting someone else to pick up the cudgels, and there were many prestigious lawyers who had volunteered their assistance, but I feared it would prove to be an overpowering burden, and frankly, I did not believe anyone could do it as well as I could.

I had met my brother for the first time in New York. We were the oldest and youngest of 11 children. His departure from our home was not on the friendliest terms, and there was an estrangement between him and my parents which did not endear me to him before our meeting. He did not come to the boat to meet me as Jimmy and Frank did, and when I met him later that evening in the boarding house of Mrs. McGuire on 145 West 103rd Street, I was introduced to a stranger.

It was not family or point of common origin which brought us closer together. He had long rejected the idea of being a tribesman. He had very little in common with Ireland and even later when he paid a visit, it seemed more out of an obligation imposed on him than any sense of fealty or relationship to a homeland. He enjoyed the family members who came here, but it was as if they had joined him in the new culture in the new world, the New York culture, to which each quickly adjusted.

As I got to spend more time in his company, I thought many of the sentiments he expressed were irritating and provoking. His views were strange, I thought. He discouraged denigrating other races and questioned the comparative value of his own. It was a bit shocking to one who was raised in the middle of a nationalist-inspired revolution. But he also questioned the church, which seemed very appropriate to me, and his criticism of St. Nathy's College, whence we both had graduated, was more than acceptable.

His shortcomings were many. He did not seem to be able to keep appointments and did not seem to feel contrite about having caused inconvenience to others, and he lacked any sense of obligation to family or friend. It was in his vast store of knowledge of history and his capacity for recounting even minute details that gave one the feeling that there was a depth to him, which was far beyond what might be expected from his earlier, or even later, environment. At times I was inwardly angry at his insensitivity but at the same time attracted to him because of what to me seemed boundless knowledge and challenging views.

But that was 1925 and soon I was going to law school, and between work and study, I saw him infrequently. But I often thought about the things he said and the dreams he had and about the worth of the new life and the kind of city to which we had drifted. When the day came for me to serve my clerkship, he got me a job with the office of Holmes & Bernstien, with whom he shared offices. That's not altogether accurate; with Oscar Bernstien he also shared life. I became a partner of Holmes & Bernstien.

Several years went by and he was running for Mayor and going to win. All of us shared in the joy of victory, and he commenced to rule over the eight million crowded fellow citizens.

While he was Mayor, we had many quarrels. I am not sure now what the details were, but when he was about to move in a political direction which was less, in my mind, than the commitment to the basic liberal principles, he would pick a quarrel with me which left me no alternative but to leave his company in anger, and the periods of our separation were several months at a time. Both Oscar Bernstien and I determined that we would in no way profit from his position. I worked harder in court during his five years as Mayor than I had ever before or since. And we bothered not at all in his appointments. I cannot recall a single position to which we made a recommendation.

When the Kefauver hearings loomed as an anti-O'Dwyer sensation-seeking campaign, I felt that it was a rank injustice. I knew how hard Bill had worked. His home life was an unhappy one, and for the first three years of his administration no more devoted or unselfish servant ever sat in the Mayor's chair. Money had never been his god, and the suggestion that in the office he sought to serve with such dedication he had fouled his nest was infuriating to me. I recognized what politics entails by way of public abuse and what cannibals it occasionally makes of ambitious men, but the distortions of truth and the attempt to create the impression of venality about him was maddening.

I knew he had become ill during the last six months of his first term. And I had seen him at times become petulant, argumentative and irritable, which were never before part of his nature. I was totally opposed to his succeeding himself as Mayor. Both Frank and I were glad when he made up his mind not to seek a second term and we were both beside ourselves with anger when Cashmore and Flynn prevailed on him to change his mind. Frank and I had come to Gracie Mansion, where we both met him after the decision. To avoid acrimony, which he knew a discussion would provoke, he simply said, "I changed my mind about running. Cashmore and Flynn were here and I told them, and there is nothing further to discuss." Frank stayed. I left.

When the Kefauver attack came, it focused on a sick man who was really not in a condition to fight back, and yet I agreed that he should come back from Mexico to face a hostile committee. I spoke with his physician, who raised serious doubts in my mind about his capacity to stand the physical and emotional strain, adding that he would not guarantee the consequences of the trip. Another lawyer not so emotionally involved might have advised the more practical path—staying away—but I felt that Dr. Lebrija could not possibly have known what it means to be pilloried in New York, with a reputation dragged in the gutter and the accusation of cowardice to top it off. And so I agreed with Bill that he should come to New York. We had come to the same conclusion but for different reasons.

His reasons sprang from his belief that the committee was, notwithstanding what I had observed and reported, interested in valuable information which he was in a position to give. I felt his appearance was imperative because he should not let his detractors say they had frightened him from coming to a town over which he had presided with such distinction for five years. It was immature reasoning, and in retrospect, I believe I would not have given that advice to a client not related to me but otherwise under the same circumstances.

On the basis of what Dr. Lebrija had told me about the complication of the flu, I called on Halley to seek an adjournment for a week. After I had made the request, he excused himself from the room, returned after an extended period, and said, "Mr. O'Dwyer, I have consulted our schedule and we cannot stay here in New York any longer. We are adjourning to Washington and therefore we will not hear from any other witnesses—only from those who have recommendations for remedial legislation. Your brother is a voluntary witness and, as such, we would like to accommodate, but we cannot hear him other than in New York. Of course, if he is not feeling up to it, I'm sure nobody would expect him to come such a long distance when it is not essential, but I have no authority to change the schedule. If you think you would like to speak to the chairman of the committee about this, I can arrange it."

"I'd welcome the opportunity, Mr. Halley," I said and requested him to make an appointment for me. "No sooner said than done," said Halley, and the following day I journeyed to Washington to meet with Kefauver. I got there at the appointed time, but Kefauver's secretary knew nothing of the appointment. The Senator, she said, was on the Senate floor. After a long wait, he appeared. I told him the purpose of my visit. He appeared very sympathetic and expressed his friendship and admiration for my brother and seemed grateful for the initial help. I told him as politely as I knew how that regretfully some of the other members of the committee apparently did not share his high regard for my brother.

He was most gracious and said he was in the habit of speaking for himself. He said there was no reason why my brother should mar his health to come here; that there would be no further testimony after they left New York, so that if my brother felt impelled to come it was necessary that he do so while the committee was in New York. I got the distinct impression from him, as I did from Halley, that they would be pleased if Bill did not come. Each of them had stressed the risk of coming such a distance while in ill health. I told Kefauver I would let him know.

By the time the committee was ready to hear from me, its timetable had already been established, with all its activities aimed at the publication of an article by the Senator in the *Saturday Evening Post*. The first draft of the article would have to be in the hands of the magazine by a certain date and, to give it the air of authenticity, it would be necessary for the article to contain quotes from the committee's report. This requirement posed a serious problem, since the committee could not possibly end its hearings before the deadline set for the delivery of the first draft. The committee got around that difficulty by arranging for the filing of an "interim report," which would accommodate both Kefauver and *Saturday Evening Post*. Bill's appearance, therefore, was endangering an extremely tight schedule. Faced with the predicament, the committee seemed very anxious to provide me with an excuse for his not coming to New York. In that way the testimony unfavorable to Bill and critical of his public life would stand uncontradicted, and the public was unlikely to believe that illness was the reason for his failure to appear.

Their statement to me that they would not receive any further testimony in Washington was an untruth. Additional testimony was, indeed, presented there after the hearings in New York had been ended. Whatever their game plan was, one thing was clear to me. Their interests did not coincide with mine or with my brother's. Bill had to come to New York even if it meant a danger to his life or health.

There were other logical witnesses to the inquiry, such as all the five city prosecutors, the State Attorney General, Mayor Impellitteri and Governor Dewey. None of them were called except the Governor.

Dewey had treated the committee with some obvious contempt. The committee had asked him to explain about the gambling in Saratoga, a racing, horsy town a short distance from Albany and a Republican stronghold. The Governor sent word that he was busy with important state affairs and invited them to Albany, offering to put them up at the palatial Governor's Mansion. The committee, however, would not have the benefit of the heavy television coverage it did in New York and declined the Governor's patronizing invitation, persisting in bringing him to New York. At this point the Governor's representative let it be known that the Governor hoped the committee would not overlook a significant gathering of New York judges and other prominent city folk at a well-known New York nightclub as the guests of Frank Costello. The reference to the incident ended the committee's desire to bring Governor Dewey before the microphones.

The event to which Governor Dewey made reference was a fund raising dinner for the benefit of the Salvation Army. It took place the year before the hearing and was arranged by Costello. The event was well within the parameters of the committee's inquiry. If its purpose was to establish Costello's association with the judiciary and the world of politics, it could not have been provided with a better example. Yet there was never any mention of it during the hearings, and for a very good reason. When Senator Kefauver was in search of a counsel, he sought out Judge Ferdinand Pecora, and Halley's name was among three recommended by Pecora to the Senator. Pecora had gained fame in the early 1930's as counsel to the Senate investigation into banking and the house of Morgan. It was an unusually well-conducted hearing. Out of it came the enactment of a law which put restrictions on the stock market and established the Securities and Exchange Commission. But that was 20 years earlier, and since then Pecora had joined the Tammany organization and was rewarded with a Supreme Court judgeship. He was one of Costello's guests on the night of the celebrated dinner.

Notwithstanding Dr. Lebrija's expressed concern, Bill wanted to return to New York, and I knew if he stayed in Mexico, no matter how poorly he felt, no one would have believed that sickness was the cause of his absence. Furthermore, notwithstanding my admonitions, he could not get himself to believe that Kefauver and Halley, whose investigation he had helped get started, would turn the investigation into a circus or a forum for his destruction. Additionally, he knew that few people could match the experience he had acquired during the prosecution of the Murder, Inc., criminals and during the investigating into fraud on the part of the suppliers of material to the armed forces. He sincerely believed that the committee was in search of facts and that he could make a real contribution to their work.

Finally, Bill reasoned that because he held the prestigious post of Ambassador to Mexico, his behavior would reflect not only on the United States but on President Truman, whose personal envoy he was. In Mexico, the American newsmen had frequently raised the question of whether he would return to face his detractors.

The hearings, held in March 1951, were televised. The job of directing the camera for full-length and close-up is a very difficult one. It requires trigger-like action, and the program director's job was highly technical and most important. In an unrehearsed program, it requires unusual skill. The director determines which camera is to be thrown on what person and for what period of time. Often under mild stress, people tap their fingers or strike their chin or touch their lips or cross their legs nervously. The director watched for these idiosyncrasies and captured them on camera. The real manipulator of those hearings was behind the scenes. He did an excellent job, and the entertainment value of the hearings proved it so.

It was hard to convince Bill that the television features of the hearing had overpowered its purpose. His testimony dragged on for two days. He made the mistake of taking the questions seriously and attempted to answer them as if the committee really wanted to know. But there was neither the time nor interest in explanations, and the only time he scored was when he, too, turned from the subject matter and told Tobey he, the Senator, had gotten contributions from sources about which he knew nothing. What Bill sought to convey was that it was impossible for any man in public life to know everything, even such important things as where his campaign money came from. Tobey became highly nervous. He jumped from his seat and demanded to be sworn in before his own committee. Then he remained silent until the next recess.

Near the end of his testimony, Bill was asked if John Crane, president of the United Firemen's Association, had given him, at Gracie Mansion, $10,000 in cash as a contribution to his 1949 campaign. He said that he had received no such contribution in cash or check in Gracie Mansion or any place else. At the very last minute the committee counsel called Crane to testify that he had indeed made such a contribution. The committee had previously called Crane. He had refused to answer the committee's questions, claiming that his answers might incriminate him, and he claimed protection under the Fifth Amendment. In his reappearance he did not claim immunity. There was no opportunity to refute Crane's testimony nor to crossexamine him on a story which was presented to the public for the first time and which contradicted three other accounts of the charge given under oath.

To dispel the charge that bookmaking flourished during Bill's administration as Mayor, Chief Magistrate John M. Murtagh came voluntarily to testify on his efforts to contain bookmaking in New York. His appearance was greeted with an avalanche of abuse. He was then made the target of two district attorneys, and for his temerity he got himself indicted for not reporting his findings to Bill in writing. The case never went to trial; the Court of Appeals dismissed it.

The committee packed up and promptly left New York to return to Washington. I protested their hit-and-run behavior, but for me the hearings were over.

Kefauver issued his report which was highly critical of Bill as Mayor. It charged, in general terms, that the atmosphere in New York during his administration was one in which crime flourished. On April 23, 1951, after his return to Mexico City, Bill wrote to the committee requesting permission to enter newspaper editorial evaluations of his public performance in various offices into the record.

Most of my interrogation concerned remote and isolated incidents in a long and active public career, and thus unfortunately produced a most distorted picture of my work, my aims and my character.

Since many of the questions asked me were prompted by or based upon New York newspaper comments, it is only fair that the editorial comments made on my work and activities during public office be given the same prominence in the record.

Particularly is this true in view of the fact that these editorial comments were made on the spot, over the years, by watchful local editors whose background, attitude and political views, in many instances, predisposed them to be keen, critical and ofttimes hostile appraisers.

It was because of the fact that the picture presented was one-sided and distorted that I requested that these editorial comments be made part of my testimony. I was thankful to the Committee for having extended that courtesy to me.

It is my hope that you will give this your consideration and if you still feel that not all of the editorial comments should be printed in the record, then, may I suggest that a member of the Committee or its counsel go over that exhibit with my brother Paul representing me. I am quite certain that the Committee desires to be fair in the matter.

After the report had been filed and the magazine article written, Senator Kefauver resigned from the committee to prepare his campaign for the Presidency. He did not succeed but was nominated at a later

Democratic Party convention as candidate for Vice-President. Halley resigned as counsel to prepare for his successful run for President of the New York City Council. However, his later bid for the office of Mayor came when the excitement was over and that campaign never got off the ground.

Senator O'Conor became the new chairman, and a man named Richard G. Moser took Halley's place as chief counsel. Both sought to give new life to the committee, but the public had lost interest and the media were on to other excitement.

Mr. Moser got around to answering Bill's letter on July 5th:

On April 23, 1951 you wrote Senator Kefauver regarding your desire to have the record of this Committee include certain newspaper clippings and other material referring to your career in public office and you suggested that we discuss the matter with your brother Paul.

Because of the pressure of other work, it has been impossible for me to turn to this until now. I have looked over the material you have in mind and I am now in a position to discuss it with your brother. I should therefore appreciate your having him communicate with me immediately in order that we may dispose of the matter as promptly as possible.

I observe that one of the loose ends regarding your testimony before the Committee was with regard to a statement of your net worth which as I recall you released to the press but did not testify about. I am wondering if you would have any objection to supplying us under oath with a statement regarding your income, assets and other financial transactions as of various dates. Perhaps I could also discuss this with your brother as well.

There was much discussion between Moser and me about the correctness and the fairness of including the editorials in the record. But nothing could convince him to include them. The best I was able to do was to submit 40 pages of favorable editorials from every New York newspaper as an exhibit.

During the hearings, efforts to present New York as a place of sin catered to the hostility towards New York which always existed throughout the nation. The committee studiously avoided conducting any inquiry in the New England area. Tobey at one time was Governor of New Hampshire and the "booze" from Canada came through that state without interference from the law. During Tobey's days there, Auburn, Portsmouth and Manchester were the centers for bookmaking and gambling, and in the summer the scene shifted temporarily to Bretton Woods.

Neither did the committee focus attention on or make any inquiry about crime in Baltimore, where O'Conor had been prosecutor and which had been a haven for many New York thugs on the run. Lepke had fled New York and was operating in Baltimore unmolested by the law until he was arrested and extradicted to New York.

Bill had been questioned at length about James Moran, the Deputy Fire Commissioner, and his relationship with him, although Fire Commissioner Quayle was never subjected to any inquiry. Moran became a target of the committee. Later he was prosecuted by District Attorney Hogan, tried before Judge Mullen, and given 12 years in jail. After his conviction and before his sentence, Hogan had him brought to the chapel of the jail. Hogan promised to see that he was given a suspended sentence if he cooperated with the prosecutor. However, the sentence was spread out so that at the end of any one term Judge Mullen could cut short the sentence if Moran chose to cooperate with authorities, and in that connection Hogan made it plain in the house of worship that Bill was the target. Later, the Federal authorities subpoenaed Moran to testify before a Federal grand jury, and he was also to be convicted of lying to it. He was given an additional five-year sentence in the Federal penitentiary. Moran served most of the sentence imposed on him. His two sons became lawyers and were successful in getting some reduction of one of the sentences.

Many persons interested in orderly procedure and in the continuance of fair play, which are necessary ingredients of democracy, were alarmed at what they saw happening during the Kefauver hearings. Prosecutors and former prosecutors joined with unyielding advocates of civil liberties in pointing out the danger that comes from such performances.

Two years after the harm was done, Senator Kefauver spoke on this subject before the Arkansas Bar Association at Little Rock:

> The whole situation which has been highlighted by Congressional hearings is most disturbing—there is no reason why fair procedures cannot exist in the Senate and House of the United States . . . One of the great weaknesses is that we have no uniform rules to establish that code of procedure. The substantive rights of witnesses before Congressional Committee hearings can be no better than their procedural rights. . . . When legitimately conducted, a legislative investigating body is not a prosecutor and it is not a Court. It seeks information only as

a basis for future legislation, or to determine how previous legislation is working out in practice, or in its legitimate function as a check upon the executive authority. Unfortunately not all legislative investigating bodies act according to this pattern. Some are shamefully used by their chairmen and by some of their members. In such cases the parent body—whether it be the Congress of the United States or a State legislature—should not be allowed to escape responsibility for the behavior of its offspring.

The Senator went on to recommend that "persons adversely affected by testimony taken in public hearings be given the right to cross-examine witnesses in public hearings, be represented by counsel, and subpoena witnesses and documents on his behalf, at the discretion of the Committee."

Another voice was heard in criticism. Frank Hogan, the prosecutor who had directed the investigation into the affairs of the Uniformed Firemen's Association and at whose invitation Bill testified before the New York County grand jury, told a reporter for the *New Yorker*:

> The Senate Committee merely rehashed my 1943 examination of Costello. Kefauver thanked the office publicly but naturally it was lost in the hippodrome.
>
> Some people think I am pleased about the O'Dwyer testimony because he double-crossed me when I was nominated for Mayor. Well, he did, but I have no bitterness in my heart.
>
> As a matter of fact, I think the hearing was unfair to O'Dwyer in the sense that he was accused of a crime on evidence insufficient for a court of law.
>
> Probably eighteen million of the twenty million people who followed the hearing on television think he took the envelope, but there was just Crane's word for it.

Several years later Drew Pearson, one of America's most widely read columnists, interviewed Kefauver, and the following is the text of Kefauver's statement as it appeared in U.S. newspapers. He gave a similar statement to Michael Ryan, reporter for the London *Empire Express*.

> Despite the fact that many people might have the idea that former Mayor O'Dwyer was charged with something before our Committee, I would like to make it clear that this was not so.

382

During the Senate crime investigation, so much was written and said that many people got the wrong impression of the role played by Mayor O'Dwyer.

I would like, therefore, to make it clear that O'Dwyer was never, at any time, charged with anything. He was merely giving evidence that helped us with our investigation. He was not under subpoena and came voluntarily from Mexico, where he was then serving as our Ambassador, to give testimony before the Senate Committee.

Our investigation proved, without any doubt, that there was a certain amount of corruption during the Mayor O'Dwyer term of office, but I would make it clear that nothing was ever proved which might associate him with that corruption.

I believe, and have always believed, that William O'Dwyer is an honest man.

Drew Pearson put it under the heading of "Righting a Wrong." Senator Kefauver must be commended for doing it. Altogether too few men in public life would have done likewise.

The avowed purpose of the investigation was to enact Federal legislation necessary to correct conditions exposed during the hearings. Not a single piece of legislation ever passed the Congress of the United States as a result of this investigation, and there was no appreciable change in the crime pattern after the inquiry ended.

For Bill, the end of the hearings was but the signal for all his old political enemies and ambitious newcomers, who had no grudge against him, to come through with a series of investigations that were unprecedented. The fact that no charges were ever preferred after numerous grand jury appearances by Bill was never the subject of fair comment by the media.

CHAPTER 48

FIGHTING THE I.R.S.

PO'D

On the heels of the Kefauver hearings Bill was requested to go to the New York office of the Intelligence Unit of the Internal Revenue Service to see Agent Kennedy. That branch of the Service is not concerned with the collection of taxes. Criminal prosecution is its exclusive purpose. He went there without counsel or other aid. He answered as many questions as were put to him. He was under oath. He also presented a net worth statement which was signed under oath and which contained a detailed account of everything he owned including his furniture and army insurance.

That was the beginning of an investigation which took a full year. Finally, I was advised that the investigation was closed, that everything checked out satisfactorily and I was asked to take back all his books, checkbooks, etc. and was referred to audit.

Then the Democrats were replaced by the Republicans who appointed Coleman Andrews to head the I.R.S. It was the signal for reopening investigations against persons close to President Truman, to go back over the closed cases and revive the investigation. The investigation took five years and an expenditure which we then estimated to be about three-quarters of a million dollars at the end of which the Revenue Commissioners imposed a tax of $20,532.00.

Accountants came to my office and spent eight months there—two of them almost every day—poring over every scrap of paper which was made available to them. Various sets of investigators were out questioning friends, associates, and practically everybody Bill had ever known.

They pursued a minute and detailed investigation into Bill's life. They called for his bank and checking account records, including cancelled checks for 10 years. I had all of them delivered to the I.R.S. offices. The investigators pursued each person to whom Bill had written a check, down to the florist from whom he occasionally ordered flowers and the tobacconist from whom he bought his cigars.

My brother Frank had been a vegetable farmer in the Imperial Valley in California for many years, and whenever Bill went to California, he dropped down to visit him. This ritual was to bring a plague of government agents down on Frank. He was not in politics and did not respond well to this continued annoyance. Furthermore, he was a rugged individualist and resented the implication that he was in any way beholden, even to a brother, for his farming and shipping operations. Nine different times agents went over his books, going back to the day he first started business. After the ninth set of investigators had finished, he called it a day. He gave public notice that he was burning the books, and he did.

The detailed information we supplied in answering their extensive questionnaire gave the investigators a starting point. Under the item of "gifts" I reported that the only gifts Bill had received came when he left New York to become the Ambassador to Mexico. Some good friends, including John Coleman, former head of the New York Stock Exchange, Morris Arnoff, who was engaged in the factoring business, Howard Johnson, the restauranteur, and David Martin, manager of the New York Athletic Club, pooled some money to purchase as gifts some furnishings and silverware which Bill and Sloane could use in the embassy in Mexico. They made the purchases, with Sloane's help, in New York stores. Now each one of them was questioned extensively in an effort to establish some consideration for the gifts, and thereby render them as taxable income which should have been reported; and for the failure to do so, Bill would be subject to indictment.

One of the agents who came from the South asked Dave Martin, who had been questioned elsewhere previously and who was known to be a very religious man, to come to the Federal Building, where he was asked to take a seat.

"Mr. Martin," the agent said, "I have placed your chair so that you are now looking at the High Altar on St. Andrews Church and I am going to ask you questions. You must be aware of the consequences of giving me an untruthful answer." Dave was a quiet man but the question was a reminder of how a century ago at the height of the anti-Catholic feeling in the United States, Americans, and Southerners particularly, believed that Catholics were idolaters who were ruled by superstition and would respond accordingly. Martin became enraged and lodged a complaint with the Internal Revenue Service about the conduct of its agent. He got nowhere with Coleman Andrews, who was then head of the agency.

One day the agent who had behaved so obnoxiously to Dave Martin called at my office and wanted an affadavit from my young niece, Joan, to the effect that she was not holding any money for me or for Bill. Joan's father, Jimmy, died before she was born and she had become the concern of everyone. I advised him if he did not leave immediately, I would physically remove him. From that date I granted the I.R.S. no further extensions of the statute of limitations.

My decision not to extend the government's time within which to take action in the case brought the issue to a climax. The mountain had labored and brought forth this determination by the Commissioner of Internal Revenue: 1) $10,000 which Crane claimed to have given to Bill as a campaign contribution in the 1949 mayoralty election should be included as part of his taxable income, although campaign contributions were non-taxable to the candidate under the law; and 2) his embassy expenses except those which were paid by the government should be disallowed, although it is generally known that the allowance made to any ambassador by the government is not nearly enough to meet his required expenses; and 3) that he had failed to report $15,000 in income covering two years.

There was a choice of either paying the taxes and end the sorry story once and for all, or fighting it and enduring the further public media stories. I chose the latter course. And so, I commenced an action against the government in the United States Tax Court.

In taking the case to the Tax Court I went against all the advice of tax lawyers who said Judge Arnold Raum, who came out of Internal Revenue Service, would never side against the government in this most political of cases. "You're only starting the whole thing up again," I was told by friends and colleagues, and I knew they were right. But there was another side to it. It was a corrupt decision and I could not accept it without going with it as far as I could. Even if I lost, and that was a probability, I would be able to bring to the forefront the unfairness about which I felt most keenly. When the government slaps a tax on a citizen, it should then at least accord the citizen the information on which the Tax Commissioner acted, and that a denial of such information was the denial of a constitutional right which should be reviewed by the United States Supreme Court, if necessary.

John James O'Toole, a rather pleasant fellow, was selected to try the case for the Service.

At about the third or fourth conference with O'Toole, he broached the subject of settlement. Settlement would not have served my purpose. I wanted to review the Treasury Department file and I wanted to cross-examine John Crane. He had made several statements which were directly contradictory of each other. The government had accepted the one which cast my brother in liability and ignored sworn statements to the contrary. However, I could not reject the idea out of hand. "I am not opposed to a settlement," I said, "but I can't buy a pig in a poke," I countered. "I'm not quite sure I understand you," he said, "What's this pig in a poke?" "I'm talking about the file in this case, all the factors on which the Internal Revenue Commissioner bases his findings that the taxpayer owed the money." "You know the I.R.S. does not reveal its files. They are confidential," he countered. "They should not be withheld from the taxpayers," I said. "However, I'll see what your witnesses have to say. They may be able to establish the file's contents. If they do, we will talk later." "Well, let it stand that way," he said. Like other meetings it was pleasant enough, but we met in court prepared to do battle.

While we were waiting for a trial date a lawyer friend of mine called. He wanted to see me but would not come to my office nor would he have me come to his. We met in the early evening in City Hall Park. Under normal circumstances such a meeting would be regarded as the product of paranoia. In the 50's it did not seem at all odd.

The snow was coming down gently and we had to brush it off the seats. He had been a close friend of Governor Dewey, but I always thought of him more as an artist than a Republican wheelhorse. It was only a few weeks earlier we had been together at an after-theatre party in an East Side apartment for some visiting Irish actors.

He said he knew that I was intent on going through with Bill's tax case, and he had been talking to a close friend of both of us who was in the Treasury Department for years and who was quite familiar with my brother's file. It was riddled with memoranda showing how far they had gone and the effort and money expended by the I.R.S. and the other government bureaus cooperating with them, in an attempt to incriminate him. He had come, he said, as a friend of Bill and myself to warn me that it would be prudence on my part to discontinue our case before the Tax Court and to pay the tax which really was not that much. He said that they both felt I was too emotional to realize the risks. I thanked him for his trouble and was sincerely impressed by what he had said.

I was haunted for a while by the suspicion that he was somehow doing a job for the I.R.S. Then on reflection I felt ashamed of myself for doubting a true friend. But that was what those times did to us. I thought about that file and I was now more determined than ever to get it and there could be no retreat. The fight would have to continue until some judge would direct the file to be produced or until by judicial edict I was denied that right.

Before the case commenced Judge Arnold Raum took us into his chambers for some informal discussions. "Mr. O'Dwyer, is this your first case in the Tax Court," he asked. I confessed that it was. "You know," said Judge Raum, "there is in every case a presumption of correctness in favor of the government." "That is unfair," I said, "and unjust. In an ordinary civil court action the plaintiff has the burden of proving his case. What you proclaim is a very different rule which at the outset of the case establishes the taxpayer is wrong and the tax assessor is right. That rule is confiscatory and violates the Constitution." "Your eloquence is impressive," said Judge Raum, "but the law is against you." "I cannot accept the premise that a bad law must be perpetuated," I said pointing out to his Honor that the battle to overrule the "Separate but Equal" rule which applied to the education of black children and which remained the law of the land for over a hundred years was changed in the Brown case.

"One more thing, your Honor. I have subpoenaed the files of the taxpayer in this case." "You can't have it," said the judge. "The law is against you." "Hear me out, Judge. The decision of the Commissioner that a taxpayer owes a certain sum of money is like a judgment in a civil court and carries even more muscle. No court judgment can be obtained without the necessity to exhibit to the judge the evidence on which the claim is based." "That is correct in a civil case, Mr. O'Dwyer, but you are in the Tax Court." "I realize that, your Honor," I argued, "but here again taking money from a taxpayer is confiscatory unless the whole file and all its contents on which the decision was based is open to the person who is required to pay." "Again, you are impressive, Mr. O'Dwyer, but the law is against you. The Commissioner is not required to honor your subpoena to produce the file. Anyway, what do you expect to get in it?" "I expect to get a direction from the Administration and/or the Republican National Committee to pursue this taxpayer. I know that Coleman Andrews is a politician, that he gave the direct orders. I mean to show animosity and bias were the motivating factors responsible for the Commissioner's findings." It was not a complete guess on my part, but I was unable to reveal the source of the information which made me so sure of my ground. If there was nothing in the file to bear out my accusation it was very simple for the Internal Revenue Service to produce it. They didn't.

At the trial, I demanded that the government produce from its files the sworn testimony Bill gave about the Crane item, and introduced it into evidence. That testimony flatly denied the receipt of the $10,000 as income or otherwise.

I then insisted that since Bill's testimony was thus far the only testimony in the case, it was up to the Commissioner to justify his assessment. The attorney for the Commissioner apparently realized the force and logic of the situation and thereupon decided to throw into the scales of justice the best proof—the only proof he relied on—and called John Crane, Terrence Dolan and Victor Wilders as witnesses to establish the Commissioner's side of the case.

A background note on these gentlemen is in order. There is an organization in New York City known as the Uniformed Firemen's Association (U.F.A.) composed of New York City firemen. This organization had a board of trustees, but its business was conducted by its board of officers which consisted of its president, secretary and treasurer. The association collected dues from its members and also raised money through the sale of tickets to the Fireman's Ball. The tickets were sold to the public by the firemen. The money from the public was collected in checks and cash. In 1949, 1950 and 1951, the officers of the association were John P. Crane, president; Gerald Purcell, secretary; and Terrence Dolan, treasurer.

With the collections in the treasury, the president would ask the membership to approve an appropriation of a set amount of money. The membership invariably agreed. Vouchers for that amount were then prepared by Purcell and signed by the trustees. Dolan then drew checks to his own order, cashed them and gave the money to Crane. Crane gave no receipts for the money delivered to him and expended the money as he saw fit without supervision or question and he never gave any accounting to the association, its executive committee, its treasurer or auditor.

Dolan, as treasurer, knew or pretended to know nothing about what money was collected or how it was disbursed by the firemen or whether it was accounted for.

Purcell was in charge of the Ball Committee. Crane and Purcell formed a corporation known as The Whitestone Estates, Inc., each investing about $50 in the company. Crane was its president and Purcell its vice-president. They bought 76 acres of land and built 179 houses, using the funds of the U.F.A. They attempted to sell the houses to firemen, but since not enough came forward, they carried on negotiations with a sister organization known as the Patrolmen's Benevolent Association, composed of New York City policemen.

During 1949 the U.F.A. was interested in passing certain legislation in Albany, known as Amendment 5, or the McNeill-Mitchell Bill, which was to be voted on in the November election of that year. Eighty-nine thousand dollars was taken out of the treasury of the U.F.A. and charged up to expenses in connection with that legislation. Out of that sum, $30,000 was withdrawn during the months of September, October and November in amounts of $5,000 each.

In 1950 and 1951 the disposition of those funds was under investigation by the District Attorney, and also by the Internal Revenue Service.

Dolan was interrogated for 15 straight days by the District Attorney about the $30,000, which had been drawn out on checks to Dolan's order, cashed by him and turned over to Crane. Crane was subpoenaed by the District Attorney to appear for questioning before the grand jury. He refused to waive immunity and retained Sol Gelb as his lawyer. Gelb was an associate of Governor Dewey when he was District Attorney and a co-assistant of District Attorney Hogan. An arrangement was made whereby Crane was permitted to go before the grand jury without waiving immunity, thus giving him immunity for any offense of dereliction to which he might testify.

In light of the foregoing circumstances, Crane testified that he received the $30,000 from Dolan and in explanation of its disposition said that on or about Columbus Day, 1949, he delivered to Bill a brown envelope containing $10,000 in cash as a contribution to his campaign for re-election. He swore that he and Bill were alone at the time and that no one was present at this occurrence.

Purcell did not receive the favored treatment that was accorded to Crane. He was convicted of larceny and sent to jail for his part in the handling of the U.F.A. funds.

When Crane was subpoenaed by the Kefauver committee and questioned about delivering money to Bill, he appeared with his attorney and pleaded the Fifth Amendment. Later he testified, repeating the story and swearing that he saw Bill alone, with no witnesses present.

In April, 1951, the I.R.S. became interested in Crane's personal finances and income, particularly with respect to the $30,000 which he admitted having received from Dolan. The Commissioner asked Crane whether he had any witnesses or any evidence to corroborate his story about delivering the money to Bill and Crane said he had none. This statement, like the similar statement before the grand jury, was made under oath.

Crane was examined by Assistant District Attorney Scotti on five occasions between January, 1951, and July, 1952. In January of 1951 Crane appeared twice within a period of a month. Scotti asked him how he got to Gracie Mansion. Crane's answer was that he wasn't sure. Scotti persisted in trying to find out who accompanied him and asked him how he got there, if anybody was with him, and Crane's response was, "I could not recall how I got there," that "I thought it was my brother who drove me there, but my brother had denied it and, therefore, I was completely at sea as to how I got up there and who was with me." Crane did not mention Jerry Finkelstein, Victor Wilders or Dolan, all of whom figured critically in later testimony, and two of whom Crane later swore were witnesses to the alleged delivery of money to Bill O'Dwyer. "When I was subpoenaed and I tried to resurrect the story in my own mind, I tried to recall how I had gotten there and I had the impression that I was driven up there by my brother so I went and asked him and he told me 'no' he didn't drive me up there. That left me completely in the dark; unable to complete the story in my own mind."

Crane's brief appearance before the Kefauver committee revealed very little about him, his circumstances or the pressure he was under.

However, in the Tax Court, the fifth telling of the tale of the occurrence that had no eyes or ears—that had no witnesses—took on a totally different shape. This time Crane told an entirely different story, full of embellishments and details. How come this strange change? It was "resurrected" for him by Wilders, a fellow fireman and an old schoolmate.

And according to their own testimony—this is how the resurrection came about.

One day in May, 1951, Crane met Wilders in Yonkers and took him for a walk around a reservoir. In the course of that walk, Wilders asked Crane whether the Gracie Mansion incident occurred on "the day I drove you up there," the day he "had an envelope with money in it." Crane remarked "that's the day," and was glad to know that Wilders "was the one that was with him."

The new story was substantially and briefly as follows: Jerry Finkelstein, Bill's campaign manager, had been soliciting a campaign contribution from Crane, who said that if he made a contribution, he would deliver it to Bill, in person. On October 10, 1949, Crane had three things in mind: he had to have his car serviced; he had to make a trip to Gracie Mansion; and he had to make a flight to St. Paul to attend a convention. That morning he took with him $10,000 which he had received from Dolan about four days prior and drove to the firehouse where Wilders was stationed to meet Wilders by appointment. They then drove to the Mezey Motors Service Station, where Wilders had some business dealing because he was having trouble with his car. Crane left the service station in Wilder's car but got out of it a block or two away to take a cab. Not finding one, Wilders invited him to get back into his car, offering to "drive him wherever he wanted to go." Crane accepted the offer, told Wilders to pick up Finkelstein, and then drive them to the mansion. In front of the mansion a woman was in the Mayor's car whom Finkelstein recognized and with whom he stopped to talk. Then, on the porch where a valet was helping Bill on with his coat, Crane gave Bill the envelope with the money and Bill, without examining it, tossed it to someone and left.

Whatever the shortcomings of the Tax Court and the strait-jacket regulations by which it is bound, in contradistinction to the Kefauver hearing, it did provide the opportunity for cross-examination. For centuries past, our system of law has recognized the absolute necessity of testing human statements by cross-examination. No other safeguard has been found to compare with it. It is a vital feature of our jurisprudence that no statement should be used or depended on as acceptable testimony until it has been *probed* and *sublimated* by the test of cross-examination. It is the greatest and most effective device ever invented for the discovery of the truth and the testing of any narrative. A story, particularly one told in answer to leading questions, assumes a different shape and different meaning after it is subjected to cross-examination.

Those who are familiar with the examination of witnesses know how extremely dangerous it is to act on the direct statement of any witness, and still more so of a witness who has been brought forward with such motives as Crane had. It is perfectly understandable that a witness in his direct examination discloses but a part of the necessary facts. What is undisclosed or suppressed may consist of qualifying circumstances, or facts which diminish the personal trustworthiness of the witness. Not infrequently, the witness is a partisan and interested in adopting his story to suit his purpose. Often the testimony is given only by way of answers to specific favorable questions. If nothing more were done to unveil all the facts known to the witness, his testimony might be half-truths or entirely false.

As often happens, the cross-examined witness supplies his own refutation. No witness or other intervention is necessary to show his unreliability. Our court records are full of examples of the dramatic contrasts between the original story told and the same tale as it appears after cross-examination.

Now, read the transcript of my cross-examination of Crane:

Q. You give us now answers to Mr. O'Toole's rather detailed information concerning the exact conversation on the step of Gracie Mansion with Finkelstein. Is that right?
Crane: Yes.
Q. And these are the details which you couldn't remember for a year and a half?
Crane: Yes.

****

Q. And about how many times did you appear before the grand jury?
Crane: Four or five times.
Q. And would you tell us over what period of time you appeared there?
Crane: I would say from January '51 to June or July '52.

392

Q. Now, in January of '51, did you appear two or three times within a period of a month or so?

Crane: Yes.

Q. And at that time did Mr. Scotti ask you how you got to Gracie Mansion?

Crane: That's right.

****

Q. Did he ask you if anybody accompanied you?

Crane: Yes, he did.

Q. And what did you tell him?

Crane: I don't recall what I told him.

Q. Well, did you tell him that Jerry Finkelstein went with you?

Crane: No, I did not.

Q. Did you mention Wilders' name or Finkelstein's name at the first session before the grand jury?

Crane: No, I did not.

Q. Were you asked about that?

Crane: Asked how I got there and if anybody was with me, yes.

Q. And you were asked if anybody was with you?

Crane: That's right.

Q. You mean by that that you responded that nobody was with you.

Crane: I responded that I could not recall how I got up there, that I had thought it was my brother who drove me up there, but my brother had denied it, and therefore, I was completely at sea on how I got up there and who was with me.

Q. But you came to the conclusion, you had a fixation in your mind, did you, at that time that your brother had come down and picked you up and driven you up?

Crane: That's right.

Q. That was your recollection of the incident, is that right?

Crane: That's right.

Q. Now, did you recall when you were before the grand jury and again before the Kefauver Committee, you had forgotten that Finkelstein had stepped out of the car and went in to make a telephone call, is that right?

Crane: I had never given it another thought.

Q. Well, had you had it in mind at the time?

Crane: No, I forgot it completely.

Q. You didn't remember it, did you?

Crane: It was just another incident of no consequence in my life.

****

Q. This was an important incident in your life, wasn't it, Mr. Crane? You were giving ten thousand dollars in cash to the Mayor of the town, isn't that so?

Crane: No; it was routine, as far as the U.F.A. is concerned.

****

Q. You remember walking right off the steps of Gracie Mansion with Finkelstein?

Crane: Yes.

Q. And you couldn't remember that before a year and a half, could you, until you and Wilders met . . .

Crane: I didn't think about it until I was called before the grand jury. At that time I could not recall it and was unable to.

Q. Let me ask you about Mr. Wilders. Did you go to school with him?

Crane: Yes, I did.

Q. Well now, are you a close friend of Wilders' today?

Crane: Yes.

Q. And have you been a close friend of his right along?

Crane: Yes.

Q. And would you go out of your way to help him?

Crane: If I could, yes.

Q. Would he go out of his way to help you?

Crane: I presume so.

Q. Now, would you tell us when it was that you first talked to Wilders and Wilders jogged your memory about having gone up there?

Crane: I would make a guess of early part of '51.

Q. And up to that time, is it a fair statement that you hadn't the foggiest notion of how you got up to Gracie Mansion?

Crane: That's right.

Q. Now, on what occasion, what was that?

Crane: That was up in Yonkers while walking around Hillview Reservoir.

Q. Around the Reservoir at Yonkers?

Crane: That's right.

Q. And it was there as you were walking around the Reservoir

394

with Mr. Wilders, that you first remembered all of the things, about Mr. Finkelstein getting out of the car and about Finkelstein talking to Miss Simpson and all of that?
Crane: It was the first time it was *resurrected*, yes.

****

Q. Now, Mr. Crane, going back to the incident where you and Wilders went around the Reservoir, you placed that in the month of May, 1951, I think?
Crane: That's right.
Q. Well, you didn't remember it all the first time, did you?
Crane: I did not remember all the details the first time, no.
Q. Did you talk to Wilders again?
Crane: Six or eight months later.
Q. And had you time to think about it in the meantime?
Crane: Yes.
Q. And did you between the time you first spoke to Wilders in May, 1951 and along about the fall of 1951, did you have a chance to mull it over in your mind to get all the details squared away?
Crane: A lot of them got squared away over a period of time.
Q. Will you tell the court how long it took to get all the pieces fitted together?
Crane: Some of them are still beginning to drop into place.

****

Q. Did you check with Finkelstein as you did with Wilders to find out if your memory might not be still a little faulty?
Crane: I was trying to tell you a . . .
Q. Did you do that, Mr. Crane? I don't want your speeches.
Crane: No, I did not.
Q. Now with respect to your conversation, I think you told Mr. O'Toole yesterday that you went to Terrence Dolan, the Treasurer, and you told him . . . what did you tell him?
Crane: I told him I wanted ten thousand dollars that week.
Q. And you didn't tell him the reason for it, did you?
Crane: No.
Q. Did you ever tell Dolan until after the Kefauver hearing what you did with the ten thousand dollars?
Crane: I don't think so, Mr. O'Dwyer.

Q. Were you asked for any additional tax by reason of your having received ten thousand dollars from Mr. Dolan in cash and not having turned over to anybody any receipt for it?

Crane: Well, I don't know how to answer that. I have been down before the Commission, discussed my personal finances with them. I went into detail on my assets and came up without any possible area of having that ten thousand dollars.

Q. What you are telling us is that when you got finished and they talked to you, they didn't attempt to assess you any taxes by reason of this cash, this cash that you had taken and given no receipt for?

Crane: That's right.

Q. How many times have they had you down there?

Crane: At least once beyond that.

Q. And was this with an idea of charging you further income tax?

Crane: That's right.

Q. Did you give them another statement, other than the one you gave on April 2?

Crane: Under oath like that, no.

Q. Was the other one typed or taken down in any way?

Crane: I don't know.

Q. Now, you knew at the time that you were taken down the second time, it was for the purpose of getting some more money from you for income tax, is that right?

Crane: I knew that it was my relationship with the Treasury Department that brought me down there. I don't know what their intentions were.

Q. And then it was that you gave them the second story that you are giving us now?

Crane: I gave them additional information, yes.

Q. Have you talked about your testimony and talked it over with Wilders?

Crane: Yes, I have.

Q. And when was that?

Crane: A few minutes ago.

Q. Did you talk about the testimony you were going to give here?

Crane: We talked about Wilders' participation in this particular incident. Yesterday, the day before, today.

Wilders on the same subject:

Q. When was the last time you spoke to Crane about this case particularly?

Wilders: About this case?

Q. Yes.

Wilders: The last time I spoke to him is about the time that the District Attorney called us down about it whenever that happened to be, 1951 or sometime around that time.

Crane's account of their meeting differed radically from his witness' account of how they got together.

Q. What arrangement did you make with Wilders?

Crane: To go over to Mezey Motors with me.

****

Q. Had you met him (Wilders) there by appointment?

Crane: Yes.

Q. Had you called him and said you wanted to meet him there?

Crane: That's right.

Wilders on the same subject:

Q. That morning, did he call you up ahead of time and tell you, "I am coming up there and I am going to leave my car with you"?

Wilders: He didn't. Not that morning.

****

Q. You mean you hadn't made any appointment to meet him there, did you?

Wilders: No definite appointment.

Q. Well, is there . . .

Wilders: No appointment. Let's say no appointment.

Q. No appointment. So that when you came to the place, to the firehouse, he was already there?

Wilders: That's right.

Q. And that was a surprise to you? You didn't expect him there?

Wilders: Well, no, I didn't. I didn't expect him to be there in person, that's right.

397

Q. Nor in spirit either, did you? You just didn't expect him to be there, isn't that true, Mr. Wilders?
Wilders: That's right. I didn't expect him to be there.

Crane testified his car was in need of repair and he needed Wilders to use his influence to see that he got a good repair job and that was why he brought Wilders along. Wilders testified it was a new car and was getting the usual thousand-mile service. The following is the testimony on the point:

Q. You were conducting business with respect to something to do with the transmission or ignition?
Crane: Yes.
Q. Something wrong with your car?
Crane: That's right.
Q. You were talking to the manager and the mechanic, I assume?
Crane: Well, the fellow that takes the car in anyway.
Q. And you were telling him what was the trouble with the car?
Crane: That's right.
Q. And you were asking him if he wouldn't fix it up and do something about it, is that right?
Crane: That's right.
Q. And you had Wilders there for a little muscle, did you?
Crane: A little influence, not muscle.
Q. And he was there to see that you got a good break and a good deal on the repair job?
Crane: Just that I got a good repair job.

Wilders testified on the same subject:
Q. Was his car, I gather from what you say that his car was able to be operated?
Wilders: That's right.
Q. It wasn't in a state . . .
Wilders: It was a new car in need of servicing, a thousand-mile service.

On the question of how Wilders happened to drive Crane to Gracie Mansion there were two diverse versions. Crane said it was not his intention to have Wilders drive him there. He said he left Wilders' car and waited for a cab, and not finding one, he accepted Wilders' invitation to drive him where he was going. Wilders testified that did not happen, that Crane never got out of his car.

Crane's testimony and that of Dolan, the treasurer, were in direct contradiction with respect to the important subject of Crane's request for the $10,000. Terrence Dolan explained that the U.F.A. was interested in the passage of the McNeill-Mitchell Bill which had nothing to do with City Hall but was in the hands of the Republican legislature and the Republican Governor; that in connection with the campaign for this bill, he withdrew over a period of time $30,000 in cash and gave it to Crane; that this sum was earmarked for the Albany bill; that it was not until more than a year later and then after some investigation had started as to the disposition of U.F.A. funds, that Crane claimed that he gave $10,000 to Bill; that the vouchers indicating the withdrawal of the $10,000 from the bank were marked as expenses for the McNeill-Mitchell Bill and that Crane never gave them any receipt for any of the money which he took.

Jerry Finkelstein testified before a New York grand jury on this subject. Mr. Finkelstein was and is a most responsible and respected business man. He was the editor of the *Civil Service Leader*, and the *Law Journal*; was chairman of the City Planning Commission and is now chairman of the Struthers Wells Corporation. The following testimony was given during contempt proceedings which resulted from his grand jury appearance:

> Q. Mr. Finkelstein, maybe this will refresh your memory. Don't you recall on the way over to Gracie Mansion you and Crane in the back, a third man driving, were discussing among other things Crane's contribution that he was going to make that very morning?
> Finkelstein: I certainly do not.
> Q. Don't you recall telling Crane, "I'd rather have you give it to him, Jack."
> Finkelstein: I certainly do not. That's absolutely untrue.
> Q. You deny that?
> Finkelstein: I certainly do completely.

****

> Q. Don't worry about terminology. We are interested in facts. Now, you don't recall that Crane in the car was discussing with you his political contribution he was making, or about to make, to Mr. O'Dwyer?
> Finkelstein: I certainly don't remember that.

Q. Well, do you deny that, or do you say it could have happened, but you have no recollection of it?
Finkelstein: I am certain that it did not happen.
Q. Now, do you recall telling Crane, "I'd rather have you give it to him, Jack"?
Finkelstein: I absolutely deny that.
Q. You deny that.
Finkelstein: Absolutely. I would certainly remember that.

Judge Valente, who presided at the contempt hearing, questioned him further:

Q. You say, Mr. Finkelstein, unequivocally, that at no time Crane went to your home and upon leaving your home entered a car with you, driven by a third man with a hearing aid and proceeded to Gracie Mansion, Crane and yourself getting out of the car, Crane going up the steps of Gracie Mansion. You remaining down on the base of the stairs, Crane in the meantime in conference with O'Dwyer within your view. You say unequivocally that these events as recited by the Court and now incorporated in my question never happened?
Finkelstein: They never happened.

****

Judge Valente: I ask you this question, Mr. Finkelstein, did Mr. Crane visit your home in the month of October, 1949, with a large manila envelope? Wait for you to dress in your apartment and did you then leave with him and enter a car with Mr. Crane that was parked at 96th Street and Park Avenue and drive in that car, which was driven by a fireman wearing a hearing aid to Gracie Mansion and following your arrival there, did you see Mr. Crane alone with Mr. O'Dwyer on the porch of Gracie Mansion?
Finkelstein: I did not.

When O'Toole examined the other assessments he knew that there was no way he could sustain the Treasury Department's claim of unreported income in the amount of $15,650.48. He immediately abandoned $14,156.48 of that item.

The next item had to do with the day-to-day expenses incurred by the Ambassador. It had been the custom from time immemorial to allow the Ambassador to deduct whatever expenditures were made over and above the limited allowance provided by the government. Men of wealth who traditionally held such posts had no problem in having massive deductions allowed. When I discussed this arbitrary decision with O'Toole I offered to be bound by the same rule which was applied to the tax return of Joseph Kennedy when he was Ambassador to the Court of St. James. No effort was made to take me up on that challenge or to demonstrate how wealthy ambassadors' returns were treated. It became plain to Judge Raum that he would have to agree with my position. He allowed expenditures of $1,957.31 in 1950 and $7,857.50 in 1951 to be deducted from the taxable income.

The end result was a reduction in the tax bill from $20,532 to $8,242.12. I had saved $12,298.88, but what was more significant was I was able to show that the Treasury Department had attempted to extract 40% more in taxes than they were entitled to according to the decision of a judge coming out of their own stable.

In the part that I found crucial, however, Judge Raum denied me the right to examine the file nor would he review the testimony of the taxpayer taken under oath by one of the government examiners.

The court's decision was handed down on November 21, 1957. I attempted to get the records through an appeal to the Circuit Court of Appeals which I argued in Richmond, Virginia. That court again denied me the right to review the government files. I made an application to have the case reviewed on constitutional grounds by the Supreme Court. The Court refused to review the case and I could take it no further. That was the end of the road. A month after they levied on his $12,000 a year pension from the City of New York. All that took place in 1957.

Many years later the Freedom of Information Act was passed. In January 1978 I wrote to the Treasury Department and the I.R.S. for the files. At that time Bill had been dead for 14 years. On January 20th I received an acknowledgement of my request from Victor Rickey, Chief, Section I, Freedom of Information Branch, in which he advised that he had sent the request to the District Director for New York. I did not get a reply from the New York District Director, so I called him. He said I could not get the information because I was not the executor of the estate. I wrote on February 13, 1978:

In the instant case a Will had been drawn and I was named Executor and Sole Distributee. Inasmuch as the size of the estate did not warrant a probate proceeding, I simply filed the Will and submitted the necessary information to the State Department of Taxation and Finance, New York State. The tax was fixed at $114.87 and was paid.

I enclosed a xerox copy of the Will and a photocopy of the receipt from the State of New York. Nothing happened until October 31, 1978, when I received a letter telling me how to go about getting the information I was seeking and what forms I must fill out. It was headed Department of the Treasury and was signed by Linda K. Zannetti, Chief, Disclosure Staff.

In compliance I sent a lengthy affidavit describing my brother and his career in and out of the service of the United States Government.

On December 4, 1978, I received a letter from Mr. Stanley Stein, Chief, Section II, Freedom of Information Branch, which enclosed copies of the law. On December 5, 1978, I received a letter from the Secret Service Department to which there was attached the order of F.D.R. in 1932 fixing the price of gold, and Secretary of the Treasury Morgenthau's note promulgating the order.

Finally, on December 6, 1978, I received a letter from Robert Vayda:

> Your letters, dated November 10 and November 14, 1978, requesting copies of all materials pertaining to your brother, William O'Dwyer and yourself have been referred to the Office of the Assistant Secretary for Enforcement and Operations for processing. Your requests were made under the Freedom of Information Act, as amended, and the Privacy Act.
>
> Please be advised that we have caused a thorough file search for information relevant to their request and have been unable to find any materials pertaining to your brother or yourself.
>
> Please contact me if I may be of any further assistance in this matter.

On December 21, 1978, I replied to Mr. Vayda:

> I have your letter of December 5th and I am not clear as to whether the communication is meant to deal with the Internal Revenue Service. If it does, it seems there is something wrong. Both my brother and I signed and submitted a Net Worth Statement back in about 1950 when a very intensive investigation was being conducted by the Intelligence Unit and the Auditors of the same. The investigation was completed under the Truman Administration, was reopened under the Eisenhower Administration on direct orders from Coleman Andrews. It covered various parts of the United States and Mexico. It took five years in all to complete the investigation and it involved the expenditure of over $750,000.00.

Knowing the purpose of a Net Worth Statement, I do not feel it easy to accept the fact that your department has difficulty in locating the file of these proportions.

On January 12, 1979, Stein said they were still looking. Finally, on February 13, 1979, Stein writes:

This refers to your letter dated December 21, 1978, in which you furnished additional information that might help us to locate the file that you are seeking.

We regret that we have not been able to locate any such file. We have searched in all possible areas, and we still do not find anything. In view of the age of the records, we presume that they must have been destroyed in accordance with normal records disposition procedures.[1]

On June 16, 1982, the Treasury Department wrote to deny access to the file implying that I was seeking "the taxpayer's tax return." They also called for documentary support of my identity. This time the letter was signed by a Tax Law Specialist, Public Services Branch.

On July 19, 1982, I received another letter from Miss Greenwell, the Tax Law Specialist, to the effect that they received some information from the F.B.I. which is exempt and I cannot have it. Also enclosed were two letters which I had sent to them two years earlier. One was a letter from Treasury Department to John Edgar Hoover, dated May 9, 1952:

Dear Mr. Hoover:

Receipt is acknowledged of your letter dated April 22, 1952, addressed to the Secretary of the Treasury, transmitting a photostatic copy of an anonymous communication dated February 5, 1952, addressed to former Special Assistant to the Attorney General Newbold Morris, relating to possible evasion of income taxes by Ambassador William O'Dwyer.

This matter will receive appropriate attention.

Very truly yours,
Frank W. Lohn
Chief, Intelligence Division

---

1. Mr. Stein did not reveal to me at what point records are destroyed, but my brother's file forwarded from the Passport Office contained papers dating back 50 years.

Exasperated, on July 21, 1982, four and a half years after my first request, I wrote to the Commissioner of Internal Revenue:

I am enclosing a copy of a communication signed by Miss Patricia A. Greenwell and dated July 19, 1982, and I appeal from this and all previous decisions which in any way denies access to the information I have sought under the appropriate provisions of law. If a further argument is necessary in connection with this matter, I will be glad to supply it.

I find it difficult to understand why, after so long a period of time has elapsed, it is necessary to withhold any information which in any way makes reference to my late brother who, in his lifetime and by personal appointment of two Presidents of the United States, held the offices of Minister to Italy, Ambassador to Mexico and General in the Army of the U.S.

That was the end of the search. Reports of five years of the most diligent and intensive investigative activity by successive agents of the Treasury Department, the most efficient of the Intelligence Units of the Internal Revenue Service, had disappeared from the face of the earth and no trace of them could be found. So I was expected to believe. Of course, I didn't. I believe that a decision had been reached by high-ranking officials to violate the Freedom of Information Act, to deny access to documents which would have exposed a scandal of major proportions and have brought the I.R.S. and other government agencies into disrepute.

When at a later time I received reports from the State Department I found an exchange of memoranda from no less a person than the Acting Secretary of the Treasury Marion B. Folsom to John Foster Dulles and a reply to George M. Humphrey, Secretary of the Treasury, and signed by Donold B. Lourie, Under Secretary for Administration.

The letter from the Acting Secretary of the Treasury contained the following allegation:

It is stated in the letter that during the time Mr. O'Dwyer was the Ambassador to Mexico (September 1, 1950 to December 7, 1952), he transferred large sums of money between Mexico City and various points in the United States, using the State Department as transfer agent.

Folsom's letter was signed in 1953. The incident to which reference was made had been publicly laid to rest on August 4, 1951, two years earlier, and it was from John Edgar Hoover himself that the memorandum emanated:

> Subject: Ambassador William O'Dwyer
>
> With reference to the phone call from the Bureau to yourself relative to the transfer of $1,000,000 from the Banco de Mexico to the Chase National Bank in the name of Ambassador William O'Dwyer, you are advised that the State Department has informed that this transaction was a payment for lend-lease goods made by the Mexican Government and was a legitimate official Government transaction.

The more the government came to a dead end by following informers' leads, the more they spread the lies around till they polluted various departments.

The exchange of memoranda came from the State Department files. It was hard to believe that the same exchange coming from so high a level could not be found in the Treasury Department.

When information which would reflect on an agency is demanded, the simplest way to handle the demand is to make the documents disappear. Even President Nixon, hard-pressed though he was, did not do that. The tapes which he could have easily caused to be destroyed were not. Underlings, however, had no such compunctions.

CHAPTER 49

PRIVATE CITIZEN

PO'D

Following his resignation as Ambassador, Bill led a generally quiet and pleasant life in Mexico. He had a great affection for the country and its people and enjoyed his continuing opportunity to live and work among them.

Oscar and Becky Bernstien had spent many summers in Mexico and had become friendly with the Correas, a well-established, old and much respected Mexican family. In 1950 its aging leader was the head of a most prestigious law firm that represented many business interests in Mexico at about the time Bill was leaving his post. Oscar brought us together with Jorge, the youngest of the Correa sons, who at that time had the urge to strike out on his own. The law firm of O'Dwyer, Bernstien & Correa was formed and its office was on the top floor of the prestigious No. 1 Passeo de la Reforma, an avenue that had become the pride of the republic.

The firm failed to attract the more affluent American and Mexican business and yet it prospered, and from 1950 to 1960 it was the stopping-off point for many Americans from the West Coast as well as the New York area. North American politicians who could not resist the urge to learn how politics and government worked in Mexico also came by to talk with the man who was by now equally at home on either side of the border. And business flowed from those contacts, but it was sporadic. In a way the Mexican office had much in common with the New York office. Each depended on a wide acquaintanceship within its own environment. The number of Mexicans and resident foreigners who visited Bill was extraordinarily high. Indeed, life in Mexico was, for the former Ambassador, full of interesting things to do and lively people became part of his existence and he was in every sense a part of it.

The lifestyle of the Mexican professional or middle-class business people differed in many respects from that of their New York counterparts. New Yorkers are inclined to live in city apartments. In Mexico

City the preference is for a house. Upon taking his place in the business and professional life of Mexico, Bill followed the living pattern of his Mexican contemporaries and in due course he found a house for rent and to his liking in a quiet suburb. It was on a one-acre plot and in true Mexican fashion a housekeeper and a gardener came as part of the arrangement. To an American this was a luxury which was simply not attainable at home.

The Mexican housekeeper procured some ducks and a drake, a few hens, a rooster and a couple of geese and a gander. Maybe the idea was very Mexican or maybe it was a gesture to this Irishman, who loved them and who was admired, respected and loved in return, which was meant to bring him close to the familiar scene of his childhood in Ireland. If that was the intent, the effort was a failure. The fowl maintained a reasonably peaceful co-existence between themselves, but the geese and the gander longed for the day their wings would once again gain the strength to rise far above the city. Their discontent at having been domesticated and even confined by an eight foot concrete wall of the type that surrounded every affluent Mexican home was made known in their hourly complaints. The master of the house had become so accustomed to New York living that the song of the geese, so limited in range, and hoarse quacking of the ducks, far from giving him a sense of well-being and tranquility as the housekeeper had intended, merely irritated. The hen's incessant clucking after laying and mating was no help and the boastful rooster, crowing at the very break of day, did nothing to endear this misplaced New Yorker to the new life he had deliberately chosen.

Furthermore, his house was quite a distance from the center of town and he was frequently alone. Pancho Buck de Parada and his wife came frequently to dinner. They discovered his mood. It so happened they owned the Prince Hotel, a small modest-priced establishment right across from the Alameda (Mexico's famous park on Avenida Juarez) and within walking distance of his office on Reforma and near the Belles Artes (the stylish old showpiece and home of many cultural events). The Paradas were delighted with the prospect of having this interesting and lovable Irish American staying at their place. They went to great expense to fix up an apartment on the roof where he was the only tenant. In his constant walks he could now, to his heart's content, circle the chimneys and the airvents. Here in this convenient, quiet and unpretentious place he could entertain his friends, and he did.

To this place came the most renowned exponents of Mexico's fine and performing arts. Diego Rivera, whose work compared favorably with the world's greatest painters, and Dolores Del Rio, as admired in her advancing years as she had been in the days of youthful stardom, the world-renowned comedian Cantinflas came there to chat, sometimes in English, mostly in Spanish. Frequently Mexico's most admired musical composer, Augustin Lara, and journalist, author and artist, Pepe Romero, spent hours "on the roof." Pepe had spent his youth in the United States and was now Mexico's chief interpreter of the United States. He wrote of Mexico's northern neighbor often with criticism and always with sympathetic understanding. Romero frequently attempted to explain our confused politics and inconsistent foreign policy which fairly baffled Mexicans.

Then there were the journalists and the columnists from *Excelsior* and the other dailies and magazines, who seemed to feel in Bill a kindred spirit whom they admired for his detailed knowledge of such things as the history of the Aztec heroes, some of whom were destroyed by Cortez. Juan O'Gorman, whose family came from Ireland direct to Mexico a generation earlier, was his friend. In the eyes of the American Embassy, the President of the United States, F.B.I. and I.R.S., almost all of these creative people were rated as Communists, high up in the ranks, conspirators against the U.S. aiding and abetting our enemies. Government officials who had come from the United States where the hysteria had virtually brought a halt to the creative writer and artist, could never quite understand how the Mexican government could give such a high rating to such men as O'Gorman, Rivera and Siqueiros and could at times harbor political refugees from the United States.

Among the American friends who visited were Barry Goldwater and his wife Peggy. A friendship grew between Bill and the Goldwaters. Since their views were so divergent it was difficult to understand their friendship. This was particularly true since some of the refugees from Hollywood, victims of the House Un-American Activities Committee, were working in Mexico surreptitiously for the film industry and were Bill's friends and clients. Hollywood had suffered greatly as a result of the blacklist which the forces of hysteria had imposed on the most creative writers, artists and technicians in one of the most important industries in the United States. In order to survive, the film industry was compelled to resort to subterfuge to get appropriate scripts from these talented Americans who had sought refuge in various parts of the Mexican republic. John Bright spent many hours with Bill going over writings which were eagerly awaited by Hollywood producers. Bright wrote under a nom de plume.

The PRI party in Mexico has been the ruling political organization since the last revolution. Many of its leaders had known Bill from visits to Gracie Mansion or City Hall while he was Mayor. He was welcomed by them when he arrived in Mexico as U.S. Ambassador. They were frequent visitors to the embassy and later to his home and they met at Mexico's great social events where they exchanged opinions on current events in Latin America as well as Mexico and the U.S. Bill was an avid reader of history and the story of Mexico during the centuries before its conquest by the Spaniards fascinated him. His intimate knowledge of the culture of Mexico and his friendship with the men and women of letters and the arts, gave him the reputation of being the best informed American on the Mexican scene.

The Ambassador succeeding Bill made a serious blunder. Bill's standing with the Mexican people irked him and in a fit of pique he ordered Bill's name off the list of those invited to embassy functions. That act made him less than acceptable to the people and he was treated with politeness and nothing more by the officialdom of Mexico. His stay was short. He was succeeded by Robert Hill, who had been quite active in Republican politics in his home state of Vermont.

When Hill arrived in Mexico, he presented his credentials, as was required, to the President of the republic. While he had been briefed extensively by the State Department in preparation for taking up his post in Mexico, he felt that further briefing in Mexico would be useful. With the good sense of a politician who had been through the grind, he decided that a suggestion from the President of the country to which he was assigned would be the fastest route he could take to the fulfillment of his mission. It was an approach which shocked the professionals with the embassy and the State Department. "I would be very pleased, Mr. President," the new Ambassador explained, "if you would have your State Department recommend some member of your government or a professor at your university, who could aid me in a better understanding of Mexico. As our President's representative here, I do want my stay here to be marked with the most serious effort to maintain the kind of communication that will ensure continued goodwill between my country and this republic." The President seemed amused and his response made it clear that politics was not a lost art in Mexico and that he was one of its most able practitioners. He paused briefly and responded. "I appreciate your own personal good intentions so frankly expressed. The man who has proven his capacity in this same respect and has done more for his country than any predecessor is living here. He held your post for only a brief period and all Mexico holds him in high esteem. If you have not met him, I suggest you do so. It would be inappropriate for me to make the introduction, but I suggest you contact him directly. I know you will find him most cooperative." A few days later Ambassador Hill called to make an appointment and hardly a week passed during his stay in Mexico that did not see the two men conferring.

By 1960, our Mexican office was not doing well. Neither Oscar nor I had the time to go down there as frequently as we should have and we felt that we would be able to do better if Bill were in New York with us. In the meantime, many of the people he had known in Mexico were no longer around and he agreed to return to our offices in the Wall Street area.

In preparation for his coming I shopped around for an apartment and was not able to get a suitable one. He stayed for a while at the St. Moritz and the bills that came to the office were all out of line with the rather modest living standards of Oscar Bernstien and myself. But we could not break his habit of picking up the check of someone who visited him at the hotel and who usually was in a much better position to pay the bill than he was. He was a former mayor, a former general and a former ambassador and it was assumed he was well off. Furthermore, he had his pride and it would not permit him to have anyone pay his bill. So he invariably paid his table companions' tab as well as his own. Finally, I bought a cooperative apartment from a man who had used it for business and wanted to dispose of it. Co-ops were cheap and I closed the deal for $22,500. It was in a 15-story building on Park Avenue, 25 feet wide, with one apartment to a floor and an elevator which was less than roomy. He had the top floor and I thought it was ideal for a bachelor.

He liked the apartment, that is, until Sloane came by to visit him. "It is dark and dreary," she complained in a voice that showed much irritation. "It is not an appropriate place for a man of his sensitivity and stature," she continued. I argued, but it did no good. She hired an interior decorator. It cost our firm $8,000. Now it was my turn to be irritated. "Why don't you find out where the money is coming from," I asked in a tone I reserved for opposing lawyers. She became defensive. "He told me he had a client who was about to retain the firm from which a substantial fee would come." "Sure," I said, trying to control the sarcasm. "We have them every day. Besides, you lived with him and you know how he can dream," and that's where the discussion ended. The firm paid the bill. Bill did not enter into the discussion between Sloane and myself.

When the decorator was finished Bill did not like the apartment any better. Living on Park Avenue had no special meaning for him. He liked the new apartment buildings on East 57th Street and decided this time to forego advice and suggestions from both Sloane and myself. The building he chose was owned by the Rudin family. The receptionist was puzzled when a man presenting himself as William O'Dwyer said he wanted to look at an apartment in the building at 300 East 57th Street. The name sounded familiar to her and she felt she ought to check. Lewis Rudin came out to see for himself. "Please come in, Mr. Mayor," he said. "How can we serve you?" Years later Rudin told me of his surprise, if not bewilderment, since he expected the former Mayor to ask for a

Photo courtesy of Brooklyn Public Library/Brooklyn Eagle Collection
United Press Photo

Visiting with former President Harry S. Truman in Kansas City, Missouri, 1954

special rate. There was no special rate requested and none given.

He came every day to the office and seemed to relish associating with Oscar and with the O'Dwyer tribe that had joined the firm. He had suffered from time to time from a heart ailment, but he was able to live with it and his diversion was a weekly visit to Toots Shor's where he would meet and dine with the Runyonesque characters who frequented the place and whose company he enjoyed.

On November 24, 1964, I was on my way to City Hall (I was then New York City Councilman at Large from Manhattan) when I heard Bill had been taken ill. The doorman at his apartment said he had gone by ambulance to Beth Israel Hospital. He had declined the proffered help and walked from the door to the ambulance. He was not in pain when I saw him in the hospital a half hour later and he seemed in good spirits. *"Zei go szunt,"* he said as I left him. *"Zei me go szunt,"* I replied. A Jewish doctor assigned to him hearing the exchange, concluded that he was going into the wrong room. The salutation and response were in Yiddish and can be roughly translated as "Be healthy" and "You be healthy." However, before I got to City Hall he had a massive attack. He died later that day. I went to his apartment. His "dog tags" were there where I could find them. We had never discussed death or burial, but the Army identification was the signal. He would be buried in Arlington with the full military ritual.

Sloane arrived for a visit to New York on the day of Bill's death. It was a coincidence. At the funeral, Frank Durkan, our nephew, escorted her from St. Patrick's Cathedral to the waiting limousine. In his years in New York Bill had never been short of attractive female companions, each of whom was given an honored place at the funeral mass and was accompanied down the steps of the cathedral by a nephew.

We chartered a plane to take us to Washington and all the family went, that is, all except Joan. She was pregnant and stayed behind in terror. She explained her feelings as a plane loaded with all who were dear to her on earth became airborne. She was glued to the radio fearful of the news she might hear. Relief came only with the news of our return.

When my brother's body arrived in Washington, the Army took over. The horse with the empty saddle was led along the Roosevelt Drive to the open grave on the side of the hill overlooking the Kennedy sepulcher. A special division of the Army trained to perform the burial service conducted the ritual similar to the one that half the world viewed on television a year earlier on the day of President Kennedy's funeral. The cannon was fired and the brass shells were ejected, the American flag which had draped the coffin was neatly folded and ceremoniously handed to me as his next of kin. It was a gesture of recognition for his dedication to his adopted country at a time when his talents were needed. It was a touching performance and while our family had over the years become insensitive to rituals, we were deeply moved.

EPILOGUE

Bill had led a good life with a full share of excitement. We had suffered some indignities at the hands of former colleagues, but Bill had accepted them as the price one pays for becoming involved in the unusual happenings of his time. He was well aware that I had insisted on carrying on a running fight with the I.R.S. and did not discourage the effort. We had scored partial success in our opposition to politicians within that Service. He shared my frustration when the Tax Court, the U.S. Circuit Court of Appeals or the Supreme Court refused to grant me the right to inspect the I.R.S. files which they said established a tax liability of $8,000.

It is the custom of each newspaper office and television station to keep an obituary file on prominent people which records the most interesting aspect of their lives, while they are still alive, so that the reporter assigned to write the obituary story will have all the material at hand. Jim Clarity, then writing for the *Herald Tribune,* and now with the *New York Times* Washington Bureau, expanded on what was available in the files. His short account of Bill's life and death was considered Pulitzer Prize material. But some of the most interesting aspects of Bill's life were not then available. They were hidden deep in the files of our government bureaus to await a day when the lid could be lifted and the behavior of a hidden government revealed.

As it turned out it may have been a blessing that the government files were not laid bare during his lifetime. Up to the day of his death he was blissfully ignorant of the fact that forces within the government, even more powerful than the Revenue Service, had conspired to injure him. Some of that information was received by me many years afterwards when the Freedom of Information Act made access to those records possible. Taking advantage of the passage of that legislation, I was about to obtain at least part of those files which covered the two decades before his death. They were the dark, mean, suspicious years during which zealot or knave, or both, literally created an eroding atmosphere of suspicion and fear in our country.

If my brother had real enemies, he seemed not to be aware of it.

He wrote off the temporary antagonistic behavior of political opponents as if it had never happened. He was aware of the efforts of the politicians within the tax services to create a tax evasion charge against him. But he would be deeply hurt to know that J. Edgar Hoover had pursued much more vigorously every lead in an effort to destroy him, but much worse, that even cabinet members of the government he had served so faithfully had willingly joined in an effort to harm him.

In the post-World War I period President Woodrow Wilson appointed a man named A. Mitchell Palmer as Attorney General. He conducted a vicious campaign against people, mostly aliens, whom he suspected of being disloyal to the United States. Before the nightmare ended many reputations had been shattered and honorable citizens maligned without reason.

In the wake of World War II a similar situation prevailed. The activities of Senator Joe McCarthy, the House Committee on Un-American Activities, and other members of Congress resulted in abnormal and unreasonable suspicion about the loyalty of thousands of Americans. The first victims were people in the arts and the entertainment world and it carried over to education where its victims were counted in the thousands. Members of Congress, who could normally be expected to resist this onslaught, seemed to be congealed with fear and few had the courage to stand before this lynchlike force.[1] Legislative bodies across the country enacted the most disgraceful, repressive legislation.[2] Most of them were later repealed, but not before much harm was done.

Even President Harry S. Truman, whose record on civil rights had been commendable, became caught up in the atmosphere of fear and uncertainty which by that time had enveloped the country. He promulgated an executive order which put in question the loyalty of thousands and thousands of government employees. It was the signal for a wholesale inquisition. Faithful government workers, many of them among the lowest paid, were brought in for questioning about such things as their social life. One of the standard questions asked of white employees was, "Do you now or did you ever entertain Negroes in your home?"

There was a provision allowing suspects to have their own lawyers at bureaucratic hearings. However, if lawyers sought to take notes, the

---

1. At one time a radio station sought to feature a debate between Joseph McCarthy and another member of the House or Senate. Only one person responded. A Congressman offered to pick up the gauntlet. His name was Eugene McCarthy, a college professor and a Congressman from Minnesota.
2. New York's Feinberg Law attacked schoolteachers suspected of being Communists or fellow travellers and many in the teaching profession were discharged from their employment. In 1977, as President of the City Council, I helped to get compensation for such of the victims who were still alive 25 years later.

papers on which the notes were written were forcibly taken from them as they left the room.

Fear was struck into the hearts of government employees. When I tried the Martin Popper case for contempt of the House Committee on Un-American Activities during that period, we found it virtually impossible to select an impartial jury. The case was tried in the U.S. District Court in the District of Columbia. The vast majority of the jury panel were government employees and they were apparently frightened to near death. They feared the consequence to them should they vote acquittal in that most political of cases. In the Popper case the jury returned with a guilty verdict in less than an hour. The conviction was reversed by the Circuit Court of Appeals. It was never retried.

The files of the House Committee on Un-American Activities were filled with unsubstantiated data taken from many mentally unbalanced letter writers and bizarre accusations. Lacking was any semblance of an effort to check the veracity of the charges. Copies of these documents provided J. Edgar Hoover with memoranda to put in his files.

The investigators wallowed in the sensational publicity which the accusations generated. Inference was piled on inference and there seemed to be no end to the progression. Suspicion and accusation spread in an everwidening circle. It was only McCarthy's temerity in embarking into an investigation into the U.S. Army and his accusation against Eisenhower's close friend, General George Marshall, that succeeded in bringing him into disfavor with the President.

LOYALTY

I was well aware that the I.R.S. had been used to do my brother harm, but I had no idea, until it was exposed as a result of their partial compliance with my demand under the Freedom of Information Act, how the other agencies—the F.B.I., the State Department, the C.I.A. and the Passport Division—had cooperated with each other to destroy him. Jointly and severally they sought to impugn his loyalty to the United States, to charge him with being a kingpin of gambling syndications, and to indict him for perjury as a result of his testimony before the Kefauver committee. With the aid of a United States Senator, whom they sought to protect from exposure, they sought to rob him of his citizenship, his most prized possession.

Hoover's interest in William O'Dwyer started on the day he became Mayor and Paul Ross was appointed to his post as assistant to the Mayor with an office in City Hall adjoining the Mayor's. That attention to William O'Dwyer, the Mayor, and William O'Dwyer, the Ambassador, and William O'Dwyer, the private citizen, was not relaxed practically up to his death at age 74. There was nothing original in any of the F.B.I.'s inquiries. For the most part the information listed in Bill's file came from sources outside the Bureau and were by and large hearsay. Reports from an "informer of known reliability" or an "informant of unknown reliability" or one who was found "at times to be reliable" and at other times "unreliable" made up a substantial part of the file. In addition, there were numerous references to news articles in the *Daily Worker* (whose ownership and staff would, I'm sure, have been highly amused to know how much reliance Hoover placed in their reporting). In the case of my brother's associations, pronouncements and public appearances, the *Daily Worker* was relied upon much more than the *New York Times*, the *Post*, the *Daily News*, the Scripps Howard or the Hearst chain.

Reference was made to another source of information—anonymous letters, some with obvious bias and some plain gossip. All of these were accepted, placed on file and contributed to the Director's assessment of O'Dwyer, "the subject." Charges made by political opponents at campaign time became a part of the "derogatory information" in the file which ultimately was sent to the White House by way of the Civil Service Commission. All were meant to convince the White House that an investigation as to O'Dwyer's loyalty by the bureau was warranted. It was in this fashion that Hoover kept officials under his control. After the derogatory information was forwarded, even the President could not afford to ignore the information, nor could he conclude that a check into the loyalty of a man who had conversations with Harry Dexter White and Vito Marcantonio was above suspicion. The fact that he had by now been decorated by the Italian, the French and the American governments cut no ice.

In addition to all the reports concerning Bill's supposed contacts with Communists, there was considerable material in the F.B.I. files on his attitudes toward crime and possible involvement in criminal activities, especially gambling.

The "derogatory" information in the F.B.I. file, which served as the basis for the loyalty investigation, included numerous items. The following is a long, but by no means complete, listing of these items and gives some insight into the quality of the information that had been gathered.

—The House Committee on Un-American Activities had shown the influence of the Communist Party on the American Labor Party which in turn supported O'Dwyer, then the Democratic candidate for Mayor of New York (1945).

—"An informant of unknown reliability" revealed that in December

1940 the names of William O'Dwyer and Paul O'Dwyer of 26 Court Street, Brooklyn, N.Y., were maintained in the active roles of the National Federation for Constitutional Liberties which the Attorney General said was within the purview of Executive Order 9835.

—"A reliable confidential informant" told the New York office of the F.B.I. that Paul Ross was the head of the Communist Party in New York. Subsequently, "an informant who had supplied reliable and unreliable" information and Louis Budenz, a well known informer, reported that Ross was a secret member of the Communist Party.

—On August 1, 1945 the New York office of the Bureau was told that a man having something to do with the New Masses cited by the H.U.A.C. as a Communist Front organization, gave O'Dwyer's name as a reference on a Personal Security Questionnaire.

—Tammany Democratic organization designated as its nominee for member of the City Council one Eugene P. Connolly, a book salesman whom the F.B.I. described as "another notorious Communist Party Line follower." "O'Dwyer never did repudiate the endorsement of Connolly and became cautiously silent for five days when Tammany designated Communist Party official Ben Davis, and never made a direct repudiation."

—William Foster, National Chairman of the Communist Party, U.S.A., on September 18, 1945, proclaimed he was in support of O'Dwyer (for Mayor) when he said, "The people of New York must elect the ALP ticket all along the line, etc." O'Dwyer was endorsed by the American Labor Party.

—The *Daily Worker* on November 12, 1945, published an article which revealed that at the annual conference of American Slav Congress of Greater New York messages of support were received from a number of individuals including Mayor-Elect William O'Dwyer. The American Slav Congress was on the Attorney General's list.

—A meeting was held in Madison Square Garden of the American Committee of Jewish Writers, Artists and Scientists Incorporated on December 9, 1946, according to the *Daily Worker*, and O'Dwyer sent the organization a message of welcome.

—O'Dwyer's brother, Paul O'Dwyer, in February 1952, presided over the Civil Liberties Panel of the National Lawyers Guild in the Book Cadillac Hotel in Detroit, and that he was the President of the New York Chapter of the National Lawyers Guild. The National Lawyers Guild was cited by H.U.A.C. as a Communist Front organization on March 29, 1944. A man whose name was blotted out made application for admission to the bar in 1947 and gave Paul O'Dwyer's name as a reference.

—A meeting took place between O'Dwyer and left-wing M.C. Representative Vito Marcantonio at Harvey's Restaurant in Washington, D.C., and later they went to the farm of Julius Lully, the proprietor of Harvey's.

—"They had no proof that Paul O'Dwyer was a member of the Communist Party, but the Communist Party attempted to use his favorable attitude towards the Communist Party to influence William O'Dwyer to be friendly to the Communists and to look favorably on the Communist Party."

—"Paul O'Dwyer was listed as a member of the Testimonial Committee given by the Voice of Freedom Committee on March 3, 1949 in New York. This Committee was cited as a Communist Front in the 5th Report on Un-American Activities in California in 1949."

—An article from the *Daily Worker*, September 1947 quoted (William) O'Dwyer as "opposed to witchhunts."

—O'Dwyer attacked the Mundt Bill in 1948 at the meeting of Amalgamated Clothing Workers Union in Atlantic City. Catholic War Veterans demanded an explanation from Mayor O'Dwyer (May 13, 1948) for his stand in opposition to the Mundt Nixon Bill.

—The record contained an extract from the *Christian Science Monitor* of December 3, 1947: "Mayor O'Dwyer resists bid to purge Communists." The story in part reads as follows: "Mayor William O'Dwyer has placed himself on record as opposed to the discharge of New York City employees who are Communists solely on the basis of their political connections.

—The May 2, 1948, issue of *Counterattack* charged that Mayor William O'Dwyer had authorized the Civil Rights Congress to have their tag days April 29-30, May 1st and the Joint Anti-Fascist Committee to have their tag days May 20-21-22. Both organizations were on the Attorney General's list as subversive societies.

—On April 17, 1943, Lt. Col. William O'Dwyer was a guest of honor at a dinner held under the auspices of the American Committee for the Protection of the Foreign Born which the Attorney General had proclaimed to be a disloyal group.

—"A confidential informant of known reliability advised that in June 1945 O'Dwyer told a Liberal Party official that 'he would not repudiate the Communist Party and would make no statement to the public repudiating the Communist endorsements.' "

—"A confidential informant of known reliability advised that the Communist Party felt that O'Dwyer, though not a Communist, would be friendly and Paul O'Dwyer would exercise strong influence on his brother (Louis Budenz)."

—The *Daily Worker*, May 30, 1946, said O'Dwyer was one of the speakers at the National Council of American Soviet Friendship.

—George Silverman, "according to an informant of known reliability," said O'Dwyer offered him a job at $7,500 per annum. Elizabeth Bentley said Silverman was part of the espionage team headed by Nathan George Silvermaster.

—A reliable informant "told the F.B.I. that on June 1, 1947, O'Dwyer sent greetings to the 1st Convention of the United Negro and Allied Vets of America which was on the Attorney General's list."

—Alex Rose, head of the Liberal Party, according to the *New York Times*, said O'Dwyer repudiated Communism in the abstract but "did business with New York City Communists."

—Paul O'Dwyer represented Duncan Paris Veterans Post which was thrown out by the American Legion as Communist dominated.

—Paul O'Dwyer represented Ben Gold, president of the Fur & Leather Workers Union, who was alleged to be a Communist Party member.

The report also reveals an official pursuit of my brother, Frank O'Dwyer, a farmer in El Centro, California, and his family. "He and his two brothers," the report noted, "William and Paul, were contributing to the support of Joan O'Dwyer, a niece, 15 years and an orphan."

On July 8, 1952, Assistant Attorney General James M. McInerney reported to Hoover that on June 4th the Loyalty Review Board found William O'Dwyer "eligible on loyalty." The notification came from Hiram Burgham, Chairman of the Loyalty Review Board, to J. Edgar Hoover, Director of the F.B.I.

Apparently unhappy with the board's decision, Hoover presented further allegations concerning Paul Ross and me. I had represented Paul Ross in an action against Chester Bowles, who had previously been the Ambassador to India and later appointed by the President to head up the Price Control Program. Ross became Bowles' administrator for the New York region. He did his work well, coming down heavy on violators engaged in the black market. He stepped on too many toes and some heavy contributors to the Democratic Party complained. Bowles first gave him hints about being as aggressive as he was and later relieved him of his office. Ross and I had been friends for years and were both national and local officers in the National Lawyers Guild. When he was discharged by Bowles I commenced the action to have him reinstated. The lawsuit was publicized and was embarrassing to Bowles and the Administration. At Bowles' request we met with him in his office. Ross was reinstated to his post, but his usefulness had been impaired and he resigned shortly afterwards. That was a short time before Bill's campaign for Mayor was being organized. At my urging Ross became the research director in the campaign. He was with Bill frequently and we were both aware of his capacity as researcher and as administrator.

Immediately after his election Bill, on my urging, created a new job, "Administrative Secretary" to the Mayor, and appointed Ross to the post. When Hoover was sending to the Civil Service Commission the derogatory matters which he felt warranted a loyalty investigation, Ross' position at City Hall had been featured prominently. This memo pointed out Ross was associated with Civil Rights Congress, The Joint Anti-Fascist Refugee Committee, The National Council for American Soviet Friendship, People's Lobby and National Lawyers Guild, anti-discrimination groups and N.Y. Tenant Welfare Consumer Councils.

My "Communist affiliation" was given as a reason why Bill's loyalty should be investigated further. The following is part of the account Hoover sent to the Civil Service Commission:

> Paul O'Dwyer was born in Bohola, County Mayo, Ireland and is a partner of O'Dwyer & Bernstien since 1931.
>
> The firm of O'Dwyer & Bernstien has represented many Communists and Communist organizations in legal matters.
>
> In March 1945 Paul O'Dwyer was a member of the Executive Committee of the West Side Legislative Conference. According to a confidential informant this organization was set up to get action on anti-discrimination bills and other Civil Liberties matters.
>
> August 22, 1947 edition of 'Counterattack' describes Paul O'Dwyer as a "Party liner—a lawyer for Communist-led T.W.U. (CIO) and a backer of Communist Front Organizations."
>
> In October Paul O'Dwyer served as counsel for Michael Obermeier, active Communist and President of Local 6 of the Restaurant Workers Union who was arrested as an illegal alien by Immigration & Naturalization Service.[3] Paul O'Dwyer said Obermeier was a 'victim of the witch hunt.'

HOOVER'S FIFTH COLUMN

Hoover's intrusion into American affairs abroad is revealed in the copies of reports from an F.B.I. agent planted in the American Embassy in Mexico City. There is no reason to believe that what transpired be-

---

3. Obermeier was head of a small union of culinary workers. His son served in the Marines during World War II. His daughter was a science professor in a California college. During the war he was used by the U.S. Government to talk to Germans in the German language via the radio. At the war's end he received a decoration from the U.S. Government for his work in this regard. During the hysteria period he was arrested on the word of an informer and jailed. Then he was deported back to the Germany he had come to despise.

tween Hoover and his secret agent within the embassy in Mexico was any different from what took place in the embassies in other parts of the world.

Documents which I received in answer to my request under the provisions of the Freedom of Information Act show that on October 20, 1950, a secret F.B.I. agent, acting as the "Legal Attache" for the embassy, received a lengthy memorandum from Hoover. The subject was dubbed "Relations with the Embassy." It starts out by giving "Legat" (the pen name for the agent) some background information on the new Ambassador. It described a disagreement between the New York Police Department and the F.B.I. relative to the method of crime reporting while Bill was Mayor of New York. It proceeds to discuss the charges made in the mayoralty campaign by Jonah Goldstein, Bill's opponent, that he was supported by underworld figures. It goes on to point out that in that election (1945) Bill was supported by the American Labor Party which the House Committee on Un-American Activities charged was, in certain sectors of that party, under heavy Communist influence. After more "derogatory" information, the memo ended with an admonition to the legal attache: "It is desired that your contacts with the new Ambassador be courteous but cautious."

By and large, the reporting of what was transpiring in Mexico went on between Hoover and his satellites in the embassy. On April 25, 1951, "Legat" reported directly to the Director on the activities and reception of O'Dwyer in Mexico and how it affected the F.B.I. agents:

> The effect of this change of Ambassadors on the office of Legal Attache could not be immediately evaluated. Mr. Thurston [former Ambassador] had been a very cooperative career diplomat and he had always given us firm backing in Mexico when we desired the same.
>
> The Ambassador's [O'Dwyer's] conferences with the Legal Attache appeared to be quite routine and the Ambassador did not attempt to go into the detailed program and operations of the Bureau office in Mexico City.
>
> It was apparent that the Ambassador had been informally briefed to the effect that the Cultural section of the Embassy had many "Parlor Pinks" and homosexuals. His questions were sufficiently specific so that I perceived he had been closely briefed on this. I told him that there was an office within the Embassy which had been set up to handle matters such as that, that office being the Security office. . . . The Ambassador was disturbed by the fact that the Security office administratively

comes under the Embassy administrative officer who is a Foreign Service officer. The Ambassador felt that the security officer should be under his personal administration.

Although certain people were inclined to continue to be hostile to Ambassador O'Dwyer it was noted that by reason of his personal charm he made friends with the great majority. The Mexico City newspapers gave him extremely favorable press and Mexican officialdom from the President down seemed to be very pleased with his appointment with the possible exception of a few officials in the Mexican Foreign Office.

Several pages were devoted to the Kefauver hearings and the Ambassador's reaction to them, but what might seem to be important observations were blotted out. Then the subject of the Ambassador's contacts in Mexico are covered in a page, two-thirds of which has been blotted out. A report of the Ambassador's "day to day relationship" was submitted to the Director. It would seem clear that each time the Ambassador had a discussion with the legal attache, a full report was sent to Hoover personally.

Then in July 1951, the Attorney General and the Director got information from the Chase National Bank that on March 31, 1951, an order had come through to transfer a million dollars to William O'Dwyer from the Banco de Mexico to the Chase. Senator O'Conor, who had succeeded Kefauver, was supplied with the same information. Hoover was not going to be left out of the story. Both agencies went into action immediately. O'Conor sent the new counsel, Richard Moser, post haste to Mexico to nail down the story. Before going, he called to see me in my New York office. I told him the story was false and in keeping with the general conduct of the inquiry and that he ought to check his facts. I called Bill about it and I felt he should have someone with him when Moser got there so I went to Mexico. It was noted in the later reports that "Paul O'Dwyer had taken a defensive attitude to the Committee," and there followed another resume of my life pointing out my association with a long list of Communist Front Organizations. The item ended with the observation: "We do have a liaison agent stationed in Mexico City."

The "Million Dollar" accusation was featured by almost every media agency in the U.S. and Mexico. The *Daily News* (August 1st) got the scoop on the papers, magazines, radio and television. The headline screamed across its whole front page: "A MILLION DOLLARS TRACED TO O'DWYER."

A man named Downey Rice, working for the Kefauver committee, had written a bizarre tale to the Bureau which described Bill stuffing

$1,000,000 in pesos into a bag and taking it from the president of the Banco de Mexico.

This last information prompted a memorandum from one L. B. Nichols to Tolson. As a result Hoover instructed that a letter be immediately sent to Admiral Somers which was delivered to him at the Wardman Park Hotel on August 1st and a further memo was sent to the Attorney General.

Hoover advised the Admiral that they had information "that sometime subsequent to March 8, 1951, the president of the Banco de Mexico personally packed in two suitcases, one million dollars worth of pesos, that Ambassador O'Dwyer picked up these two suitcases personally and walked out of the bank with them."

The hunt for the details of the transaction would have caused great embarrassment and an apology if the forces involved were capable of either. Instead, *a confidential* memorandum was sent on August 2, 1951, by Hoover to the Attorney General:

> I have now received information that this transaction involving the transfer of a million dollars was in fact a government transaction. I have been informed that the State Department will probably issue a release concerning this transfer.

Two days later Hoover sent a similar message via the confidential air pouch to his agent in the embassy (never identified in the memo by name and addressed always as legal attache).

When it was all over it would seem that the F.B.I. pressed Moser and the committee to give an explanation for getting them involved and leading them into such a blunder. Moser presented one theory to L.B. Nichols, who passed it on to Tolson: "O'Dwyer," he said, "had deliberately denied this to lay a trap for the committee." It was the same Richard Moser who had dramatically reported that when he confronted Bill with the charge, "O'Dwyer was visibly shaken," and that I, who sat in on the interview, appeared not to know what they were talking about.

It did not occur to the authors that there may be an inconsistency between the observation that Bill was "visibly shaken" by the accusation and the suggestion that cleverness and slyness had led the committee and Hoover into the error of making sensational charges in writing and somehow leaking the story to the *Daily News* before any attempt was made to verify it. The third alternative given by Moser was that "O'Dwyer was thinking so hard and was so guilty that he forgot about the incident."

THE RIGHT TO TRAVEL

One might wonder how the Passport Division of the State Department could have affected the life of William O'Dwyer, but it did. Their minions tried their level best to do him in and were it not for his age and his service in the Armed Forces they would have succeeded in stripping him of the one possession he prized most dearly—his citizenship.

Our Mexican office had been established to cater to Americans and Mexicans in need of cross-border legal service. Alfred Stern and his wife Martha Dodd[4] came to the office with subpoenas to appear before the grand jury in New York. They had been accused by one of the informants in the Ethel and Julius Rosenberg case of collecting information for the Russian government. We were retained to represent them.

I appeared before the U.S. District Court in Manhattan and in an appropriate proceeding challenged the effectiveness of a subpoena served in a foreign country and the right of the government of the U.S. to serve a court process within the borders of an alien sovereign jurisdiction. The motion was denied.

It was clear that serving the Sterns with subpoenas to testify against themselves was a mere ruse to bring them into the U.S. and the Sterns were justified in their fears in the atmosphere which then prevailed. The case had been decided against them. On September 9, 1957, they were indicted for "conspiracy to receive and obtain information relating to U.S. National Defense and transmitting same to a foreign government." Two days later a warrant for their arrest was signed by the same judge who had pronounced sentence on the Rosenbergs.

While Mexicans had tolerated American refugees and were traditionally sensitive to any attempted disregard for the sovereignty of their nation, the government of Mexico was known to cooperate with the U.S. in matters which concerned American nationals residing in Mexico. Article 33 of the Mexican Constitution permits a government agent to drop an American alien over the border and into the waiting hands of American authorities.

The Sterns heard they were to be "33rd" and fled to Czechoslovakia. In 1970 the case against them was marked closed. On March 22, 1979, the indictment against them was dropped and that presumably ended their 20-year exile.

The retention of our office and particularly of my brother and me

---

4. Martha Dodd was the daughter of William E. Dodd, distinguished author, educator and historian. He was Ambassador to Germany, 1933-37, and became an outspoken opponent of Hitler and Nazi Germany. Stern was a wealthy man who had been engaged in many civil rights causes to which he made regular contributions.

was duly noted in the press. The *New York Times* reported it on August 14, 1957, and the copy of the *Times* story was sent to me by the C.I.A. from its files in June 1981.

The government agents, however, did not choose to see my brother or me in the capacity of lawyers for a client, a U.S. citizen summoned to travel to New York to appear before a Federal grand jury thousands of miles away from his residence in a foreign country. Robert D. Johnson, a State Department representative, in the summer of 1957, sent a memo to the "Passport files" to the effect that he had received a telephone call from Mr. Chase (SCA) to the effect that the "subject . . . has engaged in activities which are inimical to the interest of the U.S. He says that O'Dwyer is mixed up somehow with the Alfred Kaufman Stern matter." Mr. Chase felt that the "subject" may come under the provisions of the law which could denaturalize him pointing out that he would *"soon complete 5 years residence* Mexico"[5] Their efforts ended in frustration because "the subject's age and war record" brought him under the exception to the law which sanctioned a denaturalization proceeding on the ground of absence from the U.S.

This was the second attempt to strip William O'Dwyer's naturalized citizenship status. In 1953 Clyde Tolson, Hoover's close friend and his chief assistant, received a message from a United States Senator whose name was blotted out.[6] The memorandum remained classified until February 21, 1979. It is difficult to understand why such a memorandum should have been classified in the first place and why it should remain classified for 26 years and long after Tolson and O'Dwyer were dead. It is a fair example of how ludicrous the rules classifying such documents were in the days of the House Un-American Activities Committee and Senator McCarthy and J. Edgar Hoover.

The message dated January 8, 1953, read ". . . the Senator is desirous of knowing whether or not William O'Dwyer, American Ambassador to Mexico, is a naturalized citizen." ". . . the Senator indicated if O'Dwyer is a naturalized citizen, there is some action that can be taken by the Senator."

In a prompt reply to the Senator whose identity was again concealed, the F.B.I. confirmed that William O'Dwyer was indeed a naturalized citizen. Transmitted were the 'subject's' date and place of birth and the date of his arrival in the U.S. and continued: "He filed his declaration to become a citizen on February 8, 1911 and was admitted

5. This portion of the memorandum was underlined.
6. The blotted out portion which successfully hid the Senator's identity took up a space equal to 14 letters. Measured against the space the name Joseph McCarthy would fit perfectly.

to citizenship on September 7, 1916 under Certificate No. 757646." Before being transmitted to the Senator the memorandum had been received and reviewed by Tolson and bureau representatives.

In responding to the demand for a review of the files the Passport Office was not as devious as the Treasury Department. Copies of their total file were supplied to me including every passport application Bill had made starting with 1928. One would wonder why the files would be cluttered so. But then it was Earl Browder's earlier application for a passport using a pseudonym which led to his being incarcerated. He was then the head of the Communist Party in the U.S. It was at that time a legal party, and membership in it did not constitute a crime, so he was prosecuted for perjury.

GAMBLING AND SMUGGLING

In addition to all the reports concerning Bill's supposed contact with Communists, there was considerable material in the F.B.I. files on his attitudes toward crime and possible involvement in criminal activities, especially gambling.

The charges of political opponents that the subject was soft on gamblers was a safe one. Illicit gambling had been part of the New York political scene for three centuries. It's the sort of charge that could be leveled against the party in power particularly if that party was Democratic. Any attempt to legalize gambling was consistently met with opposition from rural New York legislators who were almost invariably Republican and who controlled the New York Senate and frequently the State Assembly.

Bill had advocated taking horse betting out of the hands of bookmakers and placing it under state control, but got nowhere. (These proposals were enacted 20 years later.) Puritanism prevailed in New York through the 1950's. In Jimmy Walker's time the legislature had, with a mighty effort against fierce opposition within the legislature, obtained approval of Sunday baseball.

During the 1945 mayoral campaign, his opponent charged that the gamblers and racketeers were supporting Bill in the campaign. These were charges that were part of every campaign through the years. They were mostly ignored by the electorate who treated bookmaking as they had treated Prohibition. It would be untrue to say that the people considered the charges and rejected them. The huge plurality which won Bill O'Dwyer the coveted position came about because of his personal charm, popularity and his record as District Attorney of Brooklyn, but above all else his excellent record during the war years. It is doubtful that the charges of being backed by gamblers was heeded in the slightest in sophisticated New York.

But Hoover did not ignore the charges. An inter-office memorandum on April 11, 1946, reported:

> In connection with vice conditions in New York, Mayor O'Dwyer has ordered a survey made by the Police Department of night club shows, movies and pool halls for the purpose of combating gambling and juvenile delinquency. Commissioner Wallander has also ordered members of the Police Department to provide him with the names of all gamblers, policy slip operators and racketeers known to them. Plain-clothes men of the department have also been ordered to raid places suspected of harboring prostitutes or games of chance.
>
> *ACTION BEING TAKEN*
>
> The possibility of a tie-up between the O'Dwyer administration and gambling elements in the City of New York is being closely followed and you will be advised immediately of any information developed along this line.

On May 10th the Department of Justice sent a letter to Hoover assessing the record of William O'Dwyer and his attitude towards gambling:

> Reference is made to Bureau letter dated May 6, 1946, requesting that there be submitted to the Bureau a memorandum setting forth information tending to prove or disprove the authenticity of newspaper accounts indicating that Mayor O'Dwyer is carrying on a sincere campaign against gambling.
>
> As background information, it is observed that in connection with the crime survey information received in the early part of 1945, from [blotted out] that FRANK COSTELLO, the outstanding racketeer in New York City, had contributed $25,000.00 toward the campaign fund of O'DWYER when he was running for District Attorney of Kings County, New York, and that while with the U.S. Army, in Italy, O'DWYER had dinner with VITO GENOVESE, a former New York racketeer now in prison on a murder charge. During the mayoralty election campaign preceding O'DWYER's election as Mayor, the charge was made that O'DWYER's election was engineered by FRANK COSTELLO, JOHN ADONIS, and IRVING SHERMAN, the latter two also being racketeers. The charge was also made that if O'DWYER was elected Mayor, there would be

much more criminal activity in New York City, particularly along gambling lines.

Because of the above information and allegations, the New York Office has followed very closely the O'DWYER Administration in order to be aware of any tie-ups with the criminal element.

After this introduction, the memo went on to outline Bill's appointments and actions with regard to the campaign against gambling. No information was presented to indicate that the campaign was not sincere or that he had any ties with criminals.

This memorandum in no way discouraged Hoover. In the succeeding 10 years he accepted and ran down all kinds of rumors which linked my brother with the gamblers in Las Vegas and with a gambling combine in Mexico and with a gambling operation on the high seas. Nothing came of them, but they were all collected and put in his file. Even now, two decades after his death, a goodly portion of the material received by me, while it is unclassified, is nevertheless removed from vision by some unnamed censor who simply blots out the information.

Material in the files on Bill's alleged involvement with slot machines and smuggling illustrate the absurdity of much of the F.B.I.'s information gathering efforts.

Hoover advised the Deputy Attorney General William Rogers on December 7, 1953, that an informant reported certain persons whose names are blotted out, but who are in the slot machine business in Idaho and Nevada, flew to Mexico City. "They contacted William O'Dwyer who is opening Mexico to slot machines. O'Dwyer is going to be the King Pin of the rackets in Mexico and will represent the slot machine interest who are attempting to open up in Mexico City."

On September 27, 1954 the Bureau, Salt Lake City office, advised Rosen that the operators of the strip hotels in Las Vegas were worried about gambling being made legal in Mexico. (Blotted) sent for O'Dwyer to come to Vegas to discuss the situation, but O'Dwyer refused and requested operators come to him. (Blotted) a prominent underworld character, has been sent to O'Dwyer as an emissary to discuss the situation.

On October 28, 1954, Hoover wrote to A.W. Fleming, Director, Intelligence Division, I.R.S., that the hotel owners had $60,000 to pay O'Dwyer to keep legalized gambling *out* of Mexico. It was said that the hotel owners wanted O'Dwyer to come to Las Vegas, etc. "In this particular the Bureau cannot vouch for the reliability of the confidential informant nor for the accuracy of the information he furnished. The Bureau has concluded no investigation, etc."

A report dated September 13, 1951, bears the subtitle *"Former Mayor William O'Dwyer of New York & Smuggling."*

> O'Dwyer visits the Key Largo Club in lower Florida. It is an exclusive club to which belong President Herbert Hoover and Dan Topping.

> The informant noted boats of larger size were moored in the Key Largo harbor. On one of the boats he saw a sailor hang wash out to dry and this was strange because "the owners of these boats do not do their laundry in this fashion." The informant felt that possibly O'Dwyer could now be engaged in the smuggling racket between Mexico and the U.S. Because of "the important people involved" it was decided not to pursue the information further.

The freedoms outlined in our Bill of Rights seemed, in 1791, to be a radical departure from the norm and if you were not an African American or a native American it went a long way towards correcting the abuses which had grown into our system under a tyrannical monarchy. During the next century the cancer of slavery cried out for correction and attempts at a change by constitutional means and by appeals to reason, based on moral grounds, proved useless. Nothing less than violence could bring about the elimination of the evil. A bloody fratricidal war finally brought an end to the institution on American soil. During the next century freedom of speech, privacy, assembly and worship gained general acceptance.

While the struggle to keep our freedoms stayed abreast of the changing times and circumstances, the rising power of bureacracies made it necessary to add one more. Freedom to know what the administration was up to. Every American child was taught in social studies classes that we were governed by three great forces which were so created to check one another lest the rights which the individual never surrendered to the state be improperly invaded. We had, the children were told, a legislative system which created our rules for living, an administrative system which carried out the mandate of the laws of our society and we had the judicial system which could be relied upon to check any abuses of the other two branches. Provisions were made for an aggrieved citizen to have full access to the courts which could, theoretically at least, nullify the use of any law which in any way curtailed the freedoms guaranteed by the Constitution.

While we proceeded happily boasting of our good fortune, bureaucracy, another power which affected the life of the citizen more than the

O'Dwyer family photographed at ceremony unveiling portrait of Bill which hangs in City Hall, 1974

legislative, spread like a disabling disease. There is scarcely a citizen who has wanted a permit or a license or who has filed a tax return, who has not at one time or another suffered a demeaning experience at its hands.

The courts which had done so nobly in dealing with legislative enactments or executive orders which invaded the citizens' rights, consistently avoided inquiry into the operation of the bureaucracies, leaving the citizen virtually at the mercy of this cancer which frequently ran roughshod over citizens without hindrance. The checks and balances which were our proudest boasts became meaningless.

This state of affairs cried out for legislative relief and a halfway measure was enacted into law by the national and state legislatures. The Freedom of Information Act was not capable of meeting this threat to liberty, but it did fill a partial need. It was meant to let the citizen know what the government bureaucracies were doing and to a limited extent it at least exposed the government's abuse and some of the crass arrogance of its minions.

INDEX

Subheadings are arranged under main headings in chronological order. *"f"* following page numbers refers to information found in footnotes at the bottom of text pages. Italic numbers indicate photographs.

comforter of the sick, 325
New York City
   see also Mayoral elections
   present-day Native American population,
      74, 75
   status of Black Americans (1940's), 80
   minority representatives in government,
      81
   judgeships in, 130-31
   street organ grinders, 134-35
   gambling and bookmaking in, 137-38,
      276-78
   naziism in, 149
   status in 1946, 228-29
   mass transit system, 233-41
   Division of Labor Relations, 239
   Idlewild Airport, 244-46
   Planning Commission, 250
   city traffic, 250-51
   Department of Traffic, 250-51
   housing in, 252-61
   East and West sides, development of, 262
   42nd St. slaughterhouse, 262
   City Hall, 284-86, 289-94
   ticker-tape parade, 289
   Golden Jubilee, 292-93
   snow removal, 300-302
   drought in, 302, 306
   sewage disposal, 302-03
   garbage disposal, 303-06
   Board of Estimate, 304
   air pollution in, 306-08
   health and hospital services, 325-28
   smallpox scare of 1947, 325-26
   Feinberg Law, 415f
New York City Hall *see* City Hall
New York City Human Rights Commission,
   324
New York City magistrate (1932-38), 126-
   40
New York City Police Department, 99-113
   in early 1900s, 100-101
   book of rules, 103-04
   old-time cop *vs.* new type, 101, 104-06
   Manhattan cop, 106
   nine-squad system, 106
   "sparrow cop," 106
   "Murphy Lieutenant," 106-07
   prohibition and, 110
   during William's administration, 271-78
New York National War Fund, 191-92
New York Port Authority, and city airports,
   244-45
New York Post editorials:
   on city Police Department (1946), 274-75
New York State

present-day Native American population,
   75
slavery in, 76
New York Thruway, 247-50
(The) New York Times, and Coleman appointment to Board of Higher Education
   (1946), 321
(The) New York Times editorials:
   on fuel oil deliverers' strike (1946), 238-
      39
   on city's Division of Labor Relations, 239
   on possibility of TWU striking (1948),
      240
   on New York Thruway (1950), 248
   on appointment of T.T. Wiley as Traffic
      Commissioner, 251
   on traffic problems in the city, 251
   on William's first year in office, 270
   on city Police Department (1946, 1947),
      274, 275
   on the city's anti-smoke rules (1950),
      307-08
   on William's hospitalization (1948), 327
   on William's decision not to run (1949),
      328-30
   on William's vacation in Florida (1949),
      334
   on William's second term (1950), 336-37
   on William's decision to resign (1950),
      338
Nichols, General, 180
Nichols, L.B., 424
Nicolls, Governor, 76
(The) Night of the Big Wind, 38, 53
Niles, Dave, 181, 193, 204
Nine-squad system, 106
Niños Héroes, 346-47
No Deal Party, 221
Norcott, Catherine *see* O'Dwyer, Catherine
   Norcott
Norman, Dr. Philip, 131, 327
Normans (people), 16f
Norris, Sir John, 62
North River *see* Hudson River
Northrup/Consolidated case, 180
Nova, Algernon I., 110, 137, 144
Null, Sam, 165, 181

Oaxaca (Mexico), 342
Obermeier, Michael, 421, 421f
O'Brien, John P.
   mayoral election of 1933 and, 129
   as mayor of New York City, 228
   dispute over portrait of, 286
O'Brien, Sophie, 9f
O'Brien, Thurmond, 93

Indexer/Mary F. Tomaselli

SELECTED READINGS

Bolton, R.P. *New York City in Indian Possession*. 2d ed. New York: Museum of the American Indian, Heye Foundation, 1975.

Bourke, Ulick J., *Pre-Christian Ireland*. Dublin: Brown and Nolan, 1887.

Buckley, John P. *The New York Irish, Their Views of American Foreign Policy*, 1914-1921. New York: Arno Press, 1976.

Coleman, Terry. *Passage to America: A History of Emigrants from Great Britain and Ireland to America in the Mid-Nineteenth Century*. Harmondsworth: Penguin Books, 1974.

Davis, Thomas J. *A Rumor of Revolt: The "Great Negro Plot" in Colonial New York*. New York: Free Press, 1985.

Devoy, John. *Recollections of an Irish Rebel: The Fenian Movement*. New York: Chas. P. Young, 1929.

Farley, James A. *Jim Farley's Story: The Roosevelt Years*. New York: McGraw-Hill, 1948.

Fernow, Berthold. *New York in the Revolution*. Cottonport, La.: Polyanthos, 1972.

Gallagher, Thomas M. *Paddy's Lament: Ireland 1846-1847, Prelude to Hatred*. New York: Harcourt Brace Jovanovich, 1982.

Hamburger, Philip P. *The Oblong Blur, and Other Odysseys*. New York: Farrar, Straus, 1949.

Healy, John. *The Death of an Irish Town*. Cork: Mercier Press, 1968.

Horsmanden, Daniel. *A Journal of the Proceedings in the Detection of the Conspiracy. . . for Burning the City of New York . . .* New York: James Parker, 1744.

Ierardi, Eric J. *Gravesend, the Home of Coney Island*. New York: Vantage Press, 1975.

Irving, Washington. *Washington Irving's Works*. 18 vols. New York: J.W. Lovell, n.d.

Kee, Robert. *Ireland, A History*. London: Weidenfeld and Nicholson, 1980.

Lauber, Almon W. *Indian Slavery in Colonial Times within the Present Limits of the United States*. Williamstown, Mass.: Corner House, 1979.

Lecky, William E.H. *A History of Ireland in the Eighteenth Century*. London: Longmans, Green, 1906.

Lyons, F.S.L. *Charles Stewart Parnell*. London: Collins, 1977.

Marx, Karl, and Frederick Engels. *Ireland and the Irish Question: A Collection of Writings*. New York: International Publishers, 1972.

McCarthy, Justin. *The Story of Gladstone's Life*. 2d ed. London: Adam and Charles Black, 1906.

McDermot, M. *History of Ireland*. London: J. McGowan, n.d.

Murphy, Denis. *Cromwell in Ireland: A History of Cromwell's Irish Campaign*. Dublin: Gill, 1902.

Myers, Andrew B. *The Worlds of Washington Irving, 1783-1859*. Tarrytown, N.Y.: Sleepy Hollow Restorations, 1974.

Neill, Kenneth. *The Irish People: An Illustrated History*. Dublin: Gill and Macmillan, 1979.

O'Donnell Peadar. *There Will Be Another Day*. Dublin: Dolemen Press, 1963.

O'Leary, Jeremiah. *My Political Trial and Experience*. New York: Jefferson Publishing, 1919.

Rodgers, Cleveland. *New York Plans For the Future*. New York: Harper and Brothers, 1943.

Shaw, Richard. *Dagger John: The Unquiet Life and Times of Archbishop John Hughes of New York*. New York: Paulist Press, 1977.

Stokes, Isaac Newton P. *The Iconography of Manhattan Island, 1498-1909*. New York: Arno Press, 1967.

Woodham Smith, Cecil B. *The Great Hunger: Ireland 1845-1849*. New York: Harper and Row, 1962.

B